Houghton Mifflin
English

Shirley Haley-James   John Warren Stewig

Marcus T. Ballenger   Jacqueline L. Chaparro   Nancy C. Millett

June Grant Shane   C. Ann Terry

HOUGHTON   MIFFLIN   COMPANY   BOSTON

Atlanta   Dallas   Geneva, Illinois   Palo Alto   Princeton   Toronto

Acknowledgments

"Animals in Advertising," adapted from *Super-Animals and Their Unusual Careers* by Virginia Phelps Clemens. Copyright © 1979 by Virginia Phelps Clemens. Adapted by permission of The Westminster Press, Philadelphia, PA.

"At the Top of My Voice," from *At the Top of My Voice and Other Poems* by Felice Holman. Text copyright © 1970 by Felice Holman. Reprinted with the permission of Charles Scribner's Sons, an imprint of Macmillan Publishing Company.

"The Beaver Pond" adapted from *The Beaver Pond* by Alvin Tresselt. Copyright © 1970 by Alvin Tresselt. Adapted by permission of Lothrop, Lee & Shepard Books (A Division of William Morrow & Company).

"City," from *The Langston Hughes Reader* by Langston Hughes. Reprinted by permission of Harold Ober Associates, Incorporated. Copyright © 1958 by Langston Hughes. Copyright renewed 1986 by George Houston Bass.

"Confessions of an Orange Octopus," adapted from *Confessions of an Orange Octopus* by Jane Sutton. Text copyright © 1983 by Jane Sutton. Reprinted by permission of the publisher, E. P. Dutton, a division of New American Library.

"Dear Sarah," from *Dear Sarah* by Elisabeth Borchers, translated and adapted from the German by Elizabeth Shub. English translation Copyright © 1981 by Elizabeth Shub. By permission of Greenwillow Books (A Division of William Morrow & Co.).

"The Emperor's Nightingale" by Hans Christian Andersen in *Fairy Tales from Hans Christian Andersen*, trans. Mrs. Edgar Lucas. (Dent, 1899)

Haiku: "The chiming river . . ." by Rokwa from *More Cricket Songs* Japanese haiku translated by Harry Behn. Copyright © 1971 by Harry Behn. All rights reserved. Reprinted by permission of Marian Reiner.

"In My New Clothing" by Basho, excerpted from *An Introduction to Haiku* by Harold G. Henderson. Copyright © 1958 by Harold G. Henderson. Reprinted by permission of Doubleday, a division of Bantam, Doubleday, Dell Publishing Group, Inc.

"Ramona's Book Report," abridged from *Ramona Quimby, Age 8* by Beverly Cleary. Copyright © 1981 by Beverly Cleary. Abridged by permission of William Morrow & Co., and Hamish Hamilton Limited.

"Sudden Storm," from *The Sparrow Bush* by Elizabeth Coatsworth. Reprinted by permission of Grosset & Dunlap, copyright © 1966 by Grosset & Dunlap, Inc.

The Tortoise" ("La Tortuga") by José Juan Tablada, from *Haiku of a Day: Anthology of Mexican Poetry*, translated by Samuel Beckett, compiled by Octavio Paz. Reprinted by permission of Indiana University Press. Further use is prohibited by law.

Trip: San Francisco," from *The Langston Hughes Reader* by Langston Hughes. Reprinted by permission of Harold Ober Associates, Incorporated. Copyright © 1958 by Langston Hughes. Copyright renewed 1986 by George Houston Bass.

"Twister" in *Do Bananas Chew Gum?* by Jamie Gilson. Copyright © 1980, 1981. Reprinted by permission of Lothrop, Lee & Shepard Books, a division of William Morrow & Co.

1998 Impression
Copyright © 1990 by Houghton Mifflin Company. All rights reserved.

Printed in U.S.A.
ISBN: 0–395–50264–0
S-VH-998

(Acknowledgments continued on page 516.)

ACKNOWLEDGMENTS

Table of Contents

UNIT 8

Literature and Writing: Description

UNIT 9

Mechanics: Capitalization and Punctuation

Strategies Handbook

Writer's Handbook

Glossaries

Getting Ready to Write

Look at the tree outside your window...
and then find words that will make another
who may not know the tree
see it as you do.

Elizabeth Yates
from *Someday You'll Write*

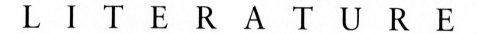

LITERATURE

What might your street look like after a tornado?

Twister

By Jamie Gilson

Sam is in the dentist chair having his braces adjusted when there is a sudden tornado warning. He jumps out of the chair and hides in the hallway with the other people in the building. Suddenly he remembers his small charges at home.

It was still dark in the hall when the all-clear sounded outside. Everybody scrambled up, feeling their way down the rough stucco walls of the hall and back into offices where there were windows. I was afraid I'd knock somebody down if I ran, so I crawled to the end of the hall where the steps were and skidded down them like a seal at the zoo.

I guess everybody else wanted to be super safe because I was the first one outside. There weren't any buildings down, but the street was a bathtub of water and the windows of the travel agency next door had blown in.

I ran like a rocket toward the Glasses' house. Branches were scattered everywhere like pick-up sticks. The telephone in front of the grocery store was swinging back and forth off its hook. Up ahead a light pole tilted, though the wind had died down and nothing was blowing it. I ran fast, panicked about the kids.

"Hey, son, watch it," somebody shouted. I turned to see the pole bending down closer to the ground, aiming itself at me.

"Over here!" It was a policeman, his car up to its hubcaps in water. As I dashed toward the squad car I could hear a long low crack, and when I looked again I saw the pole scrunch the top of a parked car, blocking the street. A shower of sparks flew up like fireworks. I turned to run again and tripped over the lid of a trash can that had blown like a flying saucer into the middle of the sidewalk. It sent me sailing, too. The concrete sandpapered the skin off my hands. My pants and shirt were soaked.

"You OK?" the policeman in the squad car yelled. I shrugged my shoulders.

"How bad is it?" I asked him.

"Dunno. Two funnels dropped down. Some damage over on Euclid Avenue, I hear. More wires down over there, too. Stay away from Euclid now, and go right home."

"Euclid *is* home!" I shouted back and started running again.

You can read the rest of this story in the book *Do Bananas Chew Gum?* by Jamie Gilson.

_____

Think and Discuss
1. What are the first five changes Sam noticed after the tornado?
2. What was the greatest danger Sam faced as he raced toward home?
3. Should Sam have behaved as he did? Was he foolish or courageous? Explain your opinion.

The Writing Process

STEP 1: PREWRITING

How to Get Ideas: Interviewing

Talking with someone is a good way to get ideas for writing. Have a writing partner ask you questions. Your answers may trigger an idea.

Susan was going to write about how to do something. She couldn't think of a topic that really excited her. Susan asked Tanya to interview her.

Tanya: What kinds of things do you like to do?
Susan: I like to go to plays and movies, and I love to read, but it might be hard to write instructions for those things.
Tanya: What are your favorite things to do outside?
Susan: I like to ice skate. I guess I could write about that.
Tanya: Have you learned to do something new recently?
Susan: Not exactly. But I did just read a story called "Twister," and I would like to find out what to do when a tornado comes.
Tanya: That sounds like a great idea.

Susan had found a topic she wanted to write about.

Questions for an Interview

- What have you learned to do recently?
- What kinds of things do you like to make?
- Is there something that you do really well?
- What are your favorite things to do outside?

Having an Interview

With a partner, take turns interviewing each other for a *how-to* paper. Jot down ideas sparked by your partner's questions. Then choose a topic.

How to Explore Your Topic: Clustering

Once you get a writing topic, how do you begin to explore it? Clustering is a helpful way to discover your ideas and to see how they fit together. Here is the cluster Susan made about preparing for a tornado.

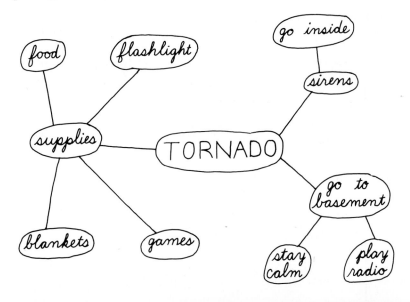

GUIDELINES FOR CLUSTERING

- Write your topic, and circle it.
- Around it, write ideas that come to mind about your topic.
- Circle your ideas, and draw lines to show how they are connected.
- Let your ideas flow freely. Do not judge them. When you write your first draft, you will decide which ones to include.

Clustering on Your Own

Make a cluster to explore the topic you chose in the last lesson. Let your ideas flow freely. Save your cluster.

How to Write a First Draft

When you write a first draft, you begin by sketching out your ideas. As you write, these ideas develop and take shape. Writing, like drawing, is a process of discovery!

This is Susan's first draft about preparing for a tornado.

Think and Discuss

- Why did Susan cross out a word?
- Does the beginning catch your interest? Explain.
- Are the steps in the right order?
- Where could Susan use more details?

> ~~There~~ A tornado is coming. Here's what you do if you are in your house. You will need suplies. You need food, a flashlight, blankets, and some games. Listen for warning sirens, and make sure everyone is inside. Hurry to the basemint. Keep the radio on, and please stay calm.

GUIDELINES FOR DRAFTING

- Keep in mind your purpose and who your audience will be.
- Write down your ideas as quickly as you can.
- Skip every other line so you can add ideas later.
- Don't worry if your paper looks messy.
- Don't worry about spelling or other mistakes. You will correct them later.

Drafting on Your Own

Use your cluster to help you write a first draft of your instructions. Be open to new ideas that come as you write.

How to Have a Writing Conference

Everyone needs a writing partner. Your partner can help you see your writing with fresh eyes.

Here is the conference Susan had with Aaron about her instructions.

Think and Discuss

- What questions did Aaron ask?
- What suggestions did he give?
- How could this conference help Susan to improve her writing?

When you are listening to someone else's writing, be sure to listen carefully. Remember to tell the writer what you like about the writing. Ask questions. Make suggestions only when you are asked. Always be polite.

Questions for a Writing Conference	
Ask your listener:	**As you listen:**
• Does my beginning catch your interest?	• Have I been listening carefully?
• Is everything clear and in order?	• What do I like about the writing?
• Where could I add details?	• What would I like to know more about?
• Should I take anything out?	• Does anything need to be made clearer?

Having a Writing Conference

Work with a partner. Take turns sharing your instructions. Ask each other questions, and make suggestions. After the conference, reread your instructions. Think about what your partner said. Make changes to improve your writing.

How to Revise Your Draft

You've sketched out your ideas in your first draft. Now look again. Can you add more details? Is your writing cluttered by extra words?

Here is part of Susan's revised draft.

A tornado may be coming if the sky turns dark yellow-green.
~~There~~ A tornado is coming. Here's what you do if you are in your house. Next, get You ~~will need suplies.~~ if you have time You need food, a a battery-operated radio flashlight, blankets, and some games.
First, Listen for warning sirens, and make sure everyone is inside. Then Hurry to the basemint. Keep the radio on, and

Think and Discuss

- Why did Susan improve her beginning?
- What sentence did she move? Why?
- What words did she add to make the order clearer?
- What details did she add?

GUIDELINES FOR REVISING

- Write new words in the lines you skipped or in the margins.
- Cross out unnecessary words. Do not erase them.
- Do not worry if your draft is messy.
- If you want to move a sentence, circle it. Then draw an arrow showing where it should go.

Revising on Your Own

Think about your partner's suggestions. Do you have any other ideas? Revise your instructions.

STEP 4: PROOFREADING

How to Proofread Your Writing

Now that you have made your writing clear and detailed, you are ready to check it for mistakes in spelling, punctuation, and grammar.

This is how Susan proofread her instructions.

Think and Discuss

- Where did Susan indent? Why?
- Why did she add a comma?
- Why did she add a period?
- Which words did she correct for spelling?
- Which capital letters did she change? Why?

A tornado may be coming if the sky turns dark yellow-green.
~~There~~ A tornado is coming. Here's what you do if you are in your house. Next, get You will need ~~suplies~~ supplies if you have time. You need food, a a battery-operated radio, flashlight, blankets, and some games. First, Listen for warning sirens, and make sure everyone is inside. Then Hurry to the basement ~~basemint~~. Keep the radio on, and please stay calm.

GUIDELINES FOR PROOFREADING

- Proofread for one kind of error at a time.
- Check that you indented where necessary.
- Check that you used capital letters and end marks correctly.
- Use a dictionary to check your spelling.
- Use proofreading marks.

Proofreading Marks

- ¶ Indent
- ∧ Add something
- ℓ Take out something
- ≡ Capitalize
- / Make a small letter

Proofreading on Your Own

Proofread your instructions. Use the guidelines.

How to Publish Your Writing

Now you are ready to publish! Use these guidelines to help you prepare your writing.

> **GUIDELINES FOR PUBLISHING**
>
> - Copy your writing neatly, and add a title.
> - Think of someone special who would enjoy your work.
> - Think of a creative way to share your writing.

Susan made a poster of tornado instructions to go with her writing. It was posted on the main school bulletin board.

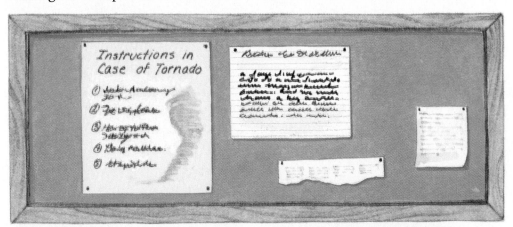

> **Ideas for Publishing**
>
> - Put your writing in cartoon form.
> - Design a note card, and tape your writing inside. Mail it to someone special.
> - Design a special frame for your work. Display it.

Publishing on Your Own

Use the guidelines to publish your instructions. Think of someone who would enjoy reading your work, and figure out a special way to share it.

Language and Usage

Look at it rain
on the windowpane!

Look at it splash
from the roof's mustache!

Look at it pour
on the field's brown floor!
    Aileen Fisher
    from "Country Window"

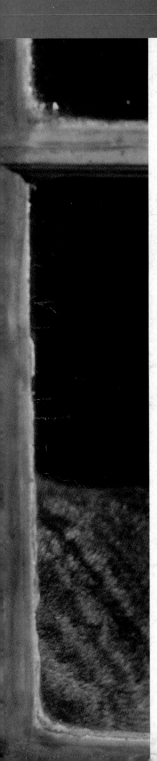

The Sentence

Getting Ready When you were very young, you used simple sentences that told, asked, commanded, or showed emotion. You still use the same kinds of sentences, but they are more interesting now. You know more words and use them in new ways. In this unit, you will learn more about the different kinds of sentences.

ACTIVITIES

Listening Listen as your teacher reads the lines of poetry on the opposite page. How many sentences are there? Do the sentences ask, tell, or make commands? What does the speaker want you to do?

Speaking Look at the picture. What do you see? Make up sentences about the picture to add to the poem.

Writing   Imagine you are looking out of this window. Write in your journal about what you might see.

1 | What Is a Sentence?

A **sentence** is a group of words that tell a complete thought. In order to tell a complete thought, a sentence must tell *who* or *what*. It must also tell *what is* or *what happens*.

WHO OR WHAT	WHAT IS OR WHAT HAPPENS
Mr. Nolan	rolled up the sleeping bags.
Your backpack	is too heavy!

SENTENCES	NOT SENTENCES
Ed likes camping.	Likes camping by the lake
Our new tent leaks.	Our new green tent.

This park   is closed.

Guided Practice Which groups of words are sentences? Which are not sentences?

Example: At Yellowstone National Park.   *not a sentence*

1. A great place for a vacation.
2. The park has famous hot springs.
3. The first national park in the world.
4. Flows through the park into the canyon.
5. Many different kinds of wildlife.
6. Jed's family camped at Yellowstone.

Summing up

▶ A **sentence** is a group of words that tell a complete thought.
▶ A sentence tells *who* or *what* and *what is* or *what happens*.

Independent Practice For each pair, write the group of words that is a sentence.

Example: Elise visited a national park.
Camping in a national park last summer.
Elise visited a national park.

Yellowstone National Park

7. Planned the trip ahead of time.
Elise's family planned for the trip.
8. Bought equipment for the trip.
Her family bought a tent.
9. Her parents sent for information.
Maps and information about the park.
10. The family camped in a meadow.
Enjoyed the view of the mountains.
11. Hiked together along the trail.
They admired the towering rocks.
12. Over sixty kinds of animals.
The hikers saw deer and bears.
13. The giant trees are famous.
Over three thousand years old.
14. The canyon is deep and narrow.
Formed by ice many years ago.
15. More than a mile above the valley.
This peak is the highest point.
16. The park has many waterfalls.
A rainbow above the falls.
17. Skiing in the winter.
The park is open all year.
18. A museum is near the entrance.
A nature center and other small museums.

Writing Application: Persuasive Writing

Pretend that you own a park or another vacation place. Write a paragraph about it. Tell what is in it, what it looks like, and what activities it offers. Try to make people want to come to your park. Be sure that all of your sentences are complete.

For Extra Practice, see p. 37.   **What Is a Sentence?**   15

2 | Statements and Questions

Different kinds of sentences have different jobs. A sentence that tells something is a **statement**. A statement ends with a **period** (.). A sentence that asks something is a **question**. A question ends with a **question mark** (?).

A sentence always begins with a capital letter.

STATEMENTS

The airport was crowded.
Her plane landed on time.
Carlos bought a ticket.

QUESTIONS

Was the airport crowded?
When did her plane land?
Did Carlos buy a ticket?

This is a statement.   Is this a question?

Guided Practice Is each sentence a statement or a question? What end mark should follow each sentence?

Example: The flight attendant welcomed all the passengers
          statement   period

1. I pushed my small brown bag under the seat
2. Have you fastened your seat belts
3. The takeoff was very smooth
4. Can you see out the window
5. How high will the plane climb
6. We will land in about an hour
7. Is this your first flight

Summing up

▶ A **statement** is a sentence that tells something. It ends with a **period** (.).
▶ A **question** is a sentence that asks something. It ends with a **question mark** (?).
▶ Every sentence begins with a capital letter.

Independent Practice

A. Write *statement* if the sentence is a statement. Write *question* if it is a question.

Example: Who made the first flight alone across the Atlantic?
question

8. Charles Lindbergh was the pilot's name.
9. A prize of $25,000 was offered.
10. What kind of plane did he fly?
11. His plane was called the *Spirit of St. Louis.*
12. Lindbergh flew from New York to Paris.
13. How long did the flight take?
14. The flight took thirty-three and one half hours.
15. Have you ever seen Lindbergh's plane?
16. His plane is in the Smithsonian Institution.

B. Write each sentence correctly.

Example: who was Amelia Earhart
Who was Amelia Earhart?

17. she was the first woman to fly across the Atlantic
18. when did Amelia Earhart complete her flight
19. she flew from Newfoundland to Ireland in 1932
20. it took fifteen hours and eighteen minutes
21. did she make any other ocean flights
22. she flew from Hawaii to California in 1935
23. she was lost at sea trying to fly around the world
24. where did her plane disappear
25. it was last seen over the Pacific Ocean

Writing Application: An Interview

Pretend that you are a newspaper reporter during the early days of flying. You are planning to interview one of the first pilots. Write three questions you would like to ask. You might ask about why the person wanted to become a pilot, what it feels like to fly, or what the person's goals are. Then write what the pilot's answers might be.

3 | Commands and Exclamations

You have learned about two kinds of sentences called statements and questions. Now you will learn about two other kinds of sentences.

A sentence that tells someone to do something is a **command**. A command ends with a period. A sentence that shows strong feeling such as surprise, excitement, or fear is an **exclamation**. It ends with an **exclamation point** (!).

Remember to begin every sentence with a capital letter.

COMMANDS	EXCLAMATIONS
Please wait at the bus stop.	The bus finally arrived!
Meet me at Page's Bookstore.	What a great store it is!
Take the subway home.	How fast the train travels!

Guided Practice Is each sentence a command or an exclamation? What end mark should be put at the end of each sentence?

Example: Planning a trip is so exciting *exclamation* !

1. Apply for your passport
2. Please answer all questions carefully
3. Have your picture taken
4. We're leaving at last
5. My dream is coming true

Summing up

> ▸ A **command** is a sentence that tells someone to do something. It ends with a period.
> ▸ An **exclamation** is a sentence that shows strong feeling. It ends with an **exclamation point** (!).
> ▸ Every sentence begins with a capital letter.

Independent Practice

A. Write each command correctly.

> Example: meet me at Kennedy Airport
> *Meet me at Kennedy Airport.*

6. be at the airport early
7. show your ticket at the gate
8. board the plane
9. find your seat quickly
10. please fasten your seat belt
11. stay in your seat until the plane lands
12. please pick up your luggage over there
13. wait here for the bus
14. take this bus to the hotel
15. decide what you want to do first

B. Write each exclamation correctly.

> Example: how noisy the airport is
> *How noisy the airport is!*

16. we'll be taking off any minute now
17. I can't wait to fly over the ocean
18. how smooth the takeoff was
19. everything looks so tiny
20. we've finally arrived in England
21. Gatwick Airport is certainly large
22. there are people here from all over the world
23. I can't wait to see the sights of London
24. there's so much to see and do
25. this is such an exciting city

Writing Application: Creative Writing

Imagine that you are flying aboard the first spaceship carrying passengers to Jupiter. During the flight, you eat dinner and breakfast, read, sleep, and talk to other passengers. Write a paragraph about what you might say during the flight. Include all four kinds of sentences.

For Extra Practice, see p. 39. **Commands and Exclamations** 19

4 | Complete Subjects and Complete Predicates

You know that a sentence must have two parts to tell a complete thought. The **subject** tells *whom* or *what* the sentence is about. The **predicate** tells what the subject *does* or *is*.

All the words in the subject make up the **complete subject**. All the words in the predicate make up the **complete predicate**. A complete subject or a complete predicate may be one word.

COMPLETE SUBJECTS	COMPLETE PREDICATES
Angela Kelly	is the captain of the boat.
We	waited at the dock.
The red ferryboat	stops.
Passengers	get off the boat.

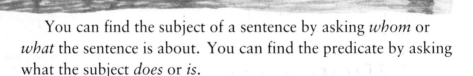

The boat stops at the dock.

You can find the subject of a sentence by asking *whom* or *what* the sentence is about. You can find the predicate by asking what the subject *does* or *is*.

Guided Practice What are the complete subject and the complete predicate of each sentence?

Example: The ocean was calm today.
subject: *The ocean* **predicate:** *was calm today*

1. Several sea gulls flew overhead.
2. They landed on the water.
3. John Day fished from the wharf.
4. He cast his line into the sea.
5. Fish swam below.
6. A large fish tugged on John's line.
7. The excited boy pulled in his catch.

► Every sentence has a subject and a predicate.
► The **complete subject** includes all the words that tell *whom* or *what* the sentence is about.
► The **complete predicate** includes all the words that tell what the subject *does* or is.

Independent Practice Write each sentence. Draw a line between the complete subject and the complete predicate.

Example: Many people enjoy the ocean in the summer.
Many people | enjoy the ocean in the summer.

 8. Children splash in the waves.
 9. Older children swim to the raft.
10. Jane Sampson works at the beach.
11. She is a lifeguard.
12. Lifeguards watch the swimmers carefully.
13. Mr. Olsen works at the beach too.
14. He runs the snack bar.
15. His children help.
16. I take long walks along the shore.
17. Sailboards skim over the waves.
18. The colorful sails flash in the sunlight.
19. Grandfather builds wonderful sand castles.
20. People stop to look at them.
21. Our whole family has a picnic on the beach.
22. The hungry gulls wait eagerly for leftovers.

Writing Application: A Story
Write another paragraph to finish the following story:

  The beach was quiet and lonely as my dog and I walked along the shore. I kept my eyes down, looking for unusual shells. Suddenly Princess began barking. I looked up and saw—

Be sure that each sentence has a subject and a predicate.

For Extra Practice, see p. 40. **Complete Subjects and Predicates 21**

5 | Simple Subjects

You have learned that the complete subject includes all the words that tell whom or what the sentence is about. In every complete subject, there is one main word. Sometimes this main word is a name. This main word or name tells exactly whom or what the sentence is about. It is called the **simple subject.** Sometimes the complete subject and the simple subject are the same. The simple subjects below are in color.

COMPLETE SUBJECTS	COMPLETE PREDICATES
Many people	watch ball games at the park.
Martin Johnson	slides into third base.
He	pitched five innings.
The palm of his glove	is torn.

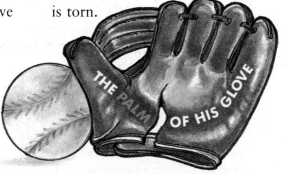

Guided Practice The complete subject of each sentence is underlined. What is the simple subject?

Example: James Naismith invented basketball in 1891.
   James Naismith

1. He was a teacher in Springfield, Massachusetts.
2. The head of the school wanted an indoor winter game.
3. Naismith tacked peach baskets to the walls of the gym.
4. The first players used soccer balls.
5. Each team had nine players.

▶ The **simple subject** is the main word in the complete subject. It tells exactly whom or what the sentence is about.

Independent Practice
The complete subject of each sentence is underlined. Write the simple subject.

Example: People all over the world play basketball.   *People*

6. Basketball is an important sport in the United States.
7. The game is fast and exciting.
8. It draws millions of fans.
9. The season is from late fall to spring.
10. A basketball court is divided in half.
11. A basket hangs at each end of the court.
12. A basketball weighs from twenty to twenty-two ounces.
13. These round balls are made of leather.
14. Players pass, dribble, and shoot the ball.
15. A toss of the ball starts the game.
16. The team with the ball tries to put it into the basket.
17. The other team tries to stop them.
18. Each team has five players.
19. The five players on a team must work together.
20. The center is usually the tallest player.
21. Wilt Chamberlain was a center.
22. He was one of the best players in history.
23. Chamberlain was the first player to score over one hundred points in a single game.
24. Many schools have basketball teams.
25. Diana plays on her school's team.
26. Diana's team won the city championship.

Writing Application: A Story
Write a story about the most exciting game you have ever played. Underline the simple subject of each sentence.

For Extra Practice, see p. 41.

6 | Simple Predicates

You know that the complete predicate includes all the words that tell what the subject does or is. In every complete predicate, there is one main word. This main word tells exactly what the subject does or is. It is called the **simple predicate**.

In each sentence below, the simple predicate is in color.

COMPLETE SUBJECTS	COMPLETE PREDICATES
Some students	go to space camp.
The camp	is in Alabama.
Campers	build rockets.
They	wear real space suits.

Guided Practice The complete predicate of each sentence is underlined. What is the simple predicate?

Example: Students come from all over the country. *come*

1. Campers are astronauts for a week.
2. They work in teams of ten.
3. The members name their teams after planets.
4. Some of the teams launch rockets into the air.
5. Other teams take a make-believe space flight.

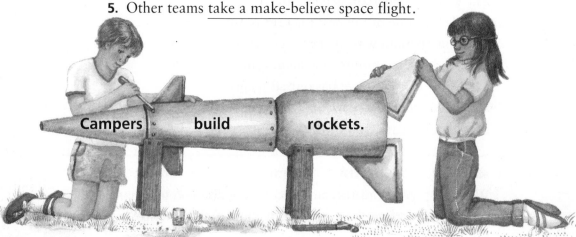

Campers build rockets.

> ▶ The **simple predicate** is the main word in the complete predicate. It tells exactly what the subject does or is.

Independent Practice
The complete predicate of each sentence is underlined. Write the simple predicate.

Example: Hundreds of boys and girls <u>attend space camp</u>.   *attend*

6. Campers <u>are twelve through fourteen years old</u>.
7. All of the students <u>stay at the camp</u>.
8. The camp <u>is in Huntsville, Alabama</u>.
9. Trained leaders <u>help the campers</u>.
10. A camper's day <u>begins about six o'clock in the morning</u>.
11. The day <u>ends about nine o'clock in the evening</u>.
12. The campers <u>do different activities each day</u>.
13. These activities <u>teach them about an astronaut's job</u>.
14. Campers <u>visit the Alabama Space and Rocket Center</u>.
15. It <u>is the world's largest space museum</u>.
16. They <u>go to the Marshall Space Flight Center</u>.
17. Astronauts <u>train at this flight center</u>.
18. Some campers <u>jump into the swimming pool</u>.
19. They <u>practice water-rescue exercises in the pool</u>.
20. The teams <u>taste different kinds of space food</u>.
21. Campers <u>use spacecraft equipment</u>.
22. One piece of equipment <u>is a robot arm</u>.
23. The robot arm <u>grabs objects in space</u>.
24. Students <u>learn answers to questions about space</u>.
25. The camp <u>opens every summer</u>.
26. The Alabama Space and Rocket Center <u>runs the camp</u>.

Writing Application: A Description
Pretend that you have just returned from a week at the summer space camp. Write a paragraph telling what you did at the camp and what you liked best. Underline each simple predicate.

For Extra Practice, see p. 42.

Simple Predicates   25

7 | Combining Sentences: Compound Sentences

One way to make sentences more interesting is to make them different lengths. Sometimes the ideas in two short sentences are related in some way. If the ideas are related, you can combine the two short sentences to make one **compound sentence**.

Britta plays the flute. Todd sings in the chorus.

Britta plays the flute , and Todd sings in the chorus.

Fred dropped the guitar. It didn't break.

Fred dropped the guitar , but it didn't break.

Should I clean my room? Should I practice the piano?

Should I clean my room , or should I practice the piano?

Notice that a **comma** (,) and the word *and, but,* or *or* were used to combine each pair of shorter sentences. The words *and, but,* and *or* are called **connecting words** because they join, or connect, the two parts of a compound sentence.

Fred dropped the guitar, but it didn't break.

Guided Practice
Combine each pair of sentences into one compound sentence, using the connecting word given.

Example: I have a guitar. Ed gives me lessons.   (and)
I have a guitar, and Ed gives me lessons.

1. You can strum. You can pluck the strings.   (or)
2. I know the notes. I cannot play any songs yet.   (but)
3. I pluck with my fingers. I use a pick.   (or)
4. Most guitars have six strings. Some have twelve.   (but)
5. Ed plays electric guitar. He is in a band.   (and)

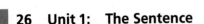

> ▶ If two short sentences are related, they can be combined to make one **compound sentence**. Use a comma (,) and the connecting word *and, but,* or *or* to combine the sentences.

Independent Practice Write each pair of sentences as one compound sentence. Use the connecting word given.

Example: Zoe went to New York City. She visited the Statue of Liberty. (and)

Zoe went to New York City, and she visited the Statue of Liberty.

 6. You may have seen pictures of it. You may have read about it in a book. (or)
 7. It is a statue of a woman. Her right hand holds a torch. (and)
 8. The statue is copper. Its frame is iron. (but)
 9. You can view it from the shore. You can go to Liberty Island. (or)
10. Visitors can climb to the crown. They cannot go into the torch. (but)
11. In 1985 the statue had stood for almost one hundred years. It needed many repairs. (and)
12. Time had aged the statue. Americans were still very proud of it. (but)
13. Money was collected. Repairs began. (and)
14. The repairs were finished in 1986. A big celebration took place on July 4. (and)
15. Were you there? Did you see it on TV? (or)

Writing Application: Persuasion
Students all over the country raised money to help repair the Statue of Liberty. Think of a way to raise money for a project. Write a paragraph persuading people to go along with your idea. Use several compound sentences.

For Extra Practice, see p. 43.   **Compound Sentences 27**

Combining Sentences: Subjects and Predicates

You have learned to combine two short sentences to make a compound sentence. There are other ways to combine sentences to make your writing more interesting. Sometimes you can combine two sentences that have different subjects but the same predicate. Join the subjects with the connecting word *and* to make one **compound subject**.

<u>Kim</u> watched.
<u>Ben</u> watched. > <u>Kim</u> and <u>Ben</u> watched.

Sometimes you can combine two sentences that have different predicates but the same subject. Join the predicates with *and* to make one **compound predicate**.

They <u>smiled</u>.
They <u>reported</u> the news. > They <u>smiled</u> and <u>reported</u> the news.

Guided Practice How would you combine each pair of sentences into one sentence with a compound subject or a compound predicate?

Example: Carl visited Hollywood. Ann visited Hollywood.
(subject)
Carl and Ann visited Hollywood.

1. Movies are filmed in Hollywood. TV shows are filmed in Hollywood. (subject)
2. Ann visited a movie studio. Ann toured the sets. (predicate)
3. She liked the special effects. Her mother liked the special effects. (subject)
4. Carl went to a TV studio. Carl saw a show. (predicate)
5. He met a director. He watched the cameras. (predicate)

> ▶ You can combine two sentences with the same predicate. Join the subjects with *and* to make a **compound subject**.
> ▶ You can combine two sentences with the same subject. Join the predicates with *and* to make a **compound predicate**.

Independent Practice

A. Write each pair of sentences as one sentence with a compound subject.

Example: Careful plans are needed to produce a show.
Many people are needed to produce a show.
Careful plans and many people are needed to produce a show.

6. Scripts must be chosen. Actors must be chosen.
7. Producers discuss ideas. Writers discuss ideas.
8. Producers need helpers. Directors need helpers.
9. Costumes must be planned. Scenery must be planned.
10. Artists work on scenery. Builders work on scenery.

B. Write each pair of sentences as one sentence with a compound predicate.

Example: Actors study lines. Actors practice scenes.
Actors study lines and practice scenes.

11. The director watches. The director makes changes.
12. Workers put up scenery. Workers set up lights.
13. Actors get made up. Actors put on their costumes.
14. The cast comes on-stage. The cast begins the show.
15. Guests sit in the audience. Guests watch the show.

Writing Application: Compare and Contrast
Choose two of your favorite TV shows. Write a paragraph telling how they are alike. How are they different? Use compound subjects and predicates.

For Extra Practice, see p. 44.

9 | Correcting Run-on Sentences

When two sentences run into each other, they make a **run-on sentence**. Do not use run-on sentences in your writing.

A run-on sentence can be corrected by writing each complete thought as a separate sentence. Remember to use capital letters and end marks correctly.

INCORRECT: Our class visited a museum we saw whaling ships.

CORRECT: Our class visited a museum. We saw whaling ships.

Guided Practice Which of the following sentences are run-on sentences? Which sentences are correct? What are the two complete thoughts in each run-on sentence?

Example: Many cities have history museums there are many different kinds.
      run-on   Many cities have history museums.
      There are many different kinds.

1. History museums are fun they teach about the past.
2. A whaling museum is one kind of history museum.
3. A whole village can sometimes be a museum.
4. People dress in costumes visitors can ask them questions.
5. Some famous people's homes become museums you can visit Paul Revere's house in Boston.

▶ A **run-on sentence** has two complete thoughts that run into each other. Correct a run-on sentence by writing each complete thought as a separate sentence.

Independent Practice Rewrite each sentence correctly.

Example: Our class went to the museum it is at Science Park.
Our class went to the museum. It is at Science Park.

6. Nick had never been there he was eager to go.
7. The museum is in a beautiful spot it overlooks the water.
8. There was a special show it was about China.
9. Ellen had read about China she was prepared.
10. People were doing crafts we could watch them work.
11. There was a huge loom two men were weaving silk.
12. They weave patterns each color has a meaning.
13. The weavers gave us a piece of silk it felt smooth.
14. Nick saw a silkworm it was eating a leaf.
15. We liked the computers they taught us Chinese words.
16. Then Ellen wrote a story on the computer she used Chinese words.
17. Kites are important in China we watched a kite maker.
18. He made a dragon kite it had a long tail.
19. Ellen liked the tiny dolls they were made from dough.
20. One woman made the dolls another woman told us about them.
21. Two men made paper they hung it up to dry.
22. We saw clothes each part of China has different clothing.
23. Afterwards Nick bought a kite Ellen bought a book.
24. Our parents went with us they enjoyed the museum too.

Writing Application: Creative Writing

Pretend that you have your own museum. What kind of museum is it? What things are in it? Write a paragraph about your museum. Be careful not to write run-on sentences.

For Extra Practice, see p. 45.   **Correcting Run-on Sentences   31**

Grammar-Writing Connection

Making Sentences Different Lengths

One way to make your writing more interesting is to make your sentences different lengths. The paragraph below sounds dull and choppy.

> Elias Howe was a machinist. His family was quite poor. His wife sewed to make money. Howe watched his wife sewing. Howe soon had a terrific idea. He invented the sewing machine.

The revised paragraph below has sentences of different lengths. This makes it more interesting than the one above.

> Elias Howe was a machinist. His family was quite poor, and his wife sewed to make money. Howe watched his wife sewing and soon had a terrific idea. He invented the sewing machine.

Notice that the writer combined two short sentences to make a compound sentence. Two other sentences were combined to make a sentence with a compound predicate.

Revising Sentences

Revise the paragraphs below by making the sentences different lengths.

1. Thomas Edison was a great inventor. He invented the light bulb. He changed the way we live.
2. Maria Mitchell was a scientist. She looked at the sky every night. She studied the stars. Maria Mitchell discovered a comet. It was named after her. She became famous.
3. Elisha G. Otis developed modern elevators. Elevators were used as early as 236 B.C. They were not used for people. Otis made them safe. His passenger elevator was the first. It was used in 1857.

Creative Writing

Carrie and Cocoa by Robert Vickrey
Courtesy Midtown Galleries

Some paintings tell a great deal, but there is much this painting does not say. Who is this girl? Where is she going on her bicycle? Does this dog belong to her? The artist Robert Vickrey has not told us. Perhaps he simply wants us to look at the lines, patterns, and shadows he has painted.

- How is the shape of the bicycle wheels repeated?
- What feelings do you have when you look at this scene?

Activities

1. **Tell the story.** Imagine that you could talk to the girl in this painting. What would she tell you about who she is and what she is doing? Write the story this girl would tell you.

2. **Write a poem.** What is it like to take a bicycle ride? Write a poem that describes this experience. You may write about an imaginary ride or one you have taken.

Check-up: Unit 1

What Is a Sentence? *(p. 14)* If a group of words below is a sentence, copy it. If not, write *not a sentence*.

1. Many people visit parks.
2. The high mountains.
3. We slept in a tent.
4. Bears visit the campsites.
5. Looking for food.

Statements and Questions *(p. 16)* Write *statement* or *question* to tell what kind of sentence each one is.

6. Airliners carry passengers, baggage, and mail.
7. Would you like to be a flight attendant?
8. My cousin is training to be an airplane pilot.
9. Have you ever flown in a plane?
10. Are you sending your package by air mail?

Commands and Exclamations *(p. 18)* Write each command or exclamation correctly.

11. the buses in London are certainly wonderful
12. take a ride on one of these double-decker buses
13. what a strange bus this is
14. give your money to the collector
15. please sit in the top of the bus
16. how high above the street we are

Complete Subjects and Complete Predicates *(p. 20)* Write each sentence. Draw a line between the complete subject and the complete predicate.

17. My family entered the sand-castle contest.
18. I used my pail and my shovel.
19. We packed it with wet sand.
20. My brother shaped a tower at the top.
21. Many beautiful castles were in the contest.
22. Three judges chose the winner.
23. Our sand castle won first prize.

Simple Subjects *(p. 22)* The complete subject of each sentence is underlined. Write the simple subject.

24. <u>My older brother</u> plays wheelchair basketball.
25. <u>His teammates</u> are in wheelchairs too.
26. <u>Their wheelchairs</u> move quickly and easily.
27. <u>The players on his team</u> practice twice a week.
28. <u>They</u> make some great shots.
29. <u>The game on Friday</u> was very exciting!
30. <u>That game</u> was the first game of the new season.

Simple Predicates *(p. 24)* The complete predicate of each sentence below is underlined. Write the simple predicate.

31. A meteor <u>is a bright streak of light in the sky</u>.
32. Meteors <u>travel through space at very great speeds</u>.
33. A meteor <u>leaves a trail of hot gas</u>.
34. Meteors <u>blaze in the sky for a few minutes</u>.
35. Sometimes they <u>explode into small pieces</u>.
36. People <u>hear the noise for many miles</u>.

Combining Sentences: Compound Sentences *(p. 26)* Write each pair of sentences as one compound sentence. Use the connecting word that is given.

37. A ferry goes from Staten Island to Manhattan. The passengers can see the Statue of Liberty.   (and)
38. The ferry used to cost only a nickel. Today the fare is twenty-five cents.   (but)
39. A bridge was built in 1964. It connects Staten Island to Brooklyn.   (and)
40. People ride the ferry every day. They drive over the bridge.   (or)
41. Part of Staten Island has hills. Most of the land is flat.   (but)

Combining Sentences: Subjects and Predicates *(p. 28)* Write each pair of sentences below as one sentence. Use either a compound subject or a compound predicate.

42. Teachers use TV equipment. Students use TV equipment.
43. School plays are taped. Speeches are taped.
44. The drama club tapes their rehearsals. The drama club watches the performances.
45. New performances can be watched. Old tapes can also be watched.
46. The actors study their good points. The actors learn from their mistakes.
47. The director looks for problems. The director makes improvements.

Correcting Sentences *(p. 30)* Rewrite each of these run-on sentences correctly.

48. The museum had many old cars my friend liked that exhibit.
49. The model whale looked huge Sally was amazed at the sharks.
50. The mummies were in a special room we wanted to see them.
51. The museum has an old-fashioned airplane it looked very small.
52. We saw a model spacecraft it had two model astronauts.

Enrichment

Using Sentences

Rhyming Couplets

Write two-line poems, called couplets, using compound sentences. Choose words that rhyme with each other for the subjects of the compound sentences. The predicates should also be words that rhyme with each other. Draw pictures to go with your couplets.

The train roars,
and the plane soars.

The frog hops,
and the dog flops.

Boats.
Boats sail.
Sleek boats sail gracefully.
Two sleek boats sail gracefully on the bay.

Pyramid Writing

Cut out a magazine picture and paste it onto paper. Then write a four-line pyramid description. Center each line as shown. First, write a simple subject. On line 2, • repeat the simple subject and add a simple predicate. For line 3, add a word to the subject and a word to the predicate. On line 4, add more words to the sentence.

Mixed-up Messages

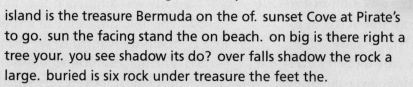

Pirate Redbeard wrote this scrambled message. Unscramble each sentence to find where his treasure is. Write the message correctly.

island is the treasure Bermuda on the of. sunset Cove at Pirate's to go. sun the facing stand the on beach. on big is there right a tree your. you see shadow its do? over falls shadow the rock a large. buried is six rock under treasure the feet the.

Extra! Write your own scrambled message for a friend to solve.

Extra Practice: Unit 1

1 | What Is a Sentence? (p. 14)

● Write *sentence* if the group of words is a sentence. Write *not a sentence* if it is not a sentence.

Example: Our camp was near a lake. *sentence*

1. My brother John.
2. We went fishing.
3. Caught a huge fish.
4. Dad cooked the fish.
5. The fish was very tasty.
6. All the campers.
7. Helped clean up the campsite.

▲ For each pair, write the group of words that is a sentence.

Example: Enjoyed driving to California.
The Lings drove to California.
The Lings drove to California.

8. They visited national parks.
National parks in the West.
9. The parks were beautiful.
Had very beautiful scenery.
10. Oldest and largest giant trees.
Many giant trees are very old.
11. Wanted to see some of the giant trees.
One giant tree is named General Grant.
12. Another tree is named General Lee.
Were named for famous generals.

■ Write one sentence for each group of words.

Example: Saw wild animals. *Todd and Jane saw wild animals.*

13. A deer.
14. Hiked through the woods.
15. A small black bear.
16. All alone in the woods.
17. Strange sounds.
18. Swam in the cool lake.

2 | Statements and Questions (p. 16)

● Write *statement* if the sentence is a statement. Write *question* if it is a question.

Example: How did the Wright brothers become famous?
question

1. They began to build gliders in the early 1900s.
2. Where did they test the gliders?
3. Kitty Hawk, North Carolina, was a good place to test gliders.
4. When did they begin to build airplanes?
5. Their first plane was built in 1903.
6. Orville Wright made the first airplane flight.

▲ Write each sentence correctly.

Example: did you read about the hot-air balloon
Did you read about the hot-air balloon?

7. two brothers in France invented the balloon
8. it carried a duck, a rooster, and a sheep
9. when was this flight
10. the flight took place in 1783
11. how long were the animals in the air
12. they landed safely after eight minutes
13. did any people fly in a balloon in 1783
14. two men flew over Paris for twenty-five minutes

■ Change each statement to a question. Change each question to a statement. Write the new sentences correctly.

Example: was Richard Byrd in the United States Navy
Richard Byrd was in the United States Navy.

15. he was also a pilot
16. was he also an explorer
17. Byrd and another pilot made a flight to the South Pole
18. his first trip to Antarctica was in 1928
19. did Byrd and his team set up a camp
20. was it at the Bay of Whales

3 || Commands and Exclamations (p. 18)

● Write *command* if the sentence is a command. Write
exclamation if it is an exclamation.

Example: Here comes the train! *exclamation*

1. Give your ticket to the conductor.
2. Let me show you to your seat.
3. What a loud noise the train makes!
4. I can't wait to eat in the dining car!
5. Please get me something to eat.
6. How fast we are moving!
7. Please let me come with you again.
8. This is such a great way to travel!

▲ Write each command or exclamation correctly.

Example: be ready for the bike trip at eight o'clock
      Be ready for the bike trip at eight o'clock.

9. let me help you pump up your tires
10. be sure to bring a water bottle
11. please show me the map
12. don't forget your helmet
13. how tired I am
14. my knees are so sore
15. what a huge blister I have
16. this bike trip was so much fun

■ Write each sentence correctly.

Example: wait in this line to board the ferry
      Wait in this line to board the ferry.

17. what a lot of cars and people there are
18. please come with me to the upper deck
19. why does the ferry open at both ends
20. it can be loaded from either end
21. it does not have to turn around
22. what a good idea that is

4 | Subjects and Predicates (p. 20)

● For each sentence, write *subject* if the subject is underlined or *predicate* if the predicate is underlined.

Example: Jan <u>went swimming in the ocean</u>.   *predicate*

1. <u>Pete</u> stayed on the beach.
2. <u>Their mother</u> called Jan.
3. The waves <u>were too high</u>.
4. <u>She</u> ran from the water.
5. The sun <u>shone</u>.
6. <u>The whole family</u> enjoyed the beach.

▲ Write each sentence. Draw a line between the subject and the predicate.

Example: A fluffy white cloud drifted across the sky.
      A fluffy white cloud|drifted across the sky.

7. Phil watched the cloud.
8. It looked like a huge white elephant.
9. Maria disagreed with Phil.
10. The cloud's shape had changed.
11. An enormous white train was now in the sky.
12. The children enjoyed the clouds' shapes.

■ Add a subject to each predicate below. Add a predicate to each subject. Write the complete sentences. Draw a line between the complete subject and the complete predicate.

Example: Streaks of lightning.
      Streaks of lightning|flashed across the sky.

13. A strong wind.
14. Pounded on the rocks.
15. Towering waves.
16. All the people on the beach.
17. The lifeguards.
18. Roared like a lion.
19. The small sailboats.
20. Fell from the clouds.

5 | Simple Subjects (p. 22)

● Choose a simple subject from the Word Box to complete each
sentence. Write the sentence. Use each subject once.
Example: My favorite ____ is baseball.
  My favorite sport is baseball.

name
Babe Ruth
games
sport
players
He
series

1. The most exciting ____ are the World Series.
2. This ____ is played in October.
3. Some baseball ____ become famous.
4. ____ was a famous player.
5. His real ____ was George.
6. ____ became a hero to many young people.

▲ The complete subject of each sentence is underlined. Write the
simple subject.
Example: The game of baseball comes from an old English sport.
  game

7. Children in colonial times played a game with two bases.
8. Abner Doubleday gave the game of baseball its name.
9. He invented the diamond-shaped field.
10. The first pro baseball team was formed in 1869.
11. The name of the team was the Cincinnati Red Stockings.
12. Eight teams formed the National League in 1876.

■ Write the complete subject of each sentence. Then underline the
simple subject.
Example: Outstanding athletes are honored in halls of fame.
  Outstanding athletes

13. Baseball has its own Hall of Fame.
14. It opened in Cooperstown, New York, in 1939.
15. Baseball players are elected to the Hall of Fame.
16. A candidate for the Hall of Fame must be retired.
17. Ten years in the major leagues is also necessary.
18. Many famous players are listed in the Hall of Fame.
19. Babe Ruth was elected to the Hall of Fame.
20. The highest honor in baseball was his.

6 | Simple Predicates (p. 24)

● Choose a simple predicate from the Word Box to complete each sentence. Write the sentence. Use each predicate once.

Example: Earth _____ a planet.
Earth is a planet.

collected
have
learned
move
means
is
landed
shines

1. Planets _____ around the sun.
2. The word *planet* _____ "wanderer."
3. Some planets _____ one or more moons.
4. Earth's moon _____ in the sky at night.
5. Astronauts _____ on our moon in 1969.
6. They _____ moon rocks and soil.
7. Scientists _____ more about the moon.

▲ The complete predicate of each sentence is underlined. Write the simple predicate.

Example: Comets are balls of dust and ice.   *are*

8. Early people called them "hairy stars."
9. A comet has a tail.
10. Comets travel around the sun.
11. Halley's Comet is a very brilliant comet.
12. People saw this comet long ago.
13. This famous comet returns about every seventy-six years.
14. Halley's Comet appeared in 1985 and 1986.
15. Many people looked for it at that time.

■ Write the complete predicate of each sentence. Then underline the simple predicate.

Example: Early people studied the sky.   *studied the sky*

16. They named groups of stars after heroes or animals.
17. We see these same star groups today.
18. The Big Dipper has seven stars.
19. It is part of the Great Bear group.
20. The handle of the dipper forms the tail of the bear.
21. Two stars in the Big Dipper point to the North Star.
22. The North Star appears in the Little Dipper's handle.

7 | Compound Sentences (p. 26)

● Write each compound sentence. Underline the two short sentences that were combined to make the compound.

Example: Ballet is dance, but it may tell a story.
  Ballet is dance, but it may tell a story.

1. My aunt takes me to the ballet, or I go with my parents.
2. Vic's family visited New York, and he saw a ballet.
3. His seat was in the front, and he could see the dancers' faces.
4. The music was great, but the dancing was the best part.
5. The dancers wore lovely costumes, and their movements were graceful.
6. Vic will go to another ballet, or he will watch one on TV.

▲ Write each pair of sentences as one compound sentence. Use the connecting word given.

Example: Ballet looks easy. Dancers work hard.   (but)
  Ballet looks easy, but dancers work hard.

7. Dancers start young. They practice often.   (and)
8. They join a class. They may take private lessons.   (or)
9. Class begins with exercises. The pupils warm up.   (and)
10. The teacher leads the exercises. The pupils follow.   (and)
11. Dancers get tired. They must keep practicing.   (but)
12. They look in a mirror. They correct their mistakes.   (and)

■ Add another sentence to each sentence below to make a compound sentence. Use the connecting word *and*, *but*, or *or*.

Example: Jenny goes to ballet class twice a week.
  Jenny goes to ballet class twice a week, but she would like to go more often.

13. She has taken ballet lessons for five years.
14. Jenny's friend Molly has just started ballet class.
15. Molly is learning the basic ballet positions.
16. Sometimes the teacher plays the piano.
17. Next month the class will give a performance.
18. Jenny will do a solo.

8 | Compound Subjs. and Pred. (p. 28)

● Write each sentence. Underline the compound subject or the compound predicate.

Example: Grandma and Grandpa like to talk about the old days.
Grandma and Grandpa like to talk about the old days.

1. People sat and listened to the radio every night.
2. Adults and children enjoyed radio programs.
3. Comedies and dramas were on the radio.
4. Radio and movies entertained people in those days.
5. Today people watch TV and play stereos.

▲ Write each pair of sentences as one sentence. Use a compound subject or a compound predicate.

Example: Meg acted in a movie. Dan acted in a movie.
Meg and Dan acted in a movie.

6. Their class made the movie. Their class showed it to us.
7. Joe wrote the script. Rosa wrote the script.
8. Mr. Grant directed the movie. Mr. Grant filmed it.
9. Meg had a big part. Meg learned her lines well.
10. Dan helped with props. Beth helped with props.

■ Combine each pair of sentences into one sentence. It may be a compound sentence, a sentence with a compound subject, or a sentence with a compound predicate.

Example: Sports fans cannot always go to games. They can watch games on TV.
Sports fans cannot always go to games, but they can watch games on TV.

11. TV brings sports into your home. TV gives you a good seat.
12. Baseball games are on TV. Tennis matches are on TV.
13. Reporters describe games. Reporters interview players.
14. Instant replays are special effects. Split screens are special effects.
15. Instant replays show you a play over again. Split screens show you two plays at once.

9 | Correcting Run-on Sentences (p. 30)

● Write *run-on* if the group of words is a run-on sentence. Write *correct* if it is correct.

Example: The White House is in Washington it is the President's home.   *run-on*

1. It was not always white it was once gray.
2. Theodore Roosevelt had the walls painted white.
3. Congress changed the name it became the White House.
4. Every President except George Washington has lived there.
5. The White House has 132 rooms you can visit five.

▲ Write each run-on sentence correctly.

Example: Mount Vernon is a famous house it was George Washington's home.
Mount Vernon is a famous house. It was George Washington's home.

6. Washington's father built Mount Vernon it was a farm.
7. Mount Vernon is on a hill trees surround the house.
8. Washington planted trees many of them are still there.
9. Each year over a million people come they visit the graves of George and Martha Washington.
10. They see Washington's furniture his books are in the study.

■ **(11–16)** Rewrite the following paragraph. Correct each run-on sentence.

Example: Congress meets in the United States Capitol it is a building in Washington.
Congress meets in the United States Capitol. It is a building in Washington.

The Capitol has two parts there is a huge dome over the center. One part is for the House of Representatives the other is for the Senate. There is a statue on top of the dome it is called the Statue of Freedom. Each year about ten million people visit the Capitol. Many rooms are open to the public. People may watch a meeting of Congress if they have a special pass.

● ▲ ■ **Three levels of practice   45**

Literature and Writing

In my new clothing
I feel so different
I must
Look like someone else.

Bashō

A Story About Yourself

Getting Ready Sharing an experience can be fun for both you and others. You can enjoy your experience a second time, and your friends can live a new experience through you. When you write a story about yourself, use details to make it come alive. In this unit, you will read one boy's story about himself and later write about an experience of your own.

ACTIVITIES

Listening Listen as the poem on the opposite page is read. Who is speaking? What experience is the speaker telling about?

Speaking Look at the picture. What special event might this girl be going to? What special times have *you* enjoyed? Which ones would be interesting to write about? Have someone write your class's ideas on a chart. Use the list for topic ideas.

Writing In your journal, write about a time that you felt different because you were wearing different clothes.

47

What Is Orange?
By Mary O'Neill

GROUP:	Orange is a tiger lily,
SOLO 1:	A carrot,
GROUP:	A feather from
	A parrot,
SOLO 2:	A flame,
GROUP:	The wildest color
	You can name.
BOTH SOLO VOICES:	Orange is a happy day
GROUP:	Saying good-by
	In a sunset that
	Shocks the sky.
SOLO 1:	Orange is brave
SOLO 2:	Orange is bold
GROUP:	It's bittersweet
	And marigold.
SOLO 1:	Orange is zip
SOLO 2:	Orange is dash
GROUP:	The brightest stripe
	In a Roman sash.

SOLO 1:   Orange is an orange
SOLO 2:   Also a mango
GROUP: Orange is music
           Of the tango.
BOTH SOLO VOICES: Orange is the fur
           Of the fiery fox,
GROUP: The brightest crayon
           In the box.
SOLO 1:   And in the fall
SOLO 2:   When the leaves are turning
GROUP: Orange is the smell
           Of a bonfire burning....

Think and Discuss

1. Which orange things mentioned in the poem can you see? Which can you hear? Which can you taste? Which can you smell?

2. How can a sunset shock the sky? What does the poet mean by "Orange is a happy day"?

3. When two words **rhyme**, they have the same last sounds. In the poem "What Is Orange?" the words *carrot* and *parrot, flame* and *name,* and *good-by* and *sky* rhyme. What other words in this poem rhyme? Where has the poet placed the words that rhyme? Do you think the poem would be as enjoyable if it did not rhyme? Why or why not?

What secret was keeping Clarence hidden in his room for four days? Why were oranges disappearing from the refrigerator? And why did Clarence want so much to surprise his family with this secret?

Confessions of an Orange Octopus

By Jane Sutton

Clarence is a nine-year-old boy who is stuck in his apartment for four days because of a cold. During that time he begins his career as an "orange octopus."

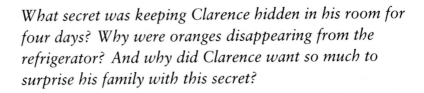

After a while, I was so bored that I started reading *How to Juggle and Feel Like a King,* the book my grandfather sent me from Cape Cod. The first part told how much fun it is to juggle and how there have been jugglers all through history. Then it gave instructions.

I got some oranges out of the refrigerator and started the first lesson. All you had to do at first was toss one orange up and down, and then pass it from one hand to the other. There was a special way to throw and catch, even a special way to hold the orange.

Then came the tough part—adding a second orange. You were supposed to remember to wait for the first orange to almost land in your hand before throwing the second one. It was really hard. I kept dropping the oranges, and it wasn't much fun. After a while, I learned to toss them back and forth, from one hand to the other, without dropping them.

When my mother knocked on my door to call me for lunch, I hid the book and the oranges. I wanted to get really good at juggling and then surprise everyone with my hidden talent. It would be neat to have a talent!

I spent the next couple of days in my room with the door shut. I practiced and practiced. My cold was almost gone, but I pretended to keep coughing so that no one would guess that I wanted to stay inside.

After four days, I was ready for three oranges. It was hard at first. But after a while, I was able to juggle three oranges for about two minutes, without dropping any. I could also juggle three tennis balls. I decided I must be one of the people the book called "naturally gifted jugglers." It was the first time I felt naturally gifted at anything. It figured that my grandfather was smart enough to know I would be good at juggling. He knows me better than anyone.

Finally, I decided I was ready to show off. After dinner, I told my parents I wanted them to see something. I asked them and my brother Bradford to sit in the living room. Then I brought out three oranges and juggled all three without dropping one. I even tried a trick I learned from the book, where you throw one of the oranges behind your back every once in a while.

When I was finished, Bradford started applauding wildly. "That was great, Clarence!" he said.

My parents just sat there with their mouths open. It was the first time I have ever left them speechless. I felt like Superboy!

"That was terrific!" my father finally said, clapping along with Bradford.

"Fantastic!" said my mother. "Where did you learn to juggle?"

"And when?" asked my father.

I reminded them about the book Gramps had sent me, and I told them I had been practicing in my room for days.

"That shows real self-discipline," said my father.

"It certainly does," said my mother. Suddenly, she slapped herself on the forehead. "Now I know why my oranges disappeared," she said. "After my Great Books class yesterday, I was looking for an orange and I couldn't find any. I just *knew* I had bought three for fifty cents at the market. 'Am I going crazy?' I wondered. Then I thought maybe I had accidentally put them in the vegetable bin instead of the fruit bin. So I checked the vegetable bin and . . ."

You can't win with grown-ups. My mother had to go on and on about the oranges—not my juggling. But those few seconds when my parents just sat there with their mouths open made all my practicing worthwhile. Now that I had a talent, I thought my parents might treat me with respect. Maybe I would win once in a while.

Think and Discuss

1. What was Clarence's secret? Why did he want to surprise his family with it?

2. What kind of person is Clarence? How can you tell?

3. "Confessions of an Orange Octopus" is told from the **first person point of view** of Clarence, the main character. Clarence tells the story. He uses first person pronouns such as *I, me,* and *my* to refer to himself. Readers see the story characters and events through Clarence's eyes. Why do you think the author chose to have Clarence tell the story? How might the story have been different if his mother or father had told it?

RESPONDING TO LITERATURE

The Reading and Writing Connection

Personal Response Clarence had four days to learn how to juggle. If you had four days to learn something new, what would you learn? Write a plan telling how you might surprise everyone with what you learned.

Creative Writing What is your favorite color? Write a poem about your favorite color. Think about these questions when you write your poem: What is the smell of your color? the sound? What are some objects of that color?

Creative Activities

Make a Collage Choose a color. Find pictures and objects of that color to make a collage. Arrange and paste your objects on a sheet of paper or poster board. Give your collage a title.

Choral Reading Choose a poem that you like. Divide it into parts for two voices. Practice reading the poem aloud with a partner, each taking a part. Practice reading with expression. When you and your partner are ready to share the poem, read it aloud to your class.

Vocabulary

Suppose your friend says, "I have to juggle my homework, my paper route, and baseball practice." Is this the same kind of juggling that Clarence did? What does your friend mean?

Looking Ahead

A Story About Yourself You will be using details to write a story about yourself. What details did Jane Sutton use to tell how Clarence learned to juggle? Turn to pages 50–51. Find these details.

VOCABULARY CONNECTION
Compound Words

Many words are made up of two or more words used as one word. These words are called **compound words.**

> It figured that my **grandfather** was smart enough. . . .
> *from "Confessions of an Orange Octopus" by Jane Sutton*

Grandfather is a compound word made from two words joined together. Some compound words are written as two or more words, and some are written with hyphens.

ONE WORD	SEPARATE WORDS	WITH HYPHENS
saucepan	living room	make-believe

You can often figure out the meanings of compound words by adding together the meanings of the words from which they are made. Use a dictionary to help you write compound words.

Vocabulary Practice

A. Find the compound word from "Confessions of an Orange Octopus" in each of these sentences. Write the word and the words from which it is made.

1. Everyone in class wanted to become a good juggler.
2. We knew the grown-ups who were teaching the class.
3. They said it would take self-discipline and practice.
4. After we learned to juggle, we felt it was a worthwhile experience and fun, too!

B. Make up four silly compound words, using these words from "What Is Orange?" Write a definition for each new word.

parrot   book   sky   carrot   tiger   flame   juggle

Speaking: Telling a Story

A good storyteller makes listeners feel as if the story is happening right in front of them. In "Confessions of an Orange Octopus," the characters and events seem to come alive.

Guides for Telling a Story

1. Think of a beginning that will get your audience interested. Plan a good ending. Memorize the events in order.
2. Choose words to help your audience see the characters, the actions, and the place where the story happens.
3. Practice your story before you tell it to an audience.
4. Speak loudly and clearly. Look at your audience.
5. Use your hands. Let your face show the characters' feelings. Change your voice for each character.
6. Pause at important points. Make your audience want to hear what will happen next.

Prewriting Practice

Work with a small group or the class. Take turns telling a story about something that happened to you. Follow the guides above.

Thinking: Putting Events in Order

What if the events in "Confessions of an Orange Octopus" had been told out of order? Clarence might have had to juggle before he even learned how! Fortunately, the events were told in an order, or **sequence,** that makes sense. Each event led to the next.

Order words such as *first, next, then, after, before, finally,* and *last* can help show the sequence of events. Do these two story parts have order words?

> After dinner, I told my parents I wanted them to see something. I asked them and my brother Bradford to sit in the living room. Then I brought out three oranges and juggled all three without dropping one.
> *from "Confessions of an Orange Octopus" by Jane Sutton*
>
> I told my parents I wanted them to see something. I asked them and my brother Bradford to sit in the living room. I brought out three oranges and juggled all three without dropping one.

• Which passage includes order words? What are they?

When you read or write a story, remember that the order of events must make sense.

Prewriting Practice

Write the following events in an order that makes sense.

1. I decided on an orange jacket and a top hat.
2. I went to a costume shop and bought a hat.
3. I found an orange jacket in the attic, but no hat.
4. I began to plan my costume for my juggling act.
5. I carried the hat from the costume shop.

Writing a Good Beginning ☑️

Surprised! Curious! That's how you feel when you get interested in a good story. A good beginning captures your interest right away. It makes you wonder what will happen next. A good beginning makes you want to read more. Which of these story beginnings is better? Why?

1. I saw a pretty good juggler the other day. He was doing a lot of things at once. His assistant just kept handing him more things to toss into the air.

2. When the three large eggs flew into the air, I gasped. The Amazing Marmaduke, billed as the greatest juggler of all time, was lost in a blur of motion. Hoops twirled from his right ankle, china plates leaped from his left hand, and the eggs were bouncing in his right hand. Then Marmaduke's assistant approached him. What on earth, I wondered, was the assistant carrying? Surely, Marmaduke couldn't handle even one more thing!

The second beginning is better than the first one. It makes you wonder about what The Amazing Marmaduke will do next. The first beginning is dull and unexciting. It does not tempt you to read the story.

Prewriting Practice

Think of an experience you have had that you would enjoy writing about. Write two good beginnings for a story about the experience. Read the two beginnings to a partner. Discuss which beginning is better and why.

Using Details ☑

Why are some stories enjoyable to read, while others are dull? Details can make the difference. Details give interesting information about the people, places, and events in a story. Read these two paragraphs. They tell how Clarence's friends reacted to his juggling act. Which paragraph holds your interest? Decide which details make it more interesting.

> **1.** Pretty soon, I had my three-orange juggling act going, and I had Gary and Louise going crazy. "Wow! *Wow!*" they kept saying. They were jumping up and down. Gary was so excited that he threw his Boston Red Sox cap in the air.
> *from* Confessions of an Orange Octopus *by Jane Sutton*
>
> **2.** My act was going very well. My friends were really excited about it. One friend was so excited that he threw his cap.

The first paragraph has many details that make it more interesting than the second one. It includes details that tell you *what* act got going, *when* the act got going, and *who* the friends were. Other details describe *how* the friends showed their excitement, *what* cap Gary threw, and *where* he threw the cap. All these details help you picture what is going on in the story.

Prewriting Practice

Rewrite this story. Add details that tell *who, what, where, when,* and *how.*

> A man delivered the box. It was for me. It looked interesting. I got excited. I opened it and found a gift from my grandfather who lives in another state.

Writing a Good Title ☑

Think of the titles of your favorite stories. Does each title give a clue about the story without telling too much? Does each one get your interest and tempt you to read the story?

Read these three titles. Why is the first one the best title for the story about Clarence?

1. Confessions of an Orange Octopus
2. The Time I Learned to Juggle
3. A Juggling Act for My Family

The first title gets your interest right away. It makes you wonder what an orange octopus might be and what an orange octopus might want to confess. The other two titles give you nothing to wonder about. They also tell too much about the story.

Prewriting Practice

Think of some stories with dull titles, such as "The Three Billy Goats Gruff" and "The Tortoise and the Hare." Write new, interesting titles for the stories. Write as many different titles as you can, and choose the one you think is best. Share your ideas with your classmates.

Using Dialogue ☑

You can learn a lot about people from what they say and how they say it. This is especially true of characters in stories. Writers can make stories seem more real by using dialogue. **Dialogue** is the exact words of the story characters. Interesting dialogue can make a story come to life.

Look at the two examples at the top of the next page. Notice how dialogue makes the second example come to life.

1.   When I was finished, Bradford started applauding wildly. He told me my act was great.

   My father, clapping along with Bradford, finally said that the act was terrific!

   My mother called the act fantastic. Then she asked where I had learned to juggle.

2.   When I was finished, Bradford started applauding wildly. "That was great, Clarence!" he said. . . .

   "That was terrific!" my father finally said, clapping along with Bradford.

   "Fantastic!" said my mother. "Where did you learn to juggle?"

from "Confessions of an Orange Octopus" by Jane Sutton

   The following rules will help you write dialogue correctly in your stories.

1. Put quotation marks (" ") around each speaker's words.
2. Identify who is speaking. Use words such as *said Jane* and *Harry yelled*.
3. When one character stops speaking and another character begins, start a new paragraph. Begin the first line a little way in from the left margin.

Prewriting Practice

Rewrite this story. Add dialogue to make it come to life. Use the rules above. Let a partner read your story. Does the dialogue make your story seem real to your partner?

   I couldn't find my juggling pins anywhere. I asked everyone in my family if they had seen them. My brother Nico said he didn't know where they were. My mother asked if I had looked under my bed. I said that I had checked my room seven times. Then my little sister Mary said that she wanted to show us something. She had painted faces on my juggling pins and tucked them in her bed with her other dolls.

The Grammar Connection

Avoiding Stringy Sentences

Stringy sentences have too many *and*'s and *and so*'s. They make writing sound wordy and are hard to read. Do not write stringy sentences. Never use *and so*.

Suppose Clarence wrote the following stringy sentence in a letter to his grandfather. Notice how he corrected it once by making two compound sentences and again by making one compound sentence and two simple sentences.

STRINGY: I had to stay in the house with my cold and I read the book you sent and I really liked it and so I decided to learn how to juggle.

BETTER: I had to stay in the house with my cold, and I read the book you sent. I really liked it, and I decided to learn how to juggle.

BETTER: I had to stay in the house with my cold. I read the book you sent, and I really liked it. I decided to learn how to juggle.

Practice Rewrite each stringy sentence two different ways.

1. My brother's birthday was coming up and I decided to make him a sweater and so I bought this book about knitting and began to read it.

2. The book told me what kind of needles to buy and how much yarn to get and it showed how to do some of the basic stitches and so I practiced those first.

3. Then I started working on the sweater and I kept stopping to count my stitches and so it took a long time to do just a few rows.

4. When I got to the sleeves I was really stuck and so I asked my father for help and he worked on them for a while and then he said he couldn't do sleeves, either.

5. My brother's birthday was almost here and I thought about what to do and I already had the yarn and the needles and so I decided to make him a scarf.

The Writing Process
How to Write a Story About Yourself

Step 1: Prewriting—Choose a Topic

Jesse wrote a list of interesting times he had had that he could remember well. He thought about each one.

fishing trip — The trip was too long to write about.

baseball game with Grandpa — It was fun, but nothing special had happened.

my dog Tina and the porcupine — He remembered it clearly. It would make a good story.

my broken arm — He really didn't want to write about this.

Jesse circled *my dog Tina and the porcupine.*

On Your Own

1. **Think and discuss** List interesting times you have had. Look at the Ideas page for suggestions. Talk about your topics with a partner.

2. **Choose** Ask yourself these questions about each topic on your list.

    Can I remember this time clearly?
    Does the topic tell about one thing that happened?
    Would it be interesting to write about?
    Circle the topic you want to write about.

3. **Explore** How will you begin? What details will you include to make your story clear? Choose an activity under "Exploring Your Topic" on the Ideas page.

Ideas for Getting Started

Choosing Your Topic

Topic Ideas

Learning a new skill
Having the flu
Singing a solo
One stormy night
A hospital visit
Lost on the trail
The soapsuds disaster

Story Starters

Do these starters give you an idea?

We were up in the sky now. I could see clouds. This was my first ride in a plane, and I felt...

It was the day of the school play. I was so nervous! I knew something would go wrong—and it did...

Exploring Your Topic

Show and Tell

Turn your topic into a filmstrip. On a wide strip of paper, draw pictures of what happened in your story. Show your filmstrip to a partner and tell your story. Here is Jesse's filmstrip.

Brainstorming

What is brainstorming? It is just letting your ideas pour out. Turn your mind into a photo album. Pretend the album is filled with snapshots of the event you have chosen to write about. For five minutes, turn the pages of this photo album. Jot down on your paper all the details you can.

Step 2: Write a First Draft

Jesse wanted to write his story for his grandfather. Grandpa had given Tina to him last year.

Jesse wrote his first draft. He wanted to get his ideas on paper. He would correct mistakes later.

Jesse's first draft

- What details did Jesse use in his story?
- Does the beginning catch your attention? Why or why not?
- Why did Jesse cross out the word *and*?

> One day last week I let Tina out. Dad went out to look for her but he came back alone then I heard Tina. I ran to the door. ~~and~~ Blood was all over her nose, and porcupine quills were in the middle of it! Dad took her to a doctor. That night I flopped on the floor beside Tina and fell asleep.

On Your Own

1. **Think about your story and your readers** Ask yourself these questions.

   Who will be reading my story?

   What is my purpose? Do I want my reader to think this experience was funny? sad? happy? frightening?

2. **Write** Write your first draft. How will the beginning catch your reader's attention? Where can you use dialogue? Write on every other line so that you can make changes later. Do not worry about mistakes. Just write as much as you can.

Step 3: Revise

Jesse read his first draft. He wrote a title that he hoped would catch his grandfather's attention. He thought his story was pretty good, but he wanted someone else to hear it. Jesse asked Ben if he would listen to the story.

Reading and responding

BEN: I could really picture how Tina looked!

JESSE: Thanks. What do you think of the beginning?

BEN: Well, it didn't really grab my attention.

JESSE: Hmm. Anything else?

BEN: How did you feel when Tina was lost?

JESSE: I felt terrible! I could tell about that. Thanks, Ben.

Jesse made more changes to his story.

Part of Jesse's revised draft

> Where's Tina?
>
> Bark? Bark?
> "All right, dog," I mumbulled. I opened the door and let Tina out.
> ~~Five hours later Dad asked,
> "Shouldn't Tina be home by now?"~~
> ~~One day last week I let Tina out.~~
>
> Dad went out to look for her but he ~~That was it. Tears came to my eyes.~~ came back alone, then I heard Tina.

Think and Discuss

- Why is Jesse's new beginning better?
- How does the dialogue help make the story interesting?
- Is Jesse's title a good one? Why?

On Your Own

Revising checklist
- ☑ Does the beginning catch my reader's attention?
- ☑ Where can I add dialogue to make my story interesting?
- ☑ Where can I add details to make my story clearer?
- ☑ Does my title give a hint about the story without telling too much?

1. **Revise** Make changes to your story. Write another beginning. Which beginning is better? Add details and dialogue that make your story come alive. Add a title that gives a hint of what your story is about. You may want to use words from the thesaurus below or the one found at the back of this book.

2. **Have a conference** Read your story to a classmate or your teacher.

Ask your listener:	As you listen:
"Does my beginning get your attention?" "Did I leave out any important details?" "Are there any sentences that do not belong?"	I must listen carefully. Does the beginning get my attention? Can I picture what is happening? Is anything unclear?

3. **Revise** Did your partner make some helpful suggestions? Do you have other ideas to make your story better? Make those changes to your story.

Thesaurus

before earlier, previously
event incident, experience
said announced, told, shouted, whispered

strange odd, peculiar, unusual, weird
surprised shocked, amazed

Step 4: Proofread

Jesse proofread his story for mistakes in spelling, capitalization, and punctuation. He used a dictionary to check spelling. He used proofreading marks to make changes.

Part of Jesse's proofread draft

Where's Tina?

Bark? Bark? mumbled
"All right, dog," I mumbulled I
opened the door and let Tina out.
Five hours later Dad asked,
"Shouldn't Tina be home by now?"
One day last week I let Tina out.

Dad went out to look for her, but he
That was it. Tears came to my eyes.
came back alone, then I heard Tina.

Think and Discuss

- Which words did Jesse correct for spelling?
- What punctuation corrections did he make?
- Which word needed a capital letter?

On Your Own

1. Proofreading Practice Proofread this paragraph. There are three spelling errors, a missing capital letter, and three punctuation errors. Write the paragraph correctly.

Proofreading Marks

- ¶ Indent
- ∧ Add something
- ℓ Take out something
- ≡ Capitalize
- / Make a small letter

Last week I went to the pet stoar for a kitten. I told the woman that I wanted a little orange cat. She asked me to wate a few minutes and then we walked past the other pets to the kitten cage. My hart sank. I saw only black kittens. Then what do you think happened a little orange head popped up. "That's the one for me!" I shouted

2. Proofreading Application Proofread your paper. Use the Proofreading Checklist and the Grammar and Spelling Hints below. You may want to use a colored pencil. Use a dictionary to check your spelling.

Proofreading Checklist

Did I

☑ **1.** begin each sentence with a capital letter?

☑ **2.** use correct end marks?

☑ **3.** use commas correctly in compound sentences?

☑ **4.** spell all words correctly?

The Grammar/Spelling Connection

Grammar Hints

Remember these rules from Unit 1 for writing sentences.

- Use a period at the end of a statement or a command.
- Use a question mark at the end of a question.
- Use a comma to combine sentences with *and*, *but*, or *or*.

Spelling Hints

- Words with the (ō) sound can be spelled *oa*, *o*-consonant-*e*, *ow*, and *o*. (*coat*, *bone*, *snow*, *go*)
- Words with the (ā) sound can be spelled *ai*, *a*-consonant-*e*, and *ay*. (*tail*, *flame*, *stay*)

Step 5: Publish

Jesse wanted to mail his story to his grandfather. First, he copied the story in his best handwriting. Then Jesse put the story in a folder. On the cover he glued a photo of Tina and a copy of her pawprint. Jesse wanted Grandpa to know that the story was from Tina too.

On Your Own

1. **Copy** Copy your story in your neatest handwriting.
2. **Check** Reread your story to make sure that you have not made any copying errors.
3. **Share** Think of a special way to share your story. You may want to use some ideas from the Ideas for Sharing box on the right.

Ideas for Sharing

- Turn your story into a book. Add illustrations and a cover.
- With friends, read aloud and act out your story.
- Begin a photo-journal. Make this story the first chapter. Add pictures.

Applying a Story About Yourself

Literature and Creative Writing

The poem "What Is Orange?" lists many ways in which the color orange can be seen, heard, smelled, and tasted. In "Confessions of an Orange Octopus," Clarence tells how he became an orange octopus when he had to stay home with a cold. He spent the time learning to juggle oranges. He surprised his family with a display of his talent.

Use what you have learned about writing stories about yourself. Choose one or more of the following activities.

> **Remember these things.** ☑
> Write a good beginning.
> Include details.
> Use dialogue.
> Write a good title.

1. **Learn from books.** Clarence learned to juggle by following the instructions in a book. What is the most useful or important thing that you have learned from a book? Write a story about what you learned and how it helped you.

2. **Write about your talent.** Clarence became good at juggling. Write a story about something you are good at doing.

3. **Give hints for the housebound.** Can you think of a time when you were ill and had to stay indoors? What did you do during this time? Write a story about your experience.

Writing Across the Curriculum
Social Studies

The things that people do every day show what is important to them. When we write about ourselves, we let other people know what is important in our lives.

Choose one or more of the following activities.

1. **Make a time line.** Time lines show important events in history. A time line can also show important events in your life. Look at Beth's time line below. What events were important to Beth? Make a time line of your life. Include events that are important to you. Then write a story about one of the best events.

Writing Steps
1. Choose a Topic
2. Write a First Draft
3. Revise
4. Proofread
5. Publish

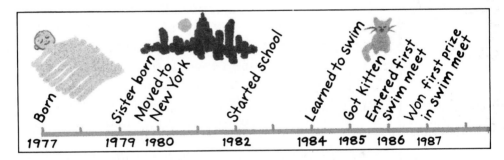

2. **Write about your life.** Are you interested in reading about how people live in other countries? Children in other countries would be interested in reading about your life too. Write about an average day in your life for a child in another country. Tell what you do and what you like best.

3. **Write about your groups.** People belong to many groups, such as families, classes, clubs, and teams. What groups do you belong to? Which are the most important to you? Write about something you have done with a group. You may want to use words from the Word Bank.

Word Bank
companions
interests
recreation
share
support

Extending Literature
Writing a Book Report

Ellie read "Confessions of an Orange Octopus" and decided that she liked Clarence a lot. Ellie wanted to read another story about a character with imagination. She chose *Henry Huggins* by Beverly Cleary. When she finished, she wrote this book report to share with her classmates.

Title Henry Huggins
Author Beverly Cleary
About the Book I just finished reading this book, and I haven't stopped laughing yet. Henry lived on Klickitat Street in a small city and felt that his life was quite boring. He changed his mind the afternoon he found a dog. Henry had been downtown at the YMCA when he found the dog. He called his mother to ask if he could keep it. She said he probably could if he could get the dog home.

That was a problem. Henry had to take a bus home. How could he get this very dirty dog on a bus? The dog was so thin its ribs showed. Henry named it Ribsy. Getting Ribsy home was just the first problem.
My Opinion This is a great book if you like funny stories! You will want to read it to find out how Henry got Ribsy home and what funny things happened after that.

Think and Discuss

- What did you learn about Henry from Ellie's report?
- Why do you think Ellie chose to tell about this part of the book?
- Did this report make you want to read the book? Explain.

Share Your Book

Write a Book Report

1. **Title and Author** Write the title and the author's name.
2. **About the Book** Think about these things when you write this part of your report.

   - Begin your report in a way that gets readers interested.
   - Let your readers know what kind of story it is—funny, exciting, scary, or sad.
   - Tell who the main characters are.
   - Choose one part of the story to share. Give an idea of what the story is about, but do not tell too much.

3. **My Opinion** Write why you liked the book and why you think others would enjoy reading it.

Other Activities

- Draw a map of the place where your book character lives. Show streets, houses, parks, and schools that are important to the story. Add labels that tell what happened in these places.
- Pretend that you and the main character in your book are friends. Think of ways to help the character solve his or her problems.
- Write a description of the main character. How does this person look and act? What does the character like to do?

 The Book Nook

Fourth-Grade Celebrity	Homer Price
by Patricia Giff Casey Valentine decides she must become famous to outdo her older sister.	*by Robert McClosky* Homer lives in a little town where his adventures keep things exciting.

Language and Usage

S un
and rain
and wind
and storms
and thunder go together.
There has to be a little bit of each
to make the weather.

Myra Cohn Livingston, "Understanding"

Nouns

Getting Ready What did you see on your way to school this morning? If you name people, places, or things, they will all be nouns. Without nouns, you would have to draw pictures to tell what you saw! In this unit, you will learn more about nouns and how to use them.

ACTIVITIES

Listening   Listen as the poem on the opposite page is read. How many nouns do you hear? Which noun is a name for all the others?

Speaking   Look at the picture. How many things can you name in this picture? Have someone list the nouns on the board. Did you list at least two nouns that have to do with weather, like the ones in the poem? The picture shows more than one of several things. What nouns name these things?

Writing   Have you ever heard of the old folk tale of making a wish when you see a white horse? In your journal, write three things you wish for.

1 | What Is a Noun?

A **noun** is a naming word. A noun names a person, a place, or a thing.

Nouns		
Persons	Polly brother dentists	**Polly** and her **brother** are **dentists**.
Places	Waterville park zoo	**Waterville** has a **park** and a **zoo**.
Things	pears plums bag	Some **pears** and **plums** are in the **bag**.

Guided Practice
What are the two nouns in each sentence? Does each noun name a person, a place, or a thing?

Example: Alex lives on an island. *Alex—person   island—place*

1. The house faces the dark blue ocean.
2. Fishing boats enter the harbor daily.
3. Many people catch lobsters.
4. Workers lift the heavy traps.
5. Gulls fly over the town.
6. Kathy stands on the shore.
7. The coast of Maine looks far away.
8. A ferry arrives from Portland.
9. Passengers step onto the dock.

Summing up

▶ A **noun** is a word that names a person, a place, or a thing.

Independent Practice Write the nouns in these sentences.

Example: Rico and Matt step off the airplane.
Rico Matt airplane

10. The warm sun shines on their faces.
11. Women greet the boys with necklaces made of flowers.
12. Graceful dancers move to the music of guitars.
13. The boys look forward to their vacation in Hawaii.
14. This state is a group of islands.
15. Honolulu is the capital and the largest city.
16. There are many shops and big hotels.
17. Shopkeepers sell clothes and jewelry.
18. Hawaii is known for its volcanoes.
19. Visitors go to the many beautiful beaches.
20. The famous Waikiki is a beach in Honolulu.
21. Swimmers enjoy the warm water.
22. Some people ride surfboards over the waves.
23. Divers look for colorful fish and plants.
24. Rico found beautiful shells along the shore.
25. Matt found a piece of pink coral.
26. Tourists can drive on twisting highways.
27. The roads pass by valleys and mountains.
28. Scientists study the earth and the rocks.
29. Sparkling waterfalls pour over tall cliffs.
30. Farms and ranches spread over the land.
31. Sugar is the most important product.
32. Some farmers raise nuts or fruits.
33. Pineapples grow in large fields.
34. Rico takes many pictures with his new camera.
35. Matt sends postcards to all his friends.

Writing Application: Instructions

Imagine that you are lost on a lonely island. Write a message to put in a bottle. Write a paragraph that tells someone how to find you. Underline all the nouns in your paragraph.

For Extra Practice, see p. 97. **What Is a Noun?**

Common and Proper Nouns

There are two kinds of nouns. A noun that names any person, place, or thing is called a **common noun**. A noun that names a particular person, place, or thing is called a **proper noun**.

	Common Nouns	Proper Nouns
Persons	girl	Marie
	uncle	Uncle George
	queen	Queen Elizabeth
Places	state	Kansas
	country	Canada
	bay	Bay of Fundy
	park	Glacier National Park
Things	pet	Patches
	day	Saturday
	holiday	Fourth of July

When you write a proper noun, always begin it with a capital letter. If a proper noun is more than one word, capitalize the first letter of each important word.

Guided Practice Find the common noun and the proper noun in each sentence. Which nouns should begin with capital letters?

Example: tanya is an explorer.
          common: explorer   **proper:** *(cap.) Tanya*

1. Her kitten magellan is too!
2. Their trips to florida are always exciting.
3. Do the alligators in the everglades national park look scary?
4. The guides at cape canaveral are helpful.
5. Is there lost treasure in the gulf of mexico?

▶ A **common noun** names any person, place, or thing.
▶ A **proper noun** names a particular person, place, or thing.
▶ Capitalize proper nouns.

Independent Practice List the common nouns and the proper nouns in these sentences. Begin the proper nouns with capital letters.

Example: christopher columbus was a famous explorer.
common: *explorer*   **proper:** *Christopher Columbus*

6. On tuesday our class read about explorers.
7. One book told about brave sailors.
8. Many people searched for the country of china.
9. Was columbus looking for gold and spices?
10. After many days at sea, one man spotted an island.
11. Now columbus day is celebrated in october.
12. People from france explored canada.
13. Their trip down the mississippi river took many months.
14. admiral peary traveled to the north pole.
15. Brave astronauts have explored space.
16. Cameras on rockets take pictures of mars.
17. Was neil armstrong the first person on the moon?
18. amelia earhart flew alone across the atlantic ocean.
19. Long ago maria mitchell observed the sky.
20. This famous woman discovered a comet.
21. Now scientists study the floor of the ocean.
22. sylvia mead discovered many new underwater plants.

Writing Application: A Description
Imagine that you are the first explorer to reach the land of Upsidedownia. What kinds of people, places, and things do you see? Write a paragraph that describes this strange land. Underline all the common nouns. Circle all the proper nouns.

3 | Singular and Plural Nouns

A noun can name one or more than one. A noun that names only one person, place, or thing is called a **singular noun**. A noun that names more than one is called a **plural noun**.

SINGULAR NOUNS

One goat is in the barn .

This hen laid one egg .

PLURAL NOUNS

Many goats are in those barns .

These hens laid a dozen eggs .

How to Form Plurals

Rules	Singular	Plural
Add *s* to most singular nouns.	one boy	two boys
	one puddle	both puddles
	a rose	ten roses
Add *es* to a singular noun that ends with *s, x, ch,* or *sh.*	one bus	three buses
	this box	some boxes
	one bunch	six bunches
	a wish	many wishes

Guided Practice
What is the plural form of each of the following singular nouns?

Example: peach *peaches*

1. brush
2. gift
3. class
4. patch
5. prize
6. circus
7. inch
8. fox

Summing up

▶ A **singular noun** names one person, place, or thing.
▶ A **plural noun** names more than one person, place, or thing.
▶ To form plural nouns, add *s* to most singular nouns. Add *es* to singular nouns that end with *s, x, ch,* or *sh.*

Independent Practice

A. Write the correct noun to complete each sentence. Label the noun *singular* or *plural*.

Example: My family works in many (business, businesses).
businesses   plural

9. Cousin Woody builds many (toolbox, toolboxes).
10. Grandmother Hooper is a basketball (coaches, coach).
11. Uncle Sandy is a lifeguard at a (beach, beaches).
12. Cousin Goldie collects all (tax, taxes) for the city.
13. My sister grows bushels of (radishes, radish).
14. Grandpa Taylor makes some silk (dress, dresses).
15. Aunt Fern owns a plant (store, stores).
16. I rest in the kitchen and eat lots of (sandwich, sandwiches)!

B. Find one noun in each sentence that should be plural. Write the noun correctly.

Example: All the student in my class have different jobs.
students

17. Gino cleans all the brush after art class.
18. Kim Lee gives out pass for the library.
19. Inez helps the librarian put all the book away.
20. Judd washes the two study table.
21. Pedro gives lunch ticket to the fourth graders.
22. Then he helps stack the dish in the cafeteria.
23. Pam's job is to straighten out all the bench.
24. Then she puts most of the lunch box in a closet.
25. Marcy announces the numbers of the four school bus.

Writing Application: An Explanation
In the year 2000, there will be many new kinds of jobs. Write a paragraph that tells what some of these new jobs might be. Use the plural form of five of the nouns from the Word Box. Underline the plural nouns.

box	house	boss	computer	watch	brush

For Extra Practice, see p. 99.   **Singular and Plural Nouns**

4 | Nouns Ending with *y*

You have already learned some rules for making nouns plural. Here are two special rules for making the plural forms of nouns that end with *y*.

How to Form Plurals

Rules	Singular	Plural
If the noun ends with a vowel and *y*, add *s*.	one toy a monkey	many toys five monkeys
If the noun ends with a consonant and *y*, change the *y* to *i* and add *es*.	one family this city a baby	some families six cities two babies

Guided Practice What is the plural form of each noun?

Example: pony *ponies*

1. berry
2. holiday
3. turkey
4. boy
5. bluejay
6. party
7. lady
8. donkey
9. puppy
10. sky
11. hobby
12. key

Summing up

▸ If a singular noun ends with a vowel and *y*, add *s* to make the noun plural.
▸ If a singular noun ends with a consonant and *y*, make it plural by changing the *y* to *i* and adding *es*.

Independent Practice Write the plural form of the noun in ( ) to complete each sentence.

Example: People are finding ____ to save energy. (way) *ways*

13. Drivers save gas by driving slower on ____. (highway)
14. We save gas by taking buses or ____ to work. (subway)
15. In some ____, workers travel by boat. (city)
16. Traveling to work on ____ helps save gas too. (ferry)
17. Newspaper ____ tell about saving energy at home. (story)
18. How can all the ____ in your town help? (family)
19. All ____ and girls can turn off extra lights. (boy)
20. People make sure that ____ are working properly. (chimney)
21. My class did several ____ about saving energy. (play)
22. We all wore matching ____. (jersey)
23. Many ____ and gentlemen enjoyed our show. (lady)
24. Mr. Watts got us books from several ____. (library)
25. We learned that many ____ are helping out. (company)
26. In some ____, bottles are washed and used again. (factory)
27. Waterfalls in deep ____ help make electricity. (valley)
28. Even ____ of sunlight are being turned into power. (ray)
29. The garbage in these ____ might be used for fuel. (alley)
30. Waves in large ____ of water might make your television work someday. (body)

Writing Application: A Story

Finish the following story:

It was a dark night on Floogle Farm when the lights suddenly went out. "Oh, no! It's a power failure!" cried poor Farmer Floogle. He worried about how he would take care of his animals with no electric power.

Luckily, Farmer Floogle had some very intelligent animals on his farm. "Leave everything to us," said the donkeys. Then—

Use the plural form of five nouns from the Word Box.

pony	puppy	turkey	bunny	bluejay	firefly

For Extra Practice, see p. 100. **Nouns Ending with *y***

5 | More Plural Nouns

You know that you add *s* or *es* to form the plurals of most nouns. There are some nouns, however, that have special plural forms. Since these words follow no spelling pattern, you must remember them.

goose

Singular and Plural Nouns

Singular	Plural	Singular	Plural
one child	two children	each tooth	five teeth
a man	many men	one goose	both geese
this woman	three women	an ox	nine oxen
that foot	these feet	a mouse	some mice

Other nouns are the same in both the singular and the plural forms.

geese

SINGULAR NOUNS

One deer nibbled the bark.

Did you see a moose ?

I have a pet sheep .

PLURAL NOUNS

Several deer ate quietly.

Two moose crossed a stream.

These sheep have soft wool.

Guided Practice Complete each sentence with the plural form of the underlined noun.

Example: One child helped both smaller ____ tie their sneakers.
          children

1. That man sang while two other ____ played guitars.
2. This sheep is my pet, and those ____ belong to Fred.
3. Pat hopped on one foot and then jumped with both ____.
4. One goose flew by, and three ____ swam in the pond.
5. Rex had a loose tooth, but his other ____ were fine.
6. Ana saw one moose in Maine and four ____ in Canada.

►Some nouns have special plural forms.
►Some nouns have the same singular and plural forms.

Independent Practice

A. Write each underlined noun. Label it *singular* or *plural*.

Example: The <u>child</u> and his grandfather stared out the window.   *child   singular*

7. Their train sped past many <u>sheep</u> grazing in a field.
8. Nearby, two <u>oxen</u> slowly pulled a plow.
9. A <u>woman</u> wearing overalls followed the animals.
10. In the distance, two <u>men</u> were cutting down trees.
11. The <u>teeth</u> of their saws gleamed in the sunlight.
12. Several <u>deer</u> watched from the edge of the forest.
13. A <u>moose</u> drank from a small watering hole.

B. Write the plural of the noun in ( ) for each sentence.

Example: Six ____ went with Opal to her grandmother's farm. (child) *children*

14. They rode in a wagon pulled by two ____.   (ox)
15. They saw four large ____ near the lake.   (moose)
16. A few ____ stepped quietly across the orchard.   (deer)
17. Norma and Ivan helped feed all the ____.   (sheep)
18. One sheep stepped on Ivan's two ____!   (foot)
19. Eric watched three ____ brushing the horses.   (man)
20. Two ____ taught Misha how to milk a cow.   (woman)

Writing Application: Creative Writing

Imagine that you are making a calendar. Write about what you would draw for five different months of the year. Use one plural noun from this lesson in each sentence, and underline it.

Example: For July, I would draw <u>children</u> swimming in the ocean.

For Extra Practice, see p. 101.   **More Plural Nouns   85**

6 | Singular Possessive Nouns

Sometimes you may want to tell what someone or something has or owns. In the sentences on the left, the words in color show one way to tell what one person or thing owns. Each shorter sentence on the right uses a singular **possessive noun** to show ownership. A noun that shows ownership is called a possessive noun.

SINGULAR NOUNS

This football belongs to Bob .

The bike the girl owns is new.

These poems by Leo are funny.

The tail of the beaver is flat.

SINGULAR POSSESSIVE NOUNS

This is Bob's football.

The girl's bike is new.

Leo's poems are funny.

The beaver's tail is flat.

Add an apostrophe and *s* (*'s*) to a singular noun to make it possessive.

Guided Practice
What is another way to make each group of words show ownership? Use the possessive form of the underlined noun.

Example: jump of one kangaroo   *one kangaroo's jump*

1. balloon of one child
2. nose of the rabbit
3. mask of Gus
4. computer of this man
5. den of one fox
6. collar of our puppy
7. basketball of a friend
8. drawings of an artist

Summing up

▶ A **possessive noun** is a noun that shows ownership.
▶ To form the possessive of a singular noun, add an apostrophe and *s* (*'s*).

Independent Practice

A. Write each phrase another way. Use the possessive form of each underlined noun.

Example: science projects of my <u>class</u>
my class's science projects

9. eyes of the <u>dinosaur</u>
10. posters drawn by <u>Patrick</u>
11. magnets owned by <u>Marita</u>
12. report written by <u>Burt</u>
13. rocks owned by <u>Chan</u>
14. telescope belonging to a <u>teacher</u>
15. hamsters owned by my <u>sister</u>
16. fur of one <u>hamster</u>
17. volcano made by <u>Doris</u>
18. bean plants grown by <u>Hernando</u>

B. Write the possessive form of each noun in ( ) to complete each sentence.

Example: ____ class put on a play. (Wendy) *Wendy's*

19. The principal helped make the ____ costume. (lion)
20. One ____ outfit was black and gold. (dancer)
21. ____ bear suit was soft and fluffy. (Tina)
22. Lee and Mike played the ____ part. (horse)
23. Were the ____ ears made of cardboard? (elephant)
24. Everyone laughed at the ____ funny speech. (mayor)
25. The audience clapped loudly after ____ song. (Ralph)
26. Then ____ wig fell onto the floor. (Timmy)
27. The ____ tail got caught in a door. (donkey)
28. The ____ tap dance stole the show! (chicken)

Writing Application: Descriptions

Imagine that you are in charge of planning costumes for a play. Write about what each character will wear. Use a singular possessive noun in each sentence.

For Extra Practice, see p. 102.   **Singular Possessive Nouns**

You have learned that a singular possessive noun shows ownership by one person or thing. Sometimes you may want to show ownership by more than one person or thing. Here are two rules for forming plural possessive nouns.

1. When a plural noun ends with *s*, add an apostrophe (').

   pumpkins owned by the boys   the boys' pumpkins
   eyes of the puppies   the puppies' eyes

2. When a plural noun does not end with *s*, add an apostrophe and *s* ('s).

   antlers of both deer   both deer's antlers
   reports by these men   these men's reports

The chart below shows the possessive forms of different kinds of nouns. Notice that the singular and plural possessive forms of some nouns are the same.

Singular	Singular possessive	Plural	Plural possessive
animal	animal's	animals	animals'
pony	pony's	ponies	ponies'
class	class's	classes	classes'
mouse	mouse's	mice	mice's
deer	deer's	deer	deer's

Guided Practice
What is another way to make each group of words show ownership? Use the possessive form of the underlined noun.

Example: hats of many <u>firefighters</u>   *many firefighters' hats*

1. canoe of two <u>women</u>
2. tails of some <u>deer</u>
3. poems of four <u>authors</u>
4. saddles of these <u>ponies</u>
5. cage of both <u>mice</u>
6. rules of many <u>coaches</u>

> ▶ To form the possessive of a plural noun that ends with *s*, add only an apostrophe (*'*)
> ▶ To form the possessive of a plural noun that does not end with *s*, add an apostrophe and *s* (*'s*).

Independent Practice

A. Write each phrase, using the possessive form of the underlined noun.

Example: awards of two <u>actresses</u>   *two actresses' awards*

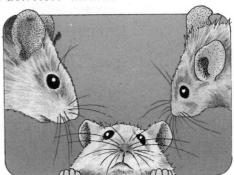

   7. whiskers of several <u>mice</u>
   8. duties of both <u>pilots</u>
   9. trucks belonging to these <u>women</u>
 10. music owned by those <u>singers</u>
 11. tools belonging to five <u>plumbers</u>
 12. wool of some <u>sheep</u>
 13. tents owned by two <u>families</u>
 14. reports by three <u>students</u>

B. Write the possessive form of each plural noun in ( ) to complete each sentence.

Example: The ＿＿ table faced the ring. (judges) *judges'*

 15. All the ＿＿ pets waited in line. (children)
 16. Then three ＿＿ monkeys pulled a wagon. (men)
 17. Two ＿＿ poodles wore pink bows. (ladies)
 18. Several ＿＿ ponies pranced along. (boys)
 19. Some ＿＿ animals did amazing tricks. (people)
 20. Did the ＿＿ goose win a prize? (girls)

Writing Application: Descriptions
The people in the town of Kazoo are having a pet show. Write a description of the pets and their owners. Use a plural possessive noun in each sentence.

        Plural Possessive Nouns   89

Grammar-Writing Connection

Telling More with Nouns

You can make your sentences more interesting by adding nouns that tell more about the subjects. This also gives your readers more information. It helps them understand what you have written.

The first sentence in each pair below tells something about the subject. In the second sentence, there is more information. A group of words follows the subject and tells more about it. That group of words includes a noun.

> Clara Barton started the American Red Cross.
>
> Clara Barton, a <u>nurse</u>, started the American Red Cross.
>
> Albert Schweitzer took care of sick people in Africa.
>
> Albert Schweitzer, a famous <u>doctor</u>, took care of sick people in Africa.

Notice that each added group of words is set off by commas.

Revising Sentences

Copy each sentence below. Fill in the blank with a noun that tells more about the subject.

1. Deb, my older ＿＿＿, wants to be a doctor.
2. Ms. Chin, her favorite ＿＿＿, encourages her.
3. Dr. Young, a ＿＿＿, takes care of sick animals.
4. Pepper, our ＿＿＿, is often Dr. Young's patient.
5. Eric, my best ＿＿＿, reads about doctors.
6. Ms. Lewis, the ＿＿＿, suggested several books for Eric to read.
7. Dr. Gomez, our next-door ＿＿＿, is Eric's hero.
8. Bill, a young ＿＿＿, works for Dr. Gomez.

Creative Writing

Banjo Lesson
by Henry Ossawa Tanner
Hampton University
Museum

The American painter Henry Tanner first began drawing when he was twelve. Many years later, he became well-known for painting gentle, shadowy pictures such as this.

• Why does the picture seem cozy and peaceful?

Activities

1. **Write a dialogue.** Imagine that the man and the boy talk after the lesson. What do they say? Perhaps they trade stories of the day's adventures. Perhaps the man tells how he learned to play the banjo long ago. Write their dialogue.
2. **Describe a special time.** Have you ever shared a special time with an older person? Write a description of that time.

Check-up: Unit 3

What Is a Noun? *(p. 76)* Write the nouns in each sentence.

1. Greenland is the largest island in the world.
2. One part is only ten miles from Canada.
3. The weather is always cold in this country.
4. Ice covers the land in the winter.
5. The people catch fish and seals for food.
6. Women wear colorful clothes on holidays.

Common and Proper Nouns *(p. 78)* Write the common nouns in these sentences in one list. Write the proper nouns in another list.

7. Pam and Jim wrote a report about the Gulf of Mexico.
8. Nancy went to the library to get some books.
9. Brian found a good map of the Atlantic Ocean.
10. His class is learning about the Gulf Stream.
11. This stream was named by Benjamin Franklin.
12. The water in the Gulf Stream is warmed by the hot sun.
13. Warm winds blow toward Europe.

Singular and Plural Nouns *(p. 80)* Write the correct form of the noun in ( ) to complete each sentence. Label the noun *singular* or *plural*.

14. Mr. Graves is a forest ___. (ranger)
15. Reporting forest fires is one of the ___ of a ranger. (chore)
16. Mr. Graves reports all forest ___ quickly. (fire)
17. Rangers clear away lots of dead ___. (branch)
18. Many bulldozers and ___ are used to clear forests. (ax)
19. People get a ___ to some parks from the park rangers. (pass)
20. Rangers find some lost ___ every day. (hiker)

Nouns Ending with *y* *(p. 82)* Write the plural form of the noun in ( ) to complete each sentence.

21. Acting is one of my favorite ___. (hobby)
22. I was in two school ___ last year. (play)
23. One play is made from three short ___. (story)
24. Two people in one story ride ___ to work. (trolley)
25. They meet during ___ on the trolley. (delay)

More Plural Nouns *(p. 84)* Write the plural form of the noun in ( ) to complete each sentence.

26. In 1850 some ___ were looking for gold. (man)
27. They walked until their ___ were sore. (foot)
28. Sometimes ___ pulled the wagons. (ox)
29. The ___ shared the work. (woman)
30. Ted had some ___ near his mine. (sheep)
31. Often he saw ___ in the distance. (deer)
32. Some field ___ nibbled his supplies of wheat flour and cornmeal. (mouse)
33. The ___ played a simple game with a string and button. (child)

Singular Possessive Nouns *(p. 86)* Write each group of words another way. Use the possessive form of each underlined noun.

34. brown horse belonging to <u>Stacy</u>
35. shiny saddle on the <u>horse</u>
36. first horse show of <u>Mike</u>
37. cheers of my <u>brother</u>
38. voice of the <u>announcer</u>
39. horse the <u>rider</u> has
40. starting point of the <u>jumper</u>
41. notebook of the <u>judge</u>
42. trophy belonging to the <u>winner</u>

Plural Possessive Nouns *(p. 88)* Write the possessive form of the plural noun in ( ) to complete each sentence.

43. My ___ grandparents live in the city. (friends)
44. Katie and John enjoyed visiting my ___ farm. (grandparents)
45. Grandfather let us pat the ___ noses. (sheep)
46. The ___ barks helped bring the sheep into the pen. (dogs)
47. The ___ chores take all day long. (workers)
48. Grandfather gets a lot of ___ milk from ten goats. (goats)
49. The ___ basket is near the warm stove. (kittens)
50. The ___ lunch is hearty. (men)
51. We peeked inside the ___ coop. (hens)
52. The ___ honking was heard all over the farm. (geese)
53. I learned about the ___ food. (cows)
54. Billy stayed away from the ___ horns. (bulls)
55. The ___ coats are brushed every day. (horses)
56. Grandmother gathers the ___ eggs each morning. (chickens)
57. Some ___ nest is underneath the coop. (mice)
58. I wrinkled my nose at the ___ food. (pigs)

Cumulative Review

Unit 1: The Sentence

Sentences *(pp. 14, 16, 18)* If a group of words below is a sentence, copy it correctly. If not, write *not a sentence.* Label each sentence *statement, question, command,* or *exclamation.*

1. my family and I ski each winter
2. my skis, boots, and poles
3. cross-country skiing is hard work
4. how thirsty you get
5. have you ever skied downhill
6. what a thrill it is
7. near the trees
8. practice on the small hill
9. would you like some help
10. watch the instructor

Subjects and Predicates *(pp. 20, 22, 24)* Write each sentence. Draw a line between the complete subject and the complete predicate. Then underline each simple subject once. Underline each simple predicate twice.

11. This book is about insects.
12. Most bees are social insects.
13. They live in groups.
14. The bees live on food from plants.
15. Colorful flowers attract the bees.
16. Beekeepers raise bees for honey.

Compound Sentences *(p. 26)* Write each pair of sentences as one compound sentence. Use the connecting word given.

17. Ruth plays in a band. She practices every day. (and)
18. She takes guitar lessons. She plays very well. (and)
19. Ruth practices in her garage. She plays in the house. (or)
20. Chico sings in the band. He also plays the drums. (and)
21. The band practiced today. Chico could not come. (but)

Compound Subjects and Predicates *(p. 28)* Write each pair of sentences as one sentence with a compound subject or a compound predicate.

22. Doctors receive training from television. Dentists receive training from television.
23. TV gives close-ups. TV shows special operations.
24. Local programs teach many subjects. Educational TV stations teach many subjects.
25. Students listen to the teacher on TV. Students study at home.
26. Students take written tests. Students receive grades.

Run-on Sentences *(p. 30)* Rewrite each run-on sentence correctly.

27. Our class visited a museum it is on Oak Street.
28. The museum is in the heart of the city I had never been there.
29. Some teachers went to the museum they liked the Navajo art.
30. The paintings were very old we had learned about them in class.
31. The blankets were colorful Dora liked their beautiful patterns.

Unit 3: Nouns

Kinds of Nouns *(pp. 76, 78)* Write the fifteen nouns in these sentences. Label each noun *common* or *proper*.

32. Mr. Grasso and his family flew over the Rocky Mountains.
33. David and Julie saw rivers, plains, and cities.
34. Their grandparents live in San Francisco.
35. Grandpa was at the airport.
36. The children and their parents enjoyed California.

Singular and Plural Nouns *(pp. 80, 82, 84)* Write the plural form of each singular noun.

37. joke
38. child
39. hunch
40. wax
41. journey
42. tooth
43. hobby
44. woman

Singular Possessive Nouns *(p. 86)* Write the possessive form of the noun in ( ) for each sentence.

45. My ___ drama club put on a play. (sister)
46. ___ scenery was great. (Kim)
47. The ___ costumes were terrific. (cast)
48. The ___ helper collected the props. (director)
49. I laughed at the ___ entrance. (captain)
50. His voice sounded like a ___ roar. (lion)
51. That ___ song was the best in the show. (man)

Plural Possessive Nouns *(p. 88)* Write the possessive form of the noun in ( ) for each sentence.

52. My twin ___ birthday party was yesterday. (brothers)
53. Everyone went to our ___ house to ride the ponies. (neighbors)
54. The ___ manes were tied with ribbons. (ponies)
55. The ___ games were fun! (children)
56. We cut ___ tails out of colored paper. (donkeys)
57. Carl tied on the ___ blindfolds. (girls)
58. We painted ___ faces on balloons. (clowns)

Enrichment

Using Nouns

Celebrity Poster

Pick a career, such as singer, athlete, or author, that has helped people to become famous. Write the name of the career in capital letters at the top of a piece of poster paper. Now look through old magazines and newspapers. Find and cut out pictures of people who have this career. Arrange the pictures in an interesting design on the poster. Write the person's name under each picture, using capital letters correctly.

Your Own Shopping Mall

Pretend to plan a shopping mall. What will you name it? Write the proper noun on your paper. Then list the names of the stores in alphabetical order. Leave some space between them. Under each name, list five things that will be sold at that store. Next, think about where the mall will be located. Draw a map of your area and show the location of the mall.

GIFT LIST

Write the names of five friends or relatives. Now go shopping in a magazine. Find something for each person. Cut out a picture of the gift, and paste it beside the person's name. Use a possessive noun to tell what it is, and include the price—for example, *Mom's book $3.95.*

Extra Practice: Unit 3

1 | **What Is a Noun? (p. 76)**

● One of the underlined words in each sentence is a noun. Write each noun.

Example: Justin learned about underwater volcanoes. *Justin*

1. First, the floor of the ocean shakes.
2. Then a long crack appears.
3. Melted rock pushes up through the crack.
4. It comes from deep inside the earth.
5. The volcano gets larger and larger.
6. Finally, the tip pushes through the water.

▲ Write the two nouns in each sentence.

Example: The students are reading about Indonesia.
students   Indonesia

7. The country is located in Asia.
8. Its many islands are on the equator.
9. Many of its great mountains are volcanoes.
10. Tigers live in some of the dark green jungles.
11. Rice is the main food.
12. Explorers once came searching for valuable spices.

■ Write the nouns in these sentences. Write *person, place,* or *thing* beside each noun.

Example: The Collinses flew to Bermuda in a jet.
Collinses—person   Bermuda—place   jet—thing

13. Then a taxi took the family to an inn.
14. Their room had a window facing the ocean.
15. Michael noticed that the beach had pink sand!
16. Maureen read from a magazine for tourists.
17. One story explained how settlers came to the island.
18. Their ship crashed on the rocks during a bad storm.

2 | Common and Proper Nouns (p. 78)

● Write each noun correctly. Next to it, write *common* or *proper*.
Example: aunt betty   *Aunt Betty—proper*

1. africa
2. maps
3. henry hudson
4. statue of liberty
5. sailor
6. forest
7. october
8. mississippi river

▲ List the common nouns and the proper nouns. Use capital letters correctly.
Example: My friends visited the grand canyon.
common: *friends*   **proper:** *Grand Canyon*

9. Visitors from many states go there daily.
10. The spectacular canyon is located in arizona.
11. Its steep walls were formed by the colorado river.
12. Wind and water gradually wore away the rock.
13. Explorers from spain found the beautiful spot long ago.
14. Later, john wesley powell took a boat down the river.
15. Now hikers climb down a trail called bright angel.
16. Some tourists ride mules instead.
17. Visitors may go to a large museum near grand canyon village.

■ Use one common noun and one proper noun to complete each sentence. Write the sentence correctly. You may add or remove words such as *a, an,* and *the.*
Example: ____ and his ____ are brave explorers!
Harvey and his sister are brave explorers!

18. They took a trip with ____ to explore the ____.
19. Harvey carefully packed the ____ that ____ gave him.
20. On ____ they finally arrived at the ____.
21. According to their map, they had to cross ____ to reach ____.
22. They walked along ____ until they saw ____.
23. Harvey quickly discovered ____ beside ____.
24. How surprised his sister was to see a huge ____ near the ____!
25. After climbing ____ they finally found ____!

3 | Singular and Plural Nouns (p. 80)

● Write each underlined noun. Beside it, write *singular* or *plural.*
   Example: Mr. Okawa sells <u>peaches</u> at his farm.   *peaches—plural*
   1. He puts the peaches in large wooden <u>boxes</u>.
   2. Mr. Okawa sells <u>pears</u> too.
   3. My <u>bus</u> passes the farm stand every day.
   4. We often see Mrs. Okawa out trimming her rose <u>bushes</u>.
   5. She has a <u>basket</u> of beautiful pink flowers beside her.
   6. Mrs. Okawa takes off her <u>hat</u> and waves it at us.
   7. Once she gave two <u>bunches</u> of flowers to our bus driver.

▲ Write the plural form of the noun in ( ) to complete each
   sentence.
   Example: Jason went to work with his two ____. (uncle) *uncles*
   8. They build ____ in the city. (skyscraper)
   9. Jason took two ____ and a pear for lunch. (sandwich)
   10. He traveled across town on three different ____. (bus)
   11. Uncle Pete introduced Jason to both of his ____. (boss)
   12. Next, Jason met several ____. (carpenter)
   13. They explained how the tools in two ____ worked. (toolbox)
   14. A woman hurried by with a box of ____. (paintbrush)

■ If the underlined noun is singular, make it plural. If it is plural,
   make it singular. Write the new sentence.
   Example: Grandmother had her own clothing <u>store</u> in Italy.
           Grandmother had her own clothing stores in Italy.
   15. She made dresses for Italy's most famous <u>actresses</u>.
   16. I hoped Grandmother would leave her <u>business</u> in Italy.
   17. I wanted her to live with my <u>cousin</u> and me in New York.
   18. My <u>wish</u> finally came true!
   19. Grandmother arrived with her <u>boxes</u> of beautiful cloth.
   20. Soon she opened her new dress <u>shop</u> downtown.
   21. Grandmother taught me to sew with her special <u>needles</u>.
   22. Then she sewed the velvet <u>patch</u> on my jeans.

4 | Nouns Ending with *y* (p. 82)

● Write the plural nouns in these sentences.

Example: The libraries in our city are closed on holidays.
libraries   holidays

1. All the factories are closed as well.
2. Some companies remain open.
3. We can still buy groceries at the corner store.
4. The drugstore will not make any deliveries.
5. The highways have very heavy traffic.
6. The subways do not run very often.
7. The airport runways are busier than usual.

▲ Write each sentence. Use the plural form of the noun in (   ).

Example: Two Presidents have _____ in February.   (birthday)
Two Presidents have birthdays in February.

8. Our class performed two short _____ about them.   (play)
9. Miss Moran read us _____ about both men.   (story)
10. We learned many facts in just a few _____.   (day)
11. Washington's army had very few _____.   (supply)
12. Lincoln carried out his many _____ honestly.   (duty)
13. He didn't want the northern and southern states to become
    _____.   (enemy)

■ Find the noun in each sentence that should be plural. Write the
noun correctly.

Example: Of all the holiday, Thanksgiving is my favorite.
holidays

14. Dad gets up very early and puts two turkey in the oven.
15. I watch puffy smoke rise from all the chimney in town.
16. My sisters and both of their family arrive first.
17. Then Cousin Rita arrives with two large tray of fruits.
18. Aunt Jo brings homemade breads made with lots of nuts,
    oranges, and cranberry.
19. Uncle Nate tells long story of when he was a boy.
20. My favorite is about the time he lost three pet donkey.

5 | More Plural Nouns (p. 84)

● Write each underlined noun. Beside it, write *singular* or *plural*.

Example: Some <u>deer</u> are good swimmers.   *deer—plural*

1. The farmer used two <u>oxen</u> to pull his plow.
2. A <u>woman</u> at the repair shop fixed our radio.
3. Six <u>sheep</u> grazed quietly in the meadow.
4. The <u>men</u> drove tractors through the fields.
5. The <u>goose</u> honked loudly at the chickens in the barnyard.
6. Are the <u>children</u> awake yet?
7. My little pet <u>mouse</u> eats seeds and nuts.
8. A duck has webbed <u>feet</u> to help it swim.
9. My front <u>tooth</u> is loose.

▲ Write each sentence correctly. Use the plural form of the noun in ( ).

Example: Two _____ showed us the pioneer village.   (woman)
Two women showed us the pioneer village.

10. We saw some _____ working at spinning wheels.   (child)
11. They made thread from the wool of many _____.   (sheep)
12. Several _____ were repairing the roof of a barn.   (man)
13. Some surprised _____ hurried across the barnyard.   (mouse)
14. Two _____ pulled a wagon filled with hay.   (ox)
15. A boy gathered eggs that all his _____ had laid.   (goose)
16. A blacksmith put new shoes on a horse's front _____.   (foot)

■ Write the correct form of the noun in ( ) for each sentence.

Example: A painting of a _____ was on the wall.   (deer)   *deer*

17. A picture of some _____ was next to it.   (moose)
18. A _____ worked quietly weaving cloth.   (woman)
19. She used wool from her flock of _____.   (sheep)
20. Two small _____ played by the fire.   (child)
21. They sat on pillows stuffed with feathers from _____.   (goose)
22. One child played with a pet white _____.   (mouse)
23. Near the window, two _____ played fiddles.   (man)
24. They tapped their _____ to the music.   (foot)

6 | Singular Possessive Nouns (p. 86)

● Write the possessive form of each singular noun.

Example: brother *brother's*

1. Monica	**7.** mouse
2. tiger	**8.** principal
3. singer	**9.** Jenny
4. Carlos	**10.** coach
5. panda	**11.** Bess
6. Charles	**12.** boy

▲ Write each group of words another way. Use the possessive form of the underlined noun.

Example: paintings by one <u>student</u> *one student's paintings*

13. picture drawn by <u>Isabel</u>

14. paintbrushes belonging to <u>Li</u>

15. crayons owned by one <u>girl</u>

16. mask painted by <u>Julio</u>

17. face of the <u>gorilla</u>

18. wings of the clay <u>dragon</u>

19. mobiles belonging to one <u>boy</u>

20. scissors owned by <u>Allison</u>

21. art show of the whole <u>class</u>

■ Write each sentence another way. Use a possessive noun to take the place of the underlined words.

Example: The club <u>of Jess</u> had a neighborhood circus.
        Jess's club had a neighborhood circus.

22. They held their circus in the yard <u>belonging to Mr. Wong.</u>

23. Posters <u>made by Chris</u> announced the circus.

24. Tickets were printed on a computer <u>owned by Marcus.</u>

25. Julia made the nose <u>of the elephant</u> from a hose.

26. The roar <u>of the lion</u> came from a tape recorder.

27. The hat <u>belonging to one clown</u> had tin cans on it.

28. A goat <u>owned by Marcy</u> pulled the circus wagon.

7 | Plural Possessive Nouns (p. 88)

● For each pair, write the group of words that has a plural possessive noun.

Example: my teacher's dictionaries
my teachers' dictionaries   *my teachers' dictionaries*

1. the butterflies' wings
   the butterfly's wings
2. our bosses' notebook
   our boss's notebook
3. the actors' costumes
   the actor's costumes
4. her brother's snowshoes
   her brothers' snowshoes
5. the woman's cameras
   the women's cameras
6. the mice's ears
   the mouse's ears

▲ Write the possessive form of the noun in ( ) for each sentence.

Example: The Young ____ Club meets after school.   (Farmers)
Farmers'

7. Everyone learns a lot about ____ habits.   (animals)
8. Each year the ____ entries win prizes at the fair.   (children)
9. Their ____ eggs are the largest in the county!   (geese)
10. People always admire the ____ dairy cows.   (girls)
11. The ____ ponies win many ribbons.   (boys)
12. Judges carefully check the ____ coats.   (ponies)
13. Who can shear the ____ wool the fastest?   (sheep)

■ Write the plural possessive form of the singular noun in ( ) to complete each sentence.

Example: Our ____ farm is next to ours.   (neighbor)
Our neighbors' farm is next to ours.

14. Their ____ goats often wander onto our lawn.   (son)
15. The goats have taken over my ____ job of mowing the lawn.   (sister)
16. Who would like my job of collecting the ____ eggs?   (chicken)
17. Maybe the boys will let me taste their ____ milk.   (goat)
18. The ____ two sheep give them lots of wool.   (girl)
19. Amy makes sweaters from the ____ wool.   (sheep)
20. She makes all the ____ sweaters for the family.   (child)

Literature and Writing

The crocodile is in the same family as the alligator. They are both reptiles. . . . Like alligators, crocodiles live in and near the water and build their nests where it is dry. The crocodile has a narrower head and a longer jaw than the alligator.

Robin B. Cano and Irving Wasserman
from *Animal Encyclopedia*

Comparison and Contrast

Getting Ready As you see and learn about new things, you may compare and contrast them with things you know. When you see two different movies and think about how they are alike, you compare them. When you think about how they are different, you contrast them. In this unit, you will read comparison and contrast paragraphs and write some of your own.

ACTIVITIES

Listening   Listen as the paragraph on the opposite page is read. In what ways are alligators and crocodiles alike? In what ways are they different?

Speaking   Look at the picture. Unless you are an expert on reptiles, you cannot tell that this animal is an alligator. What would you need to see in order to be sure which animal it is?

Writing   Think of two other animals. How are they alike? How are they different? List your ideas in your journal.

LITERATURE

Ideas can come from many different places. Ramona's idea for her book report came from a cat-food commercial. What happened when she gave her report?

All About Cats
You and Your Cat

Ramona's Book Report

By Beverly Cleary

The book, *The Left-Behind Cat,* which Mrs. Whaley had sent home for Ramona to read for her report, was divided into chapters but used babyish words. The story was about a cat that was left behind when a family moved away. Medium-boring, thought Ramona.

"Daddy, how do you sell something?" Ramona interrupted her father, who was studying, even though she knew she should not. However, her need for an answer was urgent.

Mr. Quimby did not look up from his book. "You ought to know. You see enough commercials on television."

Ramona considered his answer. She had always looked upon commercials as entertainment, but now she thought about some of her favorites—the cats that danced back and forth, the dog that pushed away brand-X dog food with his paw, the man who ate a pizza, got indigestion, and groaned that he couldn't believe he ate the *whole* thing, the six horses that pulled the Wells Fargo bank's stagecoach across deserts and over mountains.

"Do you mean I should do a book report like a T.V. commercial?" Ramona asked.

"Why not?" Mr. Quimby answered in an absentminded way.

"I don't want my teacher to say I'm a nuisance," said Ramona, needing assurance from a grown-up.

This time Mr. Quimby lifted his eyes from his book. "Look," he said, "she told you to pretend you're selling the book, so sell it. What better way than a T.V. commercial? You aren't being a nuisance if you do what your teacher asks."

Ramona went to her room and looked at her table, which the family called "Ramona's studio," because it was a clutter of crayons, different kinds of paper, tape, bits of yarn, and odds and ends that Ramona used for amusing herself. Then Ramona thought a moment, and suddenly, filled with inspiration, she went to work. She knew exactly what she wanted to do and set about doing it. She worked with paper, crayons, tape, and rubber bands. She worked so hard and with such pleasure that her cheeks grew pink. Nothing in the whole world felt as good as being able to make something from a sudden idea.

Finally, with a big sigh of relief, Ramona leaned back in her chair to admire her work: three cat masks with holes for eyes and mouths, masks that could be worn by hooking rubber bands over ears. But Ramona did not stop there. With pencil and paper, she began to write out what she would say. She was so full of ideas that she printed rather than waste time in cursive writing. Next she phoned Sara and Janet, keeping her voice low and trying not to giggle so she wouldn't disturb her father any more than necessary, and explained her plan to them. Both her friends giggled and agreed to take part in the book report. Ramona spent the rest of the evening memorizing what she was going to say.

When school started, Ramona slipped cat masks to Sara and Janet, handed her written excuse for her absence to Mrs. Whaley, and waited, fanning away escaped fruit flies, for book reports to begin.

After arithmetic, Mrs. Whaley called on several people to come to the front of the room to pretend they were selling books to the class. Most of the reports began, "This is a book about..." and many, as Beezus had predicted, ended with "...if you want to find out what happens next, read the book."

Then Mrs. Whaley said, "We have time for one more report before lunch. Who wants to be next?"

Ramona waved her hand, and Mrs. Whaley nodded.

108

Ramona beckoned to Sara and Janet, who giggled in an embarrassed way but joined Ramona, standing behind her and off to one side. All three girls slipped on their cat masks and giggled again. Ramona took a deep breath as Sara and Janet began to chant, "*Meow*, meow, meow, meow. *Meow*, meow, meow, meow," and danced back and forth like the cats they had seen in the cat-food commercial on television.

"*Left-Behind Cat* gives kids something to smile about," said Ramona in a loud clear voice, while her chorus meowed softly behind her. She wasn't sure that what she said was exactly true, but neither were the commercials that showed cats eating dry cat food without making any noise. "Kids who have tried *Left-Behind Cat* are all smiles, smiles, smiles. *Left-Behind Cat* is the book kids ask for by name. Kids can read it every day and thrive on it. The happiest kids read *Left-Behind Cat*. *Left-Behind Cat* contains cats, dogs, people—" Here Ramona caught sight of Yard Ape leaning back in his seat, grinning in the way that always flustered her. She could not help interrupting herself with a giggle, and after suppressing it she tried not to look at Yard Ape and to take up where she had left off. "... cats, dogs, people—" The giggle came back, and Ramona was lost. She could not remember what came next. "... cats, dogs, people," she repeated, trying to start and failing.

Mrs. Whaley and the class waited. Yard Ape grinned. Ramona's loyal chorus meowed and danced. This performance could not go on all morning. Ramona had to say something, anything to end the waiting, the meowing, her book report. She tried desperately to recall a cat-food commercial, any cat-food commercial, and could not. All she could remember was the man on television who ate the pizza, and so she blurted out the only sentence she could think of, "I can't believe I read the *whole* thing!"

Mrs. Whaley's laugh rang out above the laughter of the class. Ramona felt her face turn red behind her mask, and her ears, visible to the class, turned red as well.

"Thank you, Ramona," said Mrs. Whaley. "That was most entertaining. Class, you are excused for lunch."

Ramona felt brave behind her cat mask. "Mrs. Whaley," she said, as the class pushed back chairs and gathered up lunch boxes, "that wasn't the way my report was supposed to end."

"Did you like the book?" asked Mrs. Whaley.

"Not really," confessed Ramona.

"Then I think it was a good way to end your report," said the teacher. "Asking the class to sell books they really don't like isn't fair, now that I stop to think about it. I was only trying to make book reports a little livelier."

Think and Discuss

1. Did Ramona's book report turn out the way she had planned? Explain.

2. Why was Ramona's ending to her book report a good one after all?

3. Mrs. Whaley said that it wasn't fair to ask the students to sell books that they didn't like. Do you agree with her? Why or why not?

4. The story "Ramona's Book Report" is **fiction**. This means that the characters and happenings in the story are not real. The author created them from her imagination. What are some other fiction stories that you have read?

Animals in TV commercials often do some pretty amazing tricks. How are animals trained for commercials?

Animals in Advertising

By Virginia Phelps Clemens

A dog likes affection and will work for praise alone from his master. Cats and most other animals work for food. They learn to do a trick when a buzzer, clicker, or bell signals them to do it. They are rewarded with a piece of food for doing the trick correctly. Since they won't work when they are not hungry, they are fed only half of their daily food portion at mealtimes. The rest is given to them as rewards during training or working sessions.

Doubles are used for animals that have to gobble up a bowl of pet food for a commercial. Once a dog has eaten one bowl he will not do it again until hungry. This is when the double steps in and takes his place for reshooting.

A lot of time is spent teaching a cat her first trick, but after she gets the idea, she will learn new tricks even faster than a dog. Animal trainer Frank Inn says you can train a dog, but you have to "con" or fool a cat.

For a cat-food commercial, animal trainer Moe DiSesso taught four cats to play a grand piano at the Hollywood Bowl. They learned to sit on the piano bench with their front paws on the keys. When Mr. DiSesso said, "Play, play, play," they would bang on the keys as if playing a song.

Mr. DiSesso started with fifteen cats, but dropped five after three days because they did not pay attention to him. In three weeks he trained the remaining ten cats to play the piano, then picked the four best for the commercial.

Mr. DiSesso also trained a cat to open her own can of cat food with an electric can opener. However, cat-food companies did not want to use this trick because they felt it was so good that people would think it was a fake. Finally, a cat-food company in Canada bought the stunt.

Although animal advertisers may never use the product they are advertising, they are very good at making people aware of it. The animals may not be stars, but they do stand out even if they are only in the background.

Think and Discuss

1. How are dogs and cats trained for television commercials?
2. Why might some people think that a cat opening its own can of cat food with an electric can opener was a fake stunt?
3. "Animals in Advertising" is **nonfiction**. Nonfiction stories tell about events that really happened. The people or animals in the story are real. Think about the information in "Animals in Advertising." What facts do you find the most interesting? Explain.

RESPONDING TO LITERATURE

The Reading and Writing Connection

Personal Response When Ramona needed an idea for her report, she thought about her favorite commercials. What is your favorite commercial? Write several sentences telling why you like it. Does it make you want to buy the product? Why?

Creative Writing Pretend that you are making a commercial. You will use a trained kangaroo, crocodile, or other animal. Choose a product to sell and an animal to sell it. Describe what will happen in your commercial, and write the words that will be used.

Creative Activities

Make a Mobile Draw, color, and cut out objects and characters that appear in the story "Ramona's Book Report." Use thread to attach the cutouts to a coat hanger. Hang the mobile where it can move freely.

Give a Talk Choose something to "sell," and prepare a TV commercial to present to your class. Use any props that will help get your message across. Some examples of things you might "sell" are a favorite food, game, or pet.

Vocabulary

Look up the word *stunt* in a dictionary. Describe stunts that you have seen on TV. Why do some actors use trained people to do their stunts?

Looking Ahead

Comparison and Contrast You will be writing about how things are alike and different. The first paragraph of "Animals in Advertising" contrasts two things, or tells how they are different. How are dogs and cats trained differently?

VOCABULARY CONNECTION
Homophones

Some words sound alike but have different spellings and meanings. These words are called **homophones.**

> "Look," he said, "she told you to pretend **you're** selling the book, so sell it. . . ."
>
> "Then I think it was a good way to end **your** report. . . ."
> *from "Ramona's Book Report" by Beverly Cleary*

The words *you're* (contraction for *you are*) and *your* (belonging to you) are homophones. These words are pronounced the same way, but they are spelled differently and have different meanings. Here are some other homophones.

blew, blue   our, hour   write, right   for, four

When you use homophones, be sure to spell them correctly.

Vocabulary Practice

A. Write each sentence, using the correct homophones. You may use your dictionary for help.

1. The wind ____ ripples in the ____ water. (blew, blue)
2. We had been sailing on ____ boat for an ____. (hour, our)
3. We could ____ the ____ all around us. (see, sea)
4. When we got home, I felt ____ for a ____. (week, weak)

B. Each of these words from "Ramona's Book Report" is part of a homophone pair. Write another homophone to complete each pair. Then write one sentence for each word in the pair. Use a dictionary if you need help.

5. knew   **6.** one   **7.** ate   **8.** their   **9.** way

Prewriting
Comparison and Contrast

Listening: For the Main Idea

If you listen carefully to a talk, you can find out two important things. First, you can find out what the **topic** is. The topic is the one thing that the talk is about. Second, you can tell what the **main idea** is. The main idea sums up what the speaker has to say about the topic.

Guides for Listening to the Main Idea

1. Pay close attention.
2. Ask yourself these questions:
  What one thing, or **topic,** is the speaker talking about?
  What **main idea** sums up what the talk is about?

Listen as your teacher or a classmate reads aloud this group of sentences. What is the topic? What is the main idea?

A dog likes affection and will work for praise alone from his master. Cats and most other animals work for food. They learn to do a trick when a buzzer, clicker, or bell signals them to do it. They are rewarded with a piece of food for doing a trick correctly.

from "Animals in Advertising"
by Virginia Phelps Clemens

If you listened carefully, you were able to tell that the topic is *why dogs and cats work.* The main idea is *dogs work for praise, while cats and most other animals work for food.*

Prewriting Practice

Listen as your teacher reads aloud. Then write the topic and the main idea of each group of sentences. Use the guides above.

Thinking: Likenesses and Differences

When you think about how two items are alike, you **compare** them. For example, you might notice that two cats play the same way with a piece of string. If you were to compare the two cats' actions, you would begin by listing ways in which they act alike.

When you think about how two items are different, you **contrast** them. For example, you might notice how differently a dog and a cat behave, even though they live in the same house. To contrast the dog and the cat, you would begin by listing ways in which they act differently.

Think of the facts you learned in "Animals in Advertising." How would you compare the ways dogs and cats are used in advertising? You might make a list like this.

Likenesses

DOGS AND CATS
1. Get rewards for tricks
2. Require doubles when bowls of food must be gobbled
3. Stand out in commercials

Suppose, instead, that you wanted to contrast dogs and cats in advertising. Then you would make a list like the one below to show the ways in which they are different.

Differences

DOGS	CATS
1. Work for praise	1. Work for food
2. Can be trained to do tricks	2. Must be fooled to do tricks
3. Take time to learn each new trick	3. Learn first trick slowly but then learn quickly

Learn to recognize when a writer is comparing or contrasting. Read the beginnings at the top of the next page.

1. Our new cat looks just like our old one.

2. Your class and mine seem different in almost every way.

3. Books and movies are different, even when they tell the same story.

4. Everyone tells me that dogs and cats are different, but my cat and dog are very much alike.

- Which sentences tell that the writer will compare things?
- Which sentences tell that the writer will contrast things?

You will probably often write about things by comparing and contrasting them. Remember to begin by making one list to show how the things are alike and another list to show how they are different.

Prewriting Practice

A. Decide if each writer is going to compare or contrast.

   1. We celebrate my birthday and my brother's birthday in the same way.

   2. My sister and I look alike, but we are very different.

   3. Although Ben and I are the same age, we are not alike.

   4. Eva's costume was just like yours.

B. Compare and contrast the items in each pair below. First, make a list that shows how the two items are alike. Then make a list that shows how they are different.

   1. bicycle, automobile   **3.** Saturday, Monday
   2. spoon, fork   **4.** ball game, race

C. Compare and contrast radio commercials and TV commercials. First, make a list of their likenesses. Then make a list of their differences.

D. Compare and contrast lunchtime at school with lunchtime somewhere else, such as in a restaurant, your home, a park, or a friend's house. First, list the ways in which the two are alike. Then list the ways in which they are different.

Composition Skills
Comparison and Contrast

Topic Sentences and Supporting Details ☑

A **paragraph** is a group of sentences that tell about one main idea. The first line of a paragraph is **indented.** This means that it begins a few spaces to the right of the left margin. The indented line tells you that a group of related sentences follows.

The sentence that tells the main idea of a paragraph is called the **topic sentence.** It is often the first sentence in the paragraph. The other sentences in the paragraph give **supporting details** about the main idea.

Read the following paragraph. What is the topic? What is the main idea? Which sentence tells the main idea? What details do the other sentences give to support the main idea?

> All dolphins have their own personalities. Some will work with only one trainer, others will obey any trainer. Some dolphins get very jealous if their trainer pays too much attention to another dolphin, and others work well with a partner. If a dolphin is annoyed, he may slap the water with his tail, drenching his trainer, or give him a butt or even a bite.
>
> *from* Animals in Advertising *by Virginia Phelps Clemens*

Did you discover that the topic of the paragraph is *dolphins*? The main idea is *dolphins have their own personalities.* The first sentence tells the main idea. It is the topic sentence. The other sentences give supporting details, such as *some dolphins get very jealous* and *other dolphins work well with partners.*

When you write a paragraph, make sure that all of the sentences tell about the main idea. Read the following paragraph.

Huge, shaggy Newfoundland dogs are well-suited to working in water. Their front paws are webbed, which helps them to swim well. With two coats of thick fur to keep them warm and dry, they can stay in cold water a long time. Golden retrievers are good at fetching. There are many stories of Newfoundlands rescuing people from the ocean.

- What is the main idea?
- Which sentence does not keep to the main idea?

The main idea of this paragraph is *Newfoundland dogs are well-suited to working in the water.* Did you find the sentence that does not belong in the paragraph? The sentence *Golden retrievers are good at fetching* does not keep to the main idea. It does not support the topic sentence.

Prewriting Practice

These paragraphs do not have topic sentences. Write a topic sentence for each paragraph.

Chickadees and mice live in small holes in trees. The larger holes are occupied by bigger animals such as squirrels, raccoons, and chipmunks. Even ducks can be found making their homes in comfortable tree holes.

Benji, who is part poodle and part cocker spaniel, has starred in many films. He was found in an animal shelter in California. Spike was the starring pooch in a Walt Disney movie. Like Benji, he was found in a California animal shelter. Sandy is another dog who went from an animal shelter to a starring role. He appeared on Broadway in the play *Annie.*

Organizing Details to Compare and Contrast

Suppose that you have been studying about animals. You have learned several ways in which gray squirrels and chipmunks are alike and different. How can you organize these details?

One way to organize your details is to write a paragraph that compares gray squirrels and chipmunks and another paragraph that contrasts them. Your first paragraph would tell about the ways in which gray squirrels and chipmunks are alike. Your second paragraph would tell about the ways in which the two animals are different.

You have learned that your first step is to make two lists. In one, you list likenesses between gray squirrels and chipmunks. In the other, you list their differences. Look at the lists below.

Likenesses

1. Rodents of same family
2. Nervous animals
3. Live on nuts, berries, and insects
4. Excellent climbers

Differences

GRAY SQUIRREL	CHIPMUNK
1. About 20 inches long	1. About 11 inches long
2. Gray coat, light colored underneath	2. Reddish-brown coat with black stripes
3. Lives in tree holes or in nests on branches	3. Lives in underground burrows or tunnels
4. Remains active all year	4. Sleeps during cold months

After you have listed your details, you are ready to write your paragraphs. Write a good topic sentence for each paragraph. The paragraph at the top of the next page compares gray squirrels and chipmunks. Notice that it begins with a topic sentence. Why is it a good topic sentence?

The gray squirrel and the chipmunk are alike in many ways. They are both rodents and belong to the same family. They are both very nervous animals. Both live on a diet of nuts, berries, and insects. The squirrel and the chipmunk are both excellent climbers as well.

Prewriting Practice

Look back at the list of differences between a gray squirrel and a chipmunk. Use these details to write a paragraph contrasting the two animals. Begin your paragraph with a topic sentence.

The Grammar Connection

Using Exact Nouns

People who make television commercials are careful to use exact nouns. They want viewers to know exactly what they are selling. When you write, too, it is important to use exact nouns. They give your readers a clear picture of what you are writing about.

Which of these two sentences gives a clearer picture?

The trainer taught four animals to play an instrument.
The trainer taught four cats to play a piano.

The second sentence gives you a clearer picture. The exact nouns *cats* and *piano* help you see the animals' trick.

Practice Rewrite each sentence. Change the underlined noun to a more exact noun.

1. Your pet will love these tasty new treats.
2. Everyone is buying this exciting new toy.
3. Sudso detergent will get your things clean and bright.
4. This food is delicious.
5. Airway's people will fly you safely wherever you want to go in the world.

The Writing Process
How to Compare and Contrast

Step 1: Prewriting—Choose a Topic

Sara wrote a list of ideas she could compare and contrast. She thought about which one would be a good topic.

my two cats — They were too much alike.

playing soccer and kickball — They were more fun to play than to write about.

movies and plays — This topic was too broad.

two favorite actors — She really had only one favorite actor.

Sara had seen both the movie and the play *Annie*. Her third topic might be good if it were more specific. She thought about *Annie* and circled *movies and plays*.

On Your Own

1. **Think and discuss** Make a list of topics to compare and contrast. Use the activities under "Choosing Your Topic" on the Ideas page. Discuss your list with a partner.
2. **Choose** Ask yourself these questions about each topic.
   Can I compare and contrast these two things well?
   Is it too broad, or is it about something specific?
   Circle the topic you want to write about.
3. **Explore** Your topic has two parts. What is the same about both parts? What is different? Try one of the "Exploring Your Topic" activities on the Ideas page.

Ideas for Getting Started

Choosing Your Topic

Topic Ideas

Lion and tiger
My brother and myself
My left and right hands
Two kinds of cereals
Saturdays and Mondays
Pine and maple trees
Grapefruit and orange
Toothbrush and hairbrush
Magazine and newspaper
Water-skis and snow skis

Think About It

How are these things alike
and different?

Exploring Your Topic

Make Lists

Make two lists headed *Alike* and
Different. Under *Alike* write notes
that tell how the things you are
writing about are alike. Under *Different* note their differences. Here
are Sara's lists for the movie and the
play *Annie*.

Alike	Different
same story	movie better
same dog	outdoor things
same songs	better

Talk About It

Show a partner a
photo, a picture, or an
object that reminds
you of the topic of
your paragraphs.
First, tell your partner
ways in which the two
things are alike. Then
tell ways in which they
are different. Does
your partner agree
with your ideas?

Step 2: Write a First Draft

Sara's aunt had taken her to see the movie *Annie*. Sara thought that her aunt would enjoy reading her paragraphs.

Sara wrote her first draft. She used her lists of likenesses and differences. She wrote two paragraphs—one that compared the play and the movie and one that contrasted them. She did not worry about mistakes.

Sara's first draft

Think and Discuss ✓

- What are Sara's two topic sentences?
- What details does she give to support each topic sentence?
- Where could she add more details?

The play *Annie* and the movie are a lot alike ~~and~~ They both have the same storey. Annies dog sandy looks the same. They also have many of the same songs, such as "Tomorow."

The movie was better. My aunt took me to see it. The outdoor things were better.

On Your Own

1. **Think about purpose and audience** Before you write, ask yourself these questions.

   For whom shall I write my paragraphs?

   How will I make the likenesses and differences clear?

2. **Write** Write your first draft. Write one paragraph that compares and one that contrasts. Make your topic sentences clear. Use every other line. Do not worry about mistakes.

Step 3: Revise

Sara reread her first draft. The topic sentence in the second paragraph was not clear. She crossed it out and wrote a new one. Sara also thought that the second sentence did not keep to the main idea. She crossed out that one too. She also changed the word *things* to a more exact noun.

Sara asked Pedro to listen to her first draft.

Reading and responding

I really like your topic.

Are the likenesses and differences clear?

Well, why were the outdoor scenes better?

They seemed more real. I'll think about this some more.

Sara read her second paragraph again and thought about Pedro's suggestions. She decided to add more details explaining why she thought that the movie was better than the play.

Part of Sara's revised draft

> I liked the movie Annie
> ~~The movie was better.~~ My aunt
> more than the play.
> ~~took me to see it.~~ The outdoor
> scenes
> ~~things~~ were better. They seemed more
> real than in the play. Also, we could
> see the actors close up. In the play,
> they were far away.

Think and Discuss ✔

- Why did Sara cross out two sentences?
- Is Sara's new topic sentence better? Why?
- What details did Sara add?

On Your Own

Revising checklist

☑ Did I write a clear topic sentence for each paragraph?

☑ Do all of the other sentences in each paragraph support the topic sentence?

☑ Can I add more details telling how the two parts of my topic are alike? how they are different?

☑ Where can I use more exact nouns?

1. **Revise** Underline your topic sentences. Write new ones if you need to. Write the new sentences above the old ones. Cross out sentences that do not belong. Add details that you left out. Be sure to organize your details clearly. You might want to use some of the words from the thesaurus below or the one found at the back of this book.

2. **Have a conference** Read your paragraphs to a classmate or your teacher.

WRITING CONFERENCE

Ask your listener:	**As you listen:**
"Are the likenesses and differences clear?" "Can I add any details?" "Are all my sentences about the main idea?"	I must listen carefully. Did I understand the likenesses and differences? Are more details needed?

3. **Revise** Think about your listener's questions and comments. What other changes do you want to make? Revise your paragraphs.

Thesaurus

bigger greater, larger	**many** several, numerous
expensive costly, valuable	**same** equal, identical
funny amusing, comical	**smaller** littler, tinier
like enjoy, love	**think** believe, consider

Step 4: Proofread

Sara proofread her writing for errors in capitalization, punctuation, and spelling. She used the dictionary to check her spelling. She used proofreading marks to make corrections.

Part of Sara's proofread draft

¶The play *Annie* and the movie are a
lot alike. ~~and~~ They both have the
same ~~storey~~ story. Annie's dog <u>sandy</u> looks
the same. They also have many of
the same songs, such as "~~Tomorow~~ Tomorrow."

Think and Discuss

- Which words did Sara correct for spelling?
- Where did she add a capital letter? Why?
- Why did she make other changes?

On Your Own

1. **Proofreading Practice** Proofread this paragraph and write it correctly. There are three errors in spelling, two in capitalization, one in punctuation, and one incorrect possessive noun.

   My to cats, Rusty and smokey, are a
   lot alike. I got them both when they
   were only babys. Both cat's favrit
   toy is the same it is an empty thread
   spool.

2. **Proofreading Application** Proofread your paragraphs. Use the Proofreading Checklist and the Grammar and Spelling Hints on the next page. Use a dictionary to check spelling. You may want to use a colored pencil.

Proofreading Marks

¶	Indent
∧	Add something
ℓ	Take out something
=	Capitalize
/	Make a small letter

Proofreading Checklist

Did I

- ☑ **1.** indent each paragraph?
- ☑ **2.** use capital letters at the beginnings of sentences and for proper nouns?
- ☑ **3.** use apostrophes correctly with possessive nouns?
- ☑ **4.** spell all words correctly?

The Grammar/Spelling Connection

Grammar Hints

Remember these rules from Unit 3 when you use nouns.

- A proper noun begins with a capital letter. (*Andrea, Park School*)
- Add an apostrophe and *s ('s)* to a singular noun to show possession. (*the boy's horse*) Add only an apostrophe to a plural noun ending with *s*. (*the boys' bikes*)

Spelling Hints

Remember to spell plural nouns correctly.

- To form the plural of a noun ending with a consonant and *y*, change the *y* to *i* and add *es*. (*stori̲es̲, lili̲es̲*)
- To form the plural of a noun ending with a vowel and *y*, add only *s*. (*toy̲s̲, day̲s̲*)

Step 5: Publish

When Sara had finished revising and proofreading, she copied her paragraph in her neatest handwriting. Then she folded a piece of paper to look like a theater program and drew a picture of Annie and Sandy on the front. Sara added the title "Which <u>Annie</u>?" and put her paragraphs inside. She couldn't wait to show her aunt!

On Your Own

1. **Copy** Copy your paragraphs in your neatest handwriting.
2. **Check** Reread your paragraphs to check for any mistakes in your final copy.
3. **Add a title** Write a title for your paper.
4. **Share** Think of an interesting way to share your writing.

Ideas for Sharing

- Make a poster about your topic.
- Make puppets of the two parts of your topic. Read your paragraphs, using the puppets.
- Make a collage about each part of your topic.

Applying Comparison and Contrast

Literature and Creative Writing

"How do you sell something?" Ramona wanted to know. "Ramona's Book Report" tells how Ramona used a cat-food commercial to sell a medium-boring book to her classmates. Animals are often used to sell things. In "Animals in Advertising," you learned some of the ways in which they are trained for their TV appearances.

Have fun using what you learned about writing paragraphs that compare or contrast. Try one or more of these activities.

> **Remember these things** ☑
> Write a topic sentence for each paragraph.
> Give supporting details.
> Think about likenesses and differences.

1. **Find a different solution.** What did Ramona do when she forgot her lines while giving her book report? What else could she have done? What would you have done? Write a paragraph contrasting Ramona's solution with yours.

2. **Sell your lion.** Pretend that you train lions. A car company wants to make a commercial using a horse. Write a contrast paragraph telling why a lion would sell the car better than a horse.

3. **Judge two commercials.** Think of two commercials that sell the same type of product, such as cereals, cars, or sneakers. Compare the two ads in one paragraph. Contrast them in a second paragraph.

Writing Across the Curriculum
Mathematics

You often compare and contrast information with numbers. Sometimes graphs help to make the information clearer.

Choose one or both of the following activities.

1. **Compare prices.** Which of the following specials is a better buy? Write one paragraph comparing and one paragraph contrasting the two specials.

Writing Steps
1. Choose a Topic
2. Write a First Draft
3. Revise
4. Proofread
5. Publish

Joe's Special
Roast beef sandwich	$3.50
Free salad	
Milk	.75

Dinah's Special
Roast beef sandwich	$2.75
Salad	1.00
Milk	.35

2. **Make a graph.** The students in Mr. Gomez's class took a survey to find out how many students had cats, dogs, other pets, or no pets. This graph shows their findings. What was the most popular pet? How many students had dogs? cats? other pets? no pets?

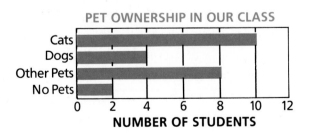

Word Bank
survey
graph
category
greatest
least
fewest

Survey the students in your class to find out how many have dogs, cats, other pets, or no pets. Draw a graph to show your findings. Write a paragraph about them.

Katrina enjoyed reading "Ramona's Book Report" by Beverly Cleary. She thought that writing a book report as a television commercial was a good way to share a book that she really liked. Katrina decided to make a commercial about the book *...and now Miguel* by Joseph Krumgold. She hoped that she could convince her classmates to read the book.

Katrina had only one minute to make her viewers curious about the book. She told about something that she thought was interesting, but she did not tell too much. This is what Katrina said in her commercial.

If you like adventure stories, you're going to love reading *... and now Miguel* by Joseph Krumgold.

Miguel Chavez lives with his parents on a sheep ranch in New Mexico. He has many adventures as he tries to prove to his father that he is grown up. When some sheep disappear in a storm, Miguel wants to help find them. Although his father sends him off to school, Miguel goes to look for the sheep.

You will enjoy reading about this and other adventures Miguel has in this exciting book. Get a copy of *... and now Miguel* at your local bookstore today.

Think and Discuss

- Why did Katrina try to interest her audience quickly?
- What did Katrina tell to get her audience interested in reading the book?
- Is *...and now Miguel* a fiction or a nonfiction book?

Share Your Book

Make a Television Commercial

1. Choose a book that you like.
2. Give yourself a one-minute time limit.
3. Tell if your book is a mystery, adventure, biography, sports book, or some other kind of book.
4. Tell the name of the book, the author, and the main characters. Also tell something interesting that happens.
5. Show a copy of the book, and tell where it can be bought.
6. You may want to write this information on note cards that you can look at while you present your commercial.

Other Activities

- Pretend that you are the author of your book. Try to sell your book to a television or radio audience. Give the name of the book and tell what you like best about it. Tell why you think everyone should read it!
- Make a magazine advertisement for your book. On a sheet of paper, copy an exciting passage from the book. Then write an advertisement to sell the book to other students. Illustrate the passage, and write the title and the author's name on the paper.

 # The Book Nook

Encyclopedia Brown Saves the Day *by Donald Sobol* A wise ten-year-old solves several puzzling mysteries by clever detective work.	**Help! I'm a Prisoner in the Library** *by Eth Clifford* Two girls have a scary experience while trapped overnight in a library.

Language and Usage

When I stamp
The ground thunders,
When I shout
The world rings,
When I sing
The air wonders
How I do such things.

   Felice Holman
      "At the Top of My Voice"

Verbs

Getting Ready Action words, or verbs, bring our language to life. You can tell that someone or something leaps, sleeps, winks, smiles, spins, twirls, tumbles, soars, or whistles! You can tell whether an action happened in the past, present, or future. In this unit, you will learn about using this lively part of our language.

ACTIVITIES

Listening
Listen as the poem on the opposite page is read. Listen for the verbs. Did you hear all seven? What are they? What does the poet mean by "The ground *thunders*" and "The world *rings*"?

Speaking
Look at the picture. Tell about it. What is the weather like? What is the girl doing? What is she saying? Have someone write the sentences on the board. What verbs were used?

Writing
Do you ever feel like stamping your feet or shouting and singing? When? Write your thoughts in your journal and notice the verbs you use.

1 | Action Verbs

You know that every sentence has a subject and a predicate. The main word in the predicate is the verb. A **verb** is a word that can show action. When a verb tells what people or things do, it is called an **action verb**.

SUBJECTS	PREDICATES
Rita and Eric	dig slowly and carefully.
The students	helped the scientists.
Rita	uncovered some pottery.
The pieces of pottery	provide clues about the past.

Guided Practice What is the action verb in each of the following sentences?

Example: Rita cleaned the pieces of pottery. *cleaned*

1. Eric found some old tools.
2. Raul made a map of the site.
3. Two students stand in the water.
4. They hold a tub with a screen in the bottom.
5. Water fills the tub.
6. Raul pours dirt into the tub.
7. Light objects float in the water.
8. Dirt goes through the screen.
9. The students take careful notes.
10. They attach labels to the objects.
11. The scientists take the objects to their lab.
12. They learn many things about early people.

Summing up

▶ An **action verb** is a word that tells what people or things do.

Independent Practice Write each action verb.

Example: Deserts cover a large part of the American Southwest.
    cover

13. Spanish explorers crossed these deserts long ago.
14. They discovered tall, steep rocks with flat tops.
15. The explorers named these rocks *mesas.*
16. They called smaller mesas *buttes.*
17. Wind and water make a mesa.
18. It takes millions of years.
19. The wind and water carve the rock.
20. The softer part of the rock disappears first.
21. The harder part forms a mesa.
22. Strong winds blow across the tops of mesas.
23. The hot desert sun beats down on them.
24. Some grasses and a few other plants grow there.
25. Flowers open only at night.
26. They protect themselves from the hot daytime sun.
27. Only a few small animals live on mesas.
28. Lizards and pack rats make their homes there.
29. Early people settled on Mesa Verde in Colorado.
30. They built homes on the flat mesa top.
31. These people disappeared long ago.
32. People tell stories about Weaver's Needle.
33. This mesa stands in the Superstition Mountains
    of Arizona.
34. A miner found a gold mine near there.
35. No one remembered the location.
36. Hundreds of people still search for the gold mine.

Writing Application: Instructions

Is there an unusual-looking rock, tree, building, or other object
near your home or school? Pretend that you are an explorer
who has made this exciting discovery. Write a paragraph of
instructions telling someone how to get there from your school
or home. Underline the action verbs.

For Extra Practice, see p. 162.   **Action Verbs 137**

2 | Main Verbs and Helping Verbs

A verb may be more than one word. The **main verb** is the most important verb. The **helping verb** comes before it.

Some Common Helping Verbs		
am	was	has
is	were	have
are	will	had

The main verbs below are in yellow. Helping verbs are in blue.

Alfredo is training for the Olympics.

He has run five miles each day.

His coach will help him next week.

Guided Practice Find each helping verb and main verb.

Example: Sara had entered the summer Olympics.
    helping verb: *had*   **main verb:** *entered*

1. She was racing in a wheelchair race.
2. Sara had joined the Wheelchair Athlete Club.
3. The racers were using special racing wheelchairs.
4. They are training several times a week.
5. They have lifted weights too.
6. Sara has raced for several years.
7. She will race many more times.
8. She is practicing for next year's Olympics.

Independent Practice Write each sentence. Draw one line under the helping verb and two lines under the main verb.

Example: I am reading about the Junior Olympics.
I am reading about the Junior Olympics.

9. The Junior Olympics are held every summer.
10. The games were started in 1967.
11. Young people will come from all parts of the country.
12. Even a six-year-old has joined in these games.
13. All of the players had won contests before.
14. They have earned a place in the Junior Olympics.
15. The children will remember the games all their lives.
16. Thousands of people will watch them.
17. Some people are watching the weight lifters.
18. One boy is lifting heavy barbells.
19. He has worked with his coach every day.
20. Two brothers will enter the table tennis event.
21. I have enjoyed table tennis.
22. I am practicing my serves.
23. I was playing with my friend yesterday.
24. Someday I will go to the Olympics.

Writing Application: An Interview

You have won first place in an event at the Junior Olympics. A reporter asks you this question: "What made you want to enter the Olympics, and how did you train for them?" Write an answer to the question. Use at least five helping verbs from the chart on page 138 and underline them. You might begin like this: All my life I <u>had</u> wanted to take part in the Junior Olympics.

For Extra Practice, see p. 163.   **Main Verbs and Helping Verbs   139**

3 | Present, Past, and Future

A verb tells when something happens. The **tense** of a verb lets you know whether something happens in the present, in the past, or in the future.

PRESENT	PAST	FUTURE
hunt, hunts	hunted	will hunt
fly, flies	flew	will fly

Verb Tenses	
A verb in the **present tense** shows action that is happening now.	Bats **hunt** at night. Now the bat **flies**.
A verb in the **past tense** shows action that has already happened. Many verbs in the past tense end with *-ed*.	It **hunted** last night. The bats **flew**.
A verb in the **future tense** shows action that will happen. Verbs in the future tense use the helping verb *will*.	They **will hunt** tonight. The bat **will fly**.

will jump

jumps

jumped

Guided Practice

What is the verb in each sentence? Is it in the present tense, the past tense, or the future tense?

Example: Sherry likes many kinds of animals.
likes—present

1. We will go to the library tomorrow.
2. I finished a book about birds yesterday.
3. Sherry will look for a book about bats.
4. She collects facts about animals.
5. The librarian always helps us.

▶ A **present tense** verb shows action that is happening now.
▶ A **past tense** verb shows action that has already happened.
▶ A **future tense** verb shows action that will happen.

Independent Practice Write the verb in each sentence.
Beside it, write *present*, *past*, or *future*.

Example: Long ago most people feared bats.
feared—past

6. Many people still fear bats today.
7. Sherry borrowed a book about bats.
8. She will give a report to the class.
9. She learned a lot about bats.
10. Bats help people a great deal.
11. Most bats eat harmful insects.
12. One scientist trained bats.
13. The bats will fly to him on command.
14. He studies the bats closely.
15. Someday he will write a book about them.
16. Bats sleep during the day.
17. They fly skillfully in the dark.
18. A flying bat makes sounds.
19. The sounds send echoes to the bat's ears.
20. The echoes direct the bat.
21. Sherry talked to a scientist.
22. The scientist will speak to our class next week.

Writing Application: Creative Writing
What is your favorite animal? Pretend that you are that animal.
Write about what you did yesterday, what you are doing today,
and what you will do tomorrow. Use the past, present, and
future tenses correctly. Underline the verb in each sentence.

For Extra Practice, see p. 164.

4 | Making Subjects and Verbs Agree

A verb in the present tense must **agree** with the subject of the sentence. This means that the subject and the verb must work together. They must both be singular or both be plural.

Subject-Verb Agreement	
Singular subjects	When the subject is a singular noun or *he*, *she*, or *it*, add *s* to the verb. A computer helps people. It solves problems.
Plural subjects	When the subject is a plural noun or *I*, *we*, *you*, or *they*, do not add *s* to the verb. Computers help people. They solve problems.

Guided Practice Which verb correctly completes each sentence?

Example: Felita (own, owns) a small computer.   *owns*

1. She (use, uses) it to do her homework.
2. The computer (help, helps) her parents too.
3. Her brothers (play, plays) games on it.
4. Many companies also (buy, buys) computers.
5. Computers (work, works) very rapidly.
6. They (store, stores) a great deal of information.
7. I (want, wants) to learn more about computers.

Summing up

▶ If the subject of a sentence is a singular noun or *he*, *she*, or *it*, add *s* to a present tense verb.
▶ If the subject is a plural noun or *I*, *we*, *you*, or *they*, do not add *s* to a present tense verb.

Independent Practice Choose the verb that correctly completes each sentence. Write the sentence.

Example: Computers (produce, produces) pictures called graphics.
Computers produce pictures called graphics.

8. Computer pictures (help, helps) people in many ways.
9. My uncle (work, works) as a pilot.
10. He (practice, practices) flying with computer graphics.
11. The screen (show, shows) a make-believe flight.
12. Sandy (play, plays) computer games with me.
13. Computer pictures (make, makes) the game exciting.
14. She (win, wins) most of the time.
15. I (beat, beats) her once in a while.
16. Computers (help, helps) in sports too.
17. A coach (film, films) a player in action.
18. Then the coach (run, runs) the film slowly.
19. Coaches (look, looks) at each action carefully.
20. They (feed, feeds) information into the computer.
21. The coach (give, gives) suggestions to the player.
22. Computers even (explore, explores) space.
23. A camera (take, takes) a picture on Mars.
24. It (send, sends) signals to a computer on Earth.
25. The computer screen (display, displays) the picture.
26. You (see, sees) sights from a faraway planet.
27. Many other workers (use, uses) computers in their jobs.
28. Doctors (learn, learns) more about the body.
29. Engineers (plan, plans) machines.
30. Some computers (steer, steers) ships on the sea.
31. A special computer (write, writes) music.
32. We (wonder, wonders) about computers in the future.

An artist drew this with a computer.

Writing Application: Compare and Contrast

Pretend that it is the year 2020. Computers do many more things than ever before. How is your life different from the way it is now? How is it the same? Write a paragraph about your life with computers. Use present tense verbs.

For Extra Practice, see p. 165.   **Making Subjects and Verbs Agree   143**

5 | Spelling the Present Tense

You have learned that you simply add *s* to most present tense verbs to make them agree with a singular subject. Some other verbs, however, add *es* when they are used with a singular noun subject or with *he, she,* or *it.*

Present Tense with Singular Subjects		
1. For most verbs: Add *s.*	sing + s	Sam sings.
	stay + s	He stays.
2. For verbs that end with *s, x, z, ch,* or *sh*: Add *es.*	pitch + es	She pitches.
	buzz + es	A bee buzzes.
3. For a verb that ends with a consonant and *y*: Change the *y* to *i* and add *es.*	study + es	Yoko studies.
	fly + es	The bird flies.

The bird flies.

Guided Practice How should you spell the verb in the present tense to complete each sentence correctly?

Example: Ben ⎯⎯ tennis at the park. (play) *plays*

1. He ⎯⎯ his serves every day. (practice)
2. His friend Rosa often ⎯⎯ him. (watch)
3. Sometimes Ben ⎯⎯ the ball. (miss)
4. Rosa ⎯⎯ his serves carefully. (study)
5. Ben ⎯⎯ his mistakes. (fix)

For spelling present tense verbs used with singular subjects:
► Add *es* to verbs that end with *s, x, z, ch,* or *sh.*
► If a verb ends with a consonant and *y,* change the *y* to *i* and add *es.*

Independent Practice

A. Write each sentence with the correct verb.

Example: Len (like, likes) the game of softball.
Len likes the game of softball.

6. Every afternoon Len (hurry, hurries) to the field.
7. First, he (dress, dresses) in the locker room.
8. Then the players (toss, tosses) the ball around.
9. Len (throw, throws) the ball to Karen.
10. The ball (fly, flies) high over her head.
11. Some more players (arrive, arrives) at the field.
12. The coach (teach, teaches) them some new plays.

B. Write each sentence. Spell the present tense verb correctly.

Example: Carol ____ in the outfield.   (stand)
Carol stands in the outfield.

13. The umpire ____, "Play ball!"   (yell)
14. Dana ____ to Len.   (pitch)
15. Len ____ at the ball.   (swing)
16. He ____ three times.   (miss)
17. The umpire ____, "You're out!"   (cry)
18. Loren ____ the ball.   (hit)
19. Carol ____ the ball easily.   (catch)
20. Carol's team ____ away the trophy.   (carry)

Writing Application: A Description
You are a sports reporter. Describe the action of a game or another sports event for your radio audience. Use present tense verbs. Underline the verbs.

6 | Spelling the Past Tense

You know that you can use a verb in the past tense to tell about an action that has already happened. The past tense is usually formed by adding *-ed* to the verb.

Rules for Spelling the Past Tense		
1. Most verbs: Add *-ed*.	play + -ed call + -ed	We played. Dad called us.
2. Verbs ending with e: Drop the e and add *-ed*.	graze + -ed rope + -ed	The cattle grazed. He roped a calf.
3. Verbs ending with a single vowel and a consonant: Double the consonant and add *-ed*.	stop + -ed tug + -ed	The horse stopped. I tugged the rope.
4. Verbs ending with a consonant and y: Change the y to i and add *-ed*.	carry + -ed hurry + -ed	Men carried ropes. They hurried out.

Guided Practice What is the past tense of each verb?

Example: splash *splashed*

1. hum
2. bake
3. fry
4. obey
5. save
6. drop
7. slap
8. study
9. talk

> ▶ Add -ed to most verbs to form the past tense.
> ▶ Remember the rules for spelling the past tense of verbs ending with e, with a single vowel and a consonant, and with a consonant and y.

Independent Practice Use the past tense of the verb to complete each sentence. Write the sentence.

Example: Luis and Kate ____ on a cattle drive.   (help)
Luis and Kate helped on a cattle drive.

10. Their grandparents ____ a cattle ranch.   (own)
11. The whole family ____ the summer drive.   (plan)
12. They ____ the cattle to new pastures.   (move)
13. Kate ____ her favorite horse.   (saddle)
14. They ____ their cousins on the drive.   (join)
15. One cow ____ away from the herd.   (walk)
16. Luis and Kate ____ after the stray.   (hurry)
17. Luis ____ up behind the cow.   (trot)
18. Kate ____ it back to the herd.   (guide)
19. Grandfather ____ the young cowhands.   (praise)
20. Their aunts and uncles ____ their hands.   (clap)
21. Before dark they ____ a water hole.   (reach)
22. They ____ there for the night.   (stop)
23. The adults ____ dinner over a campfire.   (cook)
24. Luis ____ buckets of water.   (carry)
25. Everyone ____ the delicious meal.   (enjoy)
26. After dinner Luis ____ the dishes.   (wash)
27. Kate ____ them.   (dry)
28. Everyone ____ down for the night.   (settle)

Writing Application: A Story
Luis and Kate's whole family went on the cattle drive. Write a story about a project that you have done with your family or another group. Use verbs in the past tense and underline them.

7 | The Past with Helping Verbs

You know that you can add -ed to most verbs to show action that happened in the past. There is another way to show that something has already happened. Use the helping verb *has, have,* or *had* with the past form of most verbs.

PRESENT	PAST	PAST WITH HELPING VERB
walk	walked	(has, have, had) walked
hike	hiked	(has, have, had) hiked
jog	jogged	(has, have, had) jogged
carry	carried	(has, have, had) carried

The helping verb must agree with the subject of the sentence.

Agreement with Helping Verbs	
1. With singular subjects: Use *has.*	Jo has joined a circus. She has liked it.
2. With plural subjects and *I* or *you*: Use *have.*	Horses have learned tricks. You have laughed.
3. With either singular or plural subjects: Use *had.*	Bears had danced. A clown had hurried into the ring.

Guided Practice What are the helping verb and the main verb in each sentence?

Example: We have watched the circus with Aunt Miranda.
helping verb: *have*   **main verb:** *watched*

1. She had invited us two weeks ago.
2. Ray has hurried to the circus grounds.
3. You have joined him there.
4. The first act had started.
5. The ringmaster has stepped into the ring.

▶ The helping verbs *has*, *have*, and *had* can be used with the past form of a verb to show action that has already happened.

Independent Practice

A. Write each sentence. Draw one line under the helping verb and two lines under the main verb.

Example: I have enjoyed the circus. *I have enjoyed the circus.*

6. You have liked it too.
7. The ringmaster has snapped her whip.
8. The elephants had paraded in a circle.
9. They have walked right in front of me.
10. One chimp has grinned at the audience.
11. We have clapped loudly for the performers.

B. Use *has* or *have* and the past form of the verb to complete each sentence. Write the sentence.

Example: We ____ hardest at the clowns. (laugh)
We have laughed hardest at the clowns.

12. The clowns ____ some new tricks. (try)
13. A dozen clowns ____ out of a tiny car. (hop)
14. They ____ each other around the ring. (chase)
15. One clown ____ a pail of water over another. (empty)
16. The others ____ him out of the ring. (carry)
17. Now the circus ____ for the night. (close)
18. The lion ____ up in its cage. (curl)
19. The monkeys ____ down at last. (settle)
20. All the noise ____. (stop)

Writing Application: Creative Writing

The big circus has arrived in town! Make a poster advertising the circus. Use verbs in the past with helping verbs. Decorate your poster.

For Extra Practice, see p. 168.   **The Past with Helping Verbs   149**

8 | Irregular Verbs

Verbs that do not add -*ed* to show past action are called **irregular verbs.**

I eat now.   I ate earlier.   I have eaten already.

Because irregular verbs do not follow a regular pattern, you must remember their spellings.

Irregular Verbs		
Present	**Past**	**Past with helping verb**
begin	began	(has, have, had) begun
break	broke	(has, have, had) broken
bring	brought	(has, have, had) brought
come	came	(has, have, had) come
drive	drove	(has, have, had) driven
eat	ate	(has, have, had) eaten
give	gave	(has, have, had) given
grow	grew	(has, have, had) grown
know	knew	(has, have, had) known
make	made	(has, have, had) made
say	said	(has, have, had) said
sing	sang	(has, have, had) sung
take	took	(has, have, had) taken
tell	told	(has, have, had) told
throw	threw	(has, have, had) thrown
wear	wore	(has, have, had) worn

Guided Practice What are the past tense and the past with a helping verb for each irregular verb below?

Example: sing *sang* *sung*

1. begin	**3.** know	**5.** wear	**7.** tell	**9.** drive
2. come	**4.** bring	**6.** break	**8.** make	**10.** say

> ▶ **Irregular verbs** are changed in special ways to show action that happened in the past. You must remember their spellings.

Independent Practice Write each sentence, using the correct form of the verb to show past action.

Example: Brenda has _____ many sailing trips.   (take)
Brenda has taken many sailing trips.

11. Her parents had _____ her sailing lessons.   (give)
12. Brenda _____ her friend Jean on one trip.   (bring)
13. Jean's father _____ them to the boat.   (drive)
14. The girls _____ warm clothing.   (wear)
15. The trip had _____ calmly.   (begin)
16. Soon, however, a storm _____ up.   (come)
17. The sky _____ dark.   (grow)
18. The wind _____ to blow harder.   (begin)
19. Waves _____ over the side of the boat.   (break)
20. Jean _____ that she was afraid.   (say)
21. Brenda _____ her not to worry.   (tell)
22. Her parents _____ how to handle the boat.   (know)
23. Brenda's father _____ down one of the sails.   (take)
24. That _____ the boat sail more smoothly.   (make)
25. Finally, the seas _____ calm.   (grow)
26. The boat _____ to a pleasant island.   (come)
27. They _____ a big lunch on the boat.   (eat)
28. The family _____ sea songs after sunset.   (sing)

Writing Application: A Diary Entry
That night Jean wrote in her diary, "This sailing trip was the most exciting trip I have taken in my life!" Write a diary entry about the most exciting trip you have taken. It may be a real trip or an imaginary one. Use at least five verbs from the chart on page 150, and underline them.

For Extra Practice, see p. 169.

9 | The Special Verb *be*

The verb *be,* has special forms for different subjects.

SUBJECTS	PRESENT	PAST
I	am	was
you	are	were
he, she, it	is	was
singular noun *(Lucia)*	is	was
we	are	were
they	are	were
plural noun *(stories)*	are	were

The verb *be* does not show action. It tells what someone or something is or is like.

I am a reporter.   You are a photographer.

That story was long.   Those cartoons were funny.

Guided Practice Which verb correctly completes each sentence? Is it in the present tense or the past tense?

Example: Lucia (is, are) a reporter. *is—present*

1. I (was, were) a sportswriter last year.
2. Two stories (was, were) about basketball.
3. You (is, are) in one of my stories.
4. My best story (is, are) about bikes.
5. We (was, were) winners every time!

Summing up

> ▸ The special verb *be* does not show action. It tells what someone or something is or is like.
> ▸ Use *am* or *was* with the subject *I*.
> ▸ Use *is* or *was* with singular nouns and *he, she,* or *it*.
> ▸ Use *are* or *were* with plural nouns and *we, you,* or *they*.

Independent Practice

A. Write the verb in each sentence. Then write *past* or *present* to tell the tense of the verb.

Example: The *Scoop* is our school newspaper.   *is—present*

6. I am the editor of the *Scoop*.
7. Alice is a good writer.
8. She was the writer for all the school news.
9. You are a good writer too.
10. I was happy with your last news story.
11. All the reporters were very busy.
12. The paper is ready for printing.
13. We are proud of our work.

B. Choose the verb that correctly completes each sentence. Write the sentence.

Example: Ms. Lopez (is, are) a reporter for the *Bugle*.
Ms. Lopez is a reporter for the Bugle.

14. It (is, are) the largest newspaper in the city.
15. Most readers in the city (is, are) *Bugle* fans.
16. She (is, are) the reporter for city news.
17. Her news stories (is, are) always interesting.
18. Ms. Lopez (was, were) the reporter for the fire last week.
19. The fire (was, were) in an apartment building.
20. Fire trucks (was, were) there quickly.
21. You (was, were) across the street.
22. I (was, were) with you.
23. All of the people (was, were) safe.
24. We (was, were) glad to hear that.

Writing Application: A News Story

This is the first sentence of a news story:

Today was a big day in the history of our city.

Finish the news story. Use forms of the verb *be* from this lesson and underline them.

For Extra Practice, see p. 170.   **The Special Verb *be***

Sometimes you can join a verb with the word *not*. The shortened word you make when you join the two words is called a **contraction**. An **apostrophe** (') is used to take the place of the letter or letters that you leave out.

Tim is not ready yet.   Tim isn't ready yet.

Here are some common contractions with the word *not*.

Contractions with *not*			
is not	isn't	has not	hasn't
are not	aren't	have not	haven't
was not	wasn't	had not	hadn't
were not	weren't	could not	couldn't
do not	don't	should not	shouldn't
does not	doesn't	would not	wouldn't
did not	didn't	will not	won't
cannot	can't		

Study the chart. Notice that the apostrophe replaces the letter *o* in each contraction. Look carefully at *won't* and *can't*. The spelling of the verb *will* changes when it is combined with *not* to form the contraction *won't*. The contraction *can't* is a shortened form of the single word *cannot*.

Guided Practice What is the contraction for each word or pair of words?

Example: are not   *aren't*

1. do not
2. could not
3. were not
4. have not
5. will not
6. has not
7. should not
8. did not
9. cannot
10. is not

▸ A **contraction** is the combined form of two words. An **apostrophe** (') takes the place of any missing letters.

Independent Practice

A. Write the contraction for the underlined word or words.

Example: Tim <u>cannot</u> find his gloves.   *can't*

11. They <u>are not</u> in his closet.

12. He <u>does not</u> even remember where they are.

13. He <u>had not</u> started getting ready when I called.

14. Tim <u>should not</u> wait until the last minute.

15. I <u>did not</u> expect him to be ready on time.

16. This <u>is not</u> the first time.

B. Write the word or words that make up the underlined contraction in each sentence.

Example: We <u>shouldn't</u> wait another day to clean out the attic!
         should not

17. I <u>can't</u> believe how much junk there is!

18. The old TV set <u>hasn't</u> worked for years.

19. I <u>wouldn't</u> want to get rid of these books.

20. I <u>haven't</u> even read some of them yet.

21. Dad <u>doesn't</u> play his clarinet anymore.

22. He <u>couldn't</u> bear to part with it.

23. We <u>won't</u> throw that out!

24. I <u>wasn't</u> expecting this to be such a big job.

Writing Application: A Story

Have you ever had a really bad day—perhaps a day when the sun isn't shining, the bus doesn't come on time, and you can't stay awake in class? Write a story about "The Day That Nothing Seemed to Go Right." Use at least five contractions from the chart on page 154. Underline the contractions.

For Extra Practice, see p. 171.   **Contractions with *not*   155**

Grammar-Writing Connection

Keeping Verbs in the Same Tense

Good writers try hard to make their writing clear for their readers. You, too, can help your readers to understand what you have written. Make sure that all the verbs in a paragraph are in the same tense.

In the paragraph below, three verbs are in the past tense. One verb is in the present tense. Therefore, a reader might be confused about when the action takes place.

As I dived under the water, a tadpole swam by.

Then a turtle darts in front of me. The race was on!

In the revised paragraph below, the present tense verb *darts* is changed to the past tense *darted*. Because the action of the paragraph takes place in the past, all of the verbs should be in the past tense. The revised paragraph is clearer.

As I dived under the water, a tadpole swam by.

Then a turtle darted in front of me. The race was on!

Revising Sentences

Rewrite each paragraph, keeping verbs in the same tense.

1. Last summer we camped out in the woods for a week. At night I sit and listened to the crickets. They made such a peaceful sound!
2. We fish almost every day. The best time for fishing is early in the morning. It is also good when it rained.
3. Now I remember that camping trip. I thought about the lake and the fresh air. I am ready for next summer!
4. Next summer I will enjoy each day. The sunrises will be peaceful. The sunsets are beautiful.

Creative Writing

What a wonderful, free feeling to skim along the ocean in a sailboat! Winslow Homer shows this feeling in *Breezing Up*. Homer painted many scenes of the sea off New England's coast.

- How does Homer give a feeling of the boat's speed?
- How do the clouds repeat the sea's pattern and colors?

Activities

1. **Write a sailor's yarn.** Sailors like to tell exciting stories. Sometimes they even stretch the truth a bit! Suppose you have hidden yourself away on this boat. Write a sailor's yarn, or story, about your adventures.

2. **Write a message.** Imagine that a boy in the picture sees something floating in the sea. It is a bottle with a message inside! What does the message say? Who wrote it? You decide. Then write the imaginary message.

Check-up: Unit 5

Action Verbs (p. 136) Write the action verb in each sentence.

1. We played a terrific soccer game.
2. Our team met the Pumas.
3. The Pumas play soccer well.
4. They scored a goal right away.
5. I kicked the ball hard.
6. It bounced into the net.
7. Our team tied the score.
8. Coach Yin called time out.
9. She sent in a new player.
10. Anne runs very fast.
11. She made another goal.
12. Everyone cheered loudly.
13. We beat the champions!

Main Verbs and Helping Verbs (p. 138) Write the two verbs in each sentence. Draw one line under the helping verb and two lines under the main verb.

14. Pedro had wanted a guitar.
15. He was saving up for a new one.
16. He is taking lessons.
17. He has learned many songs.
18. I am listening to Pedro.
19. He is becoming a good player.
20. I have heard this tune.
21. I have forgotten the words.
22. I will sing along anyway.
23. Pedro's friend has joined us.
24. We have formed a trio.
25. We will perform for my school.

Present, Past, and Future (p. 140) Write the verbs in these sentences. Beside each verb, write *present, past,* or *future*.

26. The circus will arrive tonight.
27. The clowns are here now.
28. We saw the lion tamer.
29. He looks very brave.
30. The panther growled fiercely.
31. The show will start at noon.

Making Subjects and Verbs Agree (p. 142) Write the verb that correctly completes each sentence.

32. Spiders (spin, spins) very fine silk threads.
33. The threads (form, forms) a web.
34. The sticky web (trap, traps) the spider's food.
35. A water spider (make, makes) its web under water.
36. It (eat, eats) tiny fish.

Spelling the Present Tense (p. 144) Write each sentence, using the correct present tense form of the verb.

37. Ray always (draw) such clever cartoons.
38. Ben (copy) his pictures.
39. He (push) hard on the pen.
40. The pen (scratch) noisily across the paper.
41. The wet ink (dry) quickly.

Spelling the Past Tense *(p. 146)*

Write each sentence. Use the past tense form of the verb in ( ).

42. Rosa (want) to buy a gift.
43. She suddenly (remember) her aunt's birthday.
44. She (save) ten dollars.
45. She (work) to earn the money.
46. She (ask) me to help her.
47. I (shop) with her yesterday.
48. We (decide) to go in the morning.
49. We (look) for hours!
50. Rosa (hope) to find a sale.
51. We (stop) only for a snack.
52. My feet (ache) from walking.
53. The glass bowl (gleam).
54. Rosa (cry), "That's perfect!"
55. The clerk (wrap) the bowl.
56. We both (carry) the present home.
57. We (try) not to drop it.
58. Rosa's aunt (love) the bowl.

Past with Helping Verbs *(p. 148)*

Write each sentence. Use *have* or *has* and the past form of the verb.

59. A busy Saturday (start).
60. The car (need) a cleaning.
61. Tyler (decide) to wash the car.
62. His friends (arrive) early to help.
63. Ali (attach) the hose.
64. Julie (drop) the bucket of water.
65. Chip (hurry) to pick it up.
66. You (spray) them with the hose!
67. The water (drip) on the windows.
68. The puddles (dry) in the sun.

Irregular Verbs *(p. 150)* Write each sentence, using the correct past form of the verb.

69. I have (give) a report on my trip.
70. Our family had (drive) to Canada.
71. Alex and I had (bring) our skis.
72. We had (know) there would be snow.
73. We (eat) wonderful food.
74. We (take) a tour of Old Montreal.
75. A guide (tell) us about its history.

The Special Verb *be* *(p. 152)*

Choose the verb that correctly completes each sentence. Write the sentence.

76. Our class play (is, are) a comedy.
77. The lines (is, are) very funny.
78. Kim (is, are) the star.
79. She (is, are) very talented.
80. You (is, are) a good actor too.
81. I (was, were) nervous on stage.
82. The seats (was, were) filled.
83. The play (was, were) a success.

Contractions with *not* *(p. 154)*

Write the contraction for the underlined word or words.

84. Karl <u>will not</u> go to the movie.
85. He <u>does not</u> want to see it again.
86. I <u>have not</u> seen this film yet.
87. You <u>cannot</u> turn me down!
88. There <u>is not</u> much time.
89. We <u>should not</u> arrive too late.
90. We <u>would not</u> find a seat.

Enrichment

◨ Past, Present, Future

Players—2–4. **You need**—index cards. Each player writes 5 sentences, each on a separate index card. Use verbs in the present tense. In addition, each player writes *past* on 5 cards and *future* on another 5 cards. **How to play**—Put all the sentence cards in one stack and all the *past* and *future* cards in another stack. Shuffle each stack separately and place the two piles face down. Take turns drawing one card at a time from each pile. If you pick a *past* card, change the verb in the sentence on the other card to past tense. If the card you draw is marked *future,* change the verb in the sentence on the other card to future tense. Change any other words you need to for the sentence to be correct. Ask other players whether the sentence is correct. **Scoring**—5 points for each correct sentence. The player with the most points wins.

Sports Scrapbook

Look through old newspapers or magazines for pictures of five of your favorite sports stars. Cut out and paste each picture onto a separate sheet of paper. Under each picture, write a sentence that describes one of the player's greatest deeds. Use an interesting past tense action verb— for example, *The player* <u>*slammed*</u> *the ball over the fence.* Make a cover, and staple the pages of the scrapbook together.

Change the Subject

Something funny has happened at school. Draw pictures to tell the story, and write sentences about the action. Use *I* as the subject with present tense verbs. Then rewrite the sentences with someone else as subject. Make subjects and verbs agree.

Party Food

A friend wants to give a party where only healthful food will be served. Share a recipe for healthful party food. On an index card, write directions for how to prepare the food. Imagine that you are actually preparing the food as you write the instructions. Use action verbs such as *peel*, *cut*, and *slice*. Underline all verbs.

TALL TALES

A **tall tale** is a humorous story that mixes real and fantastic events. The story is usually about a super hero of the past, such as Paul Bunyan, Pecos Bill, and Casey Jones. Create your own character for a tall tale. Draw a large picture of your imaginary hero on cardboard or heavy drawing paper. Think of three amazing things your character does. Then pretend that your character is speaking about these amazing deeds. Draw a large speech balloon coming from the character's mouth. Inside the balloon, write three sentences, such as "I chopped down fifty trees in one hour." Use past tense verbs and underline them.

Extra Practice: Unit 5

● The predicate of each sentence is underlined. Find the action verb in the predicate. Write the action verb.

Example: Our class <u>read about Mono Lake in California.</u>
read

1. We <u>visited this unusual lake.</u>
2. A park ranger <u>guided us around the lake.</u>
3. The lake <u>covers a large area.</u>
4. It <u>contains unusual rocks.</u>
5. People <u>call these rocks</u> *tufas.*
6. Tufas <u>grow under the lake.</u>

▲ Write the action verb in each of the following sentences.

Example: No fish at all live in the salty water of Mono Lake.
live

7. Swimmers float easily in the lake.
8. The very salty water holds them up.
9. The water also stings the swimmers' eyes.
10. Freshwater springs bubble into the lake from the bottom.
11. The fresh water mixes with the salty lake water.
12. This mixture makes the strange-looking tufa rocks.

■ Use an action verb that makes sense to complete each sentence. Write the sentences.

Example: Many kinds of birds ＿＿ Mono Lake.
Many kinds of birds visit Mono Lake.

13. The birds ＿＿ in the spring and summer.
14. Some birds ＿＿ for the whole summer.
15. Others just ＿＿ for food and rest.
16. California gulls ＿＿ their nests near the lake.
17. The eggs ＿＿ sometime in June.
18. Birdwatchers ＿＿ that Mono Lake is a great place for them.

2 | Main Verbs and Helping Verbs (p. 138)

● Copy the underlined verbs in each sentence. Write *helping* or *main* beside each verb.

Example: I am going to soccer practice.

am—helping   going—main

1. Mrs. Martinez is driving Carl and me.
2. She has coached our team for three years.
3. She has started a new job.
4. It is keeping her very busy.
5. We will play for Mr. Lewis this year.
6. He was helping Mrs. Martinez last year.

▲ Write each sentence. Draw one line under the helping verb and two lines under the main verb.

Example: Karla is signing up for soccer camp.

Karla is signing up for soccer camp.

7. Joey and Pat are thinking about it.
8. Steve was talking about the camp on Wednesday.
9. He had read a poster about it.
10. Susan has made her decision.
11. She will attend the camp for a week in July.
12. Her family had planned a vacation that week.
13. Now they have changed their plans.

■ Use a helping verb that makes sense to complete each sentence. Write the sentence.

Example: The students _____ talking about the games.

The students are talking about the games.

14. The school Olympics _____ begin on Friday.
15. They _____ held at this time every year.
16. Each class _____ planned a game.
17. Last week the classes _____ divided into two teams.
18. Each team _____ play in every game.
19. The red team _____ won the tug of war every year.
20. This year the green team _____ hoping for a victory.

● ▲ ■ **Three levels of practice   163**

3 | Present, Past, and Future (p. 140)

● Write *present*, *past*, or *future* to tell the tense of the underlined verb in each sentence.

Example: The birds <u>arrived</u> early last spring. *past*

1. I <u>watched</u> them all summer from my window.
2. Then the air <u>grew</u> cold.
3. Winter <u>will come</u> soon.
4. The birds <u>will leave</u> for their winter homes.
5. Scientists <u>call</u> this migration.
6. Some birds <u>travel</u> many miles each year.
7. They <u>will return</u> next spring.

▲ Write the verbs in these sentences. Write *present*, *past*, or *future* to describe the verb in each sentence.

Example: I watch the birds in our yard.
        watch—present

8. Last winter Dad and I built a birdhouse.
9. In the spring, some wrens made a nest in it.
10. Now a family of birds lives in the house.
11. The parent birds bring food to the babies.
12. In winter snow will cover the birds' food.
13. Then we will feed the birds.
14. Next spring a new family of birds will nest in our yard.

■ Write these sentences, using the underlined verbs in the tense shown at the end of the sentence.

Example: Jack <u>receive</u> a canary for his birthday. (past)
        Jack received a canary for his birthday.

15. Jack <u>name</u> the bird Clarence. (past)
16. Clarence <u>sang</u> to Jack all day long.   (present)
17. Jack <u>will read</u> a book about canaries. (past)
18. He <u>teach</u> Clarence tricks. (future)
19. He <u>will give</u> Clarence fresh food and water.   (present)
20. Clarence <u>stay</u> healthy with such good care. (future)

4 | Making Subjects and Verbs Agree (p. 142)

● For each sentence, write *correct* if the underlined verb agrees with the subject. Write *not correct* if it does not agree.

Example: Many schools <u>buys</u> computers.   *not correct*

1. A school <u>uses</u> computers in many different ways.
2. A teacher <u>keeps</u> records on a computer.
3. A computer <u>help</u> the school librarian.
4. Students <u>practices</u> math skills on a computer.
5. Some computers <u>make</u> writing fun and easy.
6. Sometimes we <u>play</u> games on the computer.
7. I <u>learns</u> a lot from these games.

▲ Write each sentence with the correct verb.

Example: My sister Julie (work, works) with computers.
My sister Julie works with computers.

8. She (write, writes) programs for computers.
9. The programs (tell, tells) the computer what to do.
10. Computers (change, changes) rapidly.
11. Julie (take, takes) classes to keep up with the changes.
12. I (plan, plans) to work with computers too.
13. My sister (talk, talks) to me about her job.
14. I (read, reads) all the computer books I can find.

■ Use the correct form of the verb to complete each sentence. Write the sentences.

Example: Computers ____ people plan the Olympics.   (help)
Computers help people plan the Olympics.

15. They ____ the best route for carrying the torch.   (show)
16. A computer ____ places for players to stay.   (locate)
17. It ____ rooms for thousands of people.   (find)
18. Computers ____ how much food will be needed.   (figure)
19. A computer also ____ the menus.   (plan)
20. A special computer ____ shoes for runners.   (design)
21. A computer ____ a record of all the expenses.   (keep)
22. Computers ____ the modern Olympics possible.   (make)

5 | Spelling the Present Tense (p. 144)

● Choose the verb that correctly completes each sentence. Write the sentences.

Example: Jon (watch, watches) Andy in a hockey game.
Jon watches Andy in a hockey game.

1. Andy (fix, fixes) his face mask.
2. A signal (buzzes, buzz) loudly.
3. The team (skates, skate) onto the ice.
4. Elsa (score, scores) first.
5. The crowd (cheer, cheers) for her.
6. The puck (flies, fly) toward the net.
7. The goalie (catch, catches) it in his glove.
8. Andy (tie, ties) the score in the last minute.

▲ Use the correct present tense form of the verb to complete each sentence. Write the sentences.

Example: Jill's brother ____ hockey.   (play)
Jill's brother plays hockey.

9. Jill ____ to play too.   (want)
10. Mark ____ her all the rules.   (teach)
11. Then Jill ____ out for the hockey team.   (try)
12. Mark ____ her luck.   (wish)
13. Jill ____ the hockey stick well.   (handle)
14. She ____ the puck well too.   (pass)
15. Finally, the coach ____ her the good news.   (give)

■ Write each sentence, spelling the present tense verb correctly.

Example: Jana love ice-skating. *Jana loves ice-skating.*

16. She wish for a new pair of skates.
17. She never miss a lesson.
18. Jana carry her skates to school every day.
19. She rush to the rink right after school.
20. She practice for three hours.
21. Her mother pick her up at six o'clock.
22. Then she study her lessons for school.

6 | Spelling the Past Tense (p. 146)

● Write the verb in each pair that is in the past tense.
Example: grab–grabbed *grabbed*
1. gulped–gulp
2. hemmed–hem
3. try–tried
4. trip–tripped
5. owed–owe
6. worried–worry
7. defeated–defeat
8. raise–raised

▲ Use the past tense of the verb to complete each sentence. Write the sentence.
Example: Susan ____ sandwiches for the trip.   (prepare)
Susan prepared sandwiches for the trip.
9. She ____ them in waxed paper.   (wrap)
10. Pat ____ up the backpacks.   (zip)
11. Carla ____ them to the car.   (carry)
12. Dad ____ his list one more time.   (check)
13. Mom ____ out her new camera.   (try)
14. The whole family ____ for a picture.   (pose)
15. The children ____ into the back seat.   (hop)
16. They all ____ their seat belts.   (fasten)
17. Mr. Russo ____ from his porch.   (wave)

■ Change each present tense verb to past tense. Write the sentences.
Example: Jan's family explores a museum in the desert.
Jan's family explored a museum in the desert.
18. A guide shows them around the outdoor museum.
19. Hats shade their faces from the hot sun.
20. Wolves cry in the distance.
21. Leo spots a giant cactus.
22. It stores water in its roots.
23. Bobcats and beavers live in the area.
24. Then a new dam stops the river.
25. The streams dry up.
26. The animals move to other places.

7 | The Past with Helping Verbs (p. 148)

● Copy the underlined verbs in each sentence. Write *helping* or *main* beside each verb.

Example: Jim <u>had</u> <u>received</u> tickets to the ice show.
had—helping   received—main

1. He <u>has</u> <u>offered</u> me a ticket.
2. I <u>had</u> <u>enjoyed</u> the show last year.
3. I <u>have</u> <u>thanked</u> him for the ticket.
4. Jim and I <u>had</u> <u>hurried</u> to the show.
5. An usher <u>had</u> <u>guided</u> us to our seats.
6. Now the lights <u>have</u> <u>dimmed</u>.
7. A man and a woman <u>have</u> <u>skated</u> onto the ice.

▲ Write each sentence. Draw one line under the helping verb and two lines under the main verb.

Example: Posters had advertised the ice show.
Posters <u>had</u> <u>advertised</u> the ice show.

8. Lisa and Dan have hurried ahead for good seats.
9. I had arrived in time for the first act.
10. Ten skaters in mouse costumes had scurried onto the ice.
11. A skater in a cat costume has chased after them.
12. The mice have escaped from the cat.
13. The crowd has clapped for the mice.

■ Rewrite each sentence. Use the helping verb *has*, *have*, or *had* and the past form of the verb.

Example: Two ice skaters dance in the spotlight.
Two ice skaters have danced in the spotlight.

14. Their costumes sparkle in the golden light.
15. The man lifts the woman over his head.
16. They twirl like a top together.
17. The man trips on something.
18. The crowd cries out.
19. The woman smiles at the man.
20. The man and the woman try the dance again.

8 | Irregular Verbs (p. 150)

● Choose the correct verb to complete each sentence. Write the sentences.

Example: Pam's dad had (drove, driven) for three hours.
Pam's dad had driven for three hours.

1. The car radio had (break, broken) last week.
2. Pam and Joe (sang, sung) songs to pass the time.
3. Snow had (begin, begun) to fall.
4. Their mother (say, said) that the ski lodge was not far.
5. They had (grew, grown) hungry.
6. Joe (gave, given) everyone a sandwich.
7. They (ate, eaten) supper at the lodge later.

▲ Write each sentence. Use the correct past form of the verb.

Example: Mary ____ the ski teacher a smile.   (give)
Mary gave the ski teacher a smile.

8. She ____ an upside-down *V* with her skis.   (make)
9. Then she ____ to snowplow down the small hill.   (begin)
10. The teacher ____ she was ready for a challenge.   (say)
11. She ____ Mary to a bigger hill.   (bring)
12. Mary ____ she could do it.   (know)
13. Still, she wished she had ____ more padding.   (wear)
14. Mary ____ down the hill without falling.   (come)

■ Use the correct past form of the verb from the Word Box to complete each sentence. Write the sentences.

Example: Kris had ____ about winter camping.
Kris had known about winter camping.

| begin |
| break |
| come |
| give |
| grow |
| know |
| make |
| say |
| take |

15. Nan ____ that she wanted to learn.
16. The girls ____ to winter camping school.
17. An instructor ____ them directions for building a snow shelter.
18. Nan ____ the crust of the snow with a shovel.
19. She and Kris ____ to build a shelter.
20. Soon they had ____ a good snow shelter.

9 | The Special Verb *be* (p. 152)

● Write each sentence. Underline the form of the verb *be*.
   Example: I am Jane's best friend.   *I am Jane's best friend.*

1. Jane is in my class.
2. I was at Jane's house yesterday.
3. Her mother was there too.
4. She is a sportswriter.
5. You are in her latest article.
6. It was about our basketball team.
7. We were all in the picture.

▲ Choose the verb that correctly completes each sentence. Write the sentences.
   Example: Kim Wang (is, are) a television reporter.
           Kim Wang is a television reporter.

8. She (was, were) at our school last week.
9. You (was, were) not in school that day.
10. We (was, were) in the auditorium.
11. I (was, were) in the front row.
12. I (am, is) a big fan of Ms. Wang.
13. Her stories (is, are) about young people.
14. One story (was, were) about student explorers.

■ Write each sentence. Use the correct form of the verb *be*. The word in ( ) tells which tense to use.
   Example: My father ____ a helicopter pilot.   (present)
           My father is a helicopter pilot.

15. He ____ also a traffic reporter.   (present)
16. His reports ____ on the radio.   (present)
17. Yesterday I ____ in his helicopter.   (past)
18. It ____ very exciting.   (past)
19. We ____ high above the ground.   (past)
20. You ____ far below us.   (past)
21. The news reports ____ on the air first.   (past)
22. They ____ on before the traffic report.   (present)

10 | Contractions with *not* (p. 154)

● Write the contraction in each sentence.

Example: I can't go out now.   *can't*

1. I haven't finished my homework.
2. It won't take long, though.
3. It isn't hard.
4. My sister hasn't come home yet.
5. I don't want to leave without her.
6. You shouldn't wait for us.
7. We wouldn't want you to miss the concert.

▲ Write each sentence. Use a contraction in place of the underlined word or words.

Example: We <u>were</u> <u>not</u> able to play softball today.
        We weren't able to play softball today.

8. The rain <u>did</u> <u>not</u> stop all afternoon.
9. Our team <u>could</u> <u>not</u> have been luckier.
10. We <u>did</u> <u>not</u> have a chance against the Gorillas.
11. Now we <u>will</u> <u>not</u> have to play them this year.
12. There <u>is</u> <u>not</u> enough time left in the season.
13. The Chipmunks <u>should</u> <u>not</u> be hard to beat.
14. We <u>are</u> <u>not</u> going to let anything keep us from the championship!

■ Write a sentence to answer each question. Use a contraction made up of the underlined verb and the word *not* in each one.

Example: <u>Did</u> you try out for the school musical?
        I didn't try out for the school musical.

15. <u>Were</u> Phil and Marita at the tryouts?
16. <u>Has</u> the school ever done a musical before?
17. <u>Do</u> you have a good singing voice?
18. <u>Does</u> Paul know how to dance?
19. <u>Can</u> Bob and Anna get the tickets printed?
20. <u>Will</u> Rico help build the scenery?

UNIT

6

Literature and Writing

O nce upon a time there lived a King and his wife, the Queen. They were a happy couple for they had everything in the world. However ... when the Queen's birthday came near, the King had a problem: What could he give to Someone who had Everything?

Rolf Myller
from "How Big Is a Foot?"

Story

Getting Ready Everyone likes stories. What makes a story interesting to you? Do you like funny stories? make-believe stories? Do you like stories that take place in the past? in the present? in the future? When you write a story, it can be just the way you want it to be. In this unit, you will read a story and later write one of your own.

ACTIVITIES

Listening Listen as the beginning of a story on the opposite page is read. When does the story take place? Who are the characters? What was the King's problem?

Speaking Look at the picture. What other story ideas does it make you think of? Make a class list. You may want to use some of the ideas when you write your own story.

Writing   What do you think the King will do in this story? What would you give somebody who had everything? Write your ideas in your journal. Could you make them into a story?

LITERATURE

How did a small gray bird save the life of the Emperor of China?

The Emperor's Nightingale

By Hans Christian Andersen

What I am about to tell you happened many years ago, and you should hear the story now, before it is forgotten.

The land of China, where the Chinese live, was once ruled by an Emperor. The Emperor lived in the most splendid palace in the world. The palace was made of the most delicate porcelain. Outside in the garden grew the loveliest flowers. Tiny silver bells were fastened to the most perfect blossoms so that no one passing by could fail to notice them. The garden itself was so large that even the gardener did not know where it ended. But whoever walked beyond it came to a beautiful wood with very tall trees that went on as far as the wide blue ocean. Among the trees there lived a nightingale. It sang so sweetly that the people who lived on the shore would stand still and listen to its song.

Travelers came from all parts of the world to the Emperor's city. They admired the city, the palace, and the garden. But when they heard the nightingale, they

said, "This is the best of all!" When the travelers returned home, they wrote books about the city, the palace, and the garden. And they always mentioned the nightingale.

One of these books was given to the Emperor as he sat in his golden chair. He read and read and nodded his head, for the descriptions of the city, the palace, and the garden pleased him greatly.

"But there is nothing like the nightingale," the Emperor read.

"What is this?" said the Emperor. "The nightingale? I have never heard of it. Can there be such a bird in my own country without my knowing?"

"I have never heard of this bird," said the Emperor's chamberlain.

"I wish it to come and sing for me this evening," said the Emperor. "The whole world seems to know what I have, and I do not know it myself."

"I shall find it," said the chamberlain.

But where was the nightingale to be found? The chamberlain ran up one flight of stairs and down another, through halls and through passages. Finally, he asked a young girl in the kitchen,

who said, "Oh, of course I know the nightingale. Every evening I visit my sick mother who lives near the ocean. When the nightingale sings, it is so beautiful that it makes me cry."

The kitchen maid led the chamberlain far into the wood where the nightingale sang. Half of the court attendants went with them.

"There it is," said the kitchen maid. "Listen! It is sitting up there." And she pointed to a little gray bird in the branches of a tree.

"How plain it looks," said the chamberlain. But then the nightingale began to sing and everyone was amazed. "Its voice is like glass bells," they said.

"Little nightingale," called the kitchen maid, "our Emperor wishes you to sing for him at the palace."

"My song sounds best among the green trees," answered the nightingale. But it followed them willingly to the palace.

The whole court gathered that evening in the middle of a grand hall. The nightingale was given a golden perch near the Emperor's throne. All the people wore their best clothes and all eyes were fixed upon the little gray bird. The Emperor nodded and the little gray bird began to sing.

The nightingale sang so sweetly that tears came into the Emperor's eyes. And its song touched the hearts of all who heard it.

All the city talked of the wonderful bird.

The nightingale was now to remain at the palace and have its own cage. It had permission to fly out twice a day and once a night. But twelve attendants were to go with it on these outings, and they held it by a silken band attached to its foot. The nightingale could not enjoy its outings at all.

One day, a large package arrived for the Emperor at the palace. On it was written NIGHTINGALE.

"It must be another book about our famous bird," said the Emperor.

It was not a book. It was a mechanical nightingale, a gift from the Emperor of Japan. The mechanical bird did not look gray and modest like the real nightingale. It was covered all over with diamonds and glittered with silver and gold. When the mechanical bird was wound up, it could sing one of the songs that the real nightingale sang.

"How delightful!" everybody cried. "Now they shall sing together."

And so they had to sing together, but it was not a success. Then the mechanical bird sang alone. It sang the same tune thirty-three times. Now the Emperor thought it was time the real nightingale sang once more. But where had it gone? Nobody had noticed that it had flown out of the window and back to its own green wood.

"What is the meaning of this?" said the Emperor angrily. All the court attendants called the nightingale an ungrateful creature.

"Anyway, we have the better bird," said the chamberlain. "When the real nightingale sings, you never know what is coming. Everything is settled with the mechanical bird. You know exactly what it will sing. It is prettier, too."

"That is perfectly true," the court attendants agreed. But the kitchen maid and the people from the shore said quietly, "It does sound pretty, almost like the real bird, but there is something missing."

The mechanical bird had its place on a silken cushion next to the Emperor's bed. But one evening, when the bird was singing and the Emperor was listening, there was a sudden bang and then a "whrrrrr." The music stopped. The Emperor jumped out of bed and called for the best clockmaker. At last the bird was put together again, but the clockmaker said it must not be used too much for its pegs were almost worn out.

So the mechanical bird was allowed to sing only once a year.

One day a great sorrow came to the land. The people heard that the Emperor was ill and could not live much longer. There was silence all over the palace.

The Emperor lay cold and pale in his golden bed. A window was open and the moon shone down on him and the mechanical bird. He opened his eyes.

"Music, music!" cried the Emperor. "You dear little mechanical bird, sing! Oh, do sing!"

But the bird was silent. There was no one to wind it up.

All at once the sweetest song was heard from the window.
The little living nightingale was sitting on a branch outside. It
had heard of the Emperor's illness and had come to comfort
him. As it sang, strength flowed through the Emperor's body.

"Thank you, thank you, wonderful bird," said the Emperor.
"I turned away from you and yet you have returned. How can I
reward you?"

"You have rewarded me," said the nightingale. "I saw tears
in your eyes when I first sang to you. Those I shall never forget.
But sleep now and awake fresh and healthy. I will sing you to
sleep."

The nightingale sang and the Emperor fell into a deep sleep.
When he awoke strong and healthy, the sun was shining in at
the window. The nightingale was still sitting there and singing.

"You must stay with me," said the Emperor. "I will break
the mechanical bird into a thousand pieces."

"Don't do that," said the nightingale. "It has done its best.
Keep it and take care of it. I cannot stay at your palace, for I
need my freedom and the green wood. But I shall come when I
like. I shall sit on a branch close to your window in the evening
and will sing to you. I shall sing to you of the happy people and

of the sorrowful ones in your land. I know your heart and love it better than your crown. But you must promise me something."

"Anything," said the Emperor. "Anything you like."

"I ask only one thing," said the nightingale. "Let no one know that you have a little bird who tells you of the good and bad in the world. Let them all think you are wise."

And with that the nightingale flew away.

Quietly the attendants came in, for they had expected that the Emperor would die during the night. But there stood the Emperor at a window!

"Good morning!" he said.

Think and Discuss

1. What did the nightingale do to save the Emperor's life?
2. In what ways was the mechanical nightingale different from the real nightingale?
3. Why do you think the nightingale returned? Would you have returned if you had been the nightingale?
4. The people or animals in a story are called **characters**. They can be real or make-believe. You can tell what characters are like from their words and actions. Which three of these words describe the nightingale: *selfish, loyal, kind, mean, forgiving*? What words and actions of the nightingale helped you to decide?

RESPONDING TO LITERATURE

The Reading and Writing Connection

Personal Response The Emperor did not know about the nightingale in his own woods. Like the Emperor, we may not notice beautiful things around us. Think of something you see every day. Write about it as if you were seeing it for the first time.

Creative Writing Unlike the mechanical bird, the real nightingale could sing many different songs. When the Emperor was ill, the nightingale returned to sing a song of comfort and hope. Write words, or lyrics, to this song. Choose a tune or write one of your own.

Creative Activities

Draw Read the first paragraph of the story again. How does it describe the Emperor's palace? How do you imagine the palace? Draw a picture of the Emperor's palace.

Oral Reading With two classmates, read the last part of the story as a play. Begin with paragraph 1 on page 179. Quotation marks set off the parts of the Emperor and the nightingale. The narrator reads the other parts of the story. Read with expression.

Vocabulary

The Emperor's palace "was made of the most delicate porcelain." Look up the meaning of the word *delicate*. List all the delicate things you can think of.

Looking Ahead

Story In this unit you will write your own story. You will describe where the story takes place. Read the first two paragraphs of "The Emperor's Nightingale." Notice the words that describe where this story takes place.

VOCABULARY CONNECTION
Using Word Clues

Can you figure out the meaning of *mechanical* in the quotation below?

> When the **mechanical** bird was wound up, it could sing one of the songs that the real nightingale sang.
>
> *from "The Emperor's Nightingale"*
> *by Hans Christian Andersen*

One way to find the meaning of a new word is to look at the rest of the words in the sentence. Both *mechanical* and *wound up* describe the bird. *Wound up* gives you a clue to the meaning of *mechanical*.

You know that a real bird cannot be wound up, but a bird that works like a machine can. So you can guess that the word *mechanical* probably means "acting as if by machine."

Vocabulary Practice

A. Write the meaning of each underlined word from "The Emperor's Nightingale." Use the word clues in the rest of the sentence.

1. An emperor painted a picture of his <u>splendid</u> palace with its golden roof and jeweled walls.
2. People were <u>amazed</u> by the painting's great size and beauty.
3. They <u>admired</u> the emperor's talent as an artist.

B. Choose four new words from "The Emperor's Nightingale." Write a sentence using each word. Include word clues to help your reader.

Prewriting
Story

Listening: Predicting Outcomes

When you hear thunder, you can **predict**, or tell ahead of time, that it will probably rain. The thunder is a **clue.** Your own experience tells you that it usually means rain.

In the same way, when you read a story, you can use clues and your experience to help you predict what will happen.

Listen as a classmate reads the following paragraphs.

> The Emperor lay cold and pale in his golden bed. . . .
> "Music, music!" cried the Emperor. "You dear little mechanical bird, sing! Oh, do sing!"
> But the bird was silent. There was no one to wind it up.
> All at once the sweetest song was heard from the window.
>
> *from "The Emperor's Nightingale"*
> *by Hans Christian Andersen*

• What do you think will happen? What clues helped you?

Use the following guides to help you predict outcomes.

Guides for Predicting Outcomes

1. Notice clues the author gives.
2. Use what you know from your own experiences.
3. Use this information to predict what might happen.

Prewriting Practice

Listen as your teacher reads a story. Using the guides above, write what you predict will happen in the story.

Thinking: Drawing Conclusions

Writers often use clues instead of explaining everything that happens. You can use these clues to figure out, or **draw a conclusion,** about what is happening. In the lines below, which bird's singing did the Emperor prefer?

When the mechanical bird was wound up, it could sing one of the songs that the real nightingale sang.

"How delightful!" everybody cried. "Now they shall sing together."

And so they had to sing together, but it was not a success. Then the mechanical bird sang alone. It sang the same tune thirty-three times. Now the Emperor thought it was time the real nightingale sang once more.

from "The Emperor's Nightingale"
by Hans Christian Andersen

You can guess from these lines that the Emperor preferred the real nightingale's singing. You were given these clues.

1. The mechanical bird could sing only one of the real nightingale's songs.
2. The mechanical bird sang one tune thirty-three times.
3. The Emperor wanted the real nightingale to sing again.

When you draw a conclusion, be sure that you have all the information you need. If you do not have enough information, you could reach the wrong conclusion. Read the lines below.

"I shall find it," said the chamberlain.

But where was the nightingale to be found? The chamberlain ran up one flight of stairs and down another, through halls and through passages.

from "The Emperor's Nightingale"
by Hans Christian Andersen

• What conclusion did the chamberlain draw?

The chamberlain did not have enough information to draw his conclusion. He soon learned that the nightingale lived in a wood.

When you write a story of your own, leave clues to make your reader think about the story. Be sure that your clues give enough information. When you read or listen, draw the right conclusions yourself. Follow these guides.

Guides for Drawing Conclusions

1. Look for clues. What might they mean?
2. Think about what you already know that might help you.
3. Be sure you have enough information to draw the right conclusion.
4. Decide what else you need to know.

Prewriting Practice

A. Read the clues below. What conclusion could you draw about the nightingale's feelings? Write your conclusion.

The nightingale said its song sounded best in the wood.
The nightingale was taken to the palace and had to stay in a cage.
It had permission to fly out three times a day.
On the bird's outings, attendants held it by a silken band attached to its foot.

B. Read the paragraph and answer the questions.

Bob walked up the stone steps carrying an armload of books. He entered the big, silent room and walked past rows of tables where people sat quietly reading. At the other end of the room, Bob put the books on a desk. A woman at the desk stamped a card in the back of each one. Then Bob went to look for more books.

Where was Bob? What clues and experiences helped you draw your conclusion?

Composition Skills
Story

Beginning, Middle, and End ☑

What kinds of stories do you like? fairy tales like "The Emperor's Nightingale"? mysteries? sports stories?

Each kind of story is different, but all stories are alike in some ways. Every story is about one main idea. Every story has a beginning, a middle, and an end, which make up the **plot**.

The **beginning** of a story sets the stage. It introduces the main characters and tells where and when the story takes place. A good beginning captures the reader's interest. The **middle** of a story tells the main events. There is often a problem that must be solved. The **end** finishes the story so that it makes sense. If there was a problem, the ending tells how it was solved.

The Three Parts of "The Emperor's Nightingale"	
Beginning	**Who:** Emperor, amazing nightingale **When:** Long ago **Where:** China; Emperor's palace, garden, and wood
Middle	**Main events:** Nightingale brought to palace; mechanical bird arrives; real bird flies away; Emperor becomes ill **Problem:** Mechanical bird is broken.
End	**Problem solved:** Real nightingale returns and saves Emperor's life.

Prewriting Practice

Think of a topic for a story you might like to write. Write ideas for a beginning, a middle, and an end. Make a chart like the one in this lesson.

Writing a Good Ending ☑

What would you have thought if "The Emperor's Nightingale" had ended when the Emperor became ill? You would probably have wondered what happened. The story would not be complete. The ending is an important part of a story. It should finish the story in a way that makes sense.

Read the beginning and middle of the short story below.

Long ago, a king had an enemy who did many evil things, so the king made him leave the country. Before he left, he said, "I will get even! Wait and see!"

The king had a handsome son. On the prince's sixteenth birthday, his parents gave him a huge party. Near the end of the party, the prince suddenly turned into an ugly frog. "Heh-heh-heh! Now we are even!" came the voice of the king's old enemy. "Only I know 'the one' who can make this frog a prince again."

Many years passed. Every day the frog sat by the roadside. Each time someone passed, he croaked, "Are you 'the one' who can make me a prince again?"

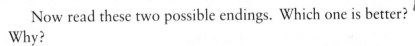

Now read these two possible endings. Which one is better? Why?

1. One day one of the prince's old friends came past. When he saw the frog-prince sitting by the roadside, he shouted, "What are you doing here, you ugly frog? Shoo!" After that, the prince's friend left the country.

2. One day a beautiful princess named Theone passed by. The frog-prince croaked, "Are you 'the one'?"

"Why yes," Princess Theone replied, "but that's not how I say my name."

Then she touched the frog-prince. He became a prince again. Not long after that, he and the princess married and lived happily ever after.

Prewriting Practice

Look at the story chart you made for Prewriting Practice in the last lesson. Write two other endings for your story. Discuss with a partner which ending is better and why.

Setting and Characters ☑

You know that every story has a plot with a beginning, a middle, and an end. Every story also has a setting and characters.

The **setting** of a story is where and when the story takes place. The setting can be real or imaginary. It can be in the past, the present, or the future. "The Emperor's Nightingale" is set in the land of China, many years ago. Look back at your story chart. What is the setting of your story?

The **characters** in a story can be people or animals, real or make-believe, young or old. Characters you make up can be just like the people and animals in your own neighborhood, or they can be from faraway lands. Who are some characters that you would like to write about?

How do you know what the characters in a story are like? How does a writer make them seem real? One way is through dialogue—exact words characters say. Read these paragraphs.

1. "What is this?" said the Emperor. "The nightingale? I have never heard of it. Can there be such a bird in my own country without my knowing?"
2. "Thank you, thank you, wonderful bird," said the Emperor. "I turned away from you and yet you have returned. How can I reward you?"

from "The Emperor's Nightingale"
by Hans Christian Andersen

- What does the first paragraph tell you about the Emperor?
- What does the second paragraph tell you?

Prewriting Practice

Look at the picture below. What is the setting? Who are the characters? Write a short description of the setting. Then write a dialogue between the characters. Use the dialogue to show what the characters are like.

The Grammar Connection

Using Exact Verbs

As Hans Christian Andersen wrote his story, he might have revised a dull sentence this way.

DULL: The Emperor got out of bed and asked for the best clockmaker.

REVISED: The Emperor jumped out of bed and called for the best clockmaker.

Exact verbs like *jumped* and *called* can turn a dull story into a lively one. They help you see the actions in the story. Make your own writing lively by using exact verbs.

Practice Write each sentence twice. Use two different exact verbs to replace the underlined verb.

1. The nightingale <u>went</u> gracefully from tree to tree.
2. It <u>sat</u> on a branch of a plum tree and began to sing.
3. All who heard it <u>said</u>, "How lovely!"
4. It was the Emperor who <u>liked</u> the nightingale most.

The Writing Process
How to Write a Story

Step 1: Prewriting—Choose a Topic

Sam wanted to write a story for the school magazine. He listed his ideas. Then Sam thought about his list.

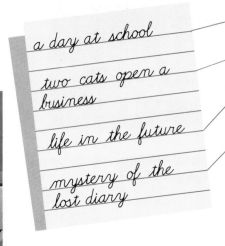

a day at school

two cats open a business

life in the future

mystery of the lost diary

⌐ This wasn't a very interesting
└ topic.

⌐ He had some ideas for this.

⌐ He had read about this. It
└ might make a good story.

⌐ He didn't have any good
└ ideas for this.

Sam liked his third topic. He had lots of ideas about the future. Sam thought it might be fun to write about a trip to Saturn. He circled *life in the future* on his list.

On Your Own

1. **Think and discuss** List some story ideas. Use the Ideas page to get started. Discuss your ideas with a partner.
2. **Choose** Ask these questions about each topic.
   Do I have enough ideas for this topic?
   Can I think of a good beginning, middle, and end?
   Which topic would make the best story?
   Circle the topic you want to write about.
3. **Explore** What will your story be about? Do one of the activities under "Exploring Your Topic" on the Ideas page.

Ideas for Getting Started

Choosing Your Topic

Topic Ideas

A zoo animal escapes
A daring rescue
The popcorn popper
  that wouldn't stop
A mystery
The day that every-
  thing was backwards
Going back in time

Story Chart

Suppose you have listed several top-ics that would be fun to write about. How can you choose the best one? Try making a story chart. First, list as many details as you can about the characters, setting, and plot for each topic. Now look at your chart. For which topic did you list the most ideas? Would it make a good story?

Exploring Your Topic

Cluster

Write your topic. Then let your ideas flow. Around your topic, write all the ideas that your topic suggests to you. What new ideas do you get? Add them to your cluster. Here is Sam's cluster.

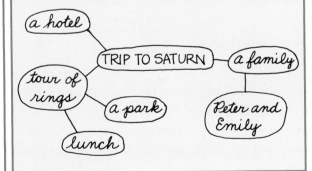

Give a Preview

Pretend that your story will be made into a movie. Give your friends a preview of your "coming attrac-tion." Tell just enough about the characters, setting, and plot to get your friends interested. Do they give you any new ideas?

Step 2: Write a First Draft

Sam wrote his first draft. He did not worry about making mistakes. Here is the first part of Sam's story.

Part of Sam's first draft

Think and Discuss

- Did Sam write a good beginning, middle, and end? Why or why not?
- Do the characters seem real? Why or why not?
- Did Sam give enough details about the setting? Where could he add more details?

> This ~~is~~ was ~~it~~ the day Peter had been waiting for. He and his famly was going to visit saturn!
>
> They finally arrived at their hotel. They toured Saturn's rings and went to a park. They ate lunch.
>
> After a week they went back to Earth. Then they went to Key West, Florida. They stayed in a big undersea hotel. They went scuba diving each day.

On Your Own

1. **Think about purpose and audience** Ask yourself: For whom shall I write this story? What is my purpose? Will my story be exciting or funny? scary or sad? an adventure or a mystery?

2. **Write** Write your first draft. Your beginning should catch a reader's interest. Your middle should tell the main events. Your ending should make sense. Write on every other line.

Step 3: Revise

Sam read his first draft. He wondered if his story would be interesting to someone else. He asked Anne to listen to it.

Reading and responding

> I like the idea, but you tell about a lot of things.

> Should I leave something out?

> Well, what is the most important part?

> The trip to Saturn! I'll just tell about that.

Sam took out the part about Key West. He thought more about the trip to Saturn. He got some new ideas. He wrote new paragraphs on another paper. Then he taped the new part over the old parts he did not want to use anymore.

Part of Sam's revised draft

going to visit saturn!
"The hotel must have an artificial gravity machine," said Peter. "We can walk just as we do on Earth!"
"Let's go swimming," said his sister Emily. When they dived into the pool, they made holes in the water. Then the holes collapsed.
Peter and Emily toured Saturn's rings. It was like walking on rainbows. They visited a park with rides. Peter liked the Spacecoaster best. They ate saturnwiches for lunch.
After a week they went back to

Think and Discuss ✔

- What details did Sam add?
- How did Sam make his characters seem more real?

On Your Own

Revising checklist

☑ Have I written an interesting beginning?

☑ Does the middle have enough events and details?

☑ Does my ending make sense?

☑ Are my setting and characters clear?

1. Revise Make changes in your draft. Add details and dialogue. Write another ending and choose the one you like better. You may want to use some of the words in the thesaurus below or the one found at the back of this book.

2. Have a conference Read your story to someone else—a classmate or your teacher.

WRITING CONFERENCE

Ask your listener:	As you listen:
"Do I have a good beginning, middle, and end?" "What parts of the story are not clear?" "Where could I add details about my setting and characters?"	I must listen carefully. Is this story about one main idea? What would I like to know more about? Does the story ending make sense?

3. Revise Think about your partner's questions. Do you have any other ideas? Make those changes.

Thesaurus

ask question, inquire
fun pleasure, entertainment, enjoyment
look seem, appear
nice agreeable, pleasant

really truly, actually
run dash, race
scary frightening, alarming, terrifying, shocking
walk march, stride, stroll

Step 4: Proofread

Sam proofread his story for mistakes in spelling, grammar, capitalization, and punctuation. He used a dictionary to check spellings. He used proofreading marks to make corrections.

Part of Sam's proofread draft

¶This ~~is~~ was ~~it~~ the day Peter had been
waiting for. He and his ~~famly~~ family were ~~was~~
going to visit saturn!

Think and Discuss

- What spelling correction did Sam make?
- What other corrections did he make? Why?

On Your Own

1. **Proofreading Practice** Proofread this paragraph. Correct the mistakes. There is one mistake in paragraph format, four spelling mistakes, two punctuation mistakes, and one missing capital letter. Write the paragraph correctly.

   One day Sid and Tom took a trip in a
   time machine the machine carryed them
   hi above the clowds. When they came
   doun, it was one hundred years ago. How
   different everything looked?

Proofreading Marks

¶	Indent
∧	Add something
ℯ	Take out something
≡	Capitalize
/	Make a small letter

2. **Proofreading Application** Now proofread your paper. Use the Proofreading Checklist and the Grammar and Spelling Hints on the next page. You may want to use a colored pencil to make your corrections. Use a dictionary to check spelling.

Proofreading Checklist

Did I

☑ **1.** indent?

☑ **2.** use capital letters correctly?

☑ **3.** use punctuation marks correctly?

☑ **4.** use verbs correctly?

☑ **5.** spell all words correctly?

The Grammar/Spelling Connection

Grammar Hints

Remember these rules from Unit 5 when you use verbs.

- With a singular subject, verbs in the present end with *s*. With a plural subject, verbs in the present do not end with *s*. (*He walks. We walk.*)
- Many verbs show past tense by adding *-ed*. (*walk— walked*)

Spelling Hints

- The (ī) sound is often spelled *i*, *igh*, or *i*-consonant-*e*. (*blind, fright, pride*)
- The (ou) sound is often spelled *ow* or *ou*. (*gown, bounce*)

Step 5: Publish

Sam copied his story and added the title "Spaceship to Saturn." He drew pictures to go with it. Then he gave the story and pictures to the editor of the school magazine.

Sam's story was accepted for the magazine. In addition, one of his pictures was chosen for the cover! When the magazine was published, Sam proudly showed it to his family.

On Your Own

1. **Copy** Copy your story in your neatest handwriting.
2. **Check** Make sure you have not left out anything or made any mistakes in copying.
3. **Add a title** Give your story a title.
4. **Share** Think of a special way to share your story. You may want to use some ideas from the Ideas for Sharing box.

Ideas for Sharing

- Make a time line. Show the main story events. Put it with your story.
- Make a book cover for your story. Attach it to the story and put it out for others to read.
- Turn your story into a radio play. Perform it with a partner or a group.

Applying Story Writing

Literature and Creative Writing

In "The Emperor's Nightingale," the Emperor had a nightingale brought to his palace to sing. The nightingale flew away when a glittering mechanical bird took its place. However, when the Emperor became ill, the real nightingale returned and saved his life with its beautiful song.

Have fun using what you learned about writing a story. Choose one or more of these activities.

> **Remember these things ☑**
> Write a beginning, a middle, and an end.
> Describe the setting.
> Create interesting characters.
> Use dialogue.

1. **Make up a mystery.** There is a mystery at the Emperor's palace. The mechanical nightingale has disappeared. Write a story about it. Tell how the kitchen maid and the real nightingale solve the mystery.

2. **Fashion a fairy tale.** Write a fairy tale about another kind of bird or animal that saves a person's life.

3. **Spin a science fiction story.** Write a science fiction story about the planet Mekanika. All the people on this planet are mechanical. Tell about the day two mechanical people of Mekanika meet a space traveler from Earth.

Writing Across the Curriculum
Health

Stories are fun to read, but they can also tell about important ideas. Ideas about health, safety, and feeling good, for example, can be shared through stories.

Choose one or more of the following activities.

1. Share your best. Look at poor Glum. He really is down in the dumps. He thinks he has no good qualities. How can you help? Think of one of *your* good qualities. Let Glum borrow it for a day. Write a story about what happens.

Writing Steps
1. Choose a Topic
2. Write a First Draft
3. Revise
4. Proofread
5. Publish

2. Sink your teeth into a story. Imagine that you are a tooth—one of your own! Write a story about a day in your life. What happens to you? Are you taken care of? What makes you feel good? You may want to use some of the words in the Word Bank.

Word Bank
floss
fluoride
cavity
plaque
enamel

3. Call for Superguard! A lifeguard at the beach sees some children being careless around the water. She tells them a story about other children who were careless and had to be rescued by Superguard. Write the story the lifeguard tells.

Extending Literature
Book Report: Puppet Play

Richard really liked Hans Christian Andersen's story "The Emperor's Nightingale." He decided to read another story by the same author. When he finished "The Ugly Duckling," Richard decided to give a puppet play to share the story with his class. Richard chose the part in which the ugly duckling hatches. Then he wrote his script and made stick puppets for the characters. This is Richard's script.

NARRATOR: Mother Duck is waiting and watching. Two of her eggs have hatched. One egg is still in the nest. It is a VERY LARGE egg.

OLD DUCK: It is time for that egg to hatch!

MOTHER DUCK: I think it is starting now!

NARRATOR: Suddenly the shell broke open. Out crawled a big clumsy-looking baby bird.

OLD DUCK: Look at that ugly creature! It isn't yellow and fuzzy. It doesn't look like a duck!

BABY DUCKS: Ugh! Go away! We don't want you here.

UGLY DUCKLING: Mother? What's the matter?

MOTHER DUCK: Don't worry. I'm sure you will turn yellow and fuzzy soon. You certainly are BIG!

NARRATOR: The ugly duckling did not turn yellow and fuzzy, but something else very interesting happened. You can find out in "The Ugly Duckling" by Hans Christian Andersen.

Think and Discuss

• What did you learn about the story from Richard's play?
• Why do you think Richard chose this part of the story?
• Did the play make you want to read the story? Explain.

Share Your Book

Put on a Puppet Play

1. First, decide which part of the book you want to share. Pick a part of the book in which the characters talk to one another.

2. Write a short script for your play. You may use the exact words of the characters, or you may want to change them a little. Be careful not to tell too much of the story.

3. Decide how many puppets you need. Then draw your puppets on heavy paper and cut them out. Finally, tape a stick or a pencil to the back of each puppet.

4. Present your puppet play to the class. Change your voice for each character.

Other Activities

- Make a stage for your puppets. You can use a big cardboard box. Cut an opening in one side for the stage. Stand the box upside down on two chairs so that you can reach up through the box top to show your characters through the opening.
- Draw or paint the scene where the action of your play takes place. If you make a stage, paste the scene at the back.

The Book Nook

Tales from Grimm	Aladdin and the Wonderful Lamp
retold by Wanda Gág Here are some favorite tales made famous many years ago by the two brothers Jakob and Wilhelm Grimm.	*by Andrew Lang* When Aladdin wipes the dust from the lamp he has found, a genie appears to grant his wishes.

Language and Usage

The chiming river changes its tune as the cold bright stars grow brighter.

Rokwa

Adjectives

Getting Ready When you draw a picture, you may color or paint it to show exactly what the objects look like. Did you know that when you speak or write you can use words that have the same effect as paint? These words are called adjectives. You can use them to describe people, places, and things. In this unit, you will learn how to use adjectives to add color to your writing.

ACTIVITIES

Listening   Listen as the poem on the opposite page is read. Which adjective describes the river? Which adjectives describe how the stars look? Which adjective compares the stars now with the way they were?

Speaking   Look at the picture. Think of words to describe the sight, sound, smell, taste, and feel of the water and ice. Share your words with the class.

Writing   In your journal, write your own poem about this picture, using descriptive words.

203

1 | What Is an Adjective?

You know that a noun is a word that names a person, a place, or a thing. In your writing, you may sometimes want to describe or give more information about a person, a place, or a thing. One way to do this is to use adjectives.

An **adjective** is a word that describes or gives more information about a noun. An adjective can tell you *what kind* or *how many*. It usually comes before the noun it describes.

WHAT KIND

We have a large dog.

The dog has a curly coat.

HOW MANY

Two dogs played in the yard.

Many dogs like children.

You can use more than one adjective to describe a noun.

We have a large, friendly dog.

The dog has five tiny puppies.

Guided Practice Find the adjectives that describe the underlined nouns. Does each adjective tell what kind, or does it tell how many?

Example: Many <u>dogs</u> can learn to do useful <u>work</u>.
        Many—how many   useful—what kind

1. Early <u>people</u> found that dogs made good <u>hunters</u>.
2. Strong <u>sheepdogs</u> help farmers with large <u>herds</u> of sheep.
3. One famous <u>dog</u> rescued forty lost <u>people</u> in the mountains.
4. Blind <u>people</u> use dogs to guide them through busy <u>streets</u>.
5. Some smart <u>dogs</u> learn to help deaf <u>people</u>.

> ► An **adjective** is a word that describes a noun. An adjective can tell what kind or how many.

Independent Practice

A. Write the adjectives that describe the underlined nouns. Write *what kind* or *how many* for each adjective.

Example: Linda Gunn has an interesting job.

interesting—what kind

6. Linda trains young dogs.
7. The dogs learn to help deaf people.
8. Two people in California found a lost dog.
9. They took the little white dog to a shelter.
10. One kind worker at the shelter named the dog Penny.
11. Linda found Penny at the shelter one day.
12. She could see that Penny was an intelligent dog.

B. Write each sentence. Draw a line under each adjective. Draw an arrow to the noun it describes.

Example: Training a dog takes about four months.

Training a dog takes about four months.

13. One big step is learning to obey simple commands.
14. Penny was a quick learner.
15. Linda and Penny practiced many times a day.
16. Linda rewarded Penny with tasty treats.
17. After four months, Penny was an excellent helper.
18. It was time to give her to a lucky owner.
19. Linda decided that Penny was a special dog.
20. Now Penny helps Linda train new dogs.

Writing Application: An Advertisement

Pretend that your pet is lost. Write a "lost-and-found" ad describing your pet. Use adjectives to describe your pet clearly.

For Extra Practice, see p. 224.   **What Is an Adjective?**

2 | Adjectives After *be*

An adjective can come after the word it describes. It usually follows a form of the verb *be*.

The project <u>is</u> ready.   I <u>am</u> excited.

You know that adjectives can describe nouns. They can also describe words like *I, it,* and *we,* which take the place of nouns.

Guided Practice Find the adjective in each sentence. What word does it describe?

Example: The weather is beautiful. *beautiful   weather*

1. The day is perfect.
2. The fair is exciting.
3. We were eager.
4. Paula is proud.
5. The chicken is fat.
6. The eggs are large.

Summing up

▶ An adjective can follow the word it describes and a form of the verb *be*.

Independent Practice Write each adjective and the word it describes.

Example: The pickles are homemade. *homemade   pickles*

7. The bread is tasty.
8. It was difficult to make.
9. The rides are popular.
10. Peter is afraid.
11. The sky is dark now.
12. I am tired.

Writing Application: A Description
Pretend that you have a project to enter in the county fair. Write a paragraph describing your project. Use adjectives after the words they describe.

3 | Using *a*, *an*, and *the*

The words *a*, *an*, and *the* are special adjectives called **articles.** Learn these rules for using articles.

With singular nouns: Use *a* if the next word begins with a consonant. Use *an* if the next word begins with a vowel. Use *the* if the noun names a particular person, place, or thing.	a flower an iris the garden
With plural nouns: Use *the*.	the flowers the irises

Guided Practice Which article or articles could be used before each word?

Example: contest   *a*   *the*

1. award   **2.** orchid   **3.** students   **4.** prize   **5.** roses

Summing up

▶ Use the articles *a* and *an* before singular nouns.
▶ Use the article *the* with both singular and plural nouns.

Independent Practice Write the articles for these words.

Example: plant   *a*   *the*

6. bushes   **7.** evergreen   **8.** seeds   **9.** area   **10.** weed

Writing Application: A Story
Finish the following story and underline the articles.

One day I discovered an unusual flower growing in the woods. All of a sudden—

For Extra Practice, see p. 226.   **Using *a*, *an*, and *the*   **

4 | Making Comparisons

Sometimes you may want to tell how things are alike or how they are different. You can use adjectives to compare.

You usually add -er to an adjective to compare two persons, places, or things, and -est to compare three or more.

Mindy took a long trip. (one trip described)

Lou's trip was longer than hers. (two trips compared)

I took the longest trip of all. (three or more compared)

Rules for Adding -er and -est	
1. If the adjective ends with e: Drop the e before adding the ending.	wide + -er = wider wide + -est = widest
2. If the adjective ends with a single vowel and a consonant: Double the consonant and add the ending.	thin + -er = thinner thin + -est = thinnest
3. If the adjective ends with a consonant and y: Change the y to i before adding the ending.	tiny + -er = tinier tiny + -est = tiniest

Guided Practice What adjective completes each sentence?

Example: Alaska is not the ____ state. (new) *newest*

1. Hawaii is ____ than Alaska. (new)
2. However, every other state is ____ than Alaska. (old)
3. Alaska is the ____ of all the states. (big)
4. It has the ____ population of all the states. (tiny)
5. There are ____ people than in my state. (few)

> ▶ Add *-er* to most adjectives to compare two persons, places, or things.
> ▶ Add *-est* to compare three or more persons, places, or things.

Independent Practice
Write the correct form of the adjective in ( ) to complete each sentence.

Example: We are visiting the ____ state of all.   (large)   *largest*

   6. It is ____ to get to Alaska than it used to be.   (easy)
   7. I will see the ____ mountains in North America.   (tall)
   8. Mount McKinley is ____ than any other peak.   (high)
   9. Alaska is ____ than many people think.   (warm)
   10. The ____ days of the year are in the middle of summer.   (long)
   11. In summer the sunlight is ____ than in the winter.   (strong)
   12. Southern Alaska has the ____ climate in the state.   (mild)
   13. In July it can get ____ than fifty-five degrees.   (hot)
   14. The southern part is also the ____ part of all.   (wet)
   15. It has the ____ average rainfall in the United States.   (high)
   16. Northern Alaska is ____ than the southern part.   (cold)
   17. It is also much ____.   (dry)
   18. Alaska is home to the ____ bears in the world.   (big)
   19. The Kodiak bear is even ____ than a grizzly bear.   (large)
   20. A Kodiak bear is also ____ than a grizzly.   (fierce)
   21. The ____ thing of all is to keep away from these bears!   (safe)
   22. Don't make the bear any ____ than it already is!   (angry)

Writing Application: A Postcard

Pretend that you are on vacation in some real or imaginary place. Write a postcard to a friend. Use adjectives with *-er* or *-est* to compare the place you are visiting with other places you have been. Use an index card. Write your message and your friend's address on one side. On the other side, draw a picture of the place you are describing.

For Extra Practice, see p. 227.

5 | Comparing with *more* and *most*

playful

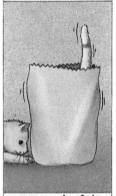

more playful

most playful

You know that you add *-er* or *-est* to some adjectives when you want to compare. With long adjectives, use the words *more* and *most* to compare persons, places, or things. Use the word *more* to compare two. Use *most* to compare three or more.

Tiger is a playful cat.   (one cat described)

Ginger is a more playful cat than Tiger.   (two cats compared)

Ike is the most playful cat of all.   (three or more compared)

Never add *-er* and *more* or *-est* and *most* to the same adjective.

INCORRECT: Tiger is more smarter then Ginger.
Tiger is the most intelligentest cat.

CORRECT: Tiger is smarter than Ginger.

Tiger is the most intelligent cat.

Guided Practice What adjective completes each sentence correctly?

Example: Cats are among the _____ of all pets.   (common)
most common

1. Only the dog is _____ than the cat.   (popular)
2. One of the _____ of all breeds of cat is the Siamese.   (popular)
3. Some people think that a Persian cat is _____ than any other cat. (beautiful)
4. However, an alley cat can be the _____ of all.   (lovable)
5. Of all the different kinds of cats in the world, the _____ is always your own.   (wonderful)

> ▶ With long adjectives, use *more* to compare two things and *most* to compare three or more.
>
> ▶ Never add *-er* and *more* or *-est* and *most* to the same adjective.

Independent Practice Write the correct form of the adjective in ( ) to complete each sentence.

Example: Cats are _____ than other pets.   (independent)
      more independent

6. An adult cat is _____ to train than a kitten is.   (difficult)
7. The _____ way of all to train a cat is with rewards and praise. (successful)
8. It takes patience, but you will have a _____ cat than you did before.   (obedient)
9. Cats are among the _____ of all animals.   (curious)
10. A cat's tricks can be _____ than a clown's.   (amusing)
11. Cats can be _____ than other pets.   (useful)
12. Some cats are _____ hunters than others.   (skillful)
13. Other cats are very lively and are _____ than others.   (playful)
14. Some people think that cats are _____ than any other pet. (intelligent)
15. Some cats seem to think that they are the _____ animals too. (intelligent)
16. The _____ event of the summer is our town's annual cat show. (exciting)

Writing Application: Compare and Contrast

Pretend that you are judging a cat show. Make up five different awards, such as *most beautiful coat*, or *more graceful than other cats*. Write about the winner of each award. Describe how it is different from the other cats. Use adjectives with *more* and *most* to describe the prize-winning cats in the show.

For Extra Practice, see p. 228.   **Comparing with *more* and *most***

6 | Comparing with *good* and *bad*

When you use the adjectives *good* and *bad* to compare, you need to change their forms. Change the adjective *good* to *better* when comparing two. Change it to *best* when comparing three or more.

> I found a good book at the library. (one book described)
>
> It is better than the last book I read. (two books compared)
>
> What is the best book you have read? (three or more compared)

Change the adjective *bad* to *worse* when comparing two. Change it to *worst* when comparing three or more.

> This is a bad story by I. M. Dull. (one story described)
>
> It is worse than her last story. (two stories compared)
>
> It may be the worst one she ever wrote! (three or more compared)

Guided Practice What adjective completes each sentence correctly?

Example: Danny is a _____ reader than his sister is.   (good)
    better

1. He thinks that the _____ thing of all on a rainy Saturday is to visit the library.   (good)
2. Danny's sister had the _____ time ever at the library last Saturday.   (bad)
3. She wanted a _____ book than her last one.   (good)
4. Every book she looked at was _____ than the one before.   (bad)
5. The one Danny chose for her was the _____ book of all.   (bad)

> ▸ When you use the adjectives *good* and *bad* to compare, you must change their forms.
> ▸ Use *better* or *worse* to compare two.
> ▸ Use *best* or *worst* to compare three or more.

Independent Practice Write the correct form of the adjective in ( ) to complete each sentence.

Example: This is the ____ weather of the week. (bad) *worst*

6. The rain today is much ____ than yesterday's. (bad)
7. Today would be the ____ day of the week to visit the library. (good)
8. May says that the ____ books of all are science fiction. (good)
9. I think that animal stories are ____ than science fiction. (good)
10. The ____ book I ever read was a science fiction book. (bad)
11. Ms. Wong is the ____ librarian I know. (good)
12. She knows which books are ____ than others. (good)
13. Ms. Wong chooses the ____ new books of all to buy for the library. (good)
14. Pete thinks that this is the ____ library in the city for him. (good)
15. It has a ____ collection of Braille books than the other libraries. (good)
16. The ____ part of all will be carrying all the books home! (bad)

Writing Application: A Story
Finish the following story:

> Last night I had the worst dream of my life. I dreamed that I got locked in the library. This is how it happened—

Use forms of *good* and *bad* in your story and underline them.

For Extra Practice, see p. 229.   **Comparing with *good* and *bad* 213**

Grammar-Writing Connection

Combining Sentences with Adjectives

Good writers try new ways to make their writing smooth and clear. You can experiment with your writing, too, by using adjectives to combine sentences.

The two choppy sentences below are both about a rabbit. They can be combined to make one smooth sentence.

A rabbit hops across the fields. A <u>brown</u> rabbit hops
    The rabbit is <u>brown</u>. across the fields.

The first two sentences below each tell something about rabbits' legs. The sentences are combined to make the third sentence by joining the adjectives *long* and *powerful*. Notice that *and* joins the two words.

   Rabbits' hind legs are <u>long</u>. Rabbits' hind legs are
Rabbits' hind legs are <u>powerful</u>. <u>long and powerful</u>.

Notice how much smoother the combined sentences are than the separate ones. They are also more interesting to read.

Revising Sentences

Rewrite these pairs of sentences by combining them.

1. Rabbits' ears are long. They are also narrow.
2. Their tails are short. Their tails are fluffy.
3. A rabbit's teeth are long. The teeth are sharp.
4. Rabbits can hide in grass. The grass is tall.
5. Some rabbits live in fields. These fields are open.
6. When baby rabbits are born, they are very weak. Baby rabbits are also hairless.
7. Look at that rabbit by the fence. The rabbit is white.
8. The rabbit hopped away. It was frightened.

Creative Writing

May, from *Les Très Riches Heures of the Duke of Berry* by The Limbourg Brothers Musée Condé, Chantilly, France

Long ago in France lived three brothers named Limbourg. They were famous for their beautiful book illustrations. This picture comes from a book the brothers made for a duke. The picture shows a month of the calendar. The people are going to celebrate a spring festival.

- How can you tell it is spring?

Activities

1. **Write a fairy tale.** Imagine that two of the people in this painting are a prince and a princess. They are riding through the enchanted woods to their kingdom. Write a fairy tale about their adventures.

2. **Describe your calendar illustration.** Suppose that the Limbourg brothers have offered to illustrate a calendar page for you. Which month would you choose? What would the picture show? Write a letter to the Limbourg brothers describing your page.

Check-up: Unit 7

What Is an Adjective? *(p. 204)*
Write the adjectives that describe the underlined nouns. Write *what kind* or *how many* for each adjective.

1. Tara has an interesting <u>hobby</u>.
2. She collects beautiful <u>seashells</u>.
3. She has found thirty different <u>kinds</u> of shells.
4. She keeps them in glass <u>boxes</u>.
5. Liz is a clever <u>artist</u>.
6. She and Tara make lovely <u>jewelry</u> from the shells.
7. They sell it at local <u>shops</u>.
8. Tara and Liz go to sandy <u>beaches</u> to hunt for new <u>shells</u>.
9. A good <u>time</u> is early <u>morning</u>.
10. Each <u>day</u> brings new <u>treasures</u>.
11. The girls look for pretty <u>objects</u> as they walk.
12. Calm <u>pools</u> are good <u>places</u> to find shells.
13. There are delicate <u>shells</u> on the clean <u>sand</u>.
14. Most <u>snails</u> have a single, twisted <u>shell</u>.
15. Empty <u>shells</u> may be homes for tiny <u>crabs</u>.
16. Tara found three pink <u>stones</u>.
17. They lay under shallow <u>water</u>.
18. They have unusual <u>markings</u>.
19. Tara will begin a new <u>collection</u>.

Adjectives After *be* *(p. 206)* Write each sentence. Draw a line under the adjective. Then draw an arrow to the word it describes.

20. Cal is eager to play the game.
21. The game is difficult.
22. It was new last year.
23. We are happy to play with Cal.
24. The questions are clever.
25. They were funny at first.
26. Now I am bored with them.

Using *a, an,* **and** *the* *(p. 207)* Write the correct article to complete each sentence.

27. (A, An) trunk was in (a, an) corner of the attic.
28. It held (a, an) old white dress with lace and ruffles.
29. There was also (a, an) old album.
30. (A, The) pictures show (a, an) young woman.
31. She is wearing (an, the) long white dress.
32. She carries (a, an) single rose.
33. She is holding (a, an) open book.
34. There is (a, an) name on one of (a, the) photos.
35. (An, The) girl is my grandmother.
36. I will write her (a, an) letter about (an, the) trunk.
37. She will tell me (a, an) story about (a, the) things in the attic.

216   Unit 7:   Adjectives

Making Comparisons *(p. 208)*
Write each sentence, using the correct form of the adjective in (   ).

38. The sun is the (close) star of all to Earth.
39. However, the sun is not the (big) star of all.
40. The (hot) stars of all look blue.
41. A blue star is (hot) than a yellow star.
42. Stars with the (low) temperatures of all appear red.
43. A red star is (cool) than the sun.
44. It is also (bright) than the sun.
45. A planet's light is (steady) than a star's.
46. All of the planets together are (small) than the sun.
47. Jupiter is (big) than any of the other planets.
48. Mercury is (tiny) than Mars.
49. Mercury is the (near) planet of all to the sun.
50. The distance from Pluto to the sun is the (great) of all.
51. Pluto is the (hard) planet to see.
52. The moon is the (bright) object of all in our nighttime sky.
53. It is the (easy) object of all to see.
54. Earth's gravity is (strong) than the moon's.
55. This makes objects (heavy) on Earth than they are on the moon.
56. You could take much (light) steps on the moon!

Comparing with *more* and *most* *(p. 210)*
Write each sentence, using the correct form of the adjective in (   ).

57. Bear cubs are (playful) than adult bears.
58. Some people think that cubs are (lovable) than grown bears.
59. However, all bears are (dangerous) than house pets.
60. The (common) bear of all is the black bear.
61. It is the (skillful) tree climber of all bears.
62. I think that polar bears are (beautiful) than black bears.
63. They are (comfortable) in the cold weather than other bears.
64. Their thick white fur is their (valuable) protection of all.

Comparing with *good* and *bad* *(p. 212)*
Write each sentence, using the correct form of the adjective in (   ).

65. I had a (good) time at summer camp this year than last year.
66. My cabin had the (good) view.
67. Insects are (bad) near the lake than in the woods.
68. That is the (bad) place in the whole camp to sleep.
69. The pool is (good) than the lake.
70. The weather was (bad) in July than in August.

Cumulative Review

Unit 1: The Sentence

Sentence, Kinds of Sentences
(pp. 14, 16, 18) If a group of words below is a sentence, write it correctly. If not, write *not a sentence*.

1. do you know how to use the computer at school
2. it is a very useful tool
3. would you like to learn
4. stores important information
5. the top row of keys
6. how quickly you learn
7. please turn the computer off now
8. makes corrections easily

Subjects and Predicates *(pp. 20, 22, 24)* Write each sentence. Draw a line between the complete subject and the complete predicate. Draw one line under the simple subject and two lines under the simple predicate.

9. Mrs. Greene has a solar house.
10. It has metal plates on the roof.
11. These metal plates are collectors.
12. They trap the sun's rays.
13. The heat of the sun warms a liquid inside the collectors.
14. The liquid heats a tank of water.
15. It is in the basement.
16. This water warms the whole solar house.

Compound Sentences *(p. 26)* Write each pair of sentences as one compound sentence. Use the connecting word given.

17. You may have read about Mozart. You may have heard some of his music.   (or)
18. He died young. He wrote over six hundred pieces of music.   (but)
19. Mozart began to play music when he was three. He wrote music at age five.   (and)
20. Mozart's father was a musician. He encouraged his son.   (and)
21. Mozart's life was hard. Much of his music is cheerful.   (but)

Compound Subjects and Predicates *(p. 28)* Write each pair of sentences as one sentence with a compound subject or a compound predicate.

22. The audience sits in the hall. The audience waits quietly for the music to start.
23. The musicians take their places. The musicians tune up.
24. The conductor lifts his baton. The conductor signals to begin.
25. The violins begin to play. The cellos begin to play.
26. Cellos are stringed instruments. Violins are stringed instruments.

Run-on Sentences *(p. 30)* Write each run-on sentence correctly as two sentences.

27. Jill and Ted were sailing a big storm suddenly came up.
28. A strong wind blew waves crashed onto the shore.
29. The lake was very rough small boats hurried toward the dock.
30. Then the thunder roared the downpour began.
31. Jill and Ted tied up the boat they had made it just in time.

Unit 3: Nouns

Common and Proper Nouns *(pp. 76, 78)* Write each noun. Beside it, write *common* or *proper*. Begin each proper noun with a capital letter.

32. On friday uncle leo brought a newspaper to our house.
33. My mother read the news.
34. One story in the paper was about the fourth of july.
35. Our town will hold a celebration on that day.
36. A big parade will march right down main street.
37. The mayor will give a speech from the grandstand.
38. A band from middletown will play at goss park.
39. People will watch fireworks over the johnstown river.

Singular and Plural Nouns *(pp. 80, 82, 84)* Write the plural form of each singular noun.

40. dish
41. mask
42. duty
43. sheep
44. compass
45. man

Singular and Plural Possessive Nouns *(pp. 86, 88)* Write the possessive form of the noun in ( ).

46. The (family) new house is being built rapidly.
47. The (carpenters) job will be done by the end of next week.
48. The (men) hammers are pounding away busily.
49. The (women) hammers are too.
50. Next week the (painters) work will start.
51. (Bert) room is in the back of the new house.
52. His (mother) office is next to it.
53. The other (children) rooms are upstairs.
54. (Dad) workshop will be in the basement.
55. The (animals) big new barn will be built next.
56. The (horses) stalls will be roomy and comfortable.
57. (Sport) new doghouse is not ready.
58. Bert is planning to build his (pet) house himself.

Cumulative Review, continued

Unit 5: Verbs

Action Verbs, Main Verbs, and Helping Verbs *(pp. 136, 138)* Write the verbs in these sentences. Write *main* or *helping* beside each verb.

59. Heidi was making a collage.
60. She had found magazine pictures.
61. We were helping her.
62. She has glued them onto cardboard.
63. The glue is drying now.

Past, Present, and Future *(p. 140)* Write each verb and label it *past, present,* or *future.*

64. Some trains carry passengers.
65. Other trains haul products.
66. The first railroads began in England in the 1820s.
67. Tomorrow's trains will be different.
68. Computers will steer those trains.

Agreement, Spelling the Present Tense *(pp. 142, 144)* Write the correct present tense form of each verb.

69. Candy (rub) the balloons on the wool rug.
70. Her brother (watch) curiously.
71. She (stick) them to the wall.
72. The balloons (stay) there!
73. Electricity (make) them stick.

Spelling the Past Tense, Past with Helping Verbs *(pp. 146, 148)* Write each sentence. Use *have* or *has* with the correct form of the verb.

74. Pete (enjoy) folk dancing.
75. This week he (try) a new dance.
76. Everyone (practice) the steps.
77. The dancers (form) a circle.
78. They (step) to the music.

Irregular Verbs *(p. 150)* Write each sentence, using the correct past form of the verb.

79. The show (begin) at two o'clock.
80. One hundred people had (come).
81. The actors (wear) shiny costumes.
82. Jen and Mike had (make) them.
83. We (take) our places on-stage.
84. I (grow) more and more nervous.
85. I had (know) my lines earlier!

The Special Verb *be (p. 152)* Write the verb that correctly completes each sentence.

86. My cousins (is, are) in Australia.
87. We (was, were) there last year.
88. Australia (is, are) a country and a continent.
89. You (was, were) in Sydney for a month last winter.
90. It (is, are) the largest city.

Contractions with *not* (*p. 154*)
Write the contractions for the following words.

91. is not   **95.** had not
92. cannot   **96.** do not
93. was not   **97.** could not
94. would not   **98.** did not

Unit 7: Adjectives

Adjectives (*p. 204*) Write each adjective and the noun it describes.

99. A giraffe is a tall animal that lives in dry areas of Africa.
100. It has a long, thin neck and four skinny legs.
101. The neck of a giraffe contains seven bones.
102. That is the same number that a human has.
103. Many people think that a giraffe cannot make a single sound.
104. However, most giraffes do make some low sounds.

Adjectives After *be* (*p. 206*) Write each adjective and the word it describes.

105. I am interested in quilting.
106. The art is old.
107. The stitches are tiny.
108. The patterns are different.
109. Mother said that Grandma was skillful at quilting.
110. Her quilts were beautiful.

Using *a, an,* and *the* (*p. 207*)
Choose the correct article or articles in ( ) to complete each sentence. Write the sentences.

111. (A, The) names of many young animals are interesting.
112. (A, An) owl's baby is called (a, an) owlet.
113. (A, An) young eagle is called (a, an) eaglet.
114. We know that (a, an) baby cat is (a, an) kitten.
115. Does that mean that (a, an) infant bat is (a, an) bitten?

Comparing with Adjectives (*pp. 208, 210, 212*) Choose the correct word in ( ) to complete each sentence. Write the sentences.

116. *Stone Fox* is the (sadder, saddest) book I have read.
117. Is it (sadder, saddest) than *Annie and the Old One*?
118. What is the (better, best) mystery story you have ever read?
119. Is *Charlotte's Web* (longer, longest) than *Stuart Little*?
120. I think it is a (better, best) story than *Stuart Little*.
121. Peg thinks that nonfiction books are the (more, most) useful kind of all.
122. Sometimes they are also the (harder, hardest) to read.

Enrichment

Using Adjectives

Self-Portrait

Draw a picture of yourself on a large sheet of paper. Leave enough room to make a one-inch frame around your picture. Look in newspapers or old magazines to find adjectives that describe the way you look and act. Cut out these adjectives and paste them inside the frame.

Pretend that you have invented a new game. It is now time to introduce your game to the public by advertising it in a popular gift catalogue. First, think of a new game. Then write a short ad that will make people want to buy it. Tell why your game is new and different. Use adjectives in your ad and underline each one. Illustrate your advertisement.

Super Sandwich

To make a super sandwich, you add layers of foods. To describe a noun, you can add adjectives. Try an adjective sandwich. Draw two slices of bread on your paper, one at the top and one at the bottom. Choose a noun and write it on each slice of bread. Then draw layers of sandwich foods on colored paper. On each layer, write an adjective to describe the noun. Cut them out and paste them into your super sandwich.

table
old
favorite
sturdy   antique
brown
wooden
table

Measure Up

Measure two objects. Write two or more sentences that compare the two objects. Then measure a third object. Write a sentence to compare this object to the others.

> My shoe is eight inches or twenty centimeters long. The full length of my watch is seven and one-half inches or eighteen centimeters. My watch is shorter than my shoe. The hour hand on my watch is the smallest object of the three.

▨ Angry Alligator

Players—3 or more. **How to play**—The first player makes up a sentence with a noun and an adjective, each beginning with the same letter, such as *a*. The next player adds *-er* or *more* to the original adjective. The third player adds *-est* or *most* to the adjective.

I saw an <u>angry alligator</u>.
I saw an <u>angrier alligator</u>.
I saw the <u>angriest alligator</u>.

The next player picks a new letter and repeats the process. A player does not score if a letter is repeated, if a sentence is incorrect, or if he or she cannot think of a new noun and adjective. **Scoring**—10 points for each new noun and adjective; 5 points for each correct sentence. The first player to reach 50 points wins.

223

Extra Practice: Unit 7

1 | What Is an Adjective? (p. 204)

● Write the adjective that describes each underlined noun.
  Example: Carlo has a new <u>puppy</u>.   *new*
   1. Carlo takes good <u>care</u> of the puppy.
   2. He gives it food in a clean <u>dish</u>.
   3. The puppy always has fresh <u>water</u>.
   4. Carlo gives the puppy four <u>meals</u> a day.
   5. He is teaching the puppy to obey simple <u>commands</u>.
   6. Carlo will have an obedient <u>companion</u>.

▲ Write each sentence. Underline each adjective. Then draw an arrow to the noun it describes.
  Example: In cold places, many people travel by sled.

  In <u>cold</u> places, <u>many</u> people travel by sled.

   7. Huskies are strong, sturdy dogs.
   8. A husky has two coats of thick fur.
   9. Large, hairy feet keep it from sinking in soft snow.
  10. There may be eight huskies in a team.
  11. They pull a long, low sled.
  12. The team may travel forty miles in one day.

■ Write each sentence. Use one or two adjectives to replace each blank. Draw one line under adjectives that tell *what kind* and two lines under adjectives that tell *how many*.
  Example: There were _____ dogs in the dog show.
    There were <u>fifty</u> <u>excited</u> dogs in the dog show.

  13. Jamie's _____ beagle Harry won a prize.
  14. He was the most _____ dog in the show.
  15. Molly's poodle Fifi won _____ ribbons.
  16. She did _____ tricks.
  17. _____ dogs pulled a _____ wagon.
  18. We all laughed at the _____ sight.

2 | Adjectives After *be* (p. 206)

● Write the adjective that describes the underlined word in each
sentence.

Example: The <u>streets</u> are crowded. *crowded*

1. The <u>sun</u> is bright.
2. The <u>music</u> is loud.
3. The <u>people</u> are happy.
4. <u>Parades</u> are exciting.

5. The <u>food</u> was delicious.
6. The <u>speeches</u> were grand.
7. <u>We</u> were delighted.
8. The <u>children</u> are sleepy.

▲ Write each sentence. Underline the adjective. Then draw an
arrow to the word that it describes.

Example: Dad is thrilled by the show.

Dad is <u>thrilled</u> by the show.

9. Before the show, the performers were nervous.
10. Under the lights, the costumes were beautiful.
11. Up on the stage, the tricks were dazzling.
12. I was amazed at one of the tricks.
13. It was unbelievable.
14. The children are speechless.
15. The jugglers are grateful for the applause.
16. I am sorry that the show has ended.

■ Write these sentences, supplying an adjective for each blank.
Then write the word that the adjective describes.

Example: The dancers were ——.
           The dancers were graceful.   dancers

17. The music was ——.
18. The dancer wearing the red costume is ——.
19. The stage decorations are ——.
20. This morning's puppet show was ——.
21. The little puppet was ——.
22. His tricks were ——.
23. After the performance, I was ——.
24. The whole street fair was ——.

3 | Using *a*, *an*, and *the* (p. 207)

● Write each word. Before it, write *a* or *an*.

Example: _____ orange   *an orange*

1. _____ bulb
2. _____ onion
3. _____ root
4. _____ stem
5. _____ edge
6. _____ carrot

7. _____ eggplant
8. _____ vegetable
9. _____ tomato
10. _____ apple
11. _____ inchworm
12. _____ orange

▲ Write each sentence, using the correct article.

Example: Mushrooms grow in (an, the) woods.
    Mushrooms grow in the woods.

13. (A, An) mushroom is (a, an) kind of plant.
14. It looks like (a, an) umbrella.
15. It does not grow from (a, an) seed.
16. (A, The) plants grow from tiny cells called *spores*.
17. Spores may be brushed off by (a, an) animal.
18. They may be blown by (an, the) wind.
19. (A, The) spores land on (an, the) warm, damp earth.
20. This is (an, the) right kind of place for (a, an) mushroom to grow well.

■ The following sentences have no articles. Rewrite the sentences, supplying the correct articles where they belong.

Example: Pitcher plant can eat insect.
    A pitcher plant can eat an insect.

21. Leaves of pitcher plant are tube-shaped.
22. Rainwater collects in plant's leaves.
23. Thick hairs grow at mouth of leaf.
24. Hairs point downward.
25. Sweet smell attracts insect.
26. Hairs keep insect from escaping.
27. Insect drowns in rainwater.
28. Then plant waits for new victim.

4 | Making Comparisons (p. 208)

● For each adjective, write the form for comparing *two* and the form for comparing *three or more*.
Example: pretty *prettier* *prettiest*

1. late	**5.** dark	**9.** wet
2. thick	**6.** hot	**10.** windy
3. safe	**7.** fine	**11.** sad
4. lucky	**8.** shiny	**12.** friendly

▲ Use the correct form of the adjective in ( ) to complete each sentence. Write the sentences.
Example: The ____ bears of all live in Alaska.   (big)
           The biggest bears of all live in Alaska.

13. Polar bears live in the ____ part of the state.   (cold)
14. Brown bears live in ____ places than the places where polar bears live.   (warm)
15. The ____ bears of all can weigh 1700 pounds.   (heavy)
16. Bears are ____ in the fall than in the summer.   (fat)
17. They eat ____ amounts of food in the fall than in the summer. (large)
18. Bears' food is the ____ of all in the winter.   (scarce)
19. Bears are the world's ____ sleepers.   (great)
20. They sleep all winter, and they are ____ in the spring.   (thin)

■ Write each incorrect sentence correctly. If a sentence is already correct, write *correct*.
Example: Bald eagles are America's mightier birds of all.
          Bald eagles are America's mightiest birds of all.

21. A bald eagle is no baldest than any other bird.
22. In earlier times than this, *bald* meant "white."
23. The eagle's body may be longest than three feet.
24. Its wingspan is greatest than six feet.
25. Eagles make their nests biggest each year than they were the year before.
26. One of the largest nests ever found weighed two tons.

5 | Comparing with *more* and *most* (p. 210)

● Choose the correct word to complete each sentence. Write the sentences.

Example: What is the (more, most) popular zoo animal?
What is the most popular zoo animal?

1. The monkeys are the (more, most) amusing of all.
2. A big cat is (more, most) exciting than a monkey.
3. Leopards are the (more, most) graceful of all big cats.
4. They are also the (more, most) skillful climbers of all.
5. A leopard may be (more, most) dangerous than a lion.

▲ Use *more* or *most* to complete each sentence. Write the sentences.

Example: The lion is ____ social than any other cat.
The lion is more social than any other cat.

6. It is ____ likely than another cat to live in a group.
7. Lions are the ____ courageous of all animals.
8. Many people think that lions are the ____ frightening of all animals.
9. The ____ beautiful part of a lion is its mane.
10. It makes the male lion ____ attractive than the female.
11. The female, however, is a ____ skillful hunter than the male.

■ Use the correct form of the adjective to complete each sentence. Write the sentences.

Example: The ____ of all cats is the tiger.   (magnificent)
The most magnificent of all cats is the tiger.

12. A tiger's roar is the ____ of all sounds.   (terrifying)
13. Tigers are ____ hunters than lions.   (fierce)
14. Tigers are ____ in the water than any of the other cats. (comfortable)
15. Tigers hunt some of the ____ animals in the jungle.   (big)
16. A tiger may even hunt an animal that is ____ than the tiger itself.   (enormous)

6 | Comparing with *good* and *bad* (p. 212)

● Write the adjective that correctly completes each sentence.

   Example: I think mystery books are (good, better) than any other
             kind.   *better*

   1. The (better, best) part of all is solving the mystery.
   2. Michael's father won a special award for the (better, best) local
       writer.
   3. I liked his last book (better, best) than his first.
   4. The first one was not the (bad, worst) book I have read.
   5. I have read a (worse, worst) book than that.

▲ Use the correct form of the adjective in ( ) to complete each
   sentence. Write the sentences.

   Example: We were the ____ readers in the school.   (bad)
             We were the worst readers in the school.

   6. We wanted to become ____ readers than we were.   (good)
   7. Ms. Lee gave us the ____ books in the whole library to read.
       (good)
   8. Some of the books were ____ than we had expected.   (bad)
   9. Others were much ____.   (good)
   10. After a month, we each reported on the ____ book we had
       read.   (good)
   11. The ____ part of all was choosing a favorite book.   (bad)

■ Rewrite each sentence, using comparisons correctly.

   Example: We wanted to be good writers than we were.
             We wanted to be better writers than we were.

   12. Mr. Diaz said that writing a newspaper would be the better
       practice of all.
   13. Our first paper had the worse mistakes of all.
   14. The second paper was much good than the first.
   15. My first story was not the better work I have done.
   16. In fact, it was the bad thing I have ever written.
   17. Janie said that her first story was even worst.
   18. I thought that it was the good story in the whole paper.

Literature and Writing

A lthough he never stirs from home
the tortoise, like a load of furniture,
jolts down the path.

Aunque jamás se muda,
A tumbos, como carro de mudanza,
Va por la senda la tortuga.

José Juan Tablada
"The Tortoise" (La Tortuga)

Description

Getting Ready A painting or a photograph can show how something looks but not how it sounds or tastes. A record can let you know how something sounds but not how it feels or smells. Words, however, can create pictures that help us imagine how something looks, sounds, feels, smells, *and* tastes. In this unit, you will read a word picture, or description, and write one of your own.

ACTIVITIES

Listening   Listen as the poem on the opposite page is read. What is the tortoise compared to? How does this help you "see" the tortoise? What verb describes how it moves? Would *crawls* or *sways* have made you see the tortoise differently?

Speaking   Look at the picture. With your class, think of sentences to describe the tortoise to someone who had never seen one.

Writing   Imagine that you are describing something else to someone who has never seen it before. Write a word picture in your journal.

Like all things, the beavers' pond changed with the passing years. What did this change mean for the beavers?

The Beaver Pond

By Alvin Tresselt

The beavers had made the pond in the first place. Here in a hidden valley, where a small stream wandered through a grove of aspen trees, the beavers built a dam.

With their sharp teeth they cut down young aspen trees to eat the bark. Then they dragged the trunks and branches to the brook for the dam. They criss-crossed the sticks just so, and plastered them over with mud and stones to hold back the rushing water of the stream.

Larger and larger the pond grew, and in the middle of the still water the beavers built their domed houses, with tunnels under the water, so no enemies could get in. In time green reeds sprang up along the shore. They waved their pointy fingers in the breeze, and redwinged blackbirds came to hide their nests in the rustly grasses.

Ducks came, too, for the beaver pond was a good place for ducklings to swim and dive. Fish swam down the stream into

232

the pond, and a blue kingfisher perched on a limb to watch for fish for his dinner. Lacy-winged dragonflies hovered and darted over the water.

It didn't matter to the beavers who used their pond. There was room for everyone, and the beavers were too busy fixing the dam and repairing their houses and raising their babies to notice their neighbors. The paddling ducks, the sunning turtles, and the slippery green frogs sitting on lily pads meant nothing to them. But while they worked, one old beaver kept careful watch for the wolf. He worried about the soft-footed lynx, and his nose warned him of the stealthy wolverine.

With a *thwack* his tail slapped the water, and the beavers dove for the shelter of their houses. Then one by one their heads popped up. Chirping and whistling they discussed the danger that was past, and back to work they went. And the beaver babies swam and splashed in the limpid green light of their underwater world.

When the late summer days felt the first nip of frost, the beavers were busier than ever cutting down more and more of the young aspens. They dragged the branches into the water and buried them in the mud at the bottom of the pond. The tender bark would be their food through the bitter days of winter.

Now was the time for the ducks and blackbirds to fly off to the southland. The sumacs flamed scarlet, the aspens turned to gold. And the frosted reeds rattled dryly in the cold wind.

The frost bit deeper and deeper into the ground as a sheet of ice spread over the top of the pond. The frozen earth slept under the snow. The pond slept under the ice, and the beavers were safe from the wolf, the prowling lynx, and the wolverine, under the icy roof of the pond and the frozen domes of their houses.

Each spring the pond came back to life. The melting winter snows and ice brought high water, and the beavers worked

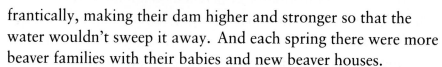

frantically, making their dam higher and stronger so that the water wouldn't sweep it away. And each spring there were more beaver families with their babies and new beaver houses.

But slowly, slowly, year by year, things changed at the pond. The ever-running stream brought more than fish and water. It carried with it fine dirt, which settled on the bottom. And little rivulets of muddy water drained into the pond every time it rained. As the years passed the pond grew smaller and more shallow. At last the pond grew too small for all the beavers. Farther and farther they had to roam from the safety of the water in search of trees to cut down for their food.

And the wolf, the lynx, and the wolverine grew bolder as they crouched and waited for their prey. So it was that in the early summer off went the beavers down the stream to find a new place for their home. They left behind their long dam of sticks and mud and their empty beaver houses sitting in the water. No longer did their chirps and whistles sound across the pond. No longer did the sharp slap of their tails warn of danger. And no longer were there bustling beavers to repair the dam when the high spring water flooded into the pond.

One early spring day, when all the snow had melted suddenly, a great flood of water came roaring down the stream into the pond. Over the old dam it poured, and the rotted sticks and branches could not hold the weight. The torrent of water raced on down the brook, and what was left of the pond went flowing out through the break in the dam.

Once more the stream ran free. Bit by bit the muddy floor of the old pond turned green. Young plants sprang up in the rich earth, and where once a pond had caught and held the blue sky there spread a green and grassy meadow with a brook meandering through it.

But farther down, the beavers had already built a new strong dam, and the new pond sparkled in the sunlight. Frogs and fishes, turtles and hovering dragonflies enjoyed its waters. Redwinged blackbirds nested in its rushes, as ducks paraded their new babies proudly. And in the cool evening light the mother deer brought their young ones to the edge of the pond to drink.

Think and Discuss

1. How did the pond change over the years? What did these changes cause the beavers to do?

2. The author uses words to create **images**, or pictures, in your mind. Images help you to picture how something looks, sounds, smells, tastes, or feels. For example, *frosted reeds rattled dryly* helps you to *hear* the sound of the reeds. *Sumacs flamed scarlet* helps you to *see* the bright red trees. What other images can you find in "The Beaver Pond"? To which sense does each one appeal?

3. What do you think will happen to the new pond? Why?

4. If you were to paint a picture of the beaver pond, which details would you choose to show? Why?

Sudden Storm

By Elizabeth Coatsworth

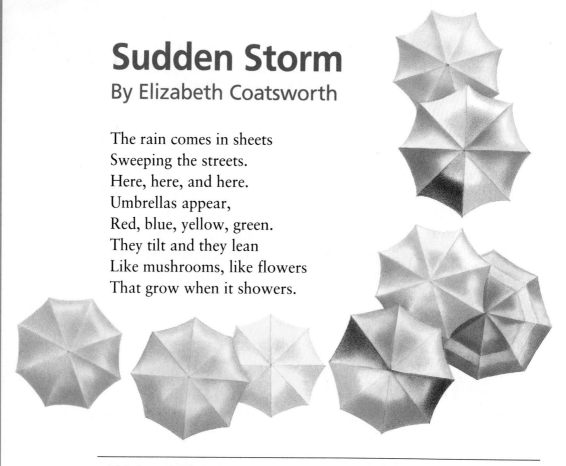

The rain comes in sheets
Sweeping the streets.
Here, here, and here.
Umbrellas appear,
Red, blue, yellow, green.
They tilt and they lean
Like mushrooms, like flowers
That grow when it showers.

Think and Discuss

1. What are red, blue, yellow, and green?

2. A **simile** compares two or more different things that are alike in some ways. The words *like* and *as* help you to recognize similes. Elizabeth Coatsworth uses this simile in "Sudden Storm" to compare umbrellas with mushrooms and flowers.

   > They tilt and they lean
   > Like mushrooms, like flowers
   > That grow when it showers.

   How are umbrellas like mushrooms? like flowers?

3. How does the poet feel about rainy days? How do you feel about rainy days? Explain.

RESPONDING TO LITERATURE

The Reading and Writing Connection

Personal Response As time passed, the beaver pond changed. Think about a place you know that has changed. Write a paragraph contrasting the way the place is now with the way it once was.

Creative Writing Imagine you are a mother or father beaver. You want to teach your youngsters how to build a dam. Write dialogue between you and your children. Reread the second paragraph of the story for help.

Creative Activities

Make a Poster "The Beaver Pond" describes many animals that lived near the pond. Choose one of these animals. Do some research to find out interesting facts about your animal. Make a poster to share with your class.

Give a News Report Pretend you are a TV or radio news reporter. You are at the scene of the flood breaking through the beavers' old dam. Give an eyewitness report to your listeners. Use details to make your story come alive.

Vocabulary

The word *thwack* sounds just like what it describes in "The Beaver Pond"—a tail slapping the water. Some other sound words are *hiss*, *buzz*, and *peep*. List as many others as you can. Write the name of something that makes each sound.

Looking Ahead

Descriptions In this unit, you will write a description. Reread the third and fourth paragraphs of "The Beaver Pond." What details help you picture the pond in your mind?

VOCABULARY CONNECTION
Words from Other Languages

Many words in the English language have come from other languages.

> The **sumacs flamed scarlet,** the aspens turned to gold.
> *from "The Beaver Pond" by Alvin Tresselt*

The word *sumacs* can be traced back to the Arabic language. *Flamed* was borrowed from French. *Scarlet* can be traced back to a Persian word that means "a kind of rich cloth." Here are more words borrowed from other languages.

zero (Italian)	menu (French)	shish kebab (Turkish)
boss (Dutch)	piano (Italian)	plaza (Spanish)
atlas (Greek)	ski (Norwegian)	yogurt (Turkish)

Dictionaries often give information about the history of a word's origins.

Vocabulary Practice

A. For each of these words from "The Beaver Pond," write the language from which the word was borrowed. Use a dictionary to help you.

1. rattle **2.** prey **3.** plaster **4.** crouch **5.** dirt

B. The word *lynx* comes from Greek. Many animal names are borrowed from different languages. Use an encyclopedia to help you find the names of four wild animals. Then use a dictionary to write the language from which each animal name comes. Compare information with a classmate.

Prewriting
Description

Speaking: Giving a Description

Think of a place where you have enjoyed spending the day. It might have been by a pond or lake, in the woods, or at the beach. You probably think first about how it looks. Think some more. How does it smell? sound? feel? Describe it clearly to a friend. Use details that appeal to the senses.

Read these two descriptions.

> **1.** Green reeds grew along the shore. They moved in the breeze, and birds built their nests in the grass.
>
> **2.** In time green reeds sprang up along the shore. They waved their pointy fingers in the breeze, and redwinged blackbirds came to hide their nests in the rustly grasses.
> *from "The Beaver Pond" by Alvin Tresselt*

- Which description gives you a clearer picture?
- What details helped you imagine the shore of the pond?

Guides for Giving a Description

1. Use details that appeal to the five senses. Describe things you see, hear, touch, taste, and smell.
2. Choose words that help create a clear picture.

Prewriting Practice

Choose something, such as a pet or your room, to describe. Using the speaking guides, describe the object to a partner. When you are finished, ask your partner to draw what you described. Does the picture look like the object you described? What details would make your description clearer?

Thinking: Observing

When you **observe,** you look at a person, place, or thing carefully. To describe things well, you must become a good observer. You must pay attention and use all of your senses to notice things.

Here are some ways to help you concentrate on details.

Make a drawing. Study an object you know well. Draw what you observe. Keep studying the object. Try to notice details you have not seen before. Make your drawing as detailed as possible.

Use a paper camera. Cut a one-inch hole in a piece of paper. Keeping one eye closed, look through the hole. Focus on one part of a scene. As you look, notice the different details. Then change your focus to another part of the scene and observe it.

Open your other senses. Close your eyes. What sounds do you hear around you? Are they near or far? Feel an object in front of you. Is it rough? smooth? soft? hard? Alert all of your senses.

Listen as your teacher reads the paragraph below. Think about the things the author observed in the scene.

> With a *thwack* his tail slapped the water, and the beavers dove for the shelter of their houses. Then one by one their heads popped up. Chirping and whistling they discussed the danger that was past, and back to work they went. And the beaver babies swam and splashed in the limpid green light of their underwater world.
>
> from *"The Beaver Pond"* by Alvin Tresselt

- How do you think the author got this information? Why do you think so?
- What senses did he use to create his description of the beavers' actions?
- What details help to make the scene real to the reader?

These guides will help you to become a good observer.

Guides for Observing

1. Know your reason for observing.
2. Decide what you want to observe.
3. Make a drawing or a paper camera to help you see details.
4. Open your other senses one at a time. How do things sound? feel? smell? taste?
5. Take notes to help you remember what you observe.

Prewriting Practice

With a partner, observe one of the scenes below. Use all of your senses and take notes on everything you observe. Compare your notes with those of your partner.

1. students in the library
2. the scene outside your classroom window
3. the school lunchroom

Composition Skills
Description

Using Sense Words ☑

Have you ever tried to describe the smell of a wet dog, the colors in a rainbow, the sound of drums, the taste of a sour pickle, or the feel of an ice cube? You will find it easier to describe how something smells, looks, sounds, tastes, and feels if you tune in your five senses. Your senses can help you find just the right words.

Read the following descriptions. Notice the underlined sense words.

> <u>Chirping</u> and <u>whistling</u> they discussed the danger that was past.
>
> In time <u>green</u> reeds sprang up along the shore. They waved their <u>pointy</u> fingers in the breeze.
>
> *from "The Beaver Pond" by Alvin Tresselt*

- Which words help you *hear* the sounds the beavers made?
- Which words help you *see* the reeds?

Here are some other sense words you can use.

Sight	Sound	Smell	Touch	Taste
blue	crack	sweet	soft	salty
foggy	hum	smoky	bumpy	minty
dark	splash	musty	furry	tangy
round	slither	stale	slick	bitter

Prewriting Practice

Write as many sense words as you can to describe each object.

1. a frog's skin
2. a rainbow
3. peanut butter
4. a lemon
5. a whistle
6. a long-stemmed rose

Writing Topic Sentences and Choosing Details ☑

The following paragraph describes spring at the pond. What is the main idea of the paragraph?

> Each spring the pond came back to life. The melting winter snows and ice brought high water, and the beavers worked frantically, making their dam higher and stronger so that the water wouldn't sweep it away. And each spring there were more beaver families with their babies and new beaver houses.
>
> *from "The Beaver Pond" by Alvin Tresselt*

The main idea is that the pond came back to life each spring. The first sentence tells the main idea. It is the topic sentence.

The author chose certain details to show how the pond came to life. Some of the details were *the beavers worked frantically* and *there were more beaver families with their babies and new beaver houses.*

Suppose that the author had had a different purpose for describing the pond in the spring. Then he would have chosen different details.

Read this paragraph. What is the main idea?

> The pond is peaceful in the spring. Fish drift lazily through the still water, and only the soothing hum of the insects breaks the silence. Slender green reeds sway rhythmically to and fro in the gentle breeze. A fat old bullfrog dozes on a lily pad, dreaming of summer.

- What is the main idea of this paragraph?
- What was the author's purpose?
- What details did the author use to support this purpose?

Prewriting Practice

A. Choose a topic from the list, or think of one yourself. Write two topic sentences about the topic. Each topic sentence should have a different purpose.

a walk in the woods   a supermarket
a birthday party   a busy street
a pet bird   the playground

B. Write three or more sentences giving supporting details for each topic sentence you wrote. List them under the topic sentences. Be sure the details fit your purpose.

Using Exact Words ☑

Read these pairs of sentences. Which sentence in each pair gives you a clearer picture?

> The <u>trees</u> turned a <u>pretty color</u>.
> The <u>aspens</u> turned to <u>gold</u>.

> The reeds <u>made noises</u> in the cold wind.
> The <u>frosted</u> reeds <u>rattled dryly</u> in the cold wind.

> The <u>ground froze</u>, and <u>some ice was on</u> the pond.
> The <u>frost bit deeper and deeper into the ground</u> as a <u>sheet of ice spread over the top</u> of the pond.

The first sentence in each pair does not give you a clear picture. These sentences do not tell you what kind of trees, what color, or how much ice. They do not help you feel the cold or hear the reeds.

The second sentence in each pair is from "The Beaver Pond" by Alvin Tresselt. These sentences use exact words such as *aspens, gold, frosted, sheet,* and *spread over the top* to help you see the trees, the reeds, and the ice on the pond. What exact words help you hear the reeds? feel the frost?

Use exact words in your own writing.

Prewriting Practice

Rewrite each sentence below. Change the underlined words to more exact ones.

Example: The woman wore a <u>colorful</u> hat.
The woman wore a purple and green hat.

1. The <u>flowers</u> smell <u>good</u>.
2. Some <u>plants</u> are growing <u>here</u>.
3. A big <u>animal</u> made a <u>noise</u>.
4. The <u>building</u> is in the <u>city</u>.
5. The <u>room</u> was quiet.
6. Some <u>children</u> were <u>playing</u>.
7. I ate a good-tasting <u>meal</u>.
8. The <u>loud</u> <u>plane</u> flew <u>by</u>.

The Grammar Connection

Varying Meaning with Adjectives

You can use different adjectives to create different pictures. Read these two sentences about the beaver pond.

The beaver pond was large and bustling.
The beaver pond was murky and deserted.

How do the different adjectives change the meaning of each sentence?

Practice Write each sentence twice, using different adjectives each time.

1. It was a _____ day in the _____ city.
2. _____ shoppers carried _____ bags.
3. A _____ girl pedaled by on a _____ bicycle.
4. A _____ man walked a _____ dog on a leash.
5. In the window of a _____ shop, many _____ things were displayed for sale.
6. The _____ shopkeeper peered at the customers through _____ glasses.

The Writing Process
How to Write a Description

Step 1: Prewriting—Choose a Topic

Rosa listed things that she would like to describe. Then she thought about each topic on her list.

my favorite poster — She couldn't describe it using all of her senses.

our old house — She had trouble remembering it clearly.

my back yard — There were a lot of ways to describe her back yard.

my soccer shoes — Her shoes didn't seem very interesting to write about.

Rosa thought about her back yard. What one thing could she write about? She thought of a great way to describe the maple tree! She circled *my back yard*.

On Your Own

1. **Think and discuss** List things you can describe. Use the Ideas page. Discuss your list with a partner.
2. **Choose** Ask yourself these questions about each topic.
   Is this topic about one thing?
   Can I describe it using several senses?
   Which topic would be the most fun to write about?
   Circle the topic you want to write about.
3. **Explore** How will you describe your topic? Do an "Exploring Your Topic" activity on the Ideas page.

Ideas for Getting Started

Choosing Your Topic

Topic Ideas

A lake or pond
An animal
A thunderstorm
My grandfather
My hiking boots
A flower garden
My favorite dinner
An old teddy bear

Picture It

Look at these pictures.
Do they give you any ideas?

Exploring Your Topic

Make a Chart

Divide a paper into five parts. Label them *Sight*, *Sound*, *Smell*, *Taste*, and *Touch*. Write your topic at the top. Then write words that describe it. Here is how Rosa started her chart.

Maple Tree

Sight	pretty leaves falling seeds
Sound	moving branches

Role Play

Pretend that you are your topic. How do you look, sound, feel, taste, and smell? Describe yourself to a partner. Use as many different senses as you can. Have your partner guess who or what you are.

Step 2: Write a First Draft

Rosa decided to write her description for Mr. Wells who lived next door. He liked the maple tree too.

Rosa thought of a good way to start. She looked back at her chart of sense words and began writing her first draft. She did not worry about making mistakes. She just wanted to get her ideas on paper.

Rosa's first draft

Think and Discuss ✓

- How could Rosa improve her topic sentence?
- Which senses did Rosa use?
- Where could she use more details?
- Which words are not exact?

> Hi! I'm Bucky Squirrel, and I live in this tree. ~~Sometimes~~ In the spring, the seeds fall to the ground. In the fall, the leaves are pretty when winter comes, I here the branchs moving in the wind.

On Your Own

1. **Think about purpose and audience** Ask yourself:
   Who will be my audience?
   What is my purpose? What kind of picture do I want my readers to imagine? What details will I choose to fit my purpose?
2. **Write** Write your first draft. Write a good topic sentence to get your readers interested. Use sense words and details. Write on every other line. Do not worry about making mistakes. Just get your ideas on paper.

Step 3: Revise

Rosa read her first draft. She made her topic sentence better. She also added a sentence to end her paragraph.

Rosa wanted to know if she needed more details in her description. She asked Jeff to listen to her paragraph.

Reading and responding

JEFF: Having a squirrel give the description was a good idea!

ROSA: Do I need more details?

JEFF: Can you tell more about the seeds?

ROSA: Anything else?

JEFF: You say the leaves are pretty, but I can't really picture them. What colors are they?

ROSA: I'll add some details. Thanks, Jeff.

Rosa pictured the maple tree in her mind. She added details and changed one word to be more exact.

Rosa's revised draft

Hi! I'm Bucky Squirrel, and I (want to show you the best maple tree on the block.) ~~live in this tree. Sometimes~~ Its rough bark tickles my paws. In the spring, the seeds fall to the ground. (look like helicopters when they) In the fall, the leaves ~~are pretty~~ (turn red and orange) When winter comes, I here the branchs, ~~moving~~ (creaking) in the wind. My tree is the perfect home for a squirrel!

> **Think and Discuss** ✓
>
> - Why is Rosa's new topic sentence better?
> - What details did she add?
> - Which detail tells how the tree feels?
> - Which word did she make more exact?

On Your Own

Revising checklist

- ☑ Have I used sense words to make my description real?
- ☑ Did I write a good topic sentence?
- ☑ Do my details support my topic sentence and make my description clear?
- ☑ Where can I use more exact words?

1. **Revise** Make changes in your first draft. Try writing a new topic sentence. Cross out weak words and write exact words above them. You might want to use some of the words from the thesaurus below or the one found at the back of this book.

2. **Have a conference** Read your description to a classmate or to your teacher.

WRITING
CONFERENCE

Ask your listener:	As you listen:
"Can you clearly picture what I am describing?" "Where do I need more details?" "Do I need more exact words?"	I must listen carefully. Can I picture this clearly? Did the writer use several senses? Does this description need more details?

3. **Revise** Think about your partner's suggestions. Can you think of any other ways to revise your writing? Make the changes on your paper.

Thesaurus

cold icy, frigid
pretty attractive, lovely, good-looking
rough bumpy, coarse, uneven

smell fragrance, aroma
smooth polished, sleek
tall high, lofty
thin skinny, lean, slim, slender

Step 4: Proofread

Rosa proofread her description. She used the dictionary to check her spelling and used proofreading marks to make changes. Here is part of Rosa's proofread draft.

Part of Rosa's proofread draft

> In the fall, the leaves ~~are pretty~~ ^{turn red and orange}
>
> when winter comes, I ~~here~~ ^{hear} the
>
> ~~branchs~~ ^{branches} moving in the wind. My tree ^{creaking}

Think and Discuss

- Which words were spelled incorrectly?
- Why did Rosa make other corrections?

On Your Own

1. **Proofreading Practice** Proofread this paragraph. There is one incorrect verb and one incorrect adjective. There are also three spelling errors and one missing punctuation mark. Write the paragraph correctly.

       The drops splash on my jaket and
   dribbles down my neck. They feel like
   melting ice cubes I stick out my tongue
   to catch a drop. It tastes cool and
   clean. Now the rain comes down in hard
   streacks. I hurrey home. This is the
   baddest storm of the year.

Proofreading Marks

- ¶ Indent
- ∧ Add something
- ℓ Take out something
- ≡ Capitalize
- / Make a small letter

2. **Proofreading Application** Now proofread your paper. Use the Proofreading Checklist and the Grammar and Spelling Hints on the next page. Use a dictionary to check spelling.

Proofreading Checklist

Did I

☑ **1.** indent my paragraph?

☑ **2.** use capital letters correctly?

☑ **3.** use correct punctuation marks?

☑ **4.** use correct adjectives when comparing?

☑ **5.** spell all words correctly?

The Grammar/Spelling Connection

Grammar Hints

Remember these rules from Unit 7 when using adjectives.

- Add *-er* when comparing two things and *-est* for three or more things. *(quick, quicker, quickest)*
- Use *more* and *most* when comparing long adjectives. *(cheerful, more cheerful, most cheerful)*
- The words *good* and *bad* have special forms for comparing. *(good, better, best; bad, worse, worst)*

Spelling Hints

Remember these rules when spelling two-syllable words.

- The final (ē) sound in a two-syllable word is often spelled *y* or *ey*. *(hungry, valley)*
- The (k) sound in a two-syllable word is often spelled *k*, *ck*, or *c*. *(mistake, locket, music)*

Step 5: Publish

Rosa was excited about sharing her description with Mr. Wells. She copied it in her neatest handwriting and added the title "My Marvelous Maple." Then she drew a large picture of Bucky Squirrel. She showed him holding her paper. She added a picture of the tree and a leaf rubbing.

On Your Own

1. **Copy** Copy your description in your neatest handwriting.
2. **Check** Read your description carefully to make sure you have not made any mistakes in copying.
3. **Add a title** Write a title for your description.
4. **Share** Think of a special way to share your description.

Ideas for Sharing

- Make a tape recording of your description. Add sound effects.
- Make a picture frame from construction paper. Decorate it. Put your description inside.
- Put photographs of your topic on a large piece of paper with your description.

Applying Description

Literature and Creative Writing

"The Beaver Pond" and "Sudden Storm" both describe changes in nature. "The Beaver Pond" describes how beavers changed a stream to a pond and how the pond finally became a stream again. "Sudden Storm" describes a heavy rainstorm, which made colorful umbrellas sprout like flowers.

Have fun using what you have learned about writing a description. Choose one or more of these activities.

Remember these things ☑
Use sense words.
Write a good topic sentence.
Choose details that fit your purpose.
Use exact words.

1. **Describe the inside story.** Imagine that you are small enough to fit inside the beavers' domed house in the middle of the pond. What do you see? hear? feel? smell? Write a paragraph describing the beavers' home from the inside.

2. **Paint a picture with a poem.** Write a poem describing your favorite outdoor spot. Use at least one simile in your poem.

3. **What's the weather?** In "Sudden Storm," the poet described one kind of weather. Look out your window. What is the weather like today? What can you see, hear, feel, and smell? Write a paragraph describing today's weather.

Writing Across the Curriculum
Art

Artists create pictures in many ways. When you enjoy a piece of art, you may want to share your feelings about it. You can do this by creating another kind of picture—a clear, exact description.

Choose one or more of the following activities.

1. **Make a movie.** What would one of your favorite stories be like as a movie? You be the director. Choose a scene from the story. Write a description of how you would film it. How would the characters and setting look? What action would take place? What voices, music, and other sounds would be heard?

Writing Steps

1. Choose a Topic
2. Write a First Draft
3. Revise
4. Proofread
5. Publish

---

2. **Slip into a scene.** The photographer who took this picture wanted you to feel as if you were there. Pretend that you are there. Write a description of the scene, using all your senses. You may wish to use words from the Word Bank.

Word Bank

velvety
silver
thunderous
blossoms
springlike
shimmering

3. **Picture a project.** Imagine that your town is having an art show. You can enter any kind of art project. Before you enter, you must describe your project to the judges. Write a description that gives them a clear and exact picture.

Ket liked "The Beaver Pond" so much that he read another book about animals. The book was *Turtle Pond* by Berniece Freschet. Ket decided to share the book with his class by making a book jacket. On the cover, he drew a picture of a turtle. On the flaps, he wrote about the book. Here is how Ket made his book jacket.

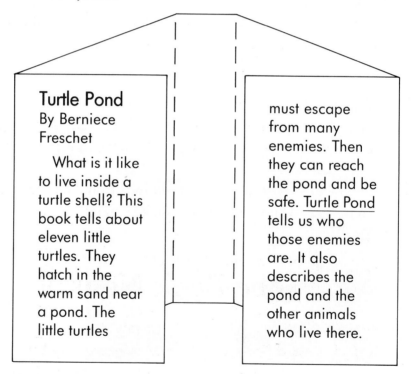

Turtle Pond
By Berniece Freschet

What is it like to live inside a turtle shell? This book tells about eleven little turtles. They hatch in the warm sand near a pond. The little turtles

must escape from many enemies. Then they can reach the pond and be safe. Turtle Pond tells us who those enemies are. It also describes the pond and the other animals who live there.

Think and Discuss

• What did you learn about the book from Ket's book jacket?
• Why is this a good way to share a book?

Share Your Book

Make a Book Jacket

1. First, get a large sheet of drawing paper. From each end, fold a flap in toward the middle. Each flap should be about four inches wide. Paste a piece of lined paper on each flap.
2. Draw a picture on the cover of the book jacket. Draw the picture with crayons and markers. Add the title and the author's name.
3. On the left flap, write the title and the author's name again. Below this, tell about interesting parts of the book. Write on a separate paper first. Then copy your work onto the flaps. Use both flaps.
4. Share your book jacket by showing the cover. Read aloud the information you have written on the flaps.

Other Activities

- From magazines and newspapers, cut out pictures and words that show what your book is about. Paste them on a large piece of paper to make a collage. Write the title and the author's name.
- Draw pictures of characters and objects from your book on heavy paper. Cut them out and make a mobile.

 # The Book Nook

Book of the Pig *by Jack Denton Scott* Pigs are among the most likable and most intelligent animals. They even have interesting jobs.	**Grizzly Bear** *by Berniece Freschet* Grizzly bear cubs, born in January, come out of their dens in spring. They must learn a lot before winter!

Mechanics

O ne hot dusty day, a fox was trotting through an orchard when he saw a bunch of grapes hanging from a very high vine. "Just the thing for my dry throat," he said. He ran and leaped his highest, but could not reach them. Finally, he trotted off in disgust. "They're probably sour, anyhow!" said he.

Aesop (retold by Marie Gaudette)
"The Fox and the Grapes"

Capitalization and Punctuation

Getting Ready Capital letters and punctuation marks are like traffic signs. We use them in our writing to tell the reader where to begin, when to pause, and where to stop. Lively writing often includes people's exact words. Punctuation marks let you show exactly what is said. Your work in this unit should help keep your writing free of traffic jams!

ACTIVITIES

Listening   Listen as your teacher reads the fable on the opposite page. Who is speaking? What does he say about the grapes? Why does he say it?

Speaking   Look at the picture. Make up a conversation about a plan to pick these grapes. Have someone write your conversation on the board. What punctuation marks do you need to use?

Writing   Do you know what the phrase "sour grapes" means? In your journal, write a conversation about "sour grapes."

1 | Correct Sentences

When you write, you must show where each sentence begins and ends. Use a capital letter to show where each sentence begins, and an end mark to show where it ends.

RUN-ON: Something smells good are you baking bread?
CORRECT: Something smells good. Are you baking bread?

You know that statements and commands end with periods. Questions end with question marks. Exclamations end with exclamation points.

We like turtle soup.   Make some turtle soup, please.
Do you like turtle soup?   What wonderful soup this is!

Guided Practice How would you write these sentences?

Example: we are making dinner would you like to help
          We are making dinner. Would you like to help?

1. how surprised Mom and Dad will be
2. put on this apron where is the large pot
3. pour in some ketchup
4. did you remember to add the peanut butter
5. i'll chop the cabbage what a great stew this will be

Summing up

> ▶ Begin every sentence with a capital letter.
> ▶ Use a period after a statement or a command.
> ▶ Use a question mark after a question.
> ▶ Use an exclamation point after an exclamation.

Independent Practice Write these sentences correctly. Add capital letters and end marks. Write each run-on sentence as two sentences.

Example: have you ever tasted soup made from a bird's nest
Have you ever tasted soup made from a bird's nest?

6. what a strange dish that must be
7. where can I taste some bird's-nest soup
8. try a Chinese restaurant
9. look for it on the menu
10. you might ask the waiter
11. what makes bird's-nest soup so special
12. taste the soup does it have an unusual flavor
13. is it really made from a bird's nest
14. only the nests of certain swiftlets are used
15. these birds are relatives of swallows and swifts
16. their nests are snow-white they make the best soup
17. swiftlets live in tall sea caves in Asia
18. they build their nests hundreds of feet above ground
19. how do people reach the nests do they climb long ladders
20. how thrilling it would be to watch people do this
21. why would people risk their lives to get the nests
22. these people make a lot of money this must be a good business
23. did you know that some nests cost $4000 a pound
24. what expensive soup this must be
25. read this book how do some countries protect the birds
26. collectors can gather nests only twice each year
27. the male birds make the nests the females lay the eggs
28. what amazing birds these small swiftlets are

Writing Application: A Description
You have gone to dinner at the home of your friend Alvin Burns. Alvin has made his famous soup, Saturday Surprise. Write a paragraph describing the soup. Include all four types of sentences. Be sure to use capital letters and end marks correctly.

For Extra Practice, see p. 283.

2 | Capitalizing Names of People and Pets

You know that you always begin a proper noun with a capital letter. Always capitalize the names of people and pets because they are proper nouns.

Sometimes a title comes before a person's name. Often you use an initial to stand for a person's name. When titles and initials are used with names, you should capitalize them.

Samuel Ames	Mrs. Carol M. Ling	Dr. Richard Wang
U. R. Wright	Miss Diane Dooley	Governor J. Bryant
Mr. Todd Rossi	Ms. E. S. Ryan	Fido

Capitalize family titles when they are used as names or as parts of names.

Today Grandmother arrived.

Did Uncle Harry bring worms?

Do not capitalize family titles when the titles are not used as names.

My grandmother took us fishing.

Our uncle paddled the canoe.

Guided Practice Where should you use capital letters?

Example: Every morning mom and aunt agnes read the newspaper.
          Mom   Aunt Agnes

1. Today a photo of mr. derek johnson is on the front page.
2. He and james p. mullen just ran a marathon.
3. There is a story about miss wanda kane on the next page.
4. Did governor garcia give her a special award?
5. My aunt read about an amazing poodle named pinky.
6. The brave dog saved the life of mrs. betty bowman!

▶ Capitalize the names of people and pets.
▶ Capitalize titles and initials that are parts of names.
▶ Capitalize family titles when they are used as names or as parts of names.

Independent Practice Write these sentences correctly.

Add capital letters where they are needed.

Example: Many students work with mr. nye on the newspaper.
Many students work with Mr. Nye on the newspaper.

7. This year leroy, sonia, and I are reporters.
8. I wrote about the math fair that ms. chan organized.
9. My friends anna cohen and john a. dixon won prizes.
10. According to principal schultz, the fair was a success!
11. I wrote my next story about freddie fraser.
12. He and melvin peabody started a pet-sitting service.
13. It all began when they visited dr. p. mortimer sloan.
14. He asked the boys to give his dog, brownie, a bath.
15. Then my brother paid them to walk his lizard, lucille.
16. Now the boys have a job feeding a goat named gulliver.
17. Today cathy murphy is writing about the city elections.
18. She heard mayor gallo talk about building a new library.
19. Then mrs. r. b. rozotta and my mother made speeches.
20. My grandfather and p. j. barnes carried large signs.
21. I told mom about an idea for my next article.
22. I want to interview grandmother winkler.
23. She and grandfather moved to our town many years ago.
24. They started a business with miss matilda moskovitz.
25. I want to find out how dad helped them after school!

Writing Application: A News Story

The headline in today's newspaper says, "Monkey Escapes: City Goes Bananas." Write a news story to go with this headline.
Use the name of a person or an animal in each sentence.

For Extra Practice, see p. 284.

3 | Capitalizing Names of Places and Things

Some proper nouns name particular places or things. Always capitalize the names of particular places and things. Whenever a proper noun is more than one word, remember to begin each important word with a capital letter.

Proper Nouns That Name Places and Things	
Places	**Things**
street – Pebble Creek Road	days – Monday
city – Dallas	Thursday
state – Colorado	months – February
country – Mexico	August
building – Museum of Science	holidays – Flag Day
mountain – Pikes Peak	Fourth of July
park – Acadia National Park	groups – Avon Garden Club
water – Indian Ocean	New York Mets

Guided Practice Which words need capital letters?

Example: My pen pal from japan is coming to visit. *Japan*

1. He plans to arrive in ocean city next tuesday.
2. We'll visit the seaside museum if he isn't too tired.
3. Then we can go to pacific park or rocky road.
4. Afterward we can watch the miami dolphins play football.
5. I'm glad he's staying until columbus day!

Summing up

▶ Capitalize the names of streets, cities, states, countries, buildings, mountains, parks, and bodies of water.
▶ Capitalize the names of days, months, holidays, and groups.

Independent Practice Write these sentences correctly.

Add capital letters where they are needed.

Example: Last saturday Melinda came to our house.
Last Saturday Melinda came to our house.

St. Lawrence River

6. We saw slides she took last june and july.
7. Melinda had traveled in north america.
8. She began her trip near the bay of fundy.
9. She drove north to forillon national park.
10. There were pictures of the st. lawrence river.
11. They showed ships heading for europe.
12. We saw slides of ottawa, the capital of canada.
13. Melinda was there for canada day!

Bay of Fundy

14. She also visited the national museum of man.
15. I recognized the slide of mount royal.
16. My father had taken me to montreal last year.
17. Melinda told us about the skyscrapers on dorchester boulevard.
18. I asked if she had seen the montreal expos play baseball.
19. Next, Melinda showed us photos of lake erie.
20. She also had pictures of farms in indiana and iowa.
21. Her slides of colorado were my favorite.
22. I had never seen anything like the rocky mountains!
23. Finally, we saw the buffalo bill wax museum.
24. It is on west manitou avenue in colorado springs.
25. Melinda's trip ended in august.
26. Then she and her family returned home to merrytown.
27. After labor day, it was time for school to start.
28. Melinda and I go to rocky road school.
29. The school is near green pond.
30. In october our class visited the merrytown museum of art.

Writing Application: An Interview

Interview someone who has taken a trip. Write a paragraph describing the trip. Include the names of particular places and things.

For Extra Practice, see p. 285. **Capitalizing Names**

4 ‖ Abbreviations

Some words have a shortened form called an **abbreviation**. An abbreviation stands for a whole word. Most abbreviations begin with a capital letter and end with a period. Use them only in special kinds of writing, such as addresses and lists.

Some Common Abbreviations				
Titles	Mr.	Mister	Mrs.	married woman
	Jr.	Junior	Ms.	any woman
	Sr.	Senior	Dr.	Doctor
Addresses	Rd.	Road	Co.	Company
	St.	Street	P. O.	Post Office
	Ave.	Avenue	Blvd.	Boulevard
Months	Jan.	January	Sept.	September
	Apr.	April	Nov.	November
Days	Sun.	Sunday	Wed.	Wednesday
	Tues.	Tuesday	Thurs.	Thursday

Special two-letter abbreviations for state names are used with ZIP Codes. Both letters are capitals, and no period is used. A list of abbreviations for states, months, and days is given in your Grammar and Usage Guide.

AL Alabama   UT Utah
OH Ohio   VT Vermont

Mr. John Smith, Jr.
1412 South St.
Burlington, VT 05401

Guided Practice What is the correct abbreviation for each underlined word?

Example: <u>January</u> 15, 1989 *Jan.*

1. Marina Boat <u>Company</u>
2. Ogden, <u>Utah</u> 84401
3. A. V. Pyke, <u>Junior</u>
4. <u>Tuesday</u>, <u>April</u> 5
5. <u>Doctor</u> Ramon
6. Grant <u>Road</u>

> ► An **abbreviation** is a short form of a word.
> ► Most abbreviations begin with a capital letter and end with a period.

Independent Practice

A. Write these groups of words, using correct abbreviations.

Example: Wednesday, November 4 *Wed., Nov. 4*

7. Doctor Ann Chang
8. Mister John Cliff, Senior
9. May Lee, a married woman
10. Rosa Sanchez
11. Sunday, November 21
12. Cooper Copper Company
13. Joseph L. Louis, Junior

14. Thursday, April 8
15. September 20, 1988
16. 19 Seneca Street
17. Mister Markham
18. Post Office Box 6
19. El Monte Avenue
20. January 1, 1989

B. Write these addresses, using an abbreviation for each underlined word.

Example: Kurt McLean, <u>Senior</u>   *Kurt McLean, Sr.*
23 Oneida <u>Road</u>   *23 Oneida Rd.*
Sunrise, <u>Florida</u> 33322   *Sunrise, FL 33322*

21. <u>Mister</u> Aram Zakian
1875 Summit <u>Street</u>
Columbus, <u>Ohio</u> 43201

22. <u>Doctor</u> Bonnie Buckman
1015 Timberlane <u>Avenue</u>
Mobile, <u>Alabama</u> 36609

23. Wayne Hubbard, <u>Junior</u>
<u>Post</u> Office Box 300
Provo, <u>Utah</u> 84603

24. Pilgrim Paint <u>Company</u>
42 Brush Hill <u>Boulevard</u>
Ely, <u>Vermont</u> 05044

Writing Application: Telegrams

You have just been elected President of the United States! You want to send two people telegrams to tell them the exciting news. Write the telegrams. Then write the names and addresses of the two people. Use correct abbreviations.

For Extra Practice, see p. 286.

5 | Commas in a Series

When you talk, you often pause briefly as you speak. When you write, you must use a **comma** (,) to tell your reader where to pause. Commas help make the meaning of your sentences clear.

INCORRECT: Al bought oatmeal bread cheese and nuts.
Connie likes to ski swim or play tennis.

How many things did Al buy? How many sports does Connie enjoy? Commas are needed to separate the items in each sentence. When you list three or more words in a sentence, the list is called a **series**. Use the word *and* or *or* before the last item in the series. Place a comma after each item except the last one.

oatmeal, bread, cheese, and nuts

CORRECT: Al bought oatmeal, bread, cheese, and nuts.
Al bought oatmeal bread, cheese, and nuts.
Connie likes to ski, swim, or play tennis.

oatmeal bread, cheese, and nuts

Guided Practice Where are commas needed in these sentences?

Example: Gold is found in California Idaho and Georgia.
Gold is found in California, Idaho, and Georgia.

1. Tim Mary and Lee are learning to pan for gold.
2. Tim watches men women and children standing in a stream.
3. They scoop shovel or toss dirt into a pan.
4. Then they sift shake and slosh the gravel.
5. Pebbles sand and gold are left in the pan.

Summing up

▶ A **series** is a list of three or more items.
▶ Use commas to separate the items in a series. Put a comma after each item in the series except the last one.

Independent Practice Write these sentences correctly. Add commas where they are needed.

Example: Marcy Ken and Pam learned about the Gold Rush.
Marcy, Ken, and Pam learned about the Gold Rush.

6. They read studied and took notes.
7. They used books articles and films.
8. People came from Ohio Virginia and Georgia.
9. Others came from Asia Europe and Australia.
10. They sailed rode or walked to California!
11. Why did people leave families friends and jobs?
12. Farmers teachers and shopkeepers hoped to become rich!
13. They sold their houses farms and shops.
14. Newspapers in Boston New York and Philadelphia told the most amazing stories!
15. Many people had found gold nuggets flakes and dust.
16. Could anyone get rich with just a shovel a pan and a dream?
17. Farmers sailors and blacksmiths wanted to find out.
18. Many people took ships fishing boats or steamboats around South America.
19. Others rode in wagons with only food clothing and tools.
20. Ed Cathy and Kuni explain how crowded the West became.
21. New hotels restaurants and stores were built quickly.
22. We wrote practiced and acted a play about the Gold Rush.
23. Marcy Pam and Kuni played pioneers.
24. Ken planned built and painted the scenery.
25. Our friends family and teachers watched the play.
26. They clapped cheered and whistled when it was over.

Writing Application: A Letter

Pretend that you live in the 1800s in the days of the Gold Rush. You are going to California to find gold. Write a letter to a friend, telling about your wagon journey to California. At least three sentences must have a series of three or more words.

For Extra Practice, see p. 287.

6 | More Uses for Commas

You know that a comma tells you to pause between words. When you speak, you pause briefly if you begin the answer to a question with *yes, no,* or *well.* Use a comma after these words to show the pause in your writing.

> Yes, I gave the horse some oats.
> No, I haven't brushed his coat.
> Well, you can clean his hoofs tomorrow.

Sometimes you use a person's name when you address, or speak directly to, that person. When you write, use a comma or commas to set off the name of the person who is being addressed.

> Alice, are you going riding with us?
> We wondered, Alice, which trail we should take.
> We're really happy that you're joining us, Alice!

Guided Practice Where are commas needed?

Example: Kwan have we always had horses in this country?
Kwan, have we always had horses in this country?

1. No Spanish explorers brought them in the 1500s.
2. They left some of their horses here Tony.
3. Well did many people use the horses?
4. Yes the Plains Indians rode horses.
5. Later Eric horses pulled the pioneers' wagons.

Summing up

> ▸ Use a comma to set off the words *yes, no,* and *well* when they are at the beginning of a sentence.
> ▸ Use a comma or commas to set off the names of people who are addressed directly.

Independent Practice Write these sentences correctly.
Add commas where they are needed.

Example: Do wild horses live together in herds Jake?
Do wild horses live together in herds, Jake?

6. Yes they roam large ranges in the West.
7. Marcos is there enough grass for them to eat?
8. No the horses share the food with many other animals.
9. Amy how are people helping the horses?
10. Well the government is rounding up some horses.
11. They hope Liza that some people will adopt a horse.
12. Well that sounds like a good idea.
13. Yes I hope that the horses find good homes.
14. You love horses Jake.
15. Well wouldn't you like to adopt one?
16. Do wild horses live in other places Matt?
17. Yes some wild ponies live on an island.
18. The island Amy is off the coast of Virginia.
19. Yes the island's name is Chincoteague.
20. Have you read the book *Misty of Chincoteague* Rafael?
21. Well the book tells about a pony from that island.
22. No I have not read that book.
23. May I borrow your copy Amy?
24. Does anyone know where the ponies came from Ara?
25. Well some people say a ship was wrecked in a storm.
26. Yes the ship was carrying some ponies.
27. Each year Meg the ponies are rounded up.
28. Yes they swim to a nearby island.
29. Michael wouldn't you like to have a wild pony for a pet?
30. Well I couldn't keep one in a city apartment!

Writing Application: Creative Writing

Imagine that you are a wild pony. You have been adopted by a family. Write a paragraph telling the other ponies back in the herd about your new life. Begin each sentence with *yes*, *no*, *well*, or a pony's name.

For Extra Practice, see p. 288.   **More Uses for Commas** 271

7 | Quotation Marks

Sometimes you may want to write a conversation between two or more people. When you write the exact words that a speaker says, you are writing a **direct quotation**.

A direct quotation can come at the beginning or at the end of a sentence. No matter where it appears, you must place **quotation marks** (" ") before and after the speaker's exact words. Do not place quotation marks around the words that explain who is talking.

> Ali asked, "Have you read about the fox and the grapes?"
> "That's my favorite fable!" I exclaimed.

Some sentences tell what someone says without using the person's exact words. Do not use quotation marks unless you give the exact words of the speaker.

> Mr. Stuart said that we would write fables today.
> Mr. Stuart said, "Today we will write fables."

Guided Practice Which sentences need quotation marks? Where should they be placed?

Example: Ms. Diaz asked, Have you read Aesop's fables?
　　　　　Ms. Diaz asked, "Have you read Aesop's fables?"

1. I've read them all! Paulo exclaimed.
2. Maureen told us that each story teaches a lesson.
3. Aesop lived over two thousand years ago, Kelly added.
4. Theo explained, The characters are talking animals.
5. Ms. Diaz said we could each read a different fable.

Summing up

> ► A **direct quotation** tells a speaker's exact words.
> ► Use **quotation marks** (" ") before and after a direct quotation.

Independent Practice

A. Add quotation marks where they are needed in these sentences. Write the sentences.

Example: I know I can win the race, the rabbit said.
"I know I can win the race," the rabbit said.

6. The turtle replied, We shall see.
7. I'm ahead already! shouted the rabbit.
8. I will do as well as I can, said the turtle.
9. The rabbit asked, Where is that turtle?
10. You are too far ahead to see him, answered the fans.
11. I'm going to win this race easily, the rabbit bragged.
12. The rabbit announced, I think I will rest for a minute.
13. The turtle whispered, Has anyone seen the rabbit?
14. The crowd answered, He is taking a nap.
15. The turtle has won the race! exclaimed the judge.

B. Write correctly the sentences that need quotation marks. Write *correct* for those that do not need quotation marks.

Example: Who knows the fable of the crow? Kimi asked.
"Who knows the fable of the crow?" Kimi asked.

16. I remember that one! exclaimed Monica.
17. Ben said, The crow had a problem to solve.
18. Karen asked, Do you remember what the crow wanted?
19. The crow was thirsty and wanted water, answered Bob.
20. Henry said, Some water was at the bottom of a jar.
21. Hal explained that the crow couldn't push the jar over.
22. The crow filled the jar with pebbles, Monica added.
23. Little by little the level of the water rose, Ben said.
24. Kimi asked if we knew what lesson the fable teaches.

Writing Application: An Interview

Imagine that a newspaper reporter interviewed either the rabbit or the turtle after the big race described in Part A of Independent Practice. Write the conversation between the reporter and the animal. Use quotation marks where they belong.

For Extra Practice, see p. 289.

8 | Quotations

You have learned how to use quotation marks to show a speaker's exact words. More punctuation marks, as well as capital letters, are needed to write quotations correctly.

Always capitalize the first word of a quotation. When a quotation comes last in a sentence, use a comma to separate the quotation from the words that tell who is speaking. Put the end mark inside the last quotation marks.

"Polly wants a cracker."

STATEMENT: Cleo said, "All birds have feathers."
QUESTION: Justin asked, "Can all birds fly?"
COMMAND: Linda said, "Look at the tiny hummingbird."
EXCLAMATION: Paul exclaimed, "It is flying backward!"

When a quotation that is a statement or a command comes first in a sentence, put a comma inside the last quotation marks. If the quotation is a question or an exclamation, put the question mark or the exclamation point inside the last quotation marks. A period always follows the last word in the sentence.

STATEMENT: "I have a new friend," Vicki said.
QUESTION: "May I meet your friend?" I asked.
COMMAND: "Say hello to Pauline," Vicki suggested.
EXCLAMATION: "Pauline is a parrot!" I exclaimed.

Guided Practice These sentences have quotations. How would you capitalize and punctuate each sentence?

Example: Jay shouted there must be thirty birds here
Jay shouted, "There must be thirty birds here!"

1. Robin said I guess they like our birdfeeder
2. Bill added they're eating all the sunflower seeds
3. I asked what kind of bird is that
4. Look it up in our bird book Robin said
5. What an unusual song it sings Jay exclaimed
6. Debbie exclaimed bird watching is a lot of fun

▶ Begin a quotation with a capital letter.

▶ When a quotation comes at the end of a sentence, use a comma to separate the quotation from the words that tell who is speaking. Put end punctuation marks inside the last quotation marks.

Independent Practice

A. These sentences have quotations. Write them correctly.

Example: Megan asked how many kinds of birds are there
Megan asked, "How many kinds of birds are there?"

7. Artie exclaimed there are over eight thousand kinds
8. Erin added different birds live in different places
9. Luis asked have you seen my list of birds
10. He explained I write down each kind of bird I see
11. Luis said try putting different seeds on the ground
12. Erin explained all birds don't like the same food
13. Artie suggested put out a pan of water too

B. These sentences have quotations. Write them correctly.

Example: Why do birds fly south in the winter Jed asked
"Why do birds fly south in the winter?" Jed asked.

14. It becomes hard for them to find food Betsy answered
15. Do all birds fly to the same place asked Kate
16. No, they head for many warmer spots Azi said
17. Tell me how far birds fly Rudi begged
18. Some birds fly thousands of miles Warren exclaimed
19. Look at those birds Warren continued
20. They will fly all the way to South America he exclaimed

Writing Application: Instructions

Imagine that you are a mother bird. You are teaching your children how to fly. Write the conversation between your children and you.

For Extra Practice, see p. 290.

9 | Titles

When you write the title of a book, a magazine, or a newspaper, capitalize the first, the last, and each important word. Capitalize words like *and, in, of, to, a,* and *the* only when they are the first or last word in the title.

The Door in the Wall   *Millions of Cats*   *News and Views*
Jack and Jill Magazine   *Boys' Life*   *The Fun Times*

In print, the titles of books, magazines, and newspapers are set off by *italics.* Since you cannot write in italics, always underline the title of a book, a magazine, or a newspaper.

Is <u>Tom Sawyer</u> your favorite book?
I am reading the magazine <u>Stone Soup</u>.

Guided Practice

A. How would you write these titles?

Example: the battle of lake erie   <u>The Battle of Lake Erie</u>

1. a family in france
2. tales of a grade four nothing
3. the rooftop reporter
4. electric company magazine
5. noisy nora
6. harbor town post
7. national geographic world
8. go up the road
9. there is no rhyme for silver
10. aladdin and the wonderful lamp

B. How would you write these sentences?

Example: Ani is reading heidi.   Ani is reading <u>Heidi</u>.

11. Chicago sun has great comics.
12. Is cricket a magazine?
13. Who wrote king of the wind?
14. Read a wrinkle in time.
15. Get walton weekly.
16. I read charlotte's web.

> ▶ Capitalize the first, the last, and each important word in the titles of books, magazines, or newspapers. Underline them.

Independent Practice

A. Write these titles correctly.

Example: nosy news   <u>Nosy News</u>

17. encyclopedia brown saves the day
18. summer of the swans
19. joytown journal
20. highlights for children
21. arrow to the sun
22. help! i'm a prisoner in the library
23. groton gazette
24. now one foot, now the other
25. stuart little
26. ranger rick

B. Write these sentences correctly.

Example: I read about the new library in village herald.
            I read about the new library in <u>Village Herald</u>.

27. The library is giving away the magazine animals.
28. Did you read a book called it's like this, cat?
29. It was on a shelf next to bright fawn and me.
30. I found an article for my report in neighborhood news.
31. I'm also using the book all kinds of families.
32. Is ben and me a good book?
33. It's almost as good as the beaver pond.
34. Is cobblestone your favorite history magazine?

Writing Application: A Friendly Letter
Your pen pal is sick. Find out what one of his or her interests is. Then write a letter telling about some books or magazines on that topic.

For Extra Practice, see p. 291.

Grammar-Writing Connection

Combining Sentences with Words in a Series

You know that a list of three or more words in a sentence is called a series. Sometimes sentences can be combined by making a series. The short sentences below are choppy.

Many dinosaurs lived in a hot climate. The climate was also wet . The climate was also steamy .

The adjectives *hot, wet,* and *steamy* all describe the climate, but they are in three separate sentences. In the revised sentence below, the three adjectives are combined to make a series. The new sentence is smoother and easier to read than the three short sentences.

Many dinosaurs lived in a hot, wet, steamy climate.

Notice how commas separate the adjectives in the series.

Revising Sentences

Rewrite each group of sentences by making a series.

1. We read about some huge dinosaurs. They were strong. They were terrifying.
2. There were also some small dinosaurs. These dinosaurs were fast. They were birdlike.
3. The first birds had thin bones. These bones were also light. These bones were hollow.
4. These birds had narrow claws on their wings. The claws were sharp. The claws were curved.
5. The museum has a new display about dinosaurs. The display is interesting. It is also popular.
6. Scientists built a large model of a dinosaur. The model is lifelike. It is also colorful.

Creative Writing

La Gare Saint Lazare, Arrivée d'un Train
by Claude Monet, The Fogg Art Museum

Over one hundred years ago, Claude Monet stood inside this train station. The French artist painted while trains and people moved all about him. Monet painted the scene quickly to capture its feeling of sunlight, smoke, and movement.

- What are the picture's main colors? What mood do they give?
- How would the picture be different without the smoke?

Activities

1. **Describe your train trip.** Imagine you are a passenger on this train. Where are you going? What happens on your trip? Write a journal entry telling about your train journey.
2. **Write a sound poem.** Imagine the sounds you might hear in the train station. For instance, you might hear people shouting and the train's whistle blowing. Write a poem that describes the sounds of the busy station.

Check-up: Unit 9

Correct Sentences *(p. 260)* Write these sentences correctly. Add capital letters and end marks. Separate run-on sentences.

1. this is a lovely new aquarium
2. how long have you had it
3. some fish have unusual shapes other fish are brightly colored
4. how huge that angelfish is
5. can you see the tiny fish they are hiding among the rocks
6. how often do you feed them
7. do not give them too much food

Capitalizing Names of People and Pets *(p. 262)* Write these sentences. Add capital letters where they are needed.

8. My uncle has a dog named nomad.
9. He leaves uncle henry very early each morning.
10. First, nomad heads downtown.
11. There he looks for mr. lee.
12. He passes the library on his way to see dr. sarah aaron.
13. At the market, miss jones gives nomad a bone.
14. She saves one for her dog, sparky.
15. The dog stops last at central high school.
16. My mother and mr. l. m. rowe are teachers there.

Capitalizing Names of Places and Things *(p. 264)* Write these sentences. Add capital letters where they are needed.

17. Cindy will go to cleveland in the middle of august.
18. She will come home shortly before labor day.
19. The terminal tower is the name of a tall building in cleveland.
20. Cindy wants to see the cleveland indians play baseball.
21. On monday the family will visit gates mills, a nearby village, and stay overnight with friends.
22. This town is on the chagrin river.

Abbreviations *(p. 266)* Write each group of words. Use an abbreviation in place of each underlined word.

23. <u>Mister</u> Scott Moe
24. <u>January</u> 9, 1944
25. 98 South Main <u>Street</u>
26. <u>Doctor</u> Jemilah Asher
27. <u>Wednesday</u>, <u>November</u> 15, 1978
28. Higgins Paper <u>Company</u>
29. 86 Ripley <u>Road</u>
30. T. J. Lavoie, <u>Junior</u>
31. Dorian Bryant, <u>Senior</u>
32. <u>Sunday</u>, <u>September</u> 14, 1834
33. <u>Post Office</u> Box 162
34. 2170 North <u>Avenue</u>

Commas in a Series *(p. 268)* Write these sentences. Add commas where they are needed.

35. Cranberries blueberries and Concord grapes grow in the northern United States.
36. Cranberries grow in bogs where there are sand moss and water.
37. They grow in Massachusetts New Jersey Wisconsin and Washington.
38. Josh Sarah and Liz are going to a bog to see the harvest.
39. They will be there on Friday Saturday and Sunday.
40. Workers will pick inspect and pack the berries for sale.
41. Cranberries are used in sauce juice and baked goods.

More Uses for Commas *(p. 270)* Write these sentences. Use commas correctly.

42. Have you heard about the new contest Chris?
43. No I have not heard about it.
44. Well each person must design a stone carving.
45. Yes the best drawing will win.
46. What will you draw Lisa?
47. Damon what do you hope to win?
48. Well the winning design will be carved in stone.
49. It will be put on the roof of a building Jon.

Quotation Marks *(p. 272)* Write correctly the sentences that need quotation marks. Write *correct* if a sentence is already correct.

50. Our class newspaper is done! announced Jonathan.
51. Tony said, My article is on the first page.
52. What is the answer to this word puzzle? wondered Jared.
53. Jim said that he likes the book reviews best.
54. Shel Silverstein is my favorite author, he explained.
55. Kristin asked who had drawn the clever illustrations.

Quotations *(p. 274)* Write these sentences. Use capital letters and punctuation marks correctly.

56. I love to ice skate announced Jeff
57. Rebecca asked is the ice thick
58. Don't be afraid to fall said Don
59. Lang answered I won't
60. Molly cried look out for the hole
61. I would much rather go roller-skating declared June

Titles *(p. 276)* Write these titles correctly.

62. a light in the attic
63. better homes and gardens
64. island of the blue dolphins
65. daily journal
66. ramona the brave

Enrichment

Using Capitalization and Punctuation

Pet Hotel

Pretend that you run a pet hotel. Fill out identification cards for five visiting animals. Make cards that include (1) name of pet; (2) name of owner; (3) owner's address; (4) description of pet that tells its size, color, and personality, and (5) dates of visit. Use correct abbreviations for titles, addresses, months, and days. Draw a picture of each pet if you wish.

Tourist Attraction

Your job is to make people want to visit your state. Draw a large outline of your state. Inside it, write the state's name and abbreviation, names of major cities, and names of interesting places to visit. Draw small pictures of these places. Around the outside, write the names and abbreviations for the surrounding states.

Talking Numbers

Imagine that numbers can talk. On index cards, write five quotations in which numbers are the speakers. Do not name the numbers. Leave blanks instead.

"I am the number of inches in a foot!" announced number ____.

Write the name of the number on the back of each card. Exchange cards with a partner. Does your partner know which numbers are talking?

Extra Practice: Unit 9

1 | Correct Sentences (p. 260)

● Each sentence is missing a capital letter or an end mark. Write each sentence correctly.

Example: have you ever seen a dolphin?
Have you ever seen a dolphin?

1. Listen to this story about a dolphin named Sandy
2. some scientists were diving near the Bahama Islands.
3. one scientist met a dolphin underwater.
4. How excited she was
5. What did the dolphin do
6. it poked her playfully with its snout.

▲ Write these sentences correctly. Add capital letters and end marks. Separate run-on sentences.

Example: dolphins breathe air how do they do it
Dolphins breathe air. How do they do it?

7. a dolphin breathes through a single nostril
8. do you know where this is it is on top of the head
9. a dolphin can stay underwater for six minutes
10. that is a long time how long can you stay underwater
11. some scientists think that dolphins can learn to speak
12. read this article it will tell you more about dolphins

■ Write these sentences correctly. Then label each sentence *statement, question, command,* or *exclamation.*

Example: can you name a very large animal
Can you name a very large animal? question

13. the blue whale is the world's largest animal
14. is it bigger than a dinosaur
15. this animal is as large as twenty-five elephants
16. what a lot of food blue whales must eat
17. they have no teeth they strain food from seawater
18. what interesting animals they are please tell me more

● ▲ ■ **Three levels of practice** 283

2 | Names of People and Pets (p. 262)

● Write these names of people and pets correctly.

Example: aunt sally   *Aunt Sally*

1. uncle barry
2. fifi
3. queen elizabeth
4. dr. doris cortez
5. mr. joseph b. zaturka

6. betsy chun
7. miss w. r. lin
8. mayor santos
9. porky
10. p. j. levy

▲ Write these sentences. Use capital letters correctly.

Example: My aunt's cat scaredy was in the pet show.
          My aunt's cat Scaredy was in the pet show.

11. As usual, miss meyer owned the prize-winning cat.
12. Her cat's full name is lord summerfield.
13. I heard that dr. jessie jones was very disappointed.
14. My cousin told dad and me what happened that morning.
15. The doctor's cat harvey climbed a tree and stayed there.
16. Even grandmother tried to get the cat out of the tree.
17. Didn't mayor short call the fire department?
18. It was too late to enter harvey in the show.

■ Use a noun from the Word Box to complete each sentence. Use each noun once. Write the sentences. Be sure to capitalize the proper nouns.

Example: Show this article to ____.
          Show this article to Aunt Jane.

Word Box
dr. dan d. lyons
attorney m. dodd
uncle ron
aunt jane
grandmother
etta
uncle
aunt
doctor

19. It is about a veterinarian named ____.
20. The ____ has a new office in our town.
21. It is above the law office of ____.
22. My ____ will be glad.
23. Her cat ____ has not been eating well.
24. ____ says that he is worried too.
25. My aunt and ____ will take the cat to the vet.
26. ____ will stay home and take care of the other cats.

3 | Names of Places and Things (p. 264)

● Write these names of places and things correctly.
  Example: washington, d.c.   *Washington, D.C.*

  1. monday
  2. united states
  3. potomac river
  4. jefferson memorial
  5. the white house

  6. may 31
  7. pennsylvania avenue
  8. memorial day
  9. rock creek park
  10. capitol hill

▲ Write these sentences. Use capital letters correctly.
  Example: The largest city in louisiana is new orleans.
          The largest city in Louisiana is New Orleans.

  11. This city lies along the mississippi river.
  12. It is north of the gulf of mexico.
  13. A holiday called mardi gras takes place every year.
  14. Tourists come in february or march for this celebration.
  15. Jazz fans hear great music at preservation hall.
  16. The top floor of a building called the international trade mart offers a wonderful view.
  17. The largest indoor stadium is the superdome.
  18. The new orleans saints play football there.

■ Invent a city that would be fun to visit. Write a sentence to answer each question about your city. Make up names of people, places, and things to answer the questions.
  Example: What is the name of your city?
          The name of my city is Clowntown.

  19. Who is the mayor?
  20. What is the nearest body of water?
  21. In what country is it located?
  22. What is the name of the best restaurant in town?
  23. On what street is this restaurant?
  24. Who is the chef?
  25. What big holiday is celebrated in your city?
  26. When does it take place?

4 | Abbreviations (p. 266)

● Write each group of words. Underline the abbreviation.
Example: Oct. 1, 1988 *Oct. 1, 1988*

1. Mr. Daniel Gambini
2. Dr. Joyce Wong
3. Old River Rd.
4. Abbot Travel Co.
5. Sun., March 2, 1986
6. 3456 Fifth Ave.
7. Pots and Pans Co.
8. Ms. Maria Garcia
9. Third St.
10. Marvin Hogan, Jr.
11. Atlanta, GA 30043
12. Mrs. Monica Cohen
13. Leo Lyons, Sr.
14. P. O. Box 567
15. Bennington, VT 05201
16. Jan. 4, 1989

▲ Write each group of words. Use an abbreviation in place of each underlined word.
Example: Douglas Food Company *Douglas Food Co.*

17. January 12, 1874
18. Irving White, Senior
19. Mister Howard Klein
20. Doctor Harriet Correlli
21. 555 Tulip Tree Avenue
22. Cleveland, Ohio 44114
23. Thursday, July 4, 1776
24. Boston Post Road
25. Post Office Box 76
26. 6710 South Maple Street
27. Mobile, Alabama 36609
28. 5110 Clinton Avenue
29. Sporting Life Company
30. Tuesday, November 1, 1988

■ Write each group of words, using correct abbreviations. Add capital letters where they are needed.
Example: a woman named ann mack
Ms. Ann Mack / Mrs. Ann Mack

31. thursday, january 7, 1988
32. apex shipping company
33. 678 goldrush road
34. post office box 89
35. mister michael burns
36. salt lake city, utah 84101
37. sunday, november 1, 1987
38. 450 milford avenue
39. doctor lorna cook
40. hunter boulevard
41. mister john chen, senior
42. september 30, 1910
43. 45 hill street
44. santora music company

5 | Commas in a Series (p. 268)

● Complete each sentence by adding two words to form a series. Write the sentence.

Example: Rita's best friends are Kim, ____, and ____.
Rita's best friends are Kim, Tommy, and Ben.

1. They all like to swim, ____, and ____.
2. Rita likes to cook spaghetti, ____, and ____.
3. Last week she invited Kim, ____, and ____ for lunch.
4. She made salad, ____, and ____.
5. After lunch the children talked, ____, and ____.
6. Rita's pets are a bird, a ____, and a ____.
7. They are named Polly ____, and ____.

▲ Write these sentences. Use commas correctly.

Example: Farmers hunters and trappers became pioneers.
Farmers, hunters, and trappers became pioneers.

8. Pioneers settled in Kansas Nebraska and Minnesota.
9. Some of them came from Norway Sweden or Denmark.
10. They sailed rode and walked to the new land.
11. Pioneer women spun wove and sewed cloth.
12. The pioneers built their own shelters wagons and boats.
13. At first men women and children lived in sod houses.
14. Sod houses were made of grass mud and dirt.
15. Pioneers used axes shovels and picks to make their houses.

■ Write each sentence two different ways. The meaning of each sentence will change depending on where you use commas.

Example: Pioneers ate oatmeal bread and potatoes.
Pioneers ate oatmeal bread and potatoes.
Pioneers ate oatmeal, bread, and potatoes.

16. On the road, they ate cod stew pork and beans.
17. Cows gave them cream cheese and milk.
18. A good dinner included chicken soup and noodles.
19. They used cornmeal flour and eggs to make pancakes.
20. Their apple walnut and cherry breads were delicious.

6 | More Uses for Commas (p. 270)

● Write these sentences. Use commas correctly.
   Example: Well have you heard about the wild horses?
             Well, have you heard about the wild horses?

   1. Yes I read that some people are adopting them.
   2. No the horses are not still wild.
   3. Carmen the horses have been tamed.
   4. Well let's go to see them.
   5. Yes there is a horse show at the fairgrounds today.
   6. No it is not too late.
   7. Bill that girl's wild horse has become a gentle pet.
   8. No she named it Paint, not Rusty.

▲ Write these sentences. Use commas correctly.
   Example: Do you know how tall the first horses were Ann?
             Do you know how tall the first horses were, Ann?

   9. Yes this book says they were eleven inches tall.
   10. Well today's horses are much taller.
   11. Some horses grow to be seven feet tall Iris.
   12. They are giants Paul compared to the early horses.
   13. Frank did people always ride horses?
   14. No the early horses were not tall or strong enough.

■ Write correctly the sentences that need commas. Write *correct*
   for each sentence that does not need commas.
   Example: Can you tell me Mark who the nomad people were?
             Can you tell me, Mark, who the nomad people were?

   15. Nomads Jeff wandered from place to place
   16. Pete were they lost?
   17. No the nomads were looking for food.
   18. Nomads were the first people to ride horses.
   19. Well did you know that they did not use saddles?
   20. Yes I read that at first they rode bareback.
   21. Then they put animal skins on the horses' backs.
   22. Someone finally invented the saddle Jill.

7 | Quotation Marks (p. 272)

● Copy each sentence. Underline the direct quotation.
  Example: "Do you know this fable?" asked Alice.
           "Do you know this fable?" asked Alice.

  1. A fox said, "I will invite the stork for dinner."
  2. The fox added, "I will serve soup in a shallow dish."
  3. "Why did the fox use a shallow dish?" asked Michael.
  4. Tina replied, "The stork could only wet its bill."
  5. Then the stork said to the fox, "Have dinner with me."
  6. "What did the stork serve for dinner?" asked Emily.
  7. Peg answered, "It was soup in a tall, narrow jar."
  8. "Well, one bad turn deserved another!" laughed Carlos.

▲ Write each sentence correctly, using quotation marks.
  Example: Let's hear another fable, begged Jon.
           "Let's hear another fable," begged Jon.

  9. Carrie said, A crow found a nice piece of cheese.
  10. A fox exclaimed, I want that crow's cheese!
  11. You are a beautiful bird! the fox told the crow.
  12. Kee asked, Was the crow pleased with this remark?
  13. Then the fox asked the crow to sing, replied Elaine.
  14. Ned said, It opened its beak and dropped the cheese.
  15. Eric added, Do not be fooled by too much praise.

■ Write correctly each sentence that needs quotation marks. If a
  sentence is already correct, write _correct_.
  Example: A lion had caught a small mouse, said Joey.
           "A lion had caught a small mouse," said Joey.

  16. The mouse squeaked, Let me go, and I'll never forget it!
  17. The lion declared that a mouse could never help a lion.
  18. However, the lion let the mouse go, said Jason.
  19. Kirk added, Hunters later trapped the lion.
  20. The hunters tied the lion to a tree, added Lisa.
  21. Nick said, The mouse chewed the rope and freed the lion.
  22. May stated that little friends may prove great friends.

8 | Quotations (p. 274)

● Each sentence is missing a comma or a capital letter. Write each sentence correctly.

Example: Don asked, "have you ever heard of a snipe?"
              Don asked, "Have you ever heard of a snipe?"

1. "Please tell me about it" answered Julie.
2. Don said, "it is a kind of bird."
3. "The snipe is related to the gull" Ann continued.
4. Pat asked "What kind of bill does it have?"
5. "A snipe has a long, pointed bill" Don explained.
6. Lou said, "a snipe's eyes are on the top of its head."
7. Julie asked, "does it look strange when it flies?"

▲ Write each sentence correctly. Add capital letters, commas, and end marks where they are needed.

Example: Ellen exclaimed "what a funny-looking bird"
              Ellen exclaimed, "What a funny-looking bird!"

8. "what kind of bird is that" Chan asked.
9. Lora explained "it is called an umbrella bird"
10. "it has a funny hat on its head" laughed Ellen.
11. "those are feathers" explained Lora.
12. Chan said "it has long feathers hanging from its neck"
13. "they look like an umbrella handle" added Al.

■ Write these sentences. Use capital letters and punctuation marks correctly.

Example: is that bird related to a woodpecker asked jo
              "Is that bird related to a woodpecker?" asked Jo.

14. yes it is answered dan
15. please show me the picture begged les
16. its bill is almost as big as its body exclaimed kim
17. how can it fly with that huge bill asked paula
18. dan said its bill is not very heavy at all paula
19. sue asked well what kind of bird is it
20. it is called a toucan sue explained dan

9 | Titles (p. 276)

● Write each sentence. Underline each title.

Example: This week's Brookland Bugle printed a list of books.
        This week's <u>*Brookland Bugle*</u> *printed a list of books.*

1. A Cricket in Times Square was on the list.
2. Is Newsweek your dad's favorite magazine?
3. Did The Arrival of Paddington make you laugh?
4. How to Eat Fried Worms certainly did.
5. Did Scott Corbett write The Black Mask Trick?
6. Yes, a Belview News critic wrote about that book.

▲ Write these sentences correctly.

Example: I lent stowaway to the mushroom planet to Jan.
        I lent <u>*Stowaway to the Mushroom Planet*</u> *to Jan.*

7. She is reading the wind in the willows now.
8. There is a review of it in highlights for children.
9. I wrote a story about it for hale school news.
10. Another article was about the book runaway ralph.
11. Wasn't Ralph also in the mouse and the motorcycle?
12. The editor of lee times asked Jim to write a column.
13. This week's column discussed the book amos and boris.

■ Make up a title to complete each sentence. Write the sentences.
Be sure to write the titles correctly.

Example: ＿＿ is a collection of scary stories.   (book)
        <u>*Terrifying Tales*</u> *is a collection of scary stories.*

14. ＿＿ reports on all the latest scientific discoveries.
    (newspaper)
15. Read ＿＿ to learn how to make a robot from things you can
    find around the house.   (book)
16. Learn the latest news about musicians in ＿＿.   (magazine)
17. ＿＿ is the fascinating story of how a new pet changes a
    family's life.   (book)
18. Buy a copy of ＿＿ today to learn all the latest happenings at
    the zoo.   (newspaper)

I went to San Francisco.
I saw the bridges high
Spun across the water
Like cobwebs in the sky.

Langston Hughes
"Trip: San Francisco"

Persuasive Letter

Getting Ready When you are on a vacation, do you write letters to friends telling them what you are doing? What other times do you write letters? Have you ever written a letter to persuade someone to do something? In this unit you will read some letters and later write one of your own.

ACTIVITIES

Listening

Listen as the poem on the opposite page is read. Where did the poet go? What did he see? What words did he use to tell what the bridges looked like? If a friend sent you this poem on a postcard, would it make you want to go to San Francisco? Why?

Speaking

Look at the picture. Suppose you were going to write a letter to a friend about this scene. What would you write to persuade your friend to visit it?

Writing

In your journal, write a letter to a friend persuading him or her to go with you to visit a place you like.

LITERATURE

Sarah's father writes letters to her when he travels. What do you learn about him from these letters?

Dear Sarah
By Elisabeth Borchers

Sarah's father is in Europe on a business trip, but he always writes to her when he is away. On Wednesday, he is in Milan, Italy, and mails one letter there. On Sunday, he writes from Paris, France.

Wednesday in Milan

Dear Sarah,

When I arrived yesterday, the sun was shining. Now it's raining and won't stop. Four shoes, four socks, one raincoat, and one umbrella are all lying about sopping wet. I've already sneezed three times. It's no fun to sneeze in a strange city. The window is as wet as your face when you cry. I know you're not crying now, but if you were, I'd say: Look out the window. Do you see the moon! It's all wet. Now if you close your eyes, you'll see it shaking itself like a dog that's just come out of the water.

Here are two moon poems. Let me know which one you like better.

1. Poem

Come now, let me see you smiling.
All those tears will make a flood,
Wet your shoes and spot your stockings,
Surely crying does no good.

See the moon itself is hiding,
Gliding in and out of view,
Moving slowly, growing paler.
Has it really split in two?

2. Poem

Though your eyes are shut tight,
The moon still sheds its light
On your bed at night.

When day comes, it will roam
To Naples or Nome
To another child's home.

Time for bed. You get into yours and I'll get into mine here. Tuck yourself in tight so you will be warm. I'll cover myself well too. Did you hear that? I just sneezed again. No kiss tonight, so you won't catch my cold.

Your papa

P.S. I'm sure that by tomorrow everything will be all right.

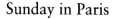

Sunday in Paris

Dear Sarah,

The Main flows through Frankfurt, the Danube through Vienna, and the Thames through London. In Paris, the Seine flows through the city in a beautiful wide curve, and there are many bridges over it leading from shore to shore. The streets on both sides of the river are lined with stalls selling flowers and clothing, pots and pans, all kinds of goods. And there are more bookstalls than any other kind. People come here to look for old books they haven't been able to find elsewhere. And sometimes they find a very special book they haven't even been looking for. I walked along until I was tired and hungry. Then I went into a restaurant and had soup, snails, fish, meat, vegetables, salad, cheese, and cake. I ate and ate until I could eat no more.

Now from my hotel window I look out on the roofs of houses and just above them is the moon. Sometimes the moon is a pumpkin, heavy and round. Sometimes it's a slipper, light and delicate. Right now it's like a swing standing still. If I were standing by your bed, I could say, "Come, Sarah, the swing is waiting." We'd only have to climb up on one of the roofs, one with a tower, and then up the tower, and we'd be at the swing. It's as simple as that. But I'll let you sleep, and see if I can get up there myself first. Next time we'll go together, you and I.

And if you get up now, and go to your window, you'll see me up there and I'll see you.

I'll be home soon.

Your papa

P.S. I love the moon even more than the beautiful stars.

296

Think and Discuss

1. What kind of person is Sarah's father? How do you know?

2. Sarah's father writes about his experiences in Milan and Paris. He also writes about his thoughts and feelings. What experiences, thoughts, and feelings does he write about in each letter?

3. Sarah's father wrote, "Sometimes the moon is a pumpkin, heavy and round." This kind of comparison is called a **metaphor**. Like a simile, a metaphor compares two different things that are alike in some way. Unlike a simile, however, a metaphor does not use the word *like* or *as*. A metaphor says that one thing *is* another. What other metaphor about the moon can you find in "Dear Sarah"? Which one do you like better? Why?

City
By Langston Hughes

In the morning the city
Spreads its wings
Making a song
In stone that sings.

In the evening the city
Goes to bed
Hanging lights
About its head.

Think and Discuss

1. What two times of day does this poem describe?
2. Some poems are divided into parts called **stanzas**. Like a paragraph, a stanza tells about one main idea. Why did the poet write "City" in two stanzas? How does he describe the city in each stanza?
3. Which stanza did you enjoy more? Why?

RESPONDING TO LITERATURE

The Reading and Writing Connection

Personal Response How did the letters in "Dear Sarah" make you feel? Would you like to receive letters like these? Why or why not? Write a paragraph describing your feelings about the letters.

Creative Writing Sarah's father wrote two poems about the moon. Would you choose to write about the moon or the stars? Write a two-stanza poem about the moon or the stars. Try to use a metaphor.

Creative Activities

Draw Draw or paint a picture of a favorite scene during the day. Make another picture of the same scene at night. How are the two pictures different?

Interpretive Reading Read "City" with a partner. You read the first stanza aloud. Try to make your voice capture the feeling of the city in the morning, as it spreads its wings and sings. Then have your partner read the second stanza, using her or his voice to show the feeling of the city going to bed in the evening.

Vocabulary

Sarah's father mentions the Main, Danube, Thames, and Seine rivers. Use a dictionary to find out how to pronounce each river's name. Then find the four rivers on a map of Europe or a globe. Which river is longest? Through which country or countries does each one flow?

Looking Ahead

Letter In this unit, you will be writing a letter. Read the letters to Sarah again. Can you find the greeting, body, and signature in each letter?

VOCABULARY CONNECTION
Figurative Language

> Now from my hotel window I look out on the roofs of houses and just above them is the moon. Sometimes **the moon is a pumpkin,** heavy and round.
>
> *from "Dear Sarah" by Elisabeth Borchers*

The moon is not really a pumpkin, but it is *like* a pumpkin because it can be thought of as *heavy and round.*

Sometimes writers use **figurative language,** words or phrases that do not mean exactly what they say, to help create a picture in the mind of the reader.

What if the writer had described the moon this way:

Sometimes **the moon is large and full.**

In this sentence the moon is described using the real, everyday meanings of words. It uses **literal language.**

Vocabulary Practice

A. Write *figurative* or *literal* to describe each of these passages from "Dear Sarah."

1. All those tears will make a flood. . . .
2. When I arrived yesterday, the sun was shining.
3. I walked along until I was tired and hungry.
4. See the moon itself is hiding. . . .

B. For each word, write a descriptive sentence using figurative language. Then rewrite each sentence, changing the figurative language to literal language.

5. sun   6. traffic light   7. river   8. furnace

Listening: For a Speaker's Purpose

A speaker always has a reason or **purpose** for speaking. A speaker may want to **persuade** you to do something, to **entertain** you, or to **inform** you of some facts. If the speaker's purpose is clear, you will better understand the talk. In the same way, a clear purpose in your writing will help your readers understand what you are saying.

Listen to these sentences. What is each speaker's purpose?

Everyone should try to travel. It is a great way to learn about the world. — MARC

Something funny happened to my aunt in Paris. Wait until you hear it. — MARIA

Paris is the capital of France. The River Seine runs through the city. — MANDY

Marc uses the words *You should*. He wants to persuade you to travel. Maria is telling a story, so she wants to entertain you. Mandy is giving you facts. Her purpose is to inform.

Guides for Listening for a Speaker's Purpose

1. Listen with attention. Do not let your mind wander.
2. Ask yourself, Does the speaker want to **persuade** me? to **entertain** me? to **inform** me of facts?

Prewriting Practice

Use the above listening guides as your teacher reads aloud. For each paragraph, write *persuade, entertain,* or *inform.*

Thinking: Telling Fact from Opinion

When someone is trying to persuade you to do or think something, it is important to know the difference between **fact** and **opinion.** A fact is a statement that can be proved. An opinion is a statement that someone believes to be true. Don't just accept what you hear or read. Think about it first.

Read these sentences.

FACT: The city of London is located on the Thames River.
OPINION: The Thames is the loveliest river in the world.

The first sentence states a fact. You can prove it by using a map, a globe, or an encyclopedia. The second sentence states an opinion. It tells what someone believes.

Certain words can help you recognize an opinion. Words like *I think, best, worst,* and *pretty* can be clues to an opinion. In the example above, *loveliest* is a clue. Since people may disagree about what is lovely, you cannot prove the statement.

Use these guides to help you tell fact from opinion.

Guides for Telling Fact from Opinion

1. Ask yourself whether the information can be proved true.
2. Watch for words such as *I think, best,* and *pretty.* These words are clues to an opinion.

Prewriting Practice

Number your paper from 1 to 6. Beside each number, write *fact* if the sentence states a fact or *opinion* if it states an opinion.

1. Paris is a very exciting city.
2. I think that the bridges over the Seine are pretty.
3. You can take an elevator up the Eiffel Tower.
4. My roof is the best place for gazing at stars.
5. The Alps border France and Italy.
6. Milan is the second largest city in Italy. F

Writing Friendly Letters ☑

You can write letters for different purposes. Sarah's father wrote **friendly letters** to tell his daughter what he was doing and to share his thoughts and feelings. A friendly letter may also be written to persuade someone to do something. In a **persuasive letter,** you must give strong reasons to convince the person to agree with you.

A friendly letter has five parts—the heading, the greeting, the body, the closing, and the signature. Study the five parts in this letter.

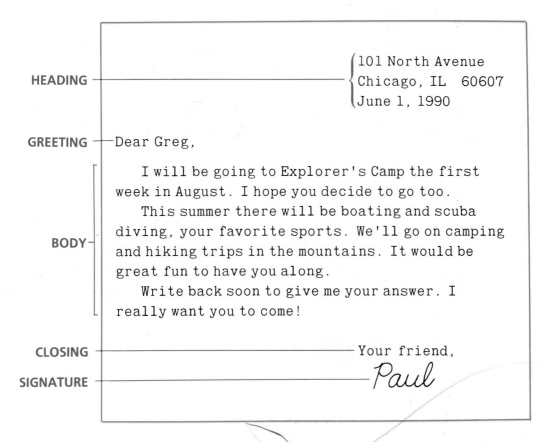

HEADING

101 North Avenue
Chicago, IL 60607
June 1, 1990

GREETING Dear Greg,

BODY

I will be going to Explorer's Camp the first week in August. I hope you decide to go too.

This summer there will be boating and scuba diving, your favorite sports. We'll go on camping and hiking trips in the mountains. It would be great fun to have you along.

Write back soon to give me your answer. I really want you to come!

CLOSING Your friend,

SIGNATURE Paul

1. **Heading:** The first two lines give your complete address. Use the special two-letter abbreviation for your state, followed by the Zip Code. The last line gives the date.

2. **Greeting:** This letter part says "hello" to your reader. It usually includes the word *Dear* and the name of the person to whom you are writing.

3. **Body:** The body is the main part of the letter. It includes all the information you want to tell your reader. Begin a new paragraph for each new idea.

4. **Closing:** This letter part says "good-by" to your reader. Here are some closings you can use: *Your niece, Love, Your friend, Always.*

5. **Signature:** Sign your name. If you are writing to someone you know well, use only your first name.

Prewriting Practice

A. Study the letter parts below. Write a letter by putting the parts in the correct order. When you are finished, label each part.

Your pen pal,   September 19, 1990

Dear Jeanne,   Hartford, CT 06101

81 Locust Street

    School has just started, and we're studying your country, France. Would you please send me a picture of the Eiffel Tower? I need it for a report about Paris.

B. Read Paul's letter to Greg again. List the reasons that Paul gives to persuade his friend to attend camp.

C. What would *you* say to persuade a friend to attend camp with you? Make a list of your reasons.

The Grammar Connection

Using Capital Letters and Commas in Letters

Read Rob's letter. Notice where he used capital letters and commas in the heading, greeting, and closing.

```
                    2300 Seaview Street
                    Palm Springs, CA  92263
                    April 27, 1990

Dear Steve,

    When you visit us this summer, could you
please bring me a badge of the Statue of Liberty?
I would like to have it to add to my collection.
    Thank you.

                    Your pal,
                    Rob
```

Use capital letters and commas correctly in the heading, greeting, and closing of a letter. Study this chart.

Letter Part	Capital Letters	Commas
Heading	Street and city State abbreviation Month	Between city and state Between day and year
Greeting	First word Name of person	After last word
Closing	First word	After last word

Practice Write a letter. Use the body given below. Write your own heading, greeting, closing, and signature. Use capital letters and commas correctly.

Mom and I are planning our San Francisco trip. We'll ride the cable cars and go to the Exploratorium. It would be such fun if you and Aunt Lisa could meet us there!

Writing and Supporting an Opinion ☑

Everyone has opinions. As you have learned, an opinion tells what someone thinks or believes.

Each of these sentences states an opinion:

1. Our class should collect canned goods for poor children in other countries.
2. Everyone should exercise for at least one hour a day.
3. You should visit our city's new museum.

You probably have many opinions of your own. Suppose that you want to persuade, or convince, someone else to agree with your opinion. The best way to do it is to state your opinion and then give strong reasons to support it. When you write a persuasive paragraph, state your opinion in the topic sentence. Then give strong reasons to support it in the other sentences. End with a strong last sentence.

Read these two paragraphs. Both were written for the same purpose. Which one is more persuasive?

1. Our class should collect canned goods for poor children in other countries. The children's families have no money to buy food. It's a good thing to do. The woman who came to speak to our class was nice. It's no fun to be hungry. I know, because I couldn't eat for three days last year. I had my tonsils taken out.

2. Our class should collect canned goods for poor children in other countries. The children's families have no money to buy milk, fruit, and vegetables. Every week, each of us could set aside a little of our allowances to buy canned food. A truck will pick up the canned goods right here at school. If you've ever seen pictures of hungry children, you know how sad they are. Our canned goods could help them to live and to be happy.

The first paragraph is not persuasive. The sentences *The woman who came to speak to our class was nice* and *I couldn't eat for three days last year* may be true, but they are not reasons for collecting canned food. They do not support the opinion. *It's a good thing to do* may also be true, but it is not convincing by itself. To make this a strong reason, the writer must tell *why* collecting food is a good thing to do.

The second paragraph is persuasive. It gives strong reasons that support the opinion. What are these reasons?

When you write a persuasive paragraph, think about your audience. Choose reasons that are important to them. The paragraphs about collecting food were written for a group of students. In the second paragraph, the writer used this reason to persuade an audience of students: *A truck will pick up the canned goods right here at school.* This reason would be important to students because many of them may not have a way to deliver the canned food.

- What other reasons in the second paragraph do you think would be important to students?
- What other reasons can you think of to persuade students to collect canned goods for poor children in other countries?

Prewriting Practice

Write one of the opinions below or an opinion of your own on a piece of paper. Think of an audience, and write it on your paper. Then list three or four reasons that might convince your audience to agree with the opinion.

1. Students should (or should not) go to school twelve months a year.
2. My town needs a new public park.
3. Our class should have a pet hamster.
4. Students should watch less (or more) television.
5. Everyone should learn a foreign language.
6. You should eat whole-grain breads and cereals.

The Writing Process
How to Write a Persuasive Letter

Step 1: Prewriting—Choose a Topic

Mandy listed things her class might like to do. For each idea, she would need to write a letter to the principal for permission. She thought about her list.

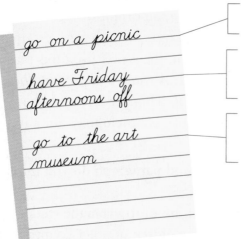

She did not feel strongly about going on a picnic.

She did not have enough strong reasons to convince Mr. Talman, the principal.

Mr. Talman might agree with this idea, since her class was studying artists.

Mandy really wanted to go to the museum, and she had strong reasons for it. She circled that topic.

On Your Own

1. **Think and discuss** What would you like to persuade someone to do? Write a list of topics. Remember, for each topic you will need to persuade someone else that it is worthwhile. Use the Ideas page to help you. Discuss your list with a partner.
2. **Choose** Ask these questions about each topic.
   Do I feel strongly about this?
   Do I have strong reasons to support this opinion?
   Circle the topic you want to write about.
3. **Explore** How will you convince your audience? Do an activity under "Exploring Your Topic" on the Ideas page.

Ideas for Getting Started

Choosing Your Topic

Topic Ideas

My town is the best place to live.

My family should go camping.

I want to take drum lessons.

I should be elected to Student Council.

Everyone should eat balanced meals.

Opinion Starters

Read the sentences and fill in the blanks. Which idea gets *you* started? Whom will you persuade?

I would really like to buy a ____ with my own money.

I wish our class could go to ____.

Everyone should learn to ____.

Exploring Your Topic

Plan It Out

Make a planning chart to help organize your thoughts. Answer these questions: To whom will you write? What action should be taken? Why is it a good idea? Here is Mandy's chart.

Who	Mr. Talman
What	class trip to museum
Why	fun place, will ask parents to go, will raise money

Act It Out

Ask a partner to pretend to be the person to whom you are writing. Try to persuade your partner of your idea. Have your partner tell why he or she might not agree.

Step 2: Write a First Draft

Mandy thought about reasons that would convince Mr. Talman to let her class go to the museum. He would want to know why the class wanted to go to the museum. He also would want to know how the class would arrange the trip. She used her planning chart and wrote her first draft. She did not worry about mistakes. She knew she could correct them later. Here is the body of Mandy's letter.

Part of Mandy's first draft

Think and Discuss ✔

- Why is Mandy's first sentence a good one?
- What are her reasons? Are they strong?
- Why do you think she changed the word *might*?

> ~~We~~ Our class would like to go to the art Museum. It's a fun place. We will ask parents to go with us. We also ~~might~~ plan to raise money to pay for a bus. Do you think these are good reasons to let us go?

On Your Own

1. **Think about purpose and audience** Ask yourself these questions.

   What is the purpose of the letter?

   Whom do I need to persuade?

   What reasons will I use to support my opinion?

2. **Write** Write the first draft of your letter. Remember to keep your audience in mind. Include the five parts of a letter. Write on every other line. Do not worry about mistakes. You can fix them later. Just get your ideas on paper.

Step 3: Revise

Mandy read her first draft. She crossed out one reason that was weak. She added another reason. She put it first because it was the best one. Then she asked Laura to listen to her letter.

Reading and responding

LAURA: The beginning of your letter sounds great. Your first reason is very strong.

MANDY: Do you think Mr. Talman will agree with me?

LAURA: It might help to tell him *how* we'll raise the money.

MANDY: That's a good idea. Is there anything else?

LAURA: The ending sounds sort of weak.

MANDY: I'll try to make it stronger. Thanks!

Mandy made the sentence about raising money more exact. She also changed her last sentence to a statement.

Part of Mandy's revised draft

~~We~~ Our class would like to go to the art Museum. ~~It's a fun place.~~ We will ask parents to go with us. We also ~~might~~ plan to _have a bake sale_ ~~raise money~~ to pay for a bus. _I'm sure you will_ ~~Do you~~ think these are good reasons to let us go? We are studying great artists, and some of their paintings are there.

Think and Discuss ✓

- What reason did Mandy add? Why?
- Why was one reason weak?
- How did she make one sentence more exact?
- Why is the last sentence better?

On Your Own

Revising checklist

- ☑ Does my topic sentence clearly say what I want to be done?
- ☑ Are all reasons in the letter strong and exact?
- ☑ Have I put the strongest reason first?
- ☑ Do I have a strong last sentence to finish the letter?

1. **Revise** Make changes in your first draft. Cross out reasons that are weak. Add reasons that make your letter more convincing. Put your strongest reasons first. Always keep your audience in mind. You may want to use some of the words in the thesaurus below or in the one found at the back of this book.

2. **Have a conference** Read your letter to a classmate or to your teacher.

WRITING CONFERENCE

Ask your listener:	As you listen:
"Is it clear what I want my reader to do?" "Which reasons are strong? weak?" "Are more reasons needed?"	I must listen carefully. Is this letter clear and convincing? Should any reasons be added? Should any be left out?

3. **Revise** Think about your partner's suggestions. Do you have any other ideas? Make other changes to your letter.

Thesaurus

agree consent, approve, comply with
dependable trustworthy, reliable, responsible
do accomplish, achieve, carry out
easy simple, uncomplicated

helpful useful, beneficial
job work, task, employment
let allow, permit
reason cause, explanation
right correct, fitting, suitable, valid
want desire, wish for

Step 4: Proofread

Mandy proofread her letter. She used a dictionary to check spelling. She used proofreading marks to make changes.

Part of Mandy's proofread draft

64 Main rd.

Boise, Id 83708

Feb. 4, 1989

Dear
~~Deer~~ Mr. Talman,

~~We~~ Our class would like to go

to the art Museum. ~~It's a fun place.~~

Think and Discuss

- Which spelling did Mandy correct?
- What punctuation marks did she add? Why?
- What other corrections did she make?

On Your Own

1. **Proofreading Practice** Proofread this letter. There are three errors in spelling, three in punctuation, and one in capitalization. Write the letter correctly.

> 500 Robins Drive
> Atlanta GA   55412
> May 4, 1990

Dear Mr. Stone

    I am starting a lawn mowing servise. I am dependable, and I trim around the hedgs. Call if you would like to hire me.

> your nieghbor
> Monica

Proofreading Marks

⌐P	Indent
∧	Add something
ℓ	Take out something
≡	Capitalize
/	Make a small letter

2. Proofreading Application Now proofread your letter. Use the Proofreading Checklist and the Grammar and Spelling Hints. Use a dictionary to check spelling.

Proofreading Checklist

Did I

☑ **1.** use the correct form for a letter?
☑ **2.** use correct punctuation in all parts of my letter?
☑ **3.** use correct abbreviations?
☑ **4.** spell all words correctly?

The Grammar/Spelling Connection

Grammar Hints

Remember these rules from Unit 9.

• Use commas to separate items in a series. *Josh planned, wrote, and mailed the letter.*
• Begin most abbreviations with capital letters and end them with periods. (*Mr., Nov., Co.*)

Spelling Hints

• The final (j) sound is usually spelled *dge* or *ge.* (*bridge, change*)
• The final (s) sound is often spelled *ce.* (*price*)

Step 5: Publish

Mandy designed her own stationery and copied her letter in her neatest writing. Then she addressed the envelope to Mr. Talman. She wrote his name and the name and address of the school in the center of the envelope. She put her own name and address in the upper left corner. Then she delivered the letter to his office.

On Your Own

1. **Copy** Copy your letter in your neatest handwriting. Address the envelope.
2. **Check** Reread your letter to make sure you have not made any mistakes in copying.
3. **Share** Think of a special way to share your letter. You may want to use some of the ideas from the Ideas for Sharing box.

Ideas for Sharing

- Make a letterhead stamp by cutting a design into a potato or a rubber eraser.
- Produce a radio show with friends. Read the letters "on the air."
- Read your letter to the class. Mail your letter and report on the response.

Literature and Creative Writing

Even though Sarah's father was away from home, the letters he wrote helped her feel close to him. In "Dear Sarah," you read his letters from Milan and Paris, two cities in Europe. In the poem "City," Langston Hughes described the same city at two different times of day.

Have fun using what you have learned about writing letters. Choose one or more of the following activities.

> **Remember these things** ☑
> Include the five parts of a letter.
> Support your opinions with convincing reasons.

1. **Write to the editor.** How can you get more people to visit your city or town? Write a letter to the editor of *Wanderer*, a travel magazine. Convince the thousands of *Wanderer* readers that your city or town is worth visiting.

2. **Persuade Sarah.** Write a letter to Sarah to persuade her that the stars are more beautiful than the moon.

3. **Write to Sarah.** Persuade her to visit you during a summer vacation.

Writing Across the Curriculum
Music

People all over the world enjoy music. One way to share our enjoyment of music is by writing letters.

Choose one or more of the following activities.

1. **Write to a disc jockey.** Radio personalities like to hear from their audience. Write a letter to your favorite disc jockey. Try to persuade the disc jockey to play your favorite record more often.

2. **Write about your music.** The children in the picture are enjoying the traditional music of their country. Write a letter to them. Tell what kind of music you enjoy and why. If you play a musical instrument, tell them what it is and what kind of music you play.

Writing Steps
1. Choose a Topic
2. Write a First Draft
3. Revise
4. Proofread
5. Publish

Word Bank
beat
lyrics
rhythm
melody
harmony
tempo
instruments

3. **Write to a music publisher.** Imagine that you have just written a song. In a letter, persuade the publisher to publish your song. Tell about your song, and explain why you think people will like it. Support your opinion with strong reasons. Send a tape of your song with your letter.

Tim enjoyed reading the letters from *Dear Sarah* by Elisabeth Borchers. He thought it would be great to get letters with poems in them. Tim had been reading the poems in *Where the Sidewalk Ends* by Shel Silverstein. He thought of his friend Pam who liked funny poems. Tim decided to share the book by writing a letter to Pam. He copied a poem on a separate piece of paper and sent it too. This is the letter Tim wrote.

> 2608 Avenue O
> Galveston, TX   77553
> April 12, 1990
>
> Dear Pam,
>
>   I was just thinking of you because I have been reading some of the funniest poems! You would like them. They are in a book of poems called *Where the Sidewalk Ends* by Shel Silverstein. The author did the drawings, too, and they are as funny as the poems. My favorite poem is "Boa Constrictor." Because I know you would like this poem too, I am sending you a copy of it. The other poems are just as good!
>
>   Your friend,
>   *Tim*

Think and Discuss

- What did Tim tell Pam about the book?
- Why did he think Pam would enjoy the book?
- What did Tim do to make Pam want to read this book?

Share Your Book

Write a Letter About a Book

1. Choose a book that you like and that you think a friend will like.
2. In your letter, write the title of the book and the author's name. Underline the title.
3. Tell about one part of the book. Tell enough about it to interest your friend in the book, but do not tell too much.
4. Explain why you liked the book. Tell your friend why you think he or she will enjoy the book.

Other Activities

- Write to the author of a book you like. Thank the author for writing such a good book. You might tell what your favorite part of the book is.
- Think of a book that you enjoyed when you were younger. Write a letter to a young child that you know. Tell what the book is about and why you think the child would enjoy it. Draw pictures in the margins to illustrate your letter.
- Pretend that you are a character in your book. Write a letter to another character. Describe something that happened to you in the book. Tell how you felt about it.

 **The Book Nook**

The First Book of Short Verse *compiled by Coralie Howard* This collection of poems includes some by children.	**There Is No Rhyme for Silver** *by Eve Merriam* This is a book of poems that play with words and make jokes with rhyme.

But still, no matter what we do,
We never have a fuss,
And so I guess it must be true
That *we* belong to *us*.

Arthur Guiterman, from "Chums"

Pronouns

Getting Ready When you talk and write, you use pronouns as a short cut to stand for the names of people and things. The words *I, you, she, he, it, we, they, me, her, him, us,* and *them* are pronouns. In this unit, you will learn how to use pronouns correctly.

ACTIVITIES

Listening   Listen as the poem on the opposite page is read. Can you hear four different pronouns? What are they?

Speaking   Look at the picture. Talk about the picture. Use sentences with pronouns. Try to use pronouns to talk about the boat, dog, water, boy, and fishing rod. Have someone write your sentences on the board and underline the pronouns.

Writing   In your journal, write about a day you spent with a friend.

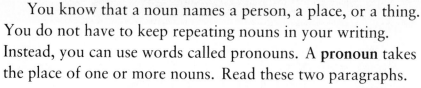

1 | What Is a Pronoun?

them

Jack collects shells.

You know that a noun names a person, a place, or a thing. You do not have to keep repeating nouns in your writing. Instead, you can use words called pronouns. A **pronoun** takes the place of one or more nouns. Read these two paragraphs.

Sara asked Jack and Leah to go to the seashore with Sara. Sara, Jack, and Leah spoke to Ms. Lanski. Ms. Lanski gave Sara, Jack, and Leah a special book. The book was about sea life.

Sara asked Jack and Leah to go to the seashore with her . They spoke to Ms. Lanski. She gave them a special book. It was about sea life.

What pronoun takes the place of the noun *Sara* in the first sentence of the second paragraph? What pronoun replaces *Sara, Jack, and Leah* in the second sentence?

Like the nouns they replace, pronouns are singular or plural. Look at the lists below. Notice that the pronoun *you* can be either singular or plural.

SINGULAR PRONOUNS: I, me, you, he, him, she, her, it
  PLURAL PRONOUNS: we, us, you, they, them

Guided Practice Which words in these sentences are pronouns? Is each pronoun singular or plural?

Example: Sara said, "Come with me to the seashore."
                me   singular

1. Leah carried a pail. She wanted to collect shells.
2. Jack took a notebook. Sara had asked him to take notes.
3. As the children walked along, they looked carefully.
4. Leah saw a starfish. Jack wrote about it in the book.
5. "You are good scientists," Sara told Leah and Jack.

▶ A **pronoun** is a word that replaces one or more nouns.
▶ A pronoun can be singular or plural.

Independent Practice Write the pronoun in each sentence that takes the place of the underlined word or words.

Example: <u>Ben</u> said, "I found a large pink shell."   *I*

6. Sara told <u>Ben</u>, "Listen to the shell. What do you hear?"
7. Ben heard <u>a noise</u>. It sounded like the ocean.
8. "Do you want to listen?" Ben asked <u>Sara and Leah</u>.
9. "Yes, please. Give the shell to me," said <u>Leah</u>.
10. Sara told <u>Ben</u> that he had found a queen conch shell.
11. "Tell us about the queen conch," begged <u>Ben and Leah</u>.
12. <u>The conch</u> is a kind of snail. It lives in the sea.
13. <u>That shell</u> is empty. The snail is no longer in it.
14. Once there were many of <u>the snails</u>. Now they are rare.
15. <u>Scientists</u> try to save the conch. Students help them.
16. <u>Marta</u> is a scientist. She works to save the conch.
17. <u>Roberto</u> is a student. He helps Marta.
18. Marta collects <u>conch eggs</u> and puts them in big tanks.
19. <u>Roberto</u> studies the eggs. He writes in a notebook.
20. Marta feeds <u>the young snails</u>. They eat tiny plants.
21. <u>Marta</u> asks Roberto to help her with the feeding.
22. One day Marta calls <u>Roberto</u> and tells him to take the snails back to the sea.
23. <u>The snails</u> are big now. They can live in the ocean.
24. <u>Ben and Leah</u> said, "We are glad the conch is being saved."

Writing Application: Creative Writing
Pretend that you found a conch shell and held it to your ear. Imagine that instead of the sound of the ocean, you heard a voice. What did the voice say? Write a paragraph telling what the voice said to you. Use at least five pronouns.

For Extra Practice, see p. 341.   **What Is a Pronoun?   323**

2 | Subject Pronouns

You have learned that a pronoun can take the place of a noun. Like a noun, a pronoun can be used as the subject of a sentence. Remember that the subject tells whom or what the sentence is about.

Juan   Lola

W E

NOUNS

Juan did a project on insects.

Lola worked with Juan.

Juan and Lola gave a report.

Vin and I enjoyed the report.

PRONOUNS

He did a project on insects.

She worked with Juan.

They gave a report.

We enjoyed the report.

Not all pronouns can be used as subjects. Only the **subject pronouns** I, *you, he, she, it, we,* and *they* can be used as the subjects of sentences.

Subject Pronouns	
Singular	**Plural**
I	we
you	you
he, she, it	they

Guided Practice Which subject pronoun could take the place of the underlined word or words in each sentence?

Example: Matt said to Barb, "Barb found a ladybug."   *You*

1. Matt and I know that ladybugs are helpful insects.
2. Matt told Barb more about ladybugs.
3. Ladybugs are not really bugs. Ladybugs are beetles.
4. This beetle eats insects that destroy plants.
5. Barb did not disturb the ladybug.
6. Barb said, "Barb should not hurt such a helpful insect."

> ▶ I, *you*, *he*, *she*, *it*, *we*, and *they* are **subject pronouns**.
> ▶ Use only subject pronouns as the subjects of sentences.

Independent Practice

A. Write the subject pronoun in each sentence.

Example: I think butterflies are beautiful. *I*

   7. They drink a sweet liquid from flowers.
   8. It is called nectar.
   9. You may see butterflies in the garden in summer.
   10. We read a good book about butterflies.
   11. Last week Joan and I saw a huge butterfly.
   12. She asked Henry to come and see the butterfly too.

B. Write each sentence. Use a subject pronoun in place of the underlined word or words.

Example: Joan and I read the book. *We read the book.*

   13. The book listed the stages in a butterfly's life.
   14. Henry learned that the first stage is an egg.
   15. Next, the egg hatches into a caterpillar.
   16. Joan said that the third stage is the pupa.
   17. The caterpillar spins a hard shell.
   18. When this shell cracks, a butterfly comes out.

Writing Application: Riddles

Question: Why did the horse jump out of the window?
 Answer: It wanted to be a horsefly.

   Many insect names are used in riddles. Choose five names from the Word Box or think of others. Write a riddle for each name. Use a subject pronoun in the question or the answer.

| butterfly | potato bug | inchworm | carpenter ant |
| dragonfly | ladybug | firefly | yellow jacket |

For Extra Practice, see p. 342.
 Subject Pronouns 325

3 Object Pronouns

You know that subject pronouns may be used as the subjects of sentences. The pronouns *me, you, him, her, it, us,* and *them* are called **object pronouns**. Object pronouns follow action verbs and words such as *to, with, for,* and *at.*

Joanna   Mabel

Please feed them carrots.

NOUNS	PRONOUNS
Ms. Rossi fed the horses .	Ms. Rossi fed them .
Sal helped Ms. Rossi .	Sal helped her .
Sal showed a pony to Ed and me .	Sal showed a pony to us .
Then Sal gave the pony a carrot.	Then Sal gave it a carrot.

Object Pronouns	
Singular	**Plural**
me	us
you	you
him, her, it	them

Never use the object pronouns *me, him, her, us,* and *them* as subjects. You can use the pronouns *you* and *it* as either subject or object pronouns.

Guided Practice
Which object pronoun could take the place of the underlined word or words in each sentence?

Example: Sally rides <u>horses</u> every day.   *them*

1. Ed said to Sally, "Please teach <u>Ed</u>."
2. Sally took Ed to the stable with <u>Sally</u>.
3. Sally told Ed, "I will teach <u>Ed</u> grooming first."
4. She handed a brush to <u>Ed</u>.
5. Then Sally and Ed brushed <u>the horse</u>.
6. Ed said, "The horse likes <u>Sally and Ed</u>."

> ▶ *Me, you, him, her, it, us,* and *them* are **object pronouns**.
> ▶ Use object pronouns after action verbs and words such as *to, with, for,* and *at.*

Independent Practice

A. Write the object pronoun in each sentence.

Example: I asked Sally to take Ed and me to the stable. *me*

   7. Ed's little brother Raul came with us.
   8. Sally's father drove her to the stable.
   9. We took the bus. We waited a long time for it.
   10. Ms. Rossi greeted us at the stable.
   11. She said, "I am so glad to see you."
   12. The horses are in the barn. Please brush them.
   13. I carefully brushed a horse and saddled it.

B. Write each sentence. Use an object pronoun in place of the underlined word or words.

Example: Ms. Rossi handed <u>Ed and me</u> hard hats.
   Ms. Rossi handed us hard hats.

   14. She said, "You must wear <u>these hats</u>."
   15. Raul led a pony into the ring and patted <u>the pony</u>.
   16. Ms. Rossi lifted <u>Raul</u> onto the pony's back.
   17. Pick up the reins and hold <u>the reins</u> like this.
   18. Ms. Rossi gave <u>Ed, Raul, and me</u> a riding lesson.
   19. We thanked <u>Ms. Rossi</u> for the lesson.
   20. We said that we had enjoyed <u>the lesson</u>.

Writing Application: Writing About Yourself
What have you learned to do well? How did you learn to do it?
Write a story about something that you have learned to do well
or something that you would like to learn to do well. Use at
least five object pronouns.

For Extra Practice, see p. 343.

4 | Using *I* and *me*

When you talk or write about yourself, you use the pronoun *I* or *me*. Do you ever have trouble deciding whether to use *I* or *me* with another noun or pronoun? For example, should you say, *Kim and me study* or *Kim and I study*? One way to check is to say the sentence to yourself with only *I* or *me*.

Kim and I study.   I study.

Mrs. Perez teaches Kim and me .   Mrs. Perez teaches me .

Ali studies with Kim and me .   Ali studies with me .

Remember to use *I* as the subject of a sentence. Use *me* after action verbs and after words such as *to*, *with*, *for*, and *at*.

When you talk about yourself and another person, always name yourself last.

INCORRECT: I and Kim help Ali. Ali thanks me and Kim.

CORRECT: Kim and I help Ali. Ali thanks Kim and me .

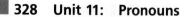

Kim and   I   set the   table .

Guided Practice Which words complete each sentence correctly?

Example: (Jen and I, I and Jen) met Maria. *Jen and I*

1. Maria invited (me and Jen, Jen and me) to her house.
2. (I and Jen, Jen and I) walked home with Maria.
3. Maria talked to (Jen and me, me and Jen) about Mexico.
4. Jen and (I, me) were very interested.
5. Maria helped prepare dinner for Jen and (I, me).
6. Jen and (I, me) ate with Maria's family.
7. The food tasted wonderful to Jen and (I, me).

> ▶ Use the pronoun *I* as the subject of a sentence.
> ▶ Use the pronoun *me* after action verbs and words such as *to*, *with*, *for*, and *at*.
> ▶ When you use the pronoun *I* or *me* with another noun or pronoun, always name yourself last.

Independent Practice

A. Write the words that correctly complete each sentence.

Example: (Sid and I, I and Sid) visited Mexico.   *Sid and I*

   8. Sid came with (me and my family, my family and me).
   9. (I and Sid, Sid and I) sat together on the plane.
   10. (Sid and I, I and Sid) became friends with Rosita.
   11. She took (Sid and me, me and Sid) on a tour.
   12. (I and he, He and I) learned about Mexico City.
   13. Rosita taught (Sid and me, me and Sid) Spanish words.

B. Write each sentence using *I* or *me*.

Example: My cousin and ____ admired the city.
   My cousin and I admired the city.

   14. Rosita took Sid and ____ to the National Palace.
   15. "Our president works here," she told Sid and ____.
   16. Sid and ____ cried, "What a beautiful building!"
   17. Then Rosita took Sid and ____ to the marketplace.
   18. She bought food for my cousin and ____.
   19. Sid and ____ bought a present for our grandmother.
   20. Sid and ____ will write to Rosita when we get home.

Writing Application: A Letter

Pretend that you and your family have just returned from visiting friends in another state or another country. Write a letter thanking the friends. Write about some things you did during the visit, and tell what you liked best. Be sure to use the pronouns *I* and *me* correctly.

For Extra Practice, see p. 344.

5 | Possessive Pronouns

You have learned that possessive nouns show ownership. You can use pronouns in place of possessive nouns. A pronoun that shows ownership is a **possessive pronoun**.

POSSESSIVE NOUNS	POSSESSIVE PRONOUNS
Pamela feeds Pamela's pet.	Pamela feeds her pet.
She fills the pet's dish.	She fills its dish.
The boys' gerbil is playful.	Their gerbil is playful.

Possessive Pronouns

Singular	Plural
my	our
your	your
her, his, its	their

Guided Practice Which possessive pronoun should you use in place of the underlined word or words?

Example: Max and I help Mr. Lee at Mr. Lee's shop.   *his*

1. Max likes Max's job at the pet store.
2. He gives the puppies the puppies' food.
3. Agnes is saving Agnes's money for a pet.
4. She will buy the parakeet and the parakeet's cage.
5. Agnes, you and Agnes's sister will like the parakeet.

Summing up

▸ A **possessive pronoun** may be used in place of a possessive noun to show ownership.

▸ *My, your, her, his, its, our,* and *their* are possessive pronouns.

Independent Practice

A. Write the possessive pronoun in each sentence.

Example: My favorite animal is the llama. *My*

6. Its close relative is the camel.
7. People use llamas to carry their packs.
8. A llama will lie down if its pack is too heavy.
9. An angry llama will spit at its owner.
10. People in our country are using llamas too.
11. Sheep ranchers use llamas to guard their flocks.
12. One man in Nebraska raises llamas on his ranch.

B. Use a possessive pronoun in place of the underlined word or words in each sentence. Write the sentences.

Example: Ranchers use dogs to guard ranchers' sheep.
Ranchers use dogs to guard their sheep.

13. Mr. Lye wanted a different kind of animal to guard Mr. Lye's sheep.
14. Mr. and Mrs. Lye bought a llama for Mr. and Mrs. Lye's ranch.
15. The llama's name is Harold.
16. Harold runs fast on Harold's long legs.
17. Adam and Adam's sister Beth visit the ranch.
18. The Lyes are Adam and Beth's grandparents.
19. Mrs. Lye shows Harold to Mrs. Lye's grandchildren.
20. Harold lets the children ride on Harold's back.
21. The Lyes are very happy with the Lyes' llama.
22. Harold seems to be happy with Harold's job too.

Writing Application: An Advertisement

Llamas carry packs in South America and guard sheep in the United States. What is another job for a llama? Pretend that you have a llama for sale. Write an advertisement. Tell what your llama can do. Try to make people want to buy it. The ad can be funny or serious. Use at least five possessive pronouns.

For Extra Practice, see p. 345.   **Possessive Pronouns   331**

6 | Contractions with Pronouns

You have learned that a contraction is the combined form of two words. A contraction may be formed by combining a pronoun and a verb. Use an apostrophe (') in place of the letter or letters that are left out.

Study this chart of contractions formed from pronouns.

Pronoun and verb	Contraction	Pronoun and verb	Contraction
I am	I'm	I have	I've
he is	he's	he has	he's
she is	she's	she has	she's
it is	it's	it has	it's
you are	you're	you have	you've
we are	we're	we have	we've
they are	they're	they have	they've
I will	I'll	I had	I'd
you will	you'll	you had	you'd
she will	she'll	he had	he'd
they will	they'll	we had	we'd

Look at the chart again. Notice what letter or letters were left out to form each contraction. Notice also that the contractions *he's*, *she's*, and *it's* are listed twice. The contractions for the pronouns *he*, *she*, and *it* with the verbs *is* and *has* are the same.

Guided Practice What is the contraction for each of the following pairs of words?

Example: he is *he's*

1. I had
2. she will
3. he had
4. we have
5. they will
6. she has
7. you have
8. it has

▶ Pronouns and verbs may be combined to form contractions.
▶ Use an apostrophe (') in place of letters that are left out.

Independent Practice

A. Write the two words for each underlined contraction.

Example: It's time for our club's dinner.   *It is*

9. We're going to have a potluck supper.
10. We've each planned to make something different.
11. We hope you'll bring your famous banana bread.
12. It's sure to be a big hit.
13. The twins said they'll bring chicken soup.
14. They're experts at making chicken soup.
15. Lori said she'll come early to decorate the hall.
16. She's planning to bring vegetables and dip.

B. Write the contraction for each underlined word.

Example: I will make lasagna and salad.   *I'll*

17. Tom said that he is coming over to help me.
18. He has made lasagna many times.
19. You are using the wrong pot for the sauce.
20. It is not big enough.
21. You have poured sauce all over the floor!
22. I forgot to watch the noodles. They have stuck to the pan.
23. It has been quite an evening!
24. I am never going to make lasagna again!

Writing Application: Instructions

Write a paragraph giving instructions for making your favorite kind of salad. Use at least five contractions from the chart on page 332. You might begin like this:

You're going to learn to make the best salad in the world.

For Extra Practice, see p. 346.

7 | Pronouns and Homophones

You know that homophones are words that sound alike but have different spellings and meanings. Writers often confuse some contractions and their homophones because these words sound alike. Study the chart below. Learn the spelling and the meaning of each homophone.

Homophone	Meaning	Sentence
it's	it is	It's a beautiful bird!
its	belonging to it	Take its picture.
they're	they are	They're odd birds.
their	belonging to them	Their wings are big!
there	in that place	There is another.
you're	you are	You're very lucky.
your	belonging to you	Get your camera.

Guided Practice Which word would you use to complete each sentence correctly?

Example: I hear (you're, your) entering the photo contest.   *you're*

1. Which of (you're, your) pictures will you enter?
2. (They're, There) all so good!
3. The puppies love having (they're, their) picture taken.
4. The picture (their, there) on your desk is interesting.
5. (It's, Its) colors are sharp and clear.
6. (It's, Its) hard to choose the best one!

Summing up

▶ Do not confuse the contractions *it's, they're,* and *you're* with their homophones *its, their, there,* and *your.*

Independent Practice Choose the word that completes each sentence correctly. Write the sentences.

Example: (It's, Its) a great day for taking pictures.
It's a great day for taking pictures.

7. Ricky and Marge have packed (their, they're) cameras.
8. (Their, They're) going to take pictures in the woods.
9. (You're, Your) invited to join them.
10. (There, They're) is a little striped chipmunk.
11. (It's, Its) the smallest member of the squirrel family.
12. (It's, Its) little cheeks are all puffed out.
13. (They're, Their) filled with nuts.
14. The chipmunk is gathering (it's, its) winter food.
15. Chipmunks store (there, their) nuts underground.
16. Can you hear (they're, their) chirping sound?
17. (You're, Your) right. They sound like birds.
18. Where is (you're, your) camera?
19. The chipmunk is still sitting (their, there).
20. You can take (it's, its) picture.
21. (You're, Your) taking a lot of good pictures.
22. They will really add to (you're, your) collection.
23. A red squirrel is over (they're, there) on that tree.
24. (It's, Its) a relative of the chipmunk.
25. (Their, There) are two more squirrels.
26. You should take (their, there) picture too.
27. (There, They're) go the squirrels!
28. (Their, They're) certainly not going to stand still for (you're, your) picture!

Writing Application: A Story

Finish the following story:

> The twins were glad they had their cameras with them that day. Otherwise, no one would have believed what happened.

Use at least five homophones from the chart in this lesson. Give your story an interesting title.

For Extra Practice, see p. 347. **Pronouns and Homophones 335**

Grammar-Writing Connection

Writing Well with Pronouns

Readers can be confused when too many pronouns are used in a paragraph. The writing can get choppy and boring. The reader may forget what or whom the writer is talking about.

> The gray wolf is the biggest wild dog in North America. It can weigh more than one hundred pounds. It is a strong runner, and it is very fast. It can run twenty miles an hour. It likes wide open spaces.

In the paragraph above, the gray wolf is named only once. The pronoun *it* is used five times. Look at the fourth sentence. A good writer might use this sentence instead:

> The gray wolf can run twenty miles an hour.

This change reminds the reader what the paragraph is about.

Revising Sentences

Rewrite these paragraphs. Replace pronouns that are unclear or are used too often.

1. Have you ever heard a coyote howl? It is famous for its lonesome-sounding cry. It is a member of the dog family, and it lives in Canada and Alaska. It also lives in many other parts of the United States.
2. Black bears are the smallest bears in the United States. They are also the most common. They weigh about two hundred to three hundred pounds, and they are about five feet in length. They live in wooded areas of North America.
3. The bobcat is sometimes called a wildcat or a bay lynx. It has a reddish-brown coat with darker spots and lines. It will climb trees to look for food. It lives in southern Canada, the United States, and northern Mexico.

Creative Writing

Trail Riders by Thomas Hart Benton
The National Gallery of Art, Washington

Can you find the trail riders among the mountains? They are hard to spot. *Trail Riders* is more a portrait of the mountains than of the people. Thomas Hart Benton loved the American landscape. He painted many views of the West and Middle West.

- What gives this picture a cool, fresh feeling?
- How do the trail riders contrast with the mountains?

Activities

1. **Write a story.** Who are these riders? Where are they traveling? Write a story about the trail riders.
2. **Write a postcard.** Imagine that you are camping in these mountains. You can see this view from your tent. Write a postcard describing the view to a friend.

Check-up: Unit 11

What Is a Pronoun? *(p. 322)* Write the pronoun in each sentence that replaces the underlined word or words.

1. Gary and Ana went to the aquarium. They saw many fish.
2. A white shark was swimming in a tank. It is the most dangerous kind of shark.
3. Many people watched the shark. The shark swam by them.
4. Sharks have many teeth. They are very long and sharp.
5. Ana said, "I don't like sharks."
6. Ana went to another tank. Gary followed her.
7. The penguins had a funny walk. Ana laughed at them.
8. A penguin is an unusual bird. It is an excellent swimmer.
9. Ana called to Gary. She pointed out the penguins.
10. Gary laughed at the penguins. He said the penguins looked like little people in black coats.
11. A penguin has short wings. They look like flippers.
12. Gary and Ana said, "We can buy a poster of the penguins."
13. Ana asked Gary, "Do you have enough money for a poster?"

Subject Pronouns *(p. 324)* Write each sentence. Use a subject pronoun in place of the underlined word or words.

14. Birds have very interesting habits.
15. My uncle and I watch birds.
16. Uncle Bill and Aunt Jenny joined a birdwatchers' club.
17. Aunt Jenny takes pictures of birds.
18. The camera has a special lens.
19. Uncle Bill and Aunt Jenny bring the pictures to their club meetings.
20. The pictures help other members learn about different birds.
21. Aunt Jenny and I write the names of the birds in a notebook.
22. The notebook is very full now.

Object Pronouns *(p. 326)* Write each sentence. Use object pronouns for the underlined words.

23. Mark took May and me riding.
24. May asked Mark for help.
25. Mark gave May a horse.
26. I gave a saddle to May.
27. She put a pad under the saddle.
28. The horse suddenly backed away from May and Mark.
29. Mark spoke softly to the horse.
30. The horse stood still for Mark.
31. May smiled at Mark and me.

Using *I* and *me* *(p. 328)* **Choose the word or words that complete each sentence correctly. Then write the sentences.**

32. (Jeff and I, I and Jeff) visited Mr. Vega's kitchen.
33. The chef gave a lesson to (Jeff and me, me and Jeff).
34. He taught (him and me, me and him) how to make tortillas.
35. Jeff and (I, me) rolled the dough into pancakes.
36. It was hard for Jeff and (I, me).
37. The chef and (I, me) filled the pancakes with beans and cheese.
38. Mr. Vega gave my friend and (I, me) some tortillas for lunch.

Possessive Pronouns *(p. 330)* **Write each sentence. Use a possessive pronoun in place of the underlined word or words.**

39. A llama looks like a small camel without the camel's hump.
40. For many years, people have made blankets from the llama's wool.
41. Peru's craft workers sell the workers' colorful woven goods.
42. My brother spent my brother's allowance on a scarf from Peru.
43. He gave the scarf to Alice for Alice's birthday.
44. My brother and sister collected pottery on my brother and sister's trip to Peru.

Contractions with Pronouns *(p. 332)* **Write the contraction for the underlined words in each sentence.**

45. We are learning about different kinds of food in class.
46. I am cooking with new foods.
47. I have cooked corn and squash.
48. You will be surprised at what I did with them.
49. I had asked my mother for advice.
50. She has taught me how to steam all kinds of vegetables.
51. They will taste better that way.
52. They are very good for you.

Pronouns and Homophones *(p. 334)* **Write each sentence. Use the correct word for each sentence.**

53. Parrots have many colors in (there, their) feathers.
54. (You're, Your) parrot is so pretty!
55. (It's, Its) name is Hector.
56. The bird likes (it's, its) name.
57. A parrot like Hector can repeat (you're, your) words.
58. (You're, Your) speaking like him!
59. Did you ever see parrots do (their, there) tricks?
60. (They're, There) very clever tricks.
61. (It's, Its) fun to talk to parrots.
62. (They're, Their) very friendly.
63. (Their, There) is a sale on parrots at the pet store.
64. Would you like to have (you're, your) own parrot?

Enrichment

Using Pronouns

Mysterious Pronouns

Most mystery stories have a crime, a detective, and suspects—people who may have done the crime. Pretend you are a detective. You are to find a merry-go-round horse that has disappeared. You have narrowed down the search to five suspects. Describe these five people. Use pronouns in each description and underline them.

Homophone Book

Use four sheets of paper for pages. On one, write your name and *Homophone Book*. On each other page, write a sentence using a set of homophones. Make pages for *it's, its; your, you're;* and *they're, their, there.* Underline the homophones.

You're lucky to have your umbrella with you today.

Draw a picture for each sentence. Staple the pages together.

I or Me?

Will you sit beside____?

Yesterday ____ ran one mile.

Players—3. **You need**—game board, markers, 30 index cards. Draw a game board like the one here. On 10 cards, each player writes 10 sentences, using *I* or *me* in each sentence but leaving a blank for the pronoun. **How to play**—Mix the cards. Pile them face down. One player reads a card and says *I* or *me* to complete the sentence. If correct with *I*, the player moves to the next space marked *I*. If correct with *me*, the player moves to the next space marked *me*. If incorrect, the player does not move. The first to reach *Finish* wins.

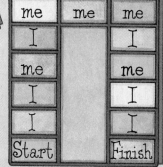

Extra Practice: Unit 11

1 | What Is a Pronoun? (p. 322)

● Write the pronoun in each sentence.

Example: Jane asked Dad to tell her about walruses. *her*

1. "Sandy and I have never seen a walrus," Jane added.
2. "What would you like to know?" Dad asked.
3. "We want to know what a walrus looks like," said Jane.
4. "A big walrus can weigh as much as a ton," he said.
5. "Please show us a picture," begged Jane.
6. Dad showed them a photograph of a walrus.
7. "Its big teeth are called tusks," said Dad.

▲ Write each pronoun. Tell whether it is singular or plural.

Example: Rays are related to sharks, but they look quite different from sharks. *they plural*

8. Here is a picture of a ray. It has a flat body.
9. "Please show me that picture," said Marco.
10. Some rays are dangerous. People get stung by them.
11. "I once saw a stingray at the beach," Kate said.
12. "What do you know about stingrays?" Tim asked Kate.
13. Kate said she knew that stingrays have poisonous tails.
14. "We would not want to get stung," Tim and Marco said.
15. "Then you should be careful," Kate told Tim and Marco.

■ (16–25) Write each pronoun and the word or words that it stands for.

Example: "Dolores and I know a lot about sea horses," said Luis.

       I Luis

    "Sea horses are strange-looking little sea animals," he told Pete.

    "A sea horse has a head like a horse's," Dolores said. "It has a pouch like a kangaroo's," she continued.

    "Can you tell me how long a sea horse is?" Pete asked her.

    "I can tell you," Dolores said to him. "It is about five inches."

● ▲ ■ **Three levels of practice   341**

2 | Subject Pronouns (p. 324)

● Write the subject pronoun in each sentence.
   Example: You must come and see the ant farm. *You*
   1. We set up the ant farm with Ms. Walton's help.
   2. She has had ant farms before.
   3. It is in the back of the classroom.
   4. Mark likes ants, and he takes care of the farm.
   5. We study the ants every day.
   6. They live inside the big plastic case.
   7. You can see the ants working busily.
   8. I like to watch the ants building tunnels and rooms.

▲ Write each sentence. Use a subject pronoun in place of the underlined word or words. Underline the subject pronoun.
   Example: Ants live in nests that the ants build.
            Ants live in nests that they build.
   9. The nests may be above ground or underground.
   10. Eli and I found an ant's nest.
   11. Eli said that an ant's nest is called a colony.
   12. A colony is a very orderly place.
   13. Eli said to Peg, "Peg will be interested in the nest."
   14. Peg was surprised at how many ants were in the colony.

■ Write each subject pronoun and tell whether it is singular or plural. Write the word or words that the pronoun stands for.
   Example: Jay and Amy were walking. They disturbed some bees.
            They   plural   Jay and Amy
   15. Amy, you just stepped on a bee's nest.
   16. Amy and Jay said, "We should be more careful."
   17. Later they talked about bees and bees' nests.
   18. "I think honeybees' nests are in trees," Amy said.
   19. They are the only bees that give honey.
   20. Jay said he had read that bumblebees nest underground.
   21. Amy said she had seen a movie about bumblebees.
   22. It showed the bees making nests in old mouse holes.

3 | Object Pronouns (p. 326)

● Write the object pronoun in each sentence.

Example: The Clarks bought the farm next door to us.   *us*

1. Sally and Chip visited us yesterday.
2. Chip showed me a beautiful horse named Sunny.
3. I fed him an apple.
4. He ate it in one bite.
5. Chip hitches him to a big sled in the winter.
6. Sally and Chip will take us for a ride sometime.
7. You will like them very much.

▲ Write each sentence. Use an object pronoun in place of the underlined word or words. Underline the object pronoun.

Example: Liz asked <u>Dan</u> about horses.
          Liz asked <u>him</u> about horses.

8. Dan knows a lot about <u>horses</u>.
9. He told <u>Liz</u> that there are about sixty kinds of horses.
10. Horses have long legs that help <u>the horses</u> run fast.
11. A horse will run if anything scares <u>the horse</u>.
12. Dan asked Liz, "What else can I tell <u>Liz</u> about horses?"
13. Liz asked, "Will you show <u>Liz</u> your new horse now?"
14. Liz told <u>Dan</u> she wanted to know what horses eat.

■ Write each pronoun. Write *subject* if it is a subject pronoun and *object* if it is an object pronoun.

Example: Draft horses are very large. Farmers use them for heavy
          work. *them   object*

15. You also see them in circuses and parades.
16. We went to a parade with draft horses in it.
17. People rode bareback and did tricks on them.
18. One huge horse had a woman on it.
19. It walked along very steadily for her.
20. "She stood on it and did somersaults," Hal said.
21. "Then the horse bowed to me," he added.
22. Ray and Mindy said, "Please take us with you next time."

4 | Using *I* and *me* (p. 328)

● Copy the sentence that is correct in each pair.

Example: My sister and I have a friend named Ian.
         I and my sister have a friend named Ian.
         My sister and I have a friend named Ian.

  1. I and my friend have never met.
     My friend and I have never met.

  2. Ian writes to Kara and me from Scotland.
     Ian writes to me and Kara from Scotland.

  3. Ian and I are the same age.
     I and Ian are the same age.

  4. Ian and me both like to play soccer.
     Ian and I both like to play soccer.

  5. I sent Ian pictures of Kara and me.
     I sent Ian pictures of Kara and I.

▲ Use *I* or *me* to complete each sentence. Write the sentences.

Example: Kara and ＿＿＿ went to visit our pen pal.
        Kara and I went to visit our pen pal.

  6. Ian met Kara and ＿＿＿ at the airport in Scotland.
  7. He asked her and ＿＿＿ what we wanted to do in Scotland.
  8. Kara told Ian and ＿＿＿ she wanted to see Loch Ness.
  9. She and ＿＿＿ had read about this lake's famous monster.
  10. Kara and ＿＿＿ asked Ian where Loch Ness is.
  11. Ian showed her and ＿＿＿ a map.

■ Write each incorrect sentence correctly and write *correct* for each sentence that has no errors.

Example: Ian took I and Kara fishing on the lake.
        Ian took Kara and me fishing on the lake.

  12. Kara caught a fish, but Ian and I did not.
  13. Ian told Kara and I about a nearby castle.
  14. I and Kara asked him to take us there.
  15. My sister and me had never seen a real castle.
  16. Kara and I learned that the castle is now a museum.

5 | Possessive Pronouns (p. 330)

● Write the possessive pronoun in each sentence.
Example: Roger enjoyed his book about llamas. *his*
1. Their soft wool was black and brown.
2. My friend Beth saw a statue of a gold llama in a museum.
3. Her guide said that the Inca people had made the statue.
4. These people made their homes in what is now Peru.
5. Our teacher told Beth how these people used the llama.
6. People used its wool to make clothing.
7. Llamas carried their heavy loads across the mountains.

▲ Write each sentence. Use a possessive pronoun to take the place of the underlined word or words.
Example: Mark showed us <u>Mark's</u> new alpaca shirt.
         Mark showed us his new alpaca shirt.
8. <u>Mark's</u> brother Dom has one just like it.
9. <u>Cheryl's</u> sister said that alpacas are related to llamas.
10. People of ancient Peru wove <u>the alpaca's</u> wool.
11. Only <u>the people's</u> royal family could wear alpaca cloth.
12. <u>Mark and Dom's</u> uncle bought the shirts in Peru.
13. Uncle George spent <u>Uncle George's</u> vacation there.

■ (14–20) Copy the paragraph. Replace the possessive nouns with possessive pronouns.
Example: Elena wrote Elena's report about the vicuña.
         Elena wrote her report about the vicuña.
    A vicuña looks something like a llama. It is a llama's smaller relative. The vicuña's home is in South America. Vicuñas' babies are able to run soon after the babies' birth. The vicuña's wool is brownish-red and very valuable. The animals had almost disappeared from the countries of South America. Then the countries' governments made a law protecting vicuñas. Over sixty years ago, a man named Señor Parades used Señor Parades's own land as a place for vicuñas to live in safety.

● ▲ ■ **Three levels of practice**   345

6 | Contractions with Pronouns (p. 332)

● Write the contraction in each sentence.

Example: I'm having a birthday next week.   *I'm*

1. I've invited some friends for dinner.
2. You're invited to come too.
3. You'll love what my sister makes.
4. She's the best cook in our whole family.
5. I hope that she'll make her famous shrimp dish.
6. It's my favorite thing to eat.
7. Sandra said she's going to come too.
8. We're going to eat around six o'clock.

▲ Write each sentence. Use a contraction in place of the underlined words.

Example: <u>We are</u> planning a special meal for our parents.
        We're planning a special meal for our parents.

9. <u>They are</u> celebrating their fifteenth wedding anniversary.
10. Fran and I hope <u>they will</u> be surprised.
11. <u>I am</u> going shopping with Fran now.
12. <u>She has</u> made a list.
13. <u>She is</u> taking a cooking course after school.
14. <u>It has</u> helped her learn how to shop for food.
15. <u>It is</u> going to be Mom and Dad's best anniversary ever!

■ Write each sentence. Use contractions whenever possible to take the place of pronouns and verbs.

Example: You are sure to enjoy the farmers' market.
        You're sure to enjoy the farmers' market.

16. It is the best place to buy fresh fruits and vegetables.
17. We are going with my parents.
18. They have been shopping there for years.
19. We will be able to buy fresh string beans.
20. They are my favorite vegetable.
21. I hope that you have brought your camera.
22. I am sure that you will get some good shots.

7 | Pronouns and Homophones (p. 334)

● Write the words in each pair of sentences that sound the same but have different spellings and meanings.

Example: I picked up your pictures at the drugstore.
            You're in for a real treat.   *your   You're*

1. They're great pictures of our trip.
   There are some pictures of our hike in the woods.
2. Look! It's a red fox!
   How did you ever get its picture?
3. My sister says they're very shy.
   It is not easy to see them outside their dens.
4. Your sister is right.
   You're looking at a lucky photographer!

▲ Write each sentence, using the correct word.

Example: Carla and Ike showed me (your, you're) pictures.
            Carla and Ike showed me your pictures.

5. (Your, You're) a very good photographer.
6. Today (their, they're) taking pictures of beavers.
7. (There, They're) are two beavers making a dam.
8. They use (there, their) sharp teeth to cut trees.
9. The dam is important. (Its, It's) to hold back water.
10. After a while, a deep pond forms (there, their).
11. A beaver will build (its, it's) home in the pond.

■ Write each incorrect sentence correctly and write *correct* for each sentence that has no errors.

Example: Quick! Get you're camera.   *Quick! Get your camera.*

12. Their is a cardinal perched on that branch.
13. It's feathers are a beautiful bright red color.
14. Your looking at the male bird.
15. It's more colorful than the female.
16. Cardinals once made their homes only in the Southeast.
17. Now its common to see them in the Northeast too.
18. They flew away. You're too late to take their picture.

Literature and Writing

There are always thunderstorms somewhere. At any moment, day or night, about eighteen hundred thunderstorms crash and flash the world over. All these storms, big and little, add up to about a hundred flashes of lightning a second, day in and day out.

Herbert S. Zim
from *Lightning and Thunder*

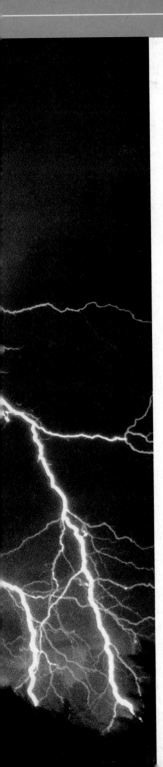

Research Report

Getting Ready What are you curious about? Do you wonder why Mars looks red? how many kinds of sharks there are? what it was like to be a knight? Writing a report is a good way to find the answers to your questions and share your findings with others. In this unit, you can choose a favorite topic to write a report.

ACTIVITIES

Listening
Listen as the paragraph on the opposite page is read. What is it about? What questions does it answer?

Speaking
Look at the picture. What ideas for a report does it make you think of? What questions do you have about each topic? Have someone list the topics and questions on chart paper. Save the paper. You can use the list for topic ideas later in the unit.

Writing
Choose something else that you are interested in, and write three questions about it in your journal.

LITERATURE

According to this story, how did Benjamin Franklin get the idea for inventing the Franklin stove?

We Invent the Franklin Stove

By Robert Lawson

Amos was the eldest of a large family of poor mice. While seeking shelter, he met Benjamin Franklin, one of America's most famous citizens. Amos soon became Dr. Franklin's good friend and adviser.

I slept late the next morning. When I woke my fur-cap home was hanging on the bedpost, and I in it.

Dr. Franklin was again crouched over the fire attempting to write, between fits of sneezing and glasses-hunting. The fire, what there was of it, was smoking, and the room was as cold as ever.

"Not wishing to be critical——" I said. "But, perhaps, a bit of wood on that smoky ember that you seem to consider a fire might——"

"WASTE NOT, WANT NOT," said he, severe, and went on writing.

350

"Well, just suppose," I said, "just suppose you spend two or three weeks in bed with pewmonia—would that be a waste or——"

"It would be," said he, putting on a log; "whatever your name might be."

"Amos," said I. . . . "And then there'd be doctors' bills——"

"BILLS!" said he, shuddering, and put on two more logs, quick. The fire blazed up then, and the room became a little better, but not much.

"Dr. Franklin," I said, "that fireplace is all wrong."

"You might call me Ben—just plain Ben," said he. . . . "What's wrong with it?"

"Well, for one thing, most of the heat goes up the chimney. And for another, you can't get *around* it. Now, outside our church there used to be a Hot-chestnut Man. Sometimes, when business was rushing, he'd drop a chestnut. Pop was always on the look-out, and almost before it touched the ground he'd have it in his sack—and down to the vestry with it. There he'd put it in the middle of the floor—and we'd all gather round for the warmth.

"Twenty-eight of us it would heat, and the room as well. It was all because it was OUT IN THE OPEN, not stuck in a hole in the wall like that fireplace."

"Amos," he interrupts, excited, "there's an idea there! But we couldn't move the fire out into the middle of the room."

"We could if there were something to put it in, iron or something."

"But the smoke?" he objected.

"PIPE," said I, and curled up for another nap.

I didn't get it, though.

Ben rushed off downstairs, came back with a great armful of junk, dumped it on the floor and was off for more. No one could have slept, not even a dormouse. After a few trips he had a big pile of things there. There were scraps of iron, tin and wire. There were a couple of old warming-pans, an iron oven, three flatirons, six pot-lids, a wire birdcage and an anvil. There were saws, hammers, pincers, files, drills, nails, screws, bolts, bricks, sand, and an old broken sword.

He drew out a sort of plan and went to work. With the clatter he made there was no chance of a nap, so I helped all I could, picking up the nuts and screws and tools that he dropped—and his glasses.

Ben was a fair terror for work, once he was interested. It was almost noon before he stopped for a bit of rest. We looked over what had been done and it didn't look so bad—considering.

It was shaped much like a small fireplace set up on legs, with two iron doors on the front and a smoke pipe running from the back to the fireplace. He had taken the andirons out of the fireplace and boarded that up so we wouldn't lose any heat up the chimney.

Ben walked around looking at it, proud as could be, but worried.

"The floor," he says. "It's the floor that troubles me, Amos. With those short legs and that thin iron bottom, the heat——"

"Down on the docks," said I, "we used to hear the shiprats telling how the sailors build their cooking fires on board ship. A layer of sand right on the deck, bricks on top of that, and——"

"Amos," he shouts, "you've got it!" and rushed for the bricks and sand. He put a layer of sand in the bottom of the affair, the bricks on top of that, and then set the andirons in.

It looked pretty promising.

352

"Eureka!" he exclaims, stepping back to admire it—and tripping over the saw. "Straighten things up a bit, Amos, while I run and get some logs."

"*Don't* try to run," I said. "And by the way, do you come through the pantry on the way up?"

"Why?" he asked.

"In some ways, Ben," I said, "you're fairly bright, but in others you're just plain dull. The joy of creating may be meat and drink to you; but as for me, a bit of cheese——"

He was gone before I finished, but when he came back with the logs he did have a fine slab of cheese.

Think and Discuss

1. In this story, who gave Benjamin Franklin the idea for the Franklin stove? Why was it better than a fireplace?

2. Conversations or dialogue in a story can tell a lot about a character. What do you learn about Amos's personality from his conversations with Dr. Franklin?

3. You know that fiction stories are created from the author's imagination. **Biographical fiction** tells about real people. However, some of the people, events, and dialogue are imaginary. How do you know that "We Invent the Franklin Stove" is biographical fiction? Why do you think Robert Lawson chose to write biographical fiction about Benjamin Franklin instead of writing only facts about Franklin's life?

What were some of Ben Franklin's big ideas?

What's the Big Idea, Ben Franklin?

By Jean Fritz

Benjamin Franklin, one of America's most famous citizens, was a printer, author, diplomat, and inventor. He was curious about everything around him, and often his curiosity turned into something very useful.

No matter how busy he was, Benjamin found time to try out new ideas. Sometimes he had ideas on why things happen the way they do. He wrote about comets. He formed a theory about hurricanes; they moved, he said, from the southwest to the northeast, contrary to the way winds usually move. Once he made an experiment with a pot of molasses and an ant. He hung the pot on a string and watched for the ant to crawl down. Soon there was a swarm of ants crawling up the string, so Benjamin concluded that ants have a way of telling each other news.

Sometimes Benjamin's ideas were for the improvement of Philadelphia. He formed the first circulating library in America. He helped organize Philadelphia's fire department. He suggested ways to light the streets, deepen the rivers, dispose of garbage, and keep people from slipping on ice in winter.

Sometimes his ideas turned into inventions. At the head of his bed he hung a cord which was connected to an iron bolt on his door. When he wanted to lock his door at night, he didn't have to get out of bed. He just pulled the cord, rolled over, and shut his eyes.

He invented a stepladder stool with a seat that turned up. And a rocking chair with a fan over it. When he rocked, the fan would turn and keep the flies off his head. He fixed up a pole with movable fingers to use when he wanted to take books down from high shelves. He cut a hole in his kitchen wall and put in a windmill to turn his meat roaster. And he invented an iron stove with a pipe leading outside. The stove produced more heat than an ordinary fireplace, cost less to operate, was less smoky, and became very popular.

In 1732, when he was 26 years old, Benjamin Franklin had one of his best ideas. He decided to publish an almanac. Every family bought an almanac each year. People read it to find out the holidays, the weather forecasts, the schedule of tides, the time the sun came up and went down, when the moon would be full, when to plant what. It was just the kind of book that Benjamin loved—full of odd pieces of information and bits of advice on this and that. It was, in addition to being a calendar, a grand how-to book and Benjamin figured he knew as many how-to's as anyone else. Besides, he knew a lot of jokes.

He put them all in his almanac, called it *Poor Richard's Almanack*, and published the first edition in 1733. His specialty was short one-line sayings.

Sometimes these one-liners were quick how-to hints for everyday living: "Eat to live, not live to eat"; "A penny saved is a penny earned."

Sometimes his one-liners were humorous comments on life: "Men and melons are hard to know"; "Fish and visitors smell in 3 days."

In a few years Franklin was selling 10,000 copies of his almanac every year. He kept it up for 25 years.

Think and Discuss

1. What were some of the big ideas that Ben Franklin had? Which one do you think was the most important? Why?
2. Many of Franklin's one-line sayings are still used. What does each of the one-liners given in this selection mean?
3. You know that nonfiction tells about real people and events. A **biography** is one type of nonfiction. It is the true story of a real person's life. How is the biography "What's the Big Idea, Ben Franklin?" different from the biographical fiction story "We Invent the Franklin Stove"? How are they alike?

RESPONDING TO LITERATURE

The Reading and Writing Connection

Personal Response Which selection about Ben Franklin did you like better? Write a paragraph giving reasons to support your opinion.

Creative Writing What new invention could make life easier for you? Write a paragraph describing your invention and explaining how it will help you.

Creative Activities

Make a Book Cover Pretend the year is 1773. Benjamin Franklin has asked you to illustrate the cover of *Poor Richard's Almanack*. Read about the contents of *Poor Richard's Almanack* again. Then draw a cover for the almanac.

Readers Theater With two other students, read "We Invent the Franklin Stove" as a play. Decide who will read the words of Amos and Ben in quotation marks. Then choose a narrator to read the rest of the story. Give extra stress to words printed in capital letters.

Vocabulary

The compound noun *Franklin stove* comes from the name of the stove's inventor. Look up these words in the dictionary: *Ferris wheel, poinsettia, teddy bear*. From what person's name does each noun come?

Looking Ahead

Reports Before you write your report, you will gather information and take notes. Reread the second paragraph of the biography. If you were taking notes on how Franklin's ideas helped Philadelphia, what six ideas would you include?

VOCABULARY CONNECTION
Synonyms

Words that have nearly the same meaning are called **synonyms.** Notice how the author of "We Invent the Franklin Stove" used two different words for *large*.

Ben rushed off downstairs, came back with a **great** armful of junk, dumped it on the floor. . . .

After a few trips he had a **big** pile of things there.
from "We Invent the Franklin Stove" by Robert Lawson

Here are some more synonyms for *large*.

huge   enormous   massive   sizable

You can vary your writing by using synonyms. Your writing will be more interesting if you do not use the same words over and over again. Use a thesaurus to look up synonyms.

Vocabulary Practice

A. Rewrite these sentences. Replace each underlined word with one of these synonyms from "We Invent the Franklin Stove."

blazed   rushed   sack   scraps

1. Jo <u>ran</u> over to the wood-burning stove.
2. She grabbed the <u>bag</u> filled with kindling.
3. Jo stacked a few <u>pieces</u> of wood in the stove.
4. Soon the fire <u>burned</u> cheerfully.

B. Find two synonyms for each of these words from "What's the Big Idea, Ben Franklin?" Use your Thesaurus Plus.

5. ordinary   **6.** crawling   **7.** operate   **8.** quick

Prewriting
Research Report

Listening and Speaking: Interviewing

One of the best ways to get facts for a report is to **interview** someone who knows the facts. An interview is a kind of conversation. One person asks questions and the other person answers them. The **interviewer** is the person who asks the questions.

To get all the facts you want from an interview, you must ask the right questions. This takes careful planning. The guides below will help you to be a good interviewer.

Guides for Interviewing

1. Decide what you want to know.
2. Make up questions that will tell you what you want to know. Ask *Who? What? Where? When? Why? How?* Do not ask questions that can be answered *yes* or *no*.
3. Write your questions in an order that makes sense. Leave space between the questions. Use this space when you take notes on the answers.
4. Before you ask your first question, tell the person the reason for your interview.
5. Ask your questions clearly and politely. Pay close attention to the answers.
6. If you don't understand something, ask more questions about it.
7. Take notes on the answers. Write only enough to help you remember what the person said. If you want to use the person's exact words, put them inside quotation marks.

Suppose you could interview Ben Franklin about *Poor Richard's Almanack*. On the next page you will find some possible questions and the interviewer's notes on the answers.

A penny saved is a penny earned.

Q: When and where did you first publish your almanac?
A: 1733, Philadelphia
Q: How successful is the almanac?
A: sells 10,000 copies a year
   —"And that's a lot of pennies earned!"
Q: What do you like most about the almanac and why?
A: giving advice and writing humorous one-line sayings
   —"People will remember them hundreds of years from now."

- What important words were used to begin the questions?
- What words of Ben Franklin's did the interviewer write down exactly? How do you know?

Prewriting Practice

A. Work with a partner. Make up three more questions you could ask Ben Franklin.

B. What inventor or other famous person would you like to interview? Choose someone. Write a list of questions for an interview. Then pick a partner. Your partner will pretend to be the famous person. Interview him or her. Follow the Guides for Interviewing.

C. Interview a parent, relative, or neighbor about that person's job or hobby. Use the Guides for Interviewing. Share your questions and notes with your class.

Thinking: Solving Problems

Ben Franklin was a skillful problem solver. He did not complain about problems. He found ways to solve them. For example, the books on his top shelves were difficult to reach. Ben invented a pole with metal fingers that could grasp the book he wanted and take it down. The people of Philadelphia had problems with slippery ice, unlighted streets, and unwanted garbage. Ben found a solution for each of these problems.

What problems do you have? Do you need a research topic for a report? Are you always late to school? These steps will help you solve your problems.

Guides for Solving Problems

1. Decide what the problem is.
2. Make a list of possible solutions. Brainstorm as many ideas as you can.
3. Evaluate the possible solutions. What are the good points of each one? the bad points?
4. Decide on a solution.
5. Carry out the solution.

Here is how one class followed the guides above to solve a problem.

1. **Decide what the problem is.** Mr. Long's class was planning a field trip to the Museum of Science. Twenty-five students were going. Mr. Long and two parents were planning to go with them, but two more adults were needed. The students had this problem: How could they get two more adults to go?
2. **Make a list of possible solutions.** Mr. Long and the class discussed the problem. They brainstormed these possible solutions.
   a. Send notes home, giving more information about the trip.
   b. Have students encourage their parents to volunteer.

   c. Have the teacher call parents on the phone.
   d. Ask senior citizens instead of parents.
   e. Change the date of the trip. Choose a date when more parents might be able to go.
3. **Evaluate the possible solutions.** The students discussed each possible solution.
   a. and b. These solutions might not work because the students had already brought notes home and discussed with their parents the importance of the trip.
   c. Having Mr. Long call their parents was a possibility, but it would take too much of his time.
   d. The fourth solution was a good possibility. Retired people might have more time than parents.
   e. A student called the Museum of Science and found that the date of the trip could not be changed.
4. **Decide on a solution.** The students agreed that the fourth possible solution was the best one. They decided to try this solution.
5. **Carry out the solution.** Mr. Long and three students visited a senior citizens' club and explained their problem. Several members of the group volunteered. Two members went on the field trip to the Museum of Science. Other members were eager to go on the class's next field trip.

Prewriting Practice

As a class or in small groups, use the Guides for Solving Problems to find a solution to one of these problems or one of your own. Brainstorm possible solutions. Evaluate each one. Then choose the solution you think is best.

1. The class library needs more books.
2. The neighborhood is becoming littered with scraps of paper, cans, and other junk.
3. Everyone enjoys playing with the class pet, but only a few students share the work of caring for it.

Composition Skills
Research Report

Finding Information ☑

How do you find facts for a report? Interviewing an expert is one way. Researching information in a library is another way.

You know that nonfiction books contain facts. You can find nonfiction books about your topic by using the card catalog. Every nonfiction book in a library has a title card, an author card, and a subject card in the card catalog. Find subject cards about your topic. They will name books that you can use.

Sometimes you may want to find a specific fact. Using reference books is a good way to do this. Some reference books that you might want to use are listed below.

Atlas—a book containing all kinds of maps
Almanac—a book of up-to-date facts published every year
Encyclopedia—a set of books with information on many topics. The topics are arranged in alphabetical order.
Special Dictionaries—books giving brief information on certain topics. The topics are arranged in alphabetical order.
  • **Biographical Dictionary**—facts about famous people
  • **Geographical Dictionary**—facts about places in the world

Follow these guides for researching facts about your topic.

1. Choose nonfiction books or reference books.
2. Check your facts in more than one source.
3. If facts about your topic change often, choose a recent book.

Prewriting Practice

Write a source you could use to find facts about each topic.

1. Ben Franklin's birthplace
2. population of Philadelphia
3. a map of your state
4. Patrick Henry's life

Taking Notes ☑

Taking notes is a way of remembering what you have heard or read. When you take notes, write just enough words to help you remember the main ideas and the important facts.

John wanted to find facts to answer the question *What did Ben Franklin print?* He read this paragraph in a book about Ben Franklin's life.

> Ben became known as one of the best printers in Philadelphia. He printed laws for the city and notices of public meetings and events. Soon he added a newspaper to his printing business. Now he was not only Benjamin Franklin, printer. He was Benjamin Franklin, editor of *The Pennsylvania Gazette.*
>
> *from* The Story of Ben Franklin *by Eve Merriam*

John took these notes to answer the question.

What did Ben Franklin print ?
— *city laws*
— *notices of meetings and events*
— *The Pennsylvania Gazette*

Prewriting Practice

Read the paragraph and the question below. Take notes to answer the question. Write only the important facts.

Philadelphia has many reminders of Benjamin Franklin, its most famous citizen. One of the city's major roads is the Benjamin Franklin Parkway. Along the Parkway is the Franklin Institute, a museum. This building also houses the Benjamin Franklin National Memorial, with a large statue of Franklin.

What reminders of Franklin can be found in Philadelphia?

Outlining ☑

An **outline** is a plan. A good outline can help you organize your ideas and arrange them in order.

An outline is made up of main ideas and details that support the main ideas. You can write an outline from notes. John took these additional notes about Ben Franklin's career.

What other jobs did Ben Franklin have?
— *statesman*
— *scientist*
— *inventor*
— *writer*

You can use notes to make an outline. Each question becomes a **main topic**. Write each main topic beside a Roman numeral.

Question ———————→ **Main Topic**
What other jobs did Ben   II. Other jobs Ben Franklin had
Franklin have?

Your notes that answer the question become the **subtopics**. Write subtopics next to capital letters, indented under the main topic.

    II. Other jobs Ben Franklin had   **Main Topic**
        A. Statesman   **Subtopic**

Each Roman numeral and capital letter is followed by a period. The first word of each main topic and subtopic begins with a capital letter. An outline also has a title.

The outline on the next page is written from the notes about Benjamin Franklin's career on this page and on page 364.

Benjamin Franklin's Career

I. What Ben Franklin printed
  A. City laws
  B. Notices of meetings and events
  C. *The Pennsylvania Gazette*
II. Other jobs Ben Franklin had
  A. Statesman
  B. Scientist
  C. Inventor
  D. Writer

- How many main topics are there?
- How many subtopics are under each main topic?

Prewriting Practice

Write an outline from the following notes. Add a title.

What did Ben Franklin publish?
—*Poor Richard's Almanack*
—*The Pennsylvania Gazette*

What did Ben Franklin invent?
—lightning rod
—Franklin stove
—bifocal eyeglasses

Writing a Paragraph from an Outline ☑

  It is easy to write a paragraph from a well-planned outline. Use the main topic to help you write a topic sentence. Change the subtopics into sentences that support the main idea.

  Read the outline below. Then compare the outline with the paragraph at the top of the next page.

I. Jobs Ben Franklin did for the American government
  A. Ran the post office
  B. Provided army with gunpowder and medicines
  C. Directed printing of money
  D. Was ambassador to France

Ben Franklin did many jobs for the American government. He ran the post office. He provided the army with gunpowder and medicines. He directed the printing of money and was ambassador to France.

- What is the topic sentence?
- What part of the outline does the topic sentence include?
- Compare the paragraph with the outline. Which sentence includes subtopic A? B? C? D?

Prewriting Practice

Write a paragraph from the outline below.

I. How Ben Franklin showed he disliked waste
   A. Invented a stove to save firewood
   B. Wrote famous one-liner, "Waste not, want not."
   C. Wrote "A penny saved is a penny earned."

The Grammar Connection

Writing Clearly with Pronouns

When you use pronouns, be sure that their meanings are clear. Read the following sentences.

Amos was a friend of Ben Franklin's. He was clever.

Who was clever? Amos or Ben Franklin? The word *He* is not clear. You must use a noun from the first sentence to make your meaning clear.

Amos was a friend of Ben Franklin's. Amos was clever.
Amos was a friend of Ben Franklin's. Ben was clever.

Practice Rewrite each pair of sentences to make the meaning of each pronoun clear.

1. The mouse gobbled the cheese. It was big and round.
2. Sumi showed her paper to her mother. She was pleased.
3. Dad called Mr. Romero. He wanted to buy his car.

Step 1: Prewriting—Choose a Topic

Ming thought of all the things he would like to learn about. He made a list of his topics. Then he thought about which topic **to research.**

model cars ————— Ming wasn't sure that he could find enough information about this.

medieval times ————— This topic was too broad.

money ————— He had always wondered where money came from.

kites ————— He wasn't very interested in this topic.

Ming chose the topic *money*. It would make an interesting report for his coin club.

On Your Own

---

1. **Think and discuss** Make a list of the things you would like to learn about. Use the Ideas page to help you. Discuss your ideas with a partner.
2. **Choose** Ask yourself these questions about each topic.
   Does this topic really interest me?
   Can I easily find information on this topic?
   Is this topic too broad? How could I narrow it?
   Circle the topic you want to write about.
3. **Explore** What information will you look for? Do one of the "Exploring Your Topic" activities on the Ideas page.

Ideas for Getting Started

Choosing Your Topic

Topic Ideas

An invention
A famous person
An occupation
An animal
A country
Bicycle racing
Underwater life

Wonder List

Make an "I wonder" list. Write down all the things you wonder about. Circle the topics that really interest you.

Exploring Your Topic

The Five *W*'s

Write four or five questions about your topic. Your questions should require answers of more than one word. Write questions that answer the Five *W*'s: *Who? What? When? Where?* and *Why?* Another important question is *How?* Here are Ming's questions about money.

1. What is money?
2. When and why was money invented?
3. What is the history of paper money?
4. What will money be like in the future?

Question Collection

Have a friend ask you questions about your topic. Which questions can you already answer? Which ones would you like to know more about? Which questions would you like to answer in your report?

Step 2: Plan

Ming wrote each of his questions on a separate note card. He went to the library and found books about money. He took notes to answer each question.

On each card, he wrote the name of the author and the title of the book he had used.

One of Ming's note cards

When and why was money invented?
—began 2500-3000 years ago
—used animals, food, and shells
— then used lumps of metal
—weight meant how much metal was worth
— king of Lydia had designs marked on
    metal—first coins
Gross, Ruth Belov. Money Money Money.

Ming could not find a book with information about the future of money. He wrote a letter to the president of a bank in his town and asked for an interview. Here are some notes Ming took during the interview.

One of Ming's note cards

What will money be like in the future?
—"In the future, there will be no need
    to carry a wallet."
—five-number code for bank
—another code for bank account
—fingerprint-reader machine
—money transferred from bank to store
Ms. May Stuart, president, Big Money Bank

After Ming gathered all his information, he made an outline to help organize his report. His questions became main topics. The notes that answered each question became subtopics. Here is part of Ming's outline.

Part of Ming's outline

Money

I. What money is
  A. Anything people agree to accept in exchange for products
  B. Usually paper and coins
  C. Some countries use stones

II. When and why money was invented
  A. Began 2500 – 3000 years ago
  B. Used animals, food, and shells
  C. Then used lumps of metal
  D. Metal's weight meant its worth
  E. King of Lydia had first coins made

Think and Discuss ✓

- What are the main topics?
- What are the subtopics?
- Do the subtopics support the main topics?

On Your Own

1. **Plan** Write three or four questions that you would like to answer in your report.

2. **Research** Gather information. Use nonfiction books, reference books, and interviews. Take notes on note cards. Write the source of your information on each card. You will need to list these sources at the end of your report.

3. **Outline** Put your questions in an order that makes sense. Then write an outline. Turn each question into a main topic. The notes will become the subtopics.

Step 3: Write a First Draft

Ming wrote the first draft of his report. He wrote a paragraph for each main section of his outline. The main topics of his outline helped him write the topic sentences. The subtopics helped him write the supporting details.

Ming did not worry about mistakes in spelling or punctuation. He would make corrections and changes later. For now, he just wanted to get all his information on paper.

Part of Ming's first draft

Think and Discuss ✓

- How did Ming's outline help him write this paragraph?
- Why did Ming cross out the words *I'm writing*?
- Where could he add more information?

~~I'm writing~~ Money began 2500 to 3000 years ago. Before that, people used animals food and shells. Metal was better. The more a lump of metal wayed, the more it was worth. Always waying it was a problim therefore, they wayed it once and marked it.

On Your Own

1. **Think about purpose and audience** Ask yourself:
   For whom shall I write this report?
   What is my purpose? What do I want my readers to learn?
2. **Write** Write your first draft. Use your outline to help you. Write a topic sentence for each paragraph. Use every other line. Do not worry about mistakes. Just write all your information.

Step 4: Revise

Ming read his first draft. He saw that he had left out some facts. He added two sentences and read the report to Tara.

Reading and responding

> Your report is very interesting.

> Is it clear? Is there anything else you want to know?

> Well, why was metal better?

> I think I can add some facts about that.

Ming added more information to his report.

Part of Ming's revised draft

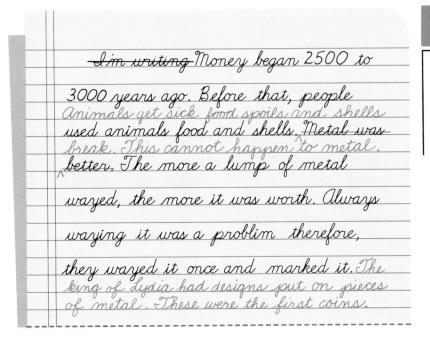

I'm writing Money began 2500 to 3000 years ago. Before that, people used animals food and shells. Animals get sick food spoils and shells break. This cannot happen to metal. Metal was better. The more a lump of metal wayed, the more it was worth. Always waying it was a problim therefore, they wayed it once and marked it. The king of Lydia had designs put on pieces of metal. These were the first coins.

Think and Discuss ✓

- What facts did Ming add to his report?
- Why did he add them?

On Your Own

Revising checklist

☑ Do I have a good topic sentence for each paragraph?
☑ Do all the sentences support the topic sentence?
☑ Have I written enough information?

1. **Revise** Make changes in your first draft. Are your topic sentences good ones? Write new ones if they are not. Make sure that you have written facts, not opinions. Check that you have not left out any information from your outline. Add more facts if you need to. You may want to use some of the words from the thesaurus below or from the one found at the back of this book.

2. **Have a conference** Read your report to a classmate or your teacher.

WRITING CONFERENCE

Ask your listener:	**As you listen:**
"Are there enough facts?" "Is my report clear?" "What else would you like to know?"	I must listen carefully. Is the information clear? What other facts would I like to know?

3. **Revise** Think about your partner's suggestions. Do you have any more ideas? Make those changes on your paper.

Thesaurus

common familiar, ordinary
discover unearth, reveal
effect consequence, result
important major, significant
invent develop, originate

main chief, principal
nearly closely, roughly, approximately
necessary essential, required
related connected, associated
sign indication, symptom

Step 5: Proofread

Ming proofread his report for mistakes in spelling, capitalization, and punctuation. He used a dictionary to check spelling. He used proofreading marks to make his changes.

Part of Ming's proofread draft

On the handwritten draft:

~~I'm writing~~ Money began 2500 to 3000 years ago. Before that, people
Animals get sick, food spoils, and shells
used animals, food, and shells. Metal was
break. This cannot happen to metal.
better. The more a lump of metal
weighed
wayed, the more it was worth. Always
weighing
waying it was a problim. therefore,
weighed
they wayed it once and marked it. The

Think and Discuss

- Where did Ming add commas? Why?
- Which words did Ming correct for spelling?
- What other corrections did Ming make? Why?

On Your Own

1. **Proofreading Practice** Proofread this paragraph. There is one mistake in paragraph format. There are two spelling mistakes and two grammar mistakes. Write the paragraph correctly.

   Jill and me studied about money. Paper money was invented because metal were too hevy to carry around. China was one of the first countries to use paper money. Marco Polo rote that the Chinese used bark as money.

Proofreading Marks

- ⊬ Indent
- ∧ Add something
- ℓ Take out something
- ≡ Capitalize
- / Make a small letter

2. Proofreading Application Now proofread your paper. Use the Proofreading Checklist and the Grammar and Spelling Hints below. Use a dictionary to check spellings.

Proofreading Checklist

Did I

☑ **1.** indent?

☑ **2.** use capital letters correctly?

☑ **3.** use punctuation marks correctly?

☑ **4.** use pronouns correctly?

☑ **5.** spell all words correctly?

The Grammar/Spelling Connection

Grammar Hints

Remember these rules from Unit 11.

- Use subject pronouns in the subject of the sentence. (*He has a new bicycle.*)
- Use object pronouns after a verb or a word such as *at* or *to.* (*Mr. Amano gave the ball to me.*)

Spelling Hint

- Some words have an unexpected consonant in their spellings. You must remember the spellings of these words. (*palm, climb, wrinkle, knight, special*)

Step 6: Publish

Ming copied his report in his neatest handwriting. On the last page, he listed the sources from which he had taken information. He added the title "Money." Then he made a display of money from around the world. In front of his display, Ming placed his report and some pamphlets from Ms. Stuart. He was ready to share his new knowledge with his coin-collecting club.

On Your Own

1. **Copy** Copy your report and list your sources.
2. **Add a title** Write a title at the top of your report.
3. **Check** Read your report again to make sure you have not left out anything or made any mistakes in copying.
4. **Share** Think of a special way to share your report.

Ideas for Sharing

- Read your report to your class. Display pictures and other materials to help explain your facts.
- Use your report to make a magazine about your topic. Include pictures and ads.

Literature and Creative Writing

Amos, a mouse who lives in Ben Franklin's old fur cap, takes the credit for inventing the Franklin stove in the story "We Invent the Franklin Stove." A slightly different explanation is given in the biography "What's the Big Idea, Ben Franklin?" This selection also discusses some of Franklin's other inventions.

Have fun using what you have learned about writing reports. Choose one or more of the following activities.

> **Remember these things** ☑
> Take clear notes.
> Make an outline.
> Write your paragraphs from the outline.

1. **Report on a famous American.** Write about a famous American. Choose one of your favorites or one of these people: Thomas Jefferson, Martin Luther King, Jr., Eleanor Roosevelt.

2. **Give facts about the flag.** Research facts about the different flags the United States has had. Include drawings of the flags in your report.

3. **Report on an invention.** Like Benjamin Franklin, many people have invented new things to make life easier or more pleasant. Write a report on an invention you are curious about or on one of these inventions: elevator, zipper, ball-point pen.

Writing Across the Curriculum
Science

Scientists write reports about the subjects they study. Through these reports, we learn about their discoveries. Scientists are very careful that their information is correct.

Choose one or more of the following activities.

1. **Revolve around this idea.** Many discoveries are being made about the planets in our solar system. Choose one planet. Find out as much about it as you can. Write a report and put it on the bulletin board.

2. **Uncover the causes.** In May, 1980, Mount St. Helens erupted. Find out more about this volcano or another one. Share your report with your class.
   Extra! Make a clay or papier-mâché model of the volcano.

Writing Steps
1. Choose a Topic
2. Plan
3. Write a First Draft
4. Revise
5. Proofread
6. Publish

Word Bank
eruption
lava
magma
crater
seismograph

3. **What is it?** Do you know what a capybara is? a manatee? an armadillo? Find out about one of these animals or another animal that you are curious about. Write a report about the animal. Draw or bring in pictures to show with your report.

Lila enjoyed reading "What's the Big Idea, Ben Franklin?" She decided to read other biographies. Lila chose *Shark Lady*, a biography of Dr. Eugenie Clark by Ann McGovern. To share her book, Lila decided to hold an imaginary interview with Dr. Clark. Here is the interview Lila and a classmate presented.

INTERVIEWER: I have read <u>Shark Lady</u> by Ann McGovern and am pleased to introduce the Shark Lady herself, Dr. Eugenie Clark. Dr. Clark, how did you become interested in fish?

DR. CLARK: When I was young, my mother often took me to the aquarium. I loved going there! I learned all I could about fish.

INTERVIEWER: You said in your book that you study fish in a laboratory. How do you do this?

DR. CLARK: We build large tanks to hold all kinds of sea life. I especially like studying sharks. One of the most interesting things I have learned is that poison from the Moses sole keeps sharks away.

INTERVIEWER: Did you learn this in your laboratory?

DR. CLARK: No, I discovered it when I was working in Israel, on the Red Sea.

INTERVIEWER: What are your plans for the future?

DR. CLARK: I want to keep on with my work. I plan to be diving when I'm ninety.

Think and Discuss

• What did you find out about Dr. Eugenie Clark?
• Why is this a good way to share a book?

Share Your Book

Interview a Book Character

1. Choose a character from a fiction or nonfiction book.
2. Write an introduction giving the title and the author's name and briefly introducing the character. Decide which part of the book to share. Write questions to ask your character about that part of the book.
3. Write answers to the questions. The answers should include information from the book.
4. Ask a classmate to read the interviewer's part. You should take the part of the character being interviewed.
5. Have the interviewer read the introduction. Then present your interview.

Other Activities

- Hold an imaginary interview with the author of your book. Ask about the author's favorite part of the book or favorite character.
- Choose a place in your book that is described with many details. Take your class on a "tour." Tell them about the place and the events that happened there.

 The Book Nook

Mary McLeod Bethune	**Daniel Inouye**
by Eloise Greenfield	*by Jane Goodsell*
This biography tells about Bethune's childhood in South Carolina, the school she started, and the work she did for a President.	This biography of a famous man from Hawaii takes readers from his island childhood to his career as a U.S. Senator.

Language and Usage

He whimpered a bit
From force of habit
While he lazily dreamed
Of chasing a rabbit.
But Old Dog happily lay in the sun
Much too lazy to rise and run.

James S. Tippett
from "Sunning"

Adverbs

Getting Ready Suppose your best friend calls and says, "Guess what! I'm going away for the summer!" The first things you would probably want to know are where, when, and how your friend is going. The words that tell these things are called adverbs. In this unit, you will learn more about these words that describe actions.

ACTIVITIES

Listening
Listen as the poetry on the opposite page is read. What word tells *how* the Old Dog dreamed? What word tells *how* he lay in the sun?

Speaking
Look at the picture. What do you see? Make up a sentence about the picture, using an action verb. Now think about the verb in your sentence. What words can you add to tell more about that verb?

Writing
In your journal, write about something you did today. Use words that tell *where* and *when* and *how*.

1 | What Is an Adverb?

You know that an adjective is a word that describes a noun or a pronoun. Another kind of describing word is called an adverb. An **adverb** can describe a verb.

Adverbs give us more information about an action verb or a form of the verb *be*. They tell *how, when,* or *where*. Adverbs can come before or after the verbs they describe.

HOW: Maggie typed the letter <u>carefully</u>.

WHEN: <u>Then</u> I sealed the envelope.

WHERE: All the stamps were <u>upstairs</u>.

Study the lists below. They show adverbs that you use often in your writing. Most adverbs telling *how* end with *-ly*.

HOW	WHEN	WHERE
angrily	always	downtown
carefully	finally	inside
fast	often	off
loudly	once	out
quickly	sometimes	there
sadly	then	upstairs

Guided Practice Find the adverb that describes each underlined verb. Does the adverb tell *how, when,* or *where*?

Example: Maggie and I <u>waited</u> inside.   *inside   where*

1. The mail carrier finally <u>arrived</u>.
2. We <u>ran</u> out to meet her.
3. Maggie <u>clapped</u> her hands excitedly.
4. I quickly <u>opened</u> the gold envelope.
5. Then Maggie <u>read</u> the letter.
6. "We won the contest!" she <u>shouted</u> proudly.

> ▸ A word that describes a verb is an **adverb**.
> ▸ An adverb can tell *how, when,* or *where.*

Independent Practice

A. Write each adverb. Label it *how, when,* or *where.*

Example: Butch always enjoys collecting stamps.
always   when

7. He keeps his collection upstairs.
8. He works on it often.
9. Sometimes friends send Butch new stamps.
10. He buys unusual stamps downtown.
11. Then Wendell Witherspoon trades with Butch.
12. Butch carefully soaks the used stamps.
13. He gently removes the wet paper.
14. Slowly the stamps dry.
15. Butch arranges the stamps neatly.

B. Write each adverb and the verb it describes.

Example: Pony express riders once carried the mail.
once   carried

16. The horseback riders bravely traveled a long route.
17. They stopped briefly at small stations.
18. There they received fresh horses.
19. The pony express riders quickly changed horses.
20. They continued ahead.
21. The daring riders rode swiftly.
22. People soon received their letters.

Writing Application: A Letter

Imagine that you have decided to bury a time capsule. Write a letter to the people who will open your time capsule twenty-five years from now. Use adverbs in your letter. Underline each adverb that you use.

For Extra Practice, see p. 402.

2 | Comparing with Adverbs

You have already learned how adjectives are used to compare people, places, and things. You can also use adverbs to make comparisons. Add -er to short adverbs to compare two actions. Add -est to compare three or more actions.

Bill skis fast . (one action)

Louise skis faster than Bill does. (two actions)

Kara skis fastest of the three. (three or more actions)

For most adverbs that end with -ly, use *more* to compare two actions. Use *most* to compare three or more actions.

Dee swam gracefully . (one action)

Did Kato swim more gracefully than Dee? (two actions)

Ty swam most gracefully of all. (three or more actions)

Do not use -er or -est to compare adverbs that end with -ly. Never use -er with *more*. Never use -est with *most*.

INCORRECT: Faith skates <u>smoothlier</u> than Don.

Don fell <u>most hardest</u> of all the skaters.

CORRECT: Faith skates more smoothly than Don.

Don fell hardest of all the skaters.

Guided Practice What form of the adverb in ( ) correctly completes each sentence?

Example: Bud arrived ____ than I did. (soon) *sooner*

1. Today we practiced ____ than we did yesterday. (long)
2. Of all the team members, Ruth skated ____. (skillfully)
3. Does Leslie skate ____ than Shawn? (quickly)
4. Andrew jumps ____ of us all. (high)
5. Of everyone on the team, Tara tries ____! (hard)

▶ Add *-er* to short adverbs to compare two actions. Add *-est* to compare three or more actions.

▶ For adverbs that end with *-ly*, use *more* to compare two actions. Use *most* to compare three or more actions.

▶ Never use *-er* with *more*. Never use *-est* with *most*.

Independent Practice Write each sentence. Use the correct form of the adverb in ( ).

Example: These Special Olympics lasted ____ than last year's. (long)
These Special Olympics lasted longer than last year's.

6. The sun shone ____ this year than last year. (brightly)
7. The fourth graders practiced ____ of all. (carefully)
8. My relay team ran ____ than my brother's team. (swiftly)
9. The runners moved ____ than the wheelchair racers. (slowly)
10. Mahalia ran ____ of all the students. (fast)
11. I watched her ____ of all the runners. (closely)
12. In the sack race, I jumped ____ of all. (eagerly)
13. Jeremy jumps ____ than I do. (smoothly)
14. He crossed the finish line ____ than I did. (soon)
15. The broad jump began ____ than the high jump. (late)
16. Roberto jumped ____ of all the boys. (high)
17. He came ____ of all to breaking a school record. (near)
18. In our class, who threw the beanbag ____ of all? (straight)
19. Dana waited ____ than Marcy for her turn. (patiently)
20. Ms. Perez blew her whistle ____ than Mr. Tanaka. (loudly)

Writing Application: A News Report

Imagine that you are a television sports reporter at a future Olympics. Write a report about the day's events, using adverbs to compare the actions of the different athletes.

For Extra Practice, see p. 403.

3 | Using *good* and *well*

Sometimes it may be hard to decide whether to use *good* or *well*. How can you make sure that you use these words correctly? Remember, *good* is an adjective that describes nouns. *Well* is an adverb that describes verbs.

ADJECTIVE

Marcia is a good pilot.

This suit is good.

ADVERB

She flies well.

I choose my suits well.

Guided Practice Which word is correct?

Example: Kipp's trips are all (good, well). *good*

1. He plans (good, well) for his adventures.
2. Kipp's guidebook is (good, well).
3. His road maps are (good, well) too.
4. He has learned to read maps (good, well).
5. Kipp speaks several languages (good, well).
6. Talking to people helps him learn (good, well) about another country.
7. Kipp is (good, well) at taking pictures.
8. Photos help him remember his trips (good, well).
9. Kipp describes his travels (good, well).
10. Everyone listens (good, well) to his stories.
11. The presents that he brings to his family are always (good, well).
12. They think that Kipp's trips are (good, well)!

Summing up

▶ Use the adjective *good* to describe nouns.
▶ Use the adverb *well* to describe verbs.

Independent Practice Use *good* or *well* to complete each sentence correctly. Write the sentences.

Example: Zelda's last vacation didn't go very ____.
Zelda's last vacation didn't go very well.

13. The train trip was not ____.
14. Her hotel room was not very ____ either.
15. She didn't sleep very ____ that night.
16. Next, Zelda discovered that she hadn't packed ____.
17. She was ____ at forgetting things!
18. She loved the water, and she swam ____.
19. The swimsuit she brought was not ____ at all.
20. How could her vacation be ____ without a swimsuit?
21. Zelda learned her lesson ____.
22. This year she has prepared ____ for her vacation.
23. Her decision to stay home was ____.
24. Zelda will spend the time ____.
25. It will be ____ to relax in the back yard.
26. The books that she plans to read are ____.
27. Zelda will finally learn to cook well.
28. The meals that she makes will be really ____.
29. Her family will eat ____ during Zelda's vacation!
30. It will be well to have many friends visit.
31. Zelda will entertain them ____.
32. She knows some games that are really ____.
33. It will be ____ to start a new hobby.
34. Zelda has always wanted to learn to use tools ____.
35. She will become ____ at carpentry on this vacation.
36. Mom's new tools are ____.
37. Zelda has promised to take care of them ____.
38. Zelda knows that this vacation will be ____.

Writing Application: An Advertisement
You own a hotel in a perfect vacation spot. Write an ad for the *Daily News* telling people why they should come to your hotel. Use the word *good* or *well* in each sentence.

For Extra Practice, see p. 404.

4 | Negatives

Sometimes when you write sentences, you use the word *no* or words that mean "no." A word that makes a sentence mean "no" is a **negative**. These sentences have negatives.

No one picked the beans.   I didn't water the garden.

The words *no, no one, nobody, none, nothing, nowhere,* and *never* are negatives. The word *not* and contractions made with *not* are also negatives. Never use two negatives together in a sentence.

Incorrect	Correct
There weren't no trees.	There weren't any trees. There were no trees.
I won't never rake leaves!	I won't ever rake leaves! I will never rake leaves!

Notice that there may be more than one correct way to write a sentence with a negative.

Guided Practice Which word in ( ) is correct?

Example: Eli doesn't want (any, no) leaves on the ground.   *any*

1. He can't go (nowhere, anywhere) until he has finished raking.
2. He never likes (anything, nothing) about yard work.
3. No one (never, ever) has time to help him.
4. Luckily there (are, aren't) no leaves left on the trees.
5. There won't be (no, any) more leaves to rake until next fall!

Summing up

▸ A **negative** is a word that means "no."
▸ Do not use two negative words together in a sentence.

Independent Practice

A. Write the correct word to complete each sentence.

Example: Elmer (hadn't, had) never collected leaves. *had*

6. Now he never goes (nowhere, anywhere) without finding some leaves.
7. He couldn't get (no, any) birch leaves at first.
8. Elmer didn't find (anything, nothing) new today.
9. Emma wouldn't show her collection to (no one, anyone).
10. She hasn't pressed (none, any) of her leaves yet.
11. She hadn't (ever, never) tried pressing them in wax paper.
12. Emma didn't know (no one, anyone) to teach her how!
13. Elsie couldn't find any red leaves (anywhere, nowhere).
14. She (hasn't, has) found no palm leaves today.
15. Didn't (anybody, nobody) find some oak leaves?

B. Each sentence has two negatives together. Write each sentence correctly. There may be more than one way to correct a sentence.

Example: Kira didn't know nothing about leaves.
Kira didn't know anything about leaves.

16. She hadn't read no books about them.
17. Nobody never told her that leaves make food for plants.
18. Leaves need sunlight, or they can't make no food.
19. Most plants couldn't live nowhere without leaves.
20. Animals couldn't never live without leaves either.
21. Some animals don't eat nothing but leaves.
22. Animals could never breathe no air without leaves.
23. Without leaves there wouldn't be enough oxygen nowhere!
24. Kira hadn't never realized leaves were so important.

Writing Application: Rules

Ranger Bud Barker is turning over a new leaf this year! He wants to do more to protect the forest. Ranger Bud has put up a list of rules for campers. Write the five rules. Use a negative word in each rule.

For Extra Practice, see p. 405.

Grammar-Writing Connection

Changing Meaning with Adverbs

Adverbs are powerful words for a writer. An adverb can add an important detail. Changing one adverb can change the meaning of an entire sentence. Read the sentences below. What do you picture when you read each sentence?

I watched Mr. Millman walk slowly and carefully .

I watched Mr. Millman walk quickly and excitedly .

Notice how changing the adverbs changes the meaning of the whole sentence.

Revising Sentences

Copy each sentence below. Fill in the blank with an adverb from the following list. Then change the meaning of the sentence by rewriting it with another adverb. You may use any adverb from the list more than once.

happily	sadly	anywhere	carefully	easily
slowly	everywhere	late	loudly	eagerly
quietly	downtown	quickly	early	noisily

1. The day began ____.
2. As dawn grew near, the robins chattered ____.
3. Subway cars ran ____.
4. The city woke up ____ as the sun rose in the sky.
5. Large buses carried workers ____.
6. Kettles whistled ____ on kitchen stoves.
7. People ate their breakfasts ____.
8. Children slammed doors and walked ____ to school.
9. The boys talked ____ as they waited for class to begin.
10. A new student walked ____ into the classroom.

Creative Writing

Beware the power of the great wave! In this picture, Katsushika Hokusai warns us of the wave's strength. He also shows us its bold beauty. *The Great Wave* is one of one hundred pictures that Hokusai made of Mount Fuji. Each picture shows a different view of the famous Japanese mountain.

- Where is the mountain? How is it like the wave?

Activities

1. **Write haiku.** A haiku is a Japanese poem. It has three unrhymed lines. The first and third lines have five syllables. The second line has seven syllables. Write haiku that describe this picture. For example: Under the great wave/The people in boats struggle/To glide free again.
2. **Write a letter.** Suppose you are a passenger on one of the boats. Write a letter to a friend about your adventure.

Check-up: Unit 13

What Is an Adverb? *(p. 384)* Write each adverb and the verb that it describes.

1. Leo called Nick early.
2. "Let's go!" he said eagerly.
3. They both dressed quickly.
4. Then they got their fishing gear.
5. The boys met outside.
6. They carried their poles easily.
7. They found the boat quickly.
8. The waves rocked it gently.
9. Leo stepped in.
10. Nick soon followed.
11. The boys rowed silently.
12. Finally, they found a good spot.
13. "Drop the anchor here," said Leo.
14. Silvery fish swam below.
15. They baited their hooks carefully.
16. Nick and Leo sat patiently.
17. Leo said, "I am often lucky."
18. "I never catch any," Nick moaned.
19. Suddenly Nick's line jerked.
20. A huge flounder had grabbed the worm greedily.
21. "I got one!" Nick cried excitedly.
22. He landed the fish smoothly.
23. Leo swiftly grabbed the fish.
24. Later the boys became hungry.
25. Leo suggested, "Let's go home."
26. Nick agreed happily.
27. "This has been a great morning for me!" he said proudly.

Comparing with Adverbs *(p. 386)* Write each sentence. Use the correct form of the adverb in ( ).

28. This year plan your garden (carefully) than last year.
29. Order vegetable seeds (soon) than you order flowers.
30. You will work (hard) of all in the spring.
31. Dig clay soil (deeply) than sand.
32. You can rake sandy soil (smoothly) than rocky soil.
33. Plant the lettuce (close) to the path.
34. Space the tomato plants (widely) apart than the rows of corn.
35. Of all spring crops, lettuce appears (soon).
36. You must wait much (long) for celery than for lettuce.
37. Parsley grows (slow) of all.
38. You will find that weeds sprout (quickly) than vegetables.
39. They grow (fast) of all the plants in the garden.
40. You can water the garden (evenly) with a sprinkler than with a hose.
41. Use the sprinkler (long) of all in the hot weather.
42. Water the plants (heavily) in the morning than at night.
43. You can harvest carrots (easily) of all when the soil is moist.

Using *good* and *well* (p. 388) Use *good* or *well* to complete each sentence.

44. The science program was ___.
45. Mr. Ray spoke ___ about animals.
46. I sat close so that I could see ___.
47. The porcupine is an animal that protects itself ___.
48. Sharp quills are hidden ___ in its soft fur.
49. The porcupine is not ___ for other animals to eat.
50. Other animals learn ___ not to attack a porcupine.
51. The quills stick ___ into anything that touches them.
52. They are ___ at protecting the porcupine from enemies.
53. Mr. Ray also described ___ what a raccoon is like.
54. This furry, ring-tailed animal is ___ at climbing trees.
55. The raccoon uses its long, sharp claws ___.
56. Raccoons can handle objects ___ with their paws.
57. A raccoon can also swim ___.
58. The raccoon hunts ___ during the night.
59. It can live ___ almost anywhere!
60. Forests, towns, and cities are all ___ for raccoons.
61. Mr. Ray is ___ to animals.
62. He knows their habits ___.
63. We listened to him very ___.

Negatives (p. 390) Each sentence has two negatives together. Write each sentence correctly.

64. Our school hasn't never had a band before.
65. No one could play no tunes well.
66. There isn't nobody to play tuba.
67. Ms. Conti didn't have no trouble finding drum players, though!
68. Most students didn't know nothing about harmony.
69. Nobody never wanted to practice.
70. Now no one can't wait to learn the new songs.
71. Sam doesn't see nothing easy about this new piece.
72. He doesn't know how to play none of the notes.
73. He won't never learn it in time.
74. Lee can't play none of the high notes on his clarinet.
75. He doesn't want to make no squeaking noises.
76. There isn't nowhere to practice.
77. Ms. Conti said, "I haven't never heard such a weak excuse!"
78. The band doesn't have no uniforms.
79. At the concert, nobody could find a seat nowhere near the stage.
80. There wasn't no sound when Ms. Conti tapped her baton.
81. The band didn't make no mistakes.
82. "Stars and Stripes Forever" hadn't never sounded so good!

Cumulative Review

Unit 1: The Sentence

Sentences, Kinds of Sentences
(pp. 14, 16, 18) If a group of words below is a sentence, write it correctly. If it is not, write *not a sentence*.

1. it was a rainy night
2. at the end of Nye Street
3. did you see the accident
4. please call the police
5. the driver of the car
6. went over the curb
7. was anyone hurt
8. how lucky they were

Subjects and Predicates *(pp. 20, 22, 24)* Write each sentence. Draw a line between the complete subject and the complete predicate. Underline each simple subject once, and each simple predicate twice.

9. Nellie Bly was a famous reporter.
10. Her news stories were daring.
11. Nellie read the book *Around the World in Eighty Days.*
12. Then she went around the world.
13. Her trip around the world took fewer than eighty days.
14. She made the trip by ship, train, cart, and donkey in 1899.
15. Many people read about her trip.

Combining Sentences *(pp. 26, 28)* Write each pair as one sentence. The words in ( ) tell you how.

16. Alex reads books. Alex knows a lot.   (compound predicate)
17. He wrote a report. Kate wrote a report.   (compound subject)
18. It was about ostriches. My class liked it.   (compound sentence)
19. An ostrich is the largest bird. An ostrich may weigh three hundred pounds.   (compound predicate)
20. The ostrich likes to eat plants. Sometimes it will eat sand. (compound sentence)

Unit 3: Nouns

Common and Proper Nouns *(pp. 76, 78)* Write each noun. Then write *common* or *proper* beside each one.

21. Di and her family live in the city.
22. Her father is a salesperson.
23. Mr. Hall makes trips to Mexico.
24. Her mother, Betty, is a lawyer.
25. On Saturdays Di visits museums.

Singular and Plural Nouns *(pp. 80, 82, 84)* Write the plural of each noun.

26. ox
27. shark
28. bush
29. glass
30. berry
31. deer

Possessive Nouns *(pp. 86, 88)* Write the possessive form of each noun.

32. men   **35.** baby
33. fox   **36.** families
34. Cindy   **37.** nurses

Unit 5: Verbs

Action Verbs, Main and Helping Verbs *(pp. 136, 138)* Write each sentence. Draw one line under the main verb and two lines under the helping verb.

38. Mr. Largo is repairing his barn.
39. Fire had damaged it.
40. The animals were roaming around the barnyard.
41. Mrs. Largo has repainted the fence.
42. The neighbors will keep some of the animals for a while.

Present, Past, and Future *(p. 140)* Write the verbs in these sentences. Label each verb *present*, *past*, or *future*.

43. Peter will tell the class about Eskimo houses.
44. The Eskimos built snow houses in the winter.
45. They called these houses igloos.
46. Peter will draw a picture of an igloo for his report.
47. Most of the Eskimos live in wooden houses today.

Using Verbs *(pp. 142, 144, 146, 148, 150, 152)* Write the verb that correctly completes each sentence.

48. Grandpa (play, plays) the violin.
49. He (try, tries) to practice daily.
50. His first concert (is, are) today.
51. I have (wore, worn) my new clothes.
52. We (has, have) found our seats.
53. Grandpa (hurry, hurried) onstage.
54. He has (took, taken) a bow.

Contractions with *not* *(p. 154)* Write contractions for these words.

55. has not   **57.** should not
56. does not   **58.** will not

Unit 7: Adjectives

What Is an Adjective?, Adjectives After *be* *(pp. 204, 206)* Write each adjective and the word it describes.

59. Cobras and vipers are two kinds of harmful snakes.
60. Cobras are slender.
61. Long, fast cobras like to fight.
62. Heads of cobras are flat.
63. Many vipers have fat bodies.

Using *a, an,* and *the* *(p. 207)* Write each correct article.

64. (a, an) alarm   **67.** (a, an) owl
65. (a, an) book   **68.** (a, an) pump
66. (a, the) trees   **69.** (an, the) oxen

Cumulative Review, *continued*

Comparisons *(pp. 208, 210, 212)*
Write the correct word in (   ).

70. Texas is (larger, largest) than Delaware is.
71. Alaska is (larger, largest) of all.
72. Is Los Angeles the (more, most) exciting city in California?
73. Florida has a (better, best) climate than New England.
74. It's the (worse, worst) trip ever.
75. The Midwestern states have the (flatter, flattest) land of all.

Unit 9: Capitalization and Punctuation

Correct Sentences, Proper Nouns, Titles *(pp. 260, 262, 264, 276)*
Write these sentences correctly.

76. have you ever seen a dolphin show
77. my aunt and I went to one near redondo beach in california
78. on friday aunt megan and mrs. feld took me my uncle met us
79. how intelligent the dolphins were
80. please get me the book creatures of the sea I would love to read it

Abbreviations *(p. 266)* Write abbreviations for these words.

81. Doctor
82. Mister
83. Road
84. April
85. Ohio
86. Utah

Commas *(pp. 268, 270)* Write these sentences correctly.

87. Ann tell me about storms.
88. Thunderstorms tornados and hurricanes are three different kinds.
89. Thunderstorms Bob are common.
90. Yes most thunderstorms take place in the spring and summer.
91. A thunderstorm brings lightning thunder and rain.

Quotation Marks *(pp. 272, 274)*
Write these sentences correctly.

92. Are we going to the fair asked Eva
93. Tad said I am working at a booth
94. I have entered a milking contest declared Ruben
95. How is it judged asked Tad
96. Ruben replied the judges will see how fast I can milk my cow

Unit 11: Pronouns

Subject and Object Pronouns *(pp. 322, 324, 326)* Write each sentence. Use a pronoun in place of the underlined word or words.

97. Mr. Hayes played a record.
98. He questioned Amy and me.
99. Amy knew the answer.
100. Johann Bach wrote the music.
101. Amy likes music by Bach.

I and *me*, Homophones *(pp. 328, 334)* Write each sentence. Use the word or words that complete each sentence correctly.

102. Luis and (I, me) are learning to roller skate.

103. (Its, It's) lots of fun.

104. Dad drives (me and Luis, Luis and me) to the rink every Saturday.

105. We have our lesson (their, there).

106. Bring (you're, your) skates and come with us.

Possessive Pronouns *(pp. 330, 334)* Write each sentence. Use a possessive pronoun in place of the underlined word or words.

107. Diane and <u>Diane's</u> brother Sam work in a pet store.

108. <u>Diane and Sam's</u> job is to feed the pets.

109. <u>Sam's</u> favorite pet is the parrot.

110. <u>The parrot's</u> feathers are orange and blue.

111. The kittens snuggle with <u>the kittens'</u> mother.

Contractions with Pronouns *(p. 332)* Write the contractions for each of the following words.

112. you will

113. I have

114. he is

115. he has

116. we had

117. they are

Unit 13: Adverbs

What Is an Adverb? *(p. 384)* Write each adverb and the verb it describes.

118. Today Benita made a skirt.

119. She sewed the stitches neatly.

120. Benita left her machine here.

121. I quickly sewed a shirt.

122. Later I surprised Benita with it.

Comparing with Adverbs *(p. 386)* Write each sentence. Use the correct form of the adverb in ( ).

123. Of all the students, Beth studied (hard) for the spelling bee.

124. I lost my turn (quickly) than Steven did.

125. Beth spelled (correctly) of all.

126. She stayed in the contest (long) than any other student.

127. Our class cheered (loudly) than Mrs. Lopez's class.

Using *good, well,* and Negatives *(pp. 388, 390)* Write the correct word to complete each sentence.

128. Pearl and Julian weren't going (nowhere, anywhere).

129. We (had, hadn't) nothing to do.

130. Can't (no one, anyone) think of something to do?

131. Pearl's idea was (good, well).

132. She studied (good, well) for her science test.

Enrichment

Using Adverbs

Well, Good!

GOOD DOG!

WELL DONE!

People often confuse the words *good* and *well*. Remember that *good* is used as an adjective and *well* is used as an adverb. Draw and write your own comic strip that uses the words *good* and *well* correctly.

Brought to You by—

ZIPPY

Your job is writing TV commercials. Explain why your toothpaste, soap, or other product is the best. Write an ad comparing your product to two other leading brands. Use adverbs with *-er* and *-est* endings or with *more* and *most*.

Brand X cleans fast.
Brand Y cleans faster.
Zippy cleans fastest of all.

Try out your commercial on a classmate.

Safety First

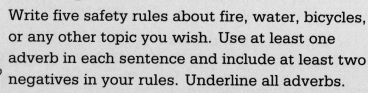

Write five safety rules about fire, water, bicycles, or any other topic you wish. Use at least one adverb in each sentence and include at least two negatives in your rules. Underline all adverbs.

Always walk carefully around the pool area.
Never swim during a storm.

Make a poster to illustrate the rules. Copy your sentences onto the poster.

Take a Look Around

Think about the landscape or the appearance of the area where you live. Are you surrounded by mountains or by tall buildings? Do you live along the coast? Fold a piece of white paper in half. On one side draw a picture that shows your landscape.

On the other side, draw a picture that shows a different type of landscape. On the back of the paper, write a paragraph that explains how your life would be different if you lived in the new place. Use adverbs and underline each one.

Act One

Find a favorite story in your reading book or in a library book. Choose a short scene from the story and write it in the form of a play. Before each character's words, write the name of the character. After the name, write an adverb telling how the character should say the lines— for example, *softly, excitedly, sadly*. Have a narrator speak the lines in the story that describe the scene or the action.

```
Margarita (loudly): The diamonds are missing!
Hernando (angrily): Who could have done this?
Narrator: Margarita and Hernando rapidly searched the
          entire building for clues. They found nothing.
```

Extra! Practice the play with a group of classmates and perform it for your class.

1 | What Is an Adverb? (p. 384)

● Write the adverb in each sentence.

Example: Kerry always got mail. *always*

1. Erin wished that sometimes she would get letters.
2. Kerry gladly told Erin about her pen pal.
3. They write letters frequently.
4. Erin then called World Pen Pals.
5. Their office is downtown.
6. This company carefully matches pen pals.
7. They could find Erin a pen pal anywhere.

▲ Write each adverb. Then write the verb it describes.

Example: Tina carefully studied the catalog.
        carefully   studied

8. She turned the pages slowly.
9. Finally, Tina spotted the perfect gift for Paco.
10. She completed the order form neatly.
11. Then she checked the name and number of the item.
12. Paco once ordered a baseball glove.
13. He carelessly wrote the wrong item number.
14. He soon received a package containing boxing gloves.

■ Use an adverb to complete each sentence. Write the sentences. The clue tells what kind of adverb to use.

Example: My uncle Jerry delivers mail ____. (where)
        My uncle Jerry delivers mail downtown.

15. He rises ____ each day and puts on his uniform. (when)
16. He greets everyone ____ as he delivers the mail. (how)
17. ____ bad weather forces businesses to close. (when)
18. Uncle Jerry dresses ____. (how)
19. He tramps ____ through snow and sleet. (how)
20. Uncle Jerry says, "I ____ deliver the mail." (when)

2 | Comparing with Adverbs (p. 386)

● Choose the word that correctly completes each sentence. Write the sentences.

Example: Lynn runs (faster, fastest) of all the runners.
Lynn runs fastest of all the runners.

1. She warms up (more carefully, most carefully) than I do.
2. Lena holds her head (higher, highest) than Lee does.
3. Sam jogs (more evenly, most evenly) than Julio does.
4. Pam runs (more gracefully, most gracefully) of all.
5. Rosa's feet pound the track (harder, hardest) than Al's.
6. Chan reaches the finish line (sooner, soonest) of all.

▲ Use the correct form of the adverb in ( ) to complete each sentence. Write the sentences.

Example: My sister skis ____ than I do.   (skillfully)
My sister skis more skillfully than I do.

7. I like to ski ____ than she does.   (slowly)
8. Kay skis ____ of everyone in the family.   (fast)
9. She started skiing ____ than Joe.   (soon)
10. Joe falls ____ of the three of us.   (frequently)
11. Of all of us, Mom skis the ____.   (expertly)
12. She turns and stops ____ than Dad does.   (smoothly)

■ For each sentence below, write two sentences. Make one compare two actions and the other compare three or more actions.

Example: Connie dives expertly.
Connie dives more expertly than Alison.
Connie dives most expertly of all the team members.

13. She reaches the end of the pool soon.
14. Kate cheers loudly for her.
15. Alex starts the race late.
16. He works hard to catch up.
17. Alex kicks his feet powerfully.
18. Coach Marcus smiles proudly.

3 | Using *good* and *well* (p. 388)

● For each sentence, write *correct* if the sentence is correct. Write *not correct* if it is not.

Example: Judy gives directions good.   *not correct*

  1. She gave us good directions to her house.
  2. I listened good.
  3. We took a good look at the directions before we started.
  4. The trip went well.
  5. Mark's sense of direction is well.
  6. He and I followed Judy's directions good.
  7. We had a good time walking along the country roads.

▲ Write each sentence, using *good* or *well* correctly.

Example: Paul and his older brother Joel get along _____.
Paul and his older brother Joel get along well.

  8. The trips they take together are _____.
  9. Joel is _____ at driving his car.
  10. Paul can read road maps _____.
  11. They are _____ as a team.
  12. Joel keeps his car running _____.
  13. The maps in his car are very _____.
  14. They help the brothers plan their trips _____.

■ Some sentences are incorrect. Write those sentences correctly. Write *correct* if a sentence has no errors.

Example: We asked Dr. Chu to speak about eating good.
We asked Dr. Chu to speak about eating well.

  15. I needed a good way to help her find our school.
  16. Then I had an idea that was well.
  17. Drawing is something I do good.
  18. I knew I could make a good map.
  19. First, I planned the map good on scrap paper.
  20. Then I made the final drawing on good paper.
  21. I labeled all the streets and landmarks good.
  22. I know the map worked good because Dr. Chu found us!

4 ‖ Negatives (p. 390)

● Write the word that makes each sentence mean *no*.

Example: Neil hadn't met Aunt Ella until last month.
hadn't

1. Nobody had told him she lived on a farm.
2. At first there weren't many things he could do.
3. He had never milked a cow.
4. He went to collect eggs and came back with none.
5. Nothing seemed to go right for Neil.
6. His aunt told him there was no need to worry.
7. A person can't do everything right the first time.

▲ Each sentence has two negatives. Write the sentences correctly. There may be more than one way to correct a sentence.

Example: Sumi didn't know nothing about gardening.
Sumi knew nothing about gardening.

8. Nobody never told her how much work it was.
9. She couldn't plant nothing until the soil was ready.
10. Nothing never grows well unless the soil is loose.
11. Sumi didn't have no experience preparing soil.
12. No one hadn't shown her how to turn it over.
13. Nothing could be no harder than digging up rocks.
14. She thought she wouldn't never get to plant seeds.

■ Answer each question with a sentence that means *no*. Use a different negative in each sentence. There may be more than one way to answer a question correctly.

Example: Have you ever planted a vegetable garden?
I have never planted a vegetable garden.

15. Do you have a good place to grow vegetables?
16. Will your plants get a lot of sunlight?
17. Have you decided what kind of vegetables to grow?
18. Could you start your own plants from seeds?
19. Is there somewhere you could buy small plants?
20. Do you know anyone who could help you?

Student's Handbook

Finding Words in a Dictionary

Alphabetical order The dictionary gives the meanings of thousands of words. The words are listed in alphabetical order.

To find a word in your dictionary, look at the first letter. Think of where in the alphabet that letter appears.

a b c d e f g **beginning**	h i j k l m n o p q **middle**	r s t u v w x y z **end**

Then turn to that part of your dictionary to begin your search. For example, the word *crank* is listed at the beginning of the dictionary with the other *c words*.

crank • crease ← guide words

entry word →

crank *noun* A rod or handle that is attached at right angles to a shaft and turned to start or run a machine.
◇ *verb* To start or run by means of a crank.
crank (krăngk) ◇ *noun, plural* **cranks** ◇ *verb* **cranked, cranking**
cranky *adjective* Easily annoyed; irritable.
crank•y (krăng′ kē) ◇ *adjective* **crankier, crankiest**
crash *verb* **1.** To fall or strike something with sudden noise and damage: *The dishes slid*

crease *noun* A mark or line, usually formed by wrinkling or folding.
◇ *verb* To make a crease in or on.
crease (krēs) ◇ *noun, plural* **creases** ◇ *verb* **creased, creasing**

When words begin the same way, look for the first different letter.

cra|nk   cra|sh

Because *n* comes before *s*, *crank* comes before *crash*.

Entry words The words in dark type are called entry words. They are usually listed without endings such as *-ed, -ing, -er, or s.*

TO FIND: cranked   TO FIND: creases

LOOK UNDER: crank   LOOK UNDER: crease

Guide words To find a word in a dictionary, look at the guide words at the top of every dictionary page. They guide you by showing the first and last entry words on the page. Look for the guide words that come before and after the word you need.

Practice

A. Write each word below. Then write *beginning, middle,* or *end* to tell where in the dictionary you would find it.

1. humor   5. curious
2. rhyme   6. jolly
3. editor   7. fault
4. wick   8. new

B. Write each group of words in alphabetical order.

9. stare   yesterday   tablet   usher
10. volume   service   rye   valve
11. parade   phrase   plume   pillow
12. prop   press   prime   praise

C. Write the entry word for each word below.

13. admired   15. singing
14. dollars   16. narrower

D. Write the words from the following list that you would find on a page with the guide words *notion–nowhere.*

noun   now   nose   November   not   novel   number

Choosing the Correct Definition

Many words have more than one meaning. Your dictionary lists all the meanings, or **definitions**, for each entry word. A number shows where a new definition begins.

> **grasp** *verb* **1.** To seize and hold firmly with or as if with the hand: *I grasped the railing so I wouldn't fall.* **2.** To take into the mind; understand: *Do you grasp the problem?*
> ◇*noun* **1.** The act of grasping. **2.** The ability to achieve; reach: *Victory seemed within the team's grasp.* **3.** Understanding: *The student has a good grasp of social studies.*

Some words are used as different parts of speech. *Grasp* can be used as a verb or as a noun. Definitions are usually given for each part of speech. Which definition of *grasp* is right for this sentence?

Did she grasp the point of the lesson?

How to Choose a Definition

1. Decide how the word is used in the sentence. In the sentence above, *grasp* is used as a verb.

2. Read the definitions for that part of speech only. There are two definitions for *grasp* as a verb.

3. Choose the meaning that makes the most sense. The second meaning of *grasp* makes the most sense.

Homographs Sometimes two entry words are spelled alike but have different meanings. These words are called homographs.

> **sash**[1] *noun* A band worn around the waist or over the shoulder as an ornament or symbol.
> **sash**[2] *noun* A frame in which the panes of a window or door are set.

Which entry word for *sash* is right in this sentence?

James painted the sash around the kitchen window.

> **How to Choose an Entry Word**
>
> **1.** Read the sentence in which the word appears.
>
> **2.** Read the definitions for both entry words.
>
> **3.** Decide which definition makes the most sense for your word.

If you chose *sash²*, you would be right.

Practice

A. Here is part of the dictionary entry for *star*. For each sentence below it, write the part of speech and the number of the right meaning for *star*.

> **star** *noun* **1.** A heavenly body that appears as a very bright point in the sky at night. **2.** A design or object that has points radiating from a center and looks like or represents a star. **3.** A performer who plays a leading role in a play, opera, or movie. **4.** An outstanding performer, as in sports.
> ◇ *verb* **1.** To decorate with stars. **2.** To play or present in the leading role.

  1. The stage was decorated with huge gold <u>stars</u>.
  2. Roberto Clemente was a famous baseball <u>star</u>.
  3. Please <u>star</u> the sentences that have proper nouns.
  4. Did you see the North <u>Star</u> in the night sky?

B. Which entry word on page 409 gives the meaning for *sash* in each sentence below? Write *sash¹* or *sash²*.

  5. Help Carmen tie her <u>sash</u> over her shoulder.
  6. Have you repaired the broken <u>sash</u> in the dining room?
  7. Everyone in the parade wore a bright yellow <u>sash</u>.

Using a Dictionary for Pronunciation

Suppose that you did not know how to pronounce the word *participate* in this sentence.

> If you join the team, you can participate in the games.

To find out, look at the special spelling in the dictionary.

Special spellings Each entry includes a special spelling given in parentheses ( ). First, the word is broken into parts, or **syllables.** Here is the special spelling for *participate*.

par•ti•ci•pate   (pär tĭs′ə pāt′)

Pronunciation key The letters and symbols of the special spelling stand for certain sounds. Each dictionary page usually has a pronunciation key that tells how to pronounce the symbols for the vowels and gives special spellings for some consonant sounds.

ă pat	ŏ pot	û fur
ā pay	ō go	*th* the
â care	ô paw, for	th thin
ä father	oi oil	hw which
ĕ pet	o͝o book	zh usual
ē be	o͞o boot	ə ago, item
ĭ pit	yo͞o cute	pencil, atom
ī ice	ou out	circus
î near	ŭ cut	ər butter

How would you use the special spelling and the pronunciation key to find out how to pronounce *participate*? On the next page are the steps you would follow. Use the same steps to figure out how to pronounce any word.

How to Use a Pronunciation Key

1. **Consonants** For most consonant letters in the special spelling, use the sound that you usually use for that letter. The *c* in *participate* is an *s* in the special spelling because you pronounce it like *s*.

2. **Vowels** Each vowel symbol in the special spelling has a special sound shown in the pronunciation key. In *(pär tĭs'ə pāt')* the *ä* sounds like the *a* in *father*. The symbol ə is a special symbol that stands for the same vowel sound of five different letters.

3. **Accent Marks** Use more **stress,** or force, to say a syllable followed by an accent mark (′). A syllable with the dark accent mark ′ is stronger than a syllable with a light accent mark. In *participate,* stress the last syllable more than the first and third syllables. Stress the second syllable most of all.

Practice

Use these special spellings to answer the questions below.

masquerade (măs′ kə **rād′**)	drowsy (**drou′** zē)
piccolo (**pĭk′**ə lō′)	traitor (**trā′** tər)
numb (nŭm)	compromise (**kŏm′** prə mīz′)

1. In masquerade, does the last syllable rhyme with mad or made?
2. Which syllable of masquerade has no stress?
3. In piccolo, does the last syllable rhyme with go or to?
4. Is the b in numb pronounced?
5. Does the first syllable of drowsy rhyme with grow or cow?
6. What is a word that rhymes with the first syllable of the word traitor?
7. Which syllable of compromise has the strongest stress?
8. Which syllable of compromise is stressed but less strongly?

Using the Library

Do you want books and magazines to read? Do you need information? Then you can go to the library.

Library materials are set up in a certain way so that you can find what you want more quickly and easily.

How to Use the Library

1. **Fiction** Books of fiction are grouped together. A fiction book is all or partly made up by the author. Fiction books are arranged alphabetically by the authors' last names. For example, *Charlotte's Web* by E. B. White would be on a shelf with other fiction books by authors whose last names begin with *W*.

2. **Nonfiction** Books that give facts about such subjects as history and science are called nonfiction books. Nonfiction books are grouped together by subject. A book about insects, for example, will be grouped with other books about insects. Each subject has a special number. This number appears under the author's name on the **spine,** or back edge, of the book.

3. **Reference** Reference books are special nonfiction books that you use for information. They are kept in a special part of the library. In the reference section, you will find dictionaries, thesauruses, and encyclopedias. Other reference books include books of maps called **atlases** and books of facts called **almanacs.** Usually you cannot take reference books out of the library.

4. **Other materials** You can usually find magazines and newspapers in the library. Records, tapes, and filmstrips may also be available.

Practice

A. Write *fiction, nonfiction,* or *reference* to describe each book.

1. *Morning Arrow* by Nanabah Chee Dodge is a story about a Navajo boy and his blind grandmother.
2. *The Paper Airplane Book* tells how to make and fly paper airplanes.
3. *Think Metric* gives a useful introduction to the metric system.
4. The *World Book Encyclopedia* is a set of books filled with facts on many subjects.
5. *The Mystery of Pony Hollow* by Lynn Hall is a story about a young girl who discovers a mystery in the woods.
6. The *Standard World Atlas* contains maps of every country in the world.
7. *Watching Birds* tells how to find and identify different kinds of birds.

B. Here is a list of fiction books. Write the word that you would use to find each one on the library shelves.

8. *Mr. Yowder and the Giant Bull Snake* by Glen Rounds
9. *A Game of Catch* by Helen Cresswell
10. *Saturdays in the City* by Ann Sharpless Bond
11. *Chooki and the Ptarmigan* by Carol Codd
12. *The Spider Plant* by Yetta Speevak
13. *Ben and Me* by Robert Lawson
14. *The Town Cats* by Lloyd Alexander

C. Here is a list of nonfiction books. Write under what subject you would look for each one.

15. *Let's Look at Reptiles*
16. *A Young Person's Guide to the Ballet*
17. *Understanding Art*
18. *How to Care for Your Pet*
19. *Kids' Gardening*
20. *Balloons: The First 200 Years*
21. *Exploring the Forests of the World*

Using the Card Catalog

In the drawers of the **card catalog** are cards that list all the books in the library. You can use these cards to help you find any book.

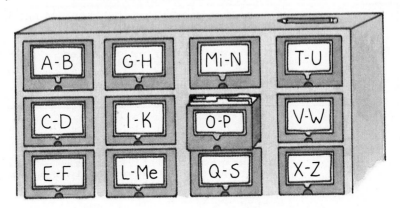

Each drawer of the card catalog is labeled with one or more letters. The letters tell you which cards are inside that drawer. The cards are in alphabetical order beginning with the letter shown on the drawer.

The card catalog has a title card and an author card for every book. It also has a subject card for every nonfiction book and for some fiction books. These cards are shown on the next page.

Every card gives the same information about a book. However, the information is arranged differently.

Title card The title appears first, at the top. Title cards are filed alphabetically, by title.

Author card The author's name is at the top. Look for the author's card if you know the author's name and want to know the title of the book.

Subject card The subject appears at the top. Look at subject cards when you want to find books on a certain subject.

Letters or **call numbers** appear on the left of most cards. They are there to help you find the book. Nonfiction books are usually arranged on the library shelves by their call numbers.

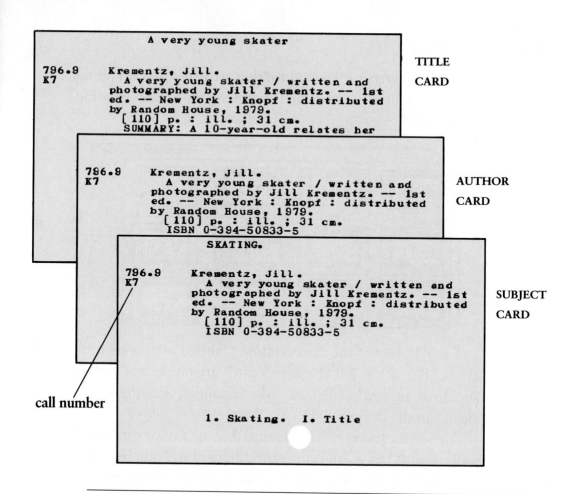

A very young skater

796.9   Krementz, Jill.
K7   A very young skater / written and
         photographed by Jill Krementz. -- 1st
         ed. -- New York : Knopf : distributed
         by Random House, 1979.
            [110] p. : ill. ; 31 cm.
            SUMMARY: A 10-year-old relates her

TITLE CARD

796.9   Krementz, Jill.
K7   A very young skater / written and
         photographed by Jill Krementz. -- 1st
         ed. -- New York : Knopf : distributed
         by Random House, 1979.
            [110] p. : ill. ; 31 cm.
            ISBN 0-394-50833-5

AUTHOR CARD

SKATING.

796.9   Krementz, Jill.
K7   A very young skater / written and
         photographed by Jill Krementz. -- 1st
         ed. -- New York : Knopf : distributed
         by Random House, 1979.
            [110] p. : ill. ; 31 cm.
            ISBN 0-394-50833-5

SUBJECT CARD

1. Skating.   I. Title

call number

Practice

In which card catalog drawer on page 415 would you look to find the answer to each question below? Write the letter or letters that appear on that drawer.

1. Does the library have any books by Rudyard Kipling?
2. What books about Germany are in the library?
3. Is the book *Frozen Fire* in the library?
4. Does the library have *Tuck Everlasting*?
5. What is the name of a book by Alan Coren?
6. What books are there on how to raise bees?
7. Would *Incredible Journey* be in the fiction or nonfiction section of the library?
8. How many Beverly Cleary books does the library have?

Using an Encyclopedia

An encyclopedia is a very useful reference. It contains articles about hundreds of people, places, things, and events. The articles answer *who*, *what*, *where*, *when*, *why*, and *how* questions.

Volumes Encyclopedia articles are arranged in alphabetical order in books called volumes. Each volume is labeled with one or more letters. The letters tell you the beginning letters of the subjects in that volume.

Key words To find information in an encyclopedia, you must first decide on a key word. The key word should name a subject that you would probably find in the encyclopedia.

QUESTION: When did James Naismith invent the game of basketball?

KEY WORD: *Naismith* or *basketball*

Practice

Which volume of the pictured encyclopedia probably would have the answer to each question? Write the volume number or numbers.

1. How many teeth do most humans have?
2. How are oranges different from tangerines?
3. What subjects did Mary Cassatt like to paint?
4. What are some books by Lewis Carroll?
5. Is rice grown only in Asia?
6. How is the land crab different from other crabs?

Parts of a Book: The Front

How do you know that a book has the information that you want? The first few pages of a book can tell you a lot about the book you have chosen.

Title page First, check the title page to be sure that you have the right book. The title page tells the title of the book, the name of the author, and the name and location of the company that made the book.

Copyright page On the back of the title page, you will usually find the copyright page. The copyright notice on this page tells the year the book was published. Check this date to make sure that the information in the book is up-to-date.

**TITLE
PAGE**

**COPYRIGHT
PAGE**

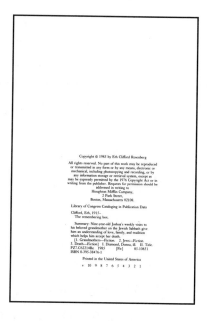

Table of contents At the front of many books, you will find a table of contents. The table of contents lists the names of the chapters or other parts of the book in order. It also gives the page number on which each part begins.

In the following table of contents from the book *This Is an Orchestra*, the chapter titles are numbered.

Use the table of contents to find out where a chapter begins or what subjects are in the book.

Practice

A. Write the answer to each question.

1. What page of a book tells who the author is?
2. What page of a book tells when the book was made?
3. What page of a book tells the title of the book?
4. What part of a book tells where each chapter begins?

B. Use the table of contents above. Write each answer.

5. Which chapter describes the families of instruments?
6. On what page does the section on the brass family begin?
7. Which chapter tells how to make your own listening library?
8. How many pages are in the chapter on practicing?
9. Which chapter tells you how to pick the right instrument?

Parts of a Book: The Back

Index Most nonfiction books have sections in the back that contain useful information. Here you will usually find an index. The index is an alphabetical list of the subjects in the book. Here is part of the index for *Turkeys, Pilgrims, and Indian Corn* by Edna Barth.

INDEX

Alden, John, 34, 37
Animals, 53–54
Bradford, William, 10,
   15, 29, 31–33, 54,
   65, 67, 86
Brewster, William, 17,
   29–30
Carver, John, 30–31,
   63–64

Massasoit, 9, 60, 63–64
Mayflower, 20, 22–28,
   30, 31; Christopher
   Jones (ship's master),
   23, 25, 28, 61;
   Mayflower II, 28
Mayflower Compact, 27
Mullins, Priscilla, 36, 37

Main topics People, places, and things that the book mentions are the main topics of the index. People are listed by their last names.

Subtopics Each subtopic gives information about a main topic. Subtopics are usually listed in alphabetical order.

Page numbers Each topic is followed by page numbers that tell where to find the information. If page numbers are given as *23–26*, for example, the information appears on pages 23, 24, 25, and 26.

Use an index to help you answer a question. Choose a key word or words. Then see if that word is in the index.

Glossary In some books you may also find a glossary at the back of the book. A glossary is an alphabetical list of words and their meanings. On the next page, you will find part of a glossary from the book *Flights*.

con·cert (**kŏn′**sûrt′) *n*. A musical performance given by one or more singers or musicians.

con·fused (kən **fyo͞ozd′**) *adj*. Mixed up: *He seemed confused by the directions.*

con·sole (kən **sōl′**) *v*. **con·soled, con·sol·ing.** To comfort during a time of disappointment or sorrow.

con·tent·ment (kən **tĕnt′**mənt) *n*. Satisfaction: *The director had a look of contentment at the end of the play.*

space that is surrounded by walls or buildings.

cross (krôs) *or* (krŏs) *adj*. Irritable or annoyed; angry.

curl·i·cue (**kûr′**lĭ kyo͞o′) *n*. A fancy twist or curl, usually made with a pen.

curt·sy (**kûrt′**sē) *n., pl.* **curt·sies.** A way of showing respect to a person by bending one's knees and lowering the body while keeping one foot forward.

When you come across an unfamiliar word in a book, check the glossary to find the word's meaning.

Practice

A. Use the index on the previous page. Write the page numbers on which you might find the answer to each question.

1. Who was Priscilla Mullins?
2. What animals did the Pilgrims find in the New World?
3. Who wrote the Mayflower Compact?
4. What was *Mayflower II*?

B. Using the glossary above, write a definition for each word.

5. console
6. curlicue
7. cross
8. confused

Summarizing

Often you will want to remember information that you read. To help you remember, you can write a summary. A **summary** sums up the main idea and the important points of a selection in just a few sentences.

Reread the first four paragraphs of "The Beaver Pond" on pages 232–233. Decide what the main idea is. Also identify the most important points. Then read the following summary of these paragraphs. The topic sentence is underlined.

> The beavers created a pond in the valley. They cut down trees and built a dam. Soon the dammed-up stream became a pond with beaver homes in the middle. In time new wildlife came to live at the pond.

The main idea of the first part of "The Beaver Pond" is that the pond was created by the beavers. The first sentence of the summary states this main idea as the topic sentence. The other sentences give the most important points about this main idea. Here are the steps to follow when you write a summary.

How to Write a Summary

1. State the main idea of the selection in a topic sentence.
2. Include only the most important points.
3. Keep the summary short.
4. Write the summary in your own words.

Practice

Turn to page 234 of "The Beaver Pond." Read the last three paragraphs on that page. Write a summary that tells how the pond changed after the beavers left. In your summary, first state the main idea in a topic sentence. Then state the most important points. Remember to use your own words.

Reading a Map

A **map** is a simple drawing of an area of the earth. The map shows only the most important details of the area. The names of cities, mountains, rivers, or other features usually appear.

Here is a map of the state of Montana.

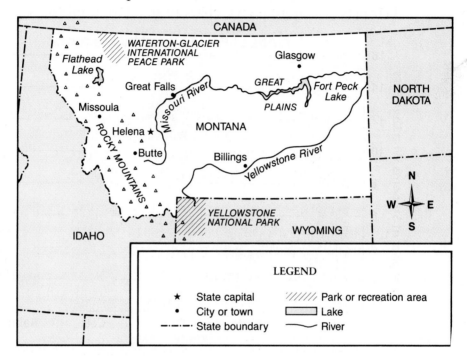

Legend The map key, or legend, explains what each special picture or symbol stands for on the map.

Compass rose You can find north (N), east (E), south (S), and west (W) on the map by looking at the compass rose.

Practice

Write the answer to each question. Use the map above.

1. What country lies to the north of Montana?
2. What are the names of two rivers in Montana?
3. What is the name of the state capital?
4. What are the names of two other cities in Montana?
5. What mountains lie in the western part of the state?

Reading a Graph

A **graph** is a drawing that gives information about amounts of things. Because it shows the information in picture form, it helps you understand and compare the numbers.

Bar graphs The students in one class made a bar graph about their pets. A bar graph uses bars to stand for numbers.

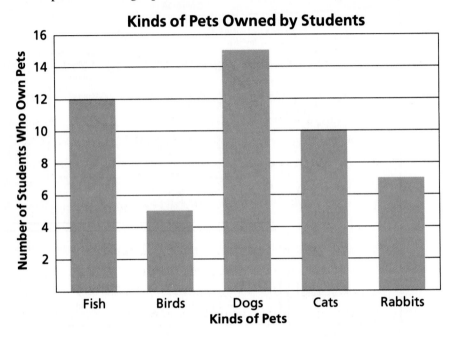

Kinds of Pets Owned by Students

Labels The title on the graph tells what the graph shows. The label at the side tells what the numbers mean. The label at the bottom tells what the bars stand for.

Look at the bar for birds. It stops between the numbers *4* and *6*. That means there are five birds as pets.

Practice

Write the answer to each question. Use the graph above.

1. How many fish do the students have?
2. What kind of pet do the most students have?
3. What kind of pet do the fewest students have?
4. Do the students own more fish or cats? How many more?

Test-Taking Tips

Each year at school you must take many kinds of tests. How can you do your best on every test? The better prepared you are for a test, the better you will do. The following tips will help you do well on any test.

How to Take a Test

Get Ready!

1. Find out what information will be covered on the test.

2. Review the information. Study your old assignments and quizzes. Look over important sections in your textbook.

3. Prepare your supplies. Have sharp pencils and an eraser.

Get Set!

1. Listen to or read the directions carefully. Ask questions if you are unsure about what to do.

2. Be sure that you know how to mark your answers. Are you to write something? underline? circle?

3. Be sure that you know where to put your answer. Do you write on the test itself? Do you write on another sheet of paper?

Go!

1. Answer the easy questions first. If you are not sure of an answer, skip the question. You can go back to it later.

2. Go back to the hard questions. Decide which answer choices are definitely wrong. Then make a good guess about the choices that are still left.

3. Do not spend too much time on any one question. If you are running out of time, you may want to skip one or two questions.

4. Check your work. Did you follow directions carefully? Did you forget to answer any questions? Are all of your answers marked correctly?

How to Follow and
Give Instructions

How do you learn to play a game or get to a friend's house? One way is to watch someone do it. Another is to read a set of instructions. Still another is to listen to instructions.

Instructions are given in steps. Here are Sam's instructions, or directions, for getting to his house from school. What are the steps?

> First, turn right when you leave the school. At the corner, where the park is, turn right again. That's Park Street. Go along Park Street for three blocks, until you get to the Pile of Pizza restaurant on a corner. Then turn right one more time, onto Third Avenue. Look for number 434. It's the fourth house from the corner.

Notice how each step leads to the next one.

1. Turn right when you leave the school.
2. At the corner, Park Street, turn right.
3. Go along Park Street for three blocks, to the Pile of Pizza.
4. Turn right onto Third Avenue.
5. Look for number 434, the fourth house from the corner.

Guides for Following Instructions

1. Listen carefully for each step.
2. Listen for the order of the steps. Words like *first, then,* and *next* will help you.
3. Picture each step.
4. Ask questions if you do not understand.

Suppose you must give instructions. Can you do as good a job as Sam did? Here are some guides that will help you.

Guides for Giving Instructions

1. Tell the purpose of your instructions.
2. Give one step at a time, in the right order. Use words such as *first, then, next.*
3. Include enough details to make each step clear.

Now read these instructions.

1. Hang a handkerchief over the edges of a glass and a saucer. Be sure to dip the handkerchief in water first and then wring it out. When you come back the next morning, all the water that was in the saucer will have moved into the glass! Before you start, make sure your glass, saucer, and handkerchief are ready.

2. How do you get water from one container to another without pouring? First, get a saucer, a glass, and a handkerchief. Next, fill the saucer with water. Then wet the handkerchief and wring it out. Twist it like a rope and hang it between the saucer and the glass. Hang it to the bottom of the saucer but only a little way into the glass. Overnight, the water will flow into the glass!

- Which set of instructions above follows the guides?
- Which set of instructions is easier to follow? Why?

Practice

A. Listen to the teacher's instructions. Then follow them. Use the Guides for Following Instructions.

B. Give a partner directions to get to a place in the classroom. Think of a roundabout way to get there. Your partner will listen and then try to follow your directions. Use the Guides for Giving Instructions.

How to Take Telephone Messages

One way to keep in touch with others is to write letters. Another way is to use the telephone. If you answer a call for someone who is not home, you should take a message.

Read the following telephone conversation.

MR. GOMEZ: Hello, Maura. This is Mr. Gomez. May I please speak to your father?

MAURA: I'm sorry, Mr. Gomez. He can't come to the phone right now. May I take a message?

MR. GOMEZ: Yes, please ask him to call me at 555-9330.

MAURA: I'll ask him to call you at 555-9330. Good-by.

Read Maura's message. Did she include all the information?

> *Dad,*
> *Please call Mr. Gomez at 555-9330.*
> *Maura*

Practice good telephone habits. Follow these guides.

Guides for Taking Telephone Messages

1. Be polite.
2. Write the caller's name and telephone number.
3. Write the message correctly and clearly.
4. Repeat the message to be sure that it is correct.

Practice

Act out this phone call with a partner. Write the message.

Mrs. Amos calls your mother to say that the picnic is at 3:00 P.M. at 11 Spring Road. Your mother should bring a salad.

How to Have a Discussion

You know that a discussion can help you improve a piece of writing. It can also help you solve a problem or learn how others feel. Follow these guides to have good discussions.

Guides for Discussing

1. Keep the discussion topic in mind, and stick to it.
2. Join in the discussion. Give your ideas, and ask questions about points that are not clear to you.
3. Listen politely to the ideas of others. Do not talk when someone else is talking.
4. Think before you speak, and speak so that everyone can hear and understand you.

A group of students had a discussion to choose a title for their class almanac. As you read their discussion, keep the discussion guides in mind.

FRANK: Let's call it *The Fourth Grade Almanac*.

TONI: I think——

LOIS: That's so dull! We can do better than that!

PEG: What were you saying, Toni?

TONI: I think we should have a more creative title.

MEL: Did you ever read *Poor Richard's Almanack*?

ANDREA: Why don't we have a title contest?

- Which students followed the discussion guides? Which students did not? Explain.

Practice

Form a group of four or five students and have a discussion. Choose one of the following topics or pick one of your own. Does everyone follow the discussion guides?

1. What time should the school day start and end?
2. Where should our class go on the next field trip?

How to Listen for Purpose, Main Idea, and Details

Listening and hearing are different. Suppose a friend is talking in a noisy room. Although you hear all the noise, you *listen* only to your friend. When you listen, you pay attention. Learn to think as you listen. Ask yourself these questions.

Why is the speaker speaking? Decide which of these is the speaker's main purpose.
1. to entertain you
2. to inform you by giving facts
3. to persuade you to do something

Why am I listening? Often your purpose is related to the speaker's purpose. Decide which of these is your main purpose.
1. to be entertained
2. to get information
3. to help you decide what to do

What kind of information should I listen for? The kind of information that you listen for will depend upon the speaker's purpose and your own.
1. If the speaker is telling a story, listen for events and details.
2. If the speaker is giving information, listen for facts that tell you what you want to know. Listen especially for facts that answer *Who? What? Where? When? Why? How?*
3. If the speaker is trying to persuade you to do something, listen for reasons.

What are the topic and the main idea? The topic is what all the sentences are about. The main idea sums up what the sentences say about the topic. A statement about the main idea often comes at the beginning of a speech.

Listen as someone reads the paragraph at the top of the next page. What is the topic? What is the main idea?

> The flea may be tiny, but it jumps like a giant. Because fleas have no wings, they must leap onto the animals on which they feed. Their strong legs can carry them 130 times higher than their height. If you were a 4-foot flea instead of a human, you could jump 520 feet!

The topic of the above paragraph is fleas. The main idea is that fleas can jump extremely high.

What details should I listen for? Once you know the main idea, listen for the supporting details. They give you information about the main idea.

Now listen as someone else reads the paragraph about fleas. Listen for details that support the main idea. Ask yourself questions that begin *Who? What? Where? When? Why?* and *How?* For example, how are fleas able to jump so high?

How are the details arranged? A good speaker puts details together in a way that makes sense. When you listen, pay attention to the way one detail follows another. For example, in a story, listen for the sequence, or order, of events. In a description, picture in your mind what the speaker is describing. Fill in more and more details as you listen.

Guides for Listening for Purpose, Main Idea, and Details

1. Pay close attention.
2. What is the purpose of the speaker?
3. What is your own purpose in listening?
4. What are the topic and main idea?
5. What details support the main idea?
6. How are the details arranged?

Practice

Your teacher will read two selections. Follow the teacher's instructions. Remember to use the guides.

How to Give a Talk

Giving a talk is not the same thing as talking. When you give a talk, you speak to many people about a certain topic. Furthermore, you plan what you are going to say.

Whenever you give a talk, use the following guides.

Guides for Giving a Talk

1. **Know your audience.** Who are they? How old are they? What are their interests?
2. **Know your purpose.** Do you want to entertain your audience? inform them? persuade them to do something?
3. **Choose a suitable topic.** Talk about something you know well. Be sure that the topic will interest your audience.
4. **Plan what you will say.** Think about your audience and purpose when you plan your talk. Are you talking to a group of children to entertain them? Are you talking to your science class to give information? You would not talk the same way or say the same thing in both cases.
5. **Write notes or key words on cards.** Do not write out what you will say. Just write words that will remind you of the order in which you want to say things.
6. **Practice your talk.** Practice until you have almost memorized your talk. Try not to say *ah, well,* and *um.* Practice not only the words but also how to say them. Do you want to be funny? to move your audience? Your speed, loudness, and expression depend on your purpose.
7. **Talk to your audience.** Speak loudly enough to be heard. Look at the people in the audience.

Practice

Think of something funny that happened to you or to someone you know. Plan a talk about it to (1) a kindergarten class, (2) your class, or (3) a parents' meeting. Give your talk.

How to Listen to Poetry

Plop! Bang! Wham! Crash! Sometimes poets use words like these to imitate sounds. **Sound words** make poems interesting and help you really hear what the poet is describing. Listen as the following poem is read aloud. What sound words do you hear?

Ululation

With a bray, with a yap,
with a grunt, snort, neigh,
with a growl, bark, yelp,
with a buzz, hiss, howl,
with a chirrup, mew, moo,
with a snarl, baa, wail,
with a blatter, hoot, bay,
with a screech, drone, yowl,
with a cackle, gaggle, guggle,
with a chuck, cluck, clack,
with a hum, gobble, quack,
with a roar, blare, bellow,
with a yip, croak, crow,
with a whinny, caw, low,
with a bleat, with a cheep, with a squawk, with a
  squeak:

animals
  —and sometimes humans—
                    speak!

Eve Merriam

Besides using sound words, poets sometimes repeat words that begin with the same sound. This gives the poem a pleasant, musical sound. Read this sentence quietly: *Sarah saved Sam from the salty blue sea.* Do you hear the repeated sound of the beginning letter *s*? Now listen as your teacher or a classmate reads aloud one stanza of a poem found in this book.

> In the morning the city
> Spreads its wings
> Making a song
> In stone that sings.
> *from "City" by Langston Hughes*

- What beginning sound is repeated in this stanza?

Have you ever listened to a poem and wanted to clap your hands to the beat? When you hear the beat in a poem, you are listening to the **rhythm**. Listen as your teacher or a classmate reads aloud part of the poem "The Yak." Tap your foot or clap your hands to the rhythm.

> Yickity-yackity, yickity-yak,
> the yak has a scriffily, scraffily back;
> some yaks are brown yaks and some yaks are black,
> yickity-yackity, yickity-yak.
>
> Sniggildy-snaggildy, sniggildy-snag,
> the yak is all covered with shiggildy-shag;
> he walks with a ziggildy-zaggildy-zag,
> sniggildy-snaggildy, sniggildy-snag.
> *from "The Yak" by Jack Prelutsky*

- How many beats did you tap for each line?

Practice

A. Listen as your teacher reads the poem "Galoshes" by Rhoda Bacmeister. Write four words that imitate sounds. Write four words with a beginning sound that is repeated. What image do these words create in your mind?

B. Listen as your teacher reads the poem "Help!" by Jack Prelutsky. Tap out the rhythm with your fingers.

How to Classify

When you put your socks in one drawer, your sweaters in another drawer, and your gloves in a third drawer, you are classifying. **Classifying** means putting things that are alike into the same group or **category.**

In what way are the things listed below alike?

Animals		
beavers	fish	dragonflies
blackbirds	kingfishers	frogs
ducks	lynxes	wolverines
deer	wolves	

The things are all alike in one way—they are all animals. Therefore, you can classify them in the category *Animals.* Would a dog fit into that category? a bike? Why or why not?

A large category like *Animals* can be broken into smaller categories too.

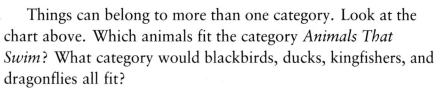

Animals		
Mammals	**Birds**	**Insects**
beavers	blackbirds	dragonflies
wolves	ducks	
lynxes	kingfishers	
wolverines		
deer		

Things can belong to more than one category. Look at the chart above. Which animals fit the category *Animals That Swim*? What category would blackbirds, ducks, kingfishers, and dragonflies all fit?

A. Write these categories across your paper: *Things for Writing, Things for Cooking, Things for Building.* Then study the lists below. Write each item under the proper category.

pen	pot	saw
hammer	screwdriver	typewriter
stove	pencil	spoon

B. Write these categories across your paper: *Fruits, Vegetables, Red Things.* Then study the lists below. Write each item under the proper category. Some items can be listed in more than one category.

string bean	banana	strawberry
stop sign	beet	cherry
fire truck	corn	sunburn

C. Decide how the items in each list are alike. Then write the name of a category in which they fit. Finally, write one more item for each category.

1. summer, winter, spring
2. scarlet, olive green, gold
3. pond, stream, river
4. dime, quarter, dollar
5. China, Spain, Canada
6. chirp, howl, growl
7. oak, maple, pine
8. circle, triangle, rectangle
9. raft, ferry, canoe
10. cotton, nylon, denim

D. Look around your classroom. Make a list of eight or ten objects you see. Think about these objects. Are any of them alike in some way? Into what categories can you classify them? Classify the objects in as many different ways as you can.

THINKING STRATEGIES

How to Identify Causes and Effects

When one thing makes something else happen, we call the events **cause** and **effect**. Suppose your alarm clock wakes you up. The alarm clock is the cause. Your waking up is the effect.

Here are some other examples of cause and effect.

CAUSE	EFFECT
You misspell a word on a test. ⟶	The teacher marks it wrong.
Someone dials your phone number. ⟶	Your phone rings.
Your friend tells you a joke. ⟶	You laugh.
The sun rises. ⟶	It becomes lighter outside.

Sometimes an event can have more than one cause.

CAUSES	EFFECT
Your friend tells you a joke.	
Someone behind her makes a face.	You laugh.
You are in a good mood.	

If you think about cause and effect, as in the paragraph below, you will better understand what you read and hear.

CAUSES — The weeks of practicing and worrying had come to a wonderful end. The sun lit up the track, and the world sparkled. Kate had won her race! To make it all perfect, her best friend, Leroy, had won his race too.

EFFECT — Kate had never felt happier.

Guides for Identifying Causes and Effects

1. To figure out the cause, ask *Why?*
2. To figure out the effect, ask *What happened as a result?*
3. Look for more than one cause or effect.

Practice

Write one effect of each event. Then write two causes.

1. a picnic
2. a baseball victory
3. a smile

THINKING STRATEGIES

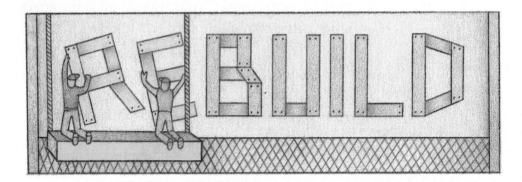

Prefixes

A **prefix** is a word part that has a special meaning. A prefix is added to the beginning of a word to make a new word. The word to which a prefix is added is called a **base word**.

A prefix changes the meaning of the base word. Add the meaning of the prefix and the meaning of the base word to get the meaning of the new word.

Prefix	Base word	New word	Meaning
un-	lucky	unlucky	not lucky
re-	build	rebuild	build again
mis-	spell	misspell	spell wrong

Practice

Write each sentence. Replace the underlined words with a word that begins with the prefix *un-*, *re-*, or *mis-*.

1. Ty <u>spelled</u> a word <u>wrong</u>.
2. The baby is <u>not</u> <u>happy</u>.
3. I <u>understood</u> you <u>wrong</u>.
4. Lu was <u>not</u> <u>kind</u> to me.

5. <u>Fill</u> the glass <u>again</u>.
6. I'll <u>write</u> the list <u>again</u>.
7. He is <u>not</u> <u>able</u> to sing.
8. <u>Heat</u> the stew <u>again</u>.

Suffixes

A **suffix** is also a word part that has meaning. A suffix is added to the end of a base word to make a new word with a different meaning.

You can usually figure out the meaning of a word that has a suffix. Just add together the meaning of the base word and the meaning of the suffix.

Base word	Suffix	New word	Meaning
climb	-er	climber	one who climbs
peace	-ful	peaceful	full of peace
hope	-less	hopeless	without hope

Practice

Add the suffix *-er*, *-ful*, or *-less* to the word in ( ) to make a new word that makes sense. Write the sentences.

1. The _____ set up her easel by the lake.   (paint)
2. An umbrella is _____ in the rain.   (use)
3. The lion tamer was brave and _____.   (fear)
4. Sandy was _____ and spilled the juice.   (care)
5. The nurse was gentle, but the shot was _____.   (pain)
6. Mr. Lopez is a _____ for the *Daily Sun*.   (report)
7. Jenny Lind was a famous _____.   (sing)
8. Nick was tired after a _____ night.   (sleep)

Homographs

Some words are spelled the same but have different meanings. They are called **homographs**. Homographs are usually listed in the dictionary as completely separate words. Look at these sentences.

The paint was a light color.   The empty box was light .

In the first sentence, the word *light* means "not dark." In the second sentence, *light* means "not heavy." These two words look the same, but they are really two different words.

Many homographs also sound different. Look at this chart.

Word	Sound	Meaning
wind	(wīnd)	blowing air
wind	(wīnd)	to twist or turn
wound	(wound)	past tense of wind
wound	(wōōnd)	an injury

Practice

Each word below has a homograph. Write a meaning for each word in each pair. Then write whether the two homographs sound alike or different. Use your dictionary for help.

1. fan **3.** live **5.** tear **7.** rose
2. jar **4.** rock **6.** clip **8.** lead

Antonyms

Antonyms are words that have opposite meanings. You can use antonyms to show how people, places, or things are different. Here are some antonyms.

stop – start	lost – found	dark – light
left – right	good – bad	night – day
shiny – dull	love – hate	top – bottom
sharp – dull	hard – easy	under – over

Practice

Choose the word in ( ) that is an antonym for the underlined word in the sentence. Write the sentence, using the antonym in place of the underlined word. You may use your dictionary for help.

1. Karen reads many <u>dull</u> books.   (interesting, long)
2. She likes to read about <u>familiar</u> places.   (strange, famous)
3. One book was about <u>modern</u> ruins in Greece.   (ancient, important)
4. She <u>disliked</u> a book about Iceland.   (enjoyed, bought)
5. I am sure that Karen would be <u>sorry</u> to visit other lands.   (glad, amazed)
6. She would like a chance to see many <u>similar</u> places.   (different, historical)

Bob is up in the air about coming with us.

Idioms

Have you ever heard people say that they were "up a tree"? They were probably not sitting on a branch of a tall, woody plant. They were just telling you that they were in a difficult situation.

An expression like *up a tree* is called an idiom. An **idiom** is an expression that has a special meaning as a whole. This special meaning is different from the meanings of the separate words added together.

IDIOM: The lesson was over my head .

MEANING: The lesson was too hard for me to understand.

IDIOM: Ira and Ann didn't hit it off .

MEANING: Ira and Ann didn't like each other.

IDIOM: What are you driving at ?

MEANING: What are you trying to say?

IDIOM: Rob is still up in the air about coming with us.

MEANING: Rob is still undecided about coming with us.

IDIOM: I will sell you my old guitar for a song .

MEANING: I will sell you my old guitar at a low price.

Practice

Write each sentence. Replace the underlined idiom with a meaning from the Word Box. Be sure that the answer makes sense in the sentence. Use your dictionary if you need help.

hurry	find	at a low price
better than	teasing you	help
fainted	agree	immediately
unable to think of	clumsy	became afraid
listening carefully	tastes good	free
exactly	trouble	undecided
easily annoyed	told me about	

1. Charlie said that he bought the used skates <u>for a song</u>.
2. Ellie couldn't <u>come up with</u> enough money for a ticket.
3. Ted was <u>up in the air</u> about which book to read for his report.
4. We'll have to <u>step on it</u> to get home in time.
5. Ms. George said, "I'm <u>all thumbs</u> at sewing."
6. I was just <u>pulling your leg</u> about going to school on Saturday.
7. Max was <u>all ears</u> when the teacher talked about space travel.
8. Karen <u>filled me in on</u> the swim meet.
9. Dan was going to dive, but he <u>got cold feet</u>.
10. Nicole was <u>at a loss for</u> a good idea for a story.
11. Please wash the dishes <u>right away</u>.
12. Mr. Lyle was grumpy and <u>out of sorts</u> on Monday.
13. The room was so stuffy that two people <u>passed out</u>.
14. This soup really <u>hits the spot</u>.
15. This book is <u>a cut above</u> other books by that author.
16. My teacher and I don't <u>see eye to eye</u> about homework.
17. Sid said that he would <u>lend a hand</u> at the book sale.
18. Tia was in <u>hot water</u> for being late again.
19. Theodore guessed the price <u>on the nose</u>.
20. The waiter said that our dinner would be <u>on the house</u>.

A diagram of a sentence is a set of lines that show how the words of that sentence work together. You will begin by diagraming the most important words in the sentence. In beginning sections of this Diagraming Guide, sentences will contain words that you have not yet learned how to diagram. Work only with the words that you are asked to diagram. You will learn about the others as you work through the other sections.

Simple Subjects and Simple Predicates *(pp. 22–25)*

The simple subject and the simple predicate are written on a line called the **base line**. The simple subject is separated from the simple predicate by an up-and-down line, or **bar**, that cuts through the line.

Find the simple subject and the simple predicate in this sentence.

Airplanes fly.

Study this diagram of the simple subject and the simple predicate from the sentence above.

Airplanes	fly

Find the simple subject and the simple predicate in this sentence.

The large jet rides smoothly.

Study this diagram. Notice which two words from the sentence are placed on the base line.

jet	rides

Practice Diagram only the simple subjects and simple predicates in these sentences.

1. Polly eats.
2. Mom sleeps.
3. A passenger smiles at a crew member.
4. The friendly pilot speaks clearly.
5. A hungry baby cries.

Compound Subjects *(pp. 28–29)*

Each part of a compound subject is written on a separate line. The word *and* is written on a dotted line that joins the two subject lines.

Find the compound subject in this sentence.

Trees and grass live.

Study this diagram of the compound subject. Notice where the word *and* is written.

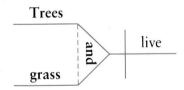

Find the compound subject in this sentence.

Acorns and colored leaves fall eventually.

Study this diagram of the compound subject. Notice which two words in the compound subject are diagramed.

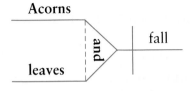

Practice Diagram the subjects and the predicate in each of the five sentences that follow.

1. Ferns and ivy grow quickly.
2. Sunlight and water help.

3. Oaks and maples live long.
4. Pretty flowers and plants fill the garden with color.
5. The young trees and the willow branches bend easily.

Compound Predicates *(pp. 28–29)*

Each part of a compound predicate is written on a separate line. The word *and* is written on a dotted line that joins the two predicate lines.

Find the compound predicate in each sentence. Then study how compound predicates are diagramed. Notice where the word *and* is written.

The noisy crowd rose suddenly and cheered.

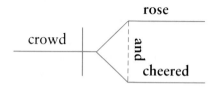

Carlos twisted and turned for a touchdown.

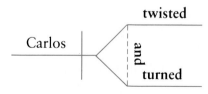

Practice Diagram only the subject and the compound predicates in each sentence.

1. Cheerleaders sang and jumped.
2. The quarterback planned and performed well.
3. The coach watched and walked toward the bench.
4. Sam laughed loudly and waved to us.
5. We smiled and shouted to our team.

Adjectives *(pp. 204–207)*

Adjectives are diagramed on a slanting line below the word that they describe. Find the adjective in this sentence.

Clever dolphins perform.

Study this diagram of the sentence.

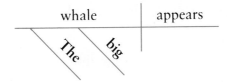

The special words *a*, *an*, and *the* are diagramed just like adjectives.

The big whale appears.

Study this diagram of the sentence.

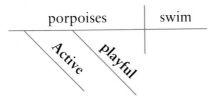

More than one adjective can describe the same word.

Active, playful porpoises swim gracefully.

Study the diagram of this sentence.

More than one adjective can describe the same word.

An adjective sometimes follows a form of the verb *be* (*am*, *are*, *is*, *was*, and *were*). Forms of the verb *be* are diagramed in the same position as action verbs. A slanting line follows the form of the verb *be*. The adjective is written on the base line after the slanting line.

Find the verb and the adjective that follows it in this sentence.

A porpoise is smart.

Study the diagram of this sentence. Notice that the slanting line points back toward the subject but does not cut through the base line.

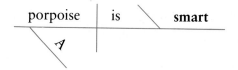

Practice Diagram only the adjectives, the subjects, and the predicates in these sentences.

1. Friendly porpoises jump.
2. Loud, funny noises echo from them.
3. A large whale dives for food.
4. Bright, alert dolphins learn tricks.
5. The three animals are interesting.

Adverbs *(pp. 384–387)*

An adverb is diagramed on a slanting line below the word that it describes.

Find the adverb and the verb that it describes in this sentence.

Pioneers lived simply.

Study this diagram of the sentence.

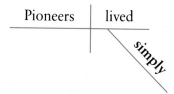

An adverb can appear anywhere in a sentence. It is not always next to the word that it describes. Find the adverb in this sentence.

Bravely the early settlers hunted.

Study this diagram of the sentence.

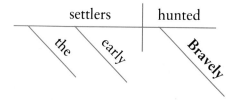

Practice Diagram the subjects, predicates, adjectives, and adverbs in these sentences.

1. Johnny Appleseed worked hard.
2. He eagerly planted seeds.
3. The young trees started slowly.
4. Carefully the young man trimmed branches.
5. The apple trees grew beautifully.

Nouns in Direct Address *(pp. 270–271)*

Diagram a noun in direct address on a short line above and just to the left of the base line.

Find the noun in direct address in this sentence.

Betty, you won.

Study this diagram of the sentence.

A noun in direct address is diagramed in the same way no matter where the word appears in the sentence.

Practice Diagram all of the words in these sentences.

1. Coach Perez, we won easily.
2. Your game, Sandy, started slowly.
3. Players work hard, Todd.
4. The other team, Katie, was excellent.
5. We cheered and yelled, Mrs. Humbolt.

How to Write a Story About Yourself

In a **story about yourself** you tell about one of your own real-life experiences. You show your reader what you saw and how you felt.

Guides for Writing a Story About Yourself

1. Think about your purpose. Do you want your reader to think your experience was funny? sad? happy? Think about your audience. Who will read your story?

2. Write a catchy beginning to capture your reader's interest. Make your reader wonder what will happen next.

3. Include details to make your story come alive. Details help your reader picture what is happening.

4. Use dialogue to make your story lively and interesting. Show what your characters are like from what they say.

5. Write a dialogue correctly. Put quotation marks around a speaker's exact words. Begin a new paragraph when one character stops speaking and another character starts.

6. Write an interesting title to capture your reader's attention. Give a hint about the story without telling too much.

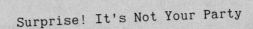

Surprise! It's Not Your Party

I can't believe that my family ever thought it would be fun to give Jack a birthday party. Jack is my older brother. He lives at school, but he comes home every weekend. "Here comes Jack. I can smell his dirty laundry," I joked as Jack's car pulled into the driveway.

Jack had no idea what we had planned for his 18th birthday. I had invited all of Jack's friends. Mom and Dad made enough food to feed fifty people.

Writing Prompt

Directions: Look at the two pictures. Some days are pleasant and others are unpleasant. What was the best day you ever had? What was the worst? What happened to make those days stand out? Choose your best or worst day, and write a story in order to share with your classmates.

How to Write Paragraphs of Comparison and Contrast

When you write a **paragraph of comparison,** you show how two things are alike. When you write a **paragraph of contrast,** you show how two things are different.

Guides for Writing: Comparison and Contrast

1. Think about your purpose. Do you want to inform, persuade, or entertain the reader? Think about your audience. For whom will you write?
2. Choose a topic. Make sure it has two things you can compare and contrast. Make one list of details that shows how the things are alike. Make a second list that shows how they are different.
3. Organize the details on your lists. Use these details to write one paragraph that compares and another that contrasts.
4. For each paragraph, write a clear topic sentence that tells the main idea.
5. Use the details on your lists to write the other sentences for each paragraph. Each sentence must support the main idea.

Making References

   A dictionary and an encyclopedia are similar. They are both reference books that contain useful and true information. Both include a large number of entries or articles arranged in alphabetical order. Both have guide words at the top of each page.
   A dictionary gives information about a word's spelling and pronunciation. It also gives definitions for each word. On the other hand, an encyclopedia contains hundreds of articles that give information about a variety of topics.

Writing Prompt

Directions: Look at the picture. It shows a lion and a tiger. How are the lion and the tiger alike? How are they different? Write two paragraphs so that someone your age can understand how a lion and a tiger are alike and different.

How to Write a Story

A **story** can be an adventure or a mystery. It can be real or make-believe and can take place in the present, the past, or the future.

Guides for Writing a Story

1. Think about your purpose. Will your story be funny? sad? Think about your audience. For whom are you writing?
2. Think about the setting, the main characters, and the plot. Where and when will the story take place? Will your characters be real or make-believe?
3. Write an interesting beginning. You can describe the setting or introduce your main characters. You can also use dialogue to make your characters seem real.
4. In the middle of your story, write about the main events. You can include a problem to solve.
5. Write a good ending. Solve the problem if there was one. Finish the story in a way that makes sense.
6. Write a catchy title for your story. Make your reader want to read more.

The Invitation

   "Come to a party on the Planet Zarumi on the tenth day of May in the year 2045," Leon read aloud for the third time. He scratched his head and decided to pinch himself to see if he was dreaming. "Ouch!" he yelled, rubbing his now sore arm.
   Leon studied the invitation's envelope for a clue. He could not identify the postmark. There was no name on the return address. All that was written on the return address was Zarumi, Planet of Your Dreams.
   "What's going on?" Leon asked himself over and over again.

Writing Prompt

Directions: Look at the picture. It shows a girl who has just discovered a very unusual picnic. What is the girl thinking? Who are these little people? What do you think will happen next? Write a story for your class about the girl and the little people.

How to Write a Description

A **description** is a word picture that helps the reader imagine how something looks, sounds, feels, smells, and tastes. A description can be of a person or animal, a place, or a thing.

Guides for Writing a Description

1. Think about your purpose. What picture do you want your reader to imagine? What details will you choose to fit your purpose? Think about your audience. Will your reader be your age? younger? older?

2. Write a topic sentence that tells the main idea of your paragraph. Choose details that support the main idea and the purpose of your description.

3. Use sense words. Help your reader see, hear, taste, touch, and smell what you are describing.

4. Use exact words in your description. Paint a clear word picture for your reader.

The Storm

Papa and I huddled together on the wooden porch swing. The sweet smell of Grandma's prize roses floated through the cool air to where we sat rocking back and forth. Crickets chirped, and the old swing creaked and groaned.

I got up from the swing and hung my head over the worn porch rail. I looked up at the sky. The bright, full moon disappeared behind a huge, dark cloud. Suddenly a bolt of lightning flashed across the sky. Almost immediately the sound of thunder exploded around us. I ran to Papa and buried my face against his chest.

Writing Prompt

Directions: Look at the picture. Imagine that you are in this crowd watching the street performer. What do you see and hear? What do you feel as you watch? Write a paragraph, describing the scene to someone who has not seen this picture.

How to Write a Persuasive Letter

A **persuasive letter** is a letter that tries to persuade or convince someone to agree with and support your ideas.

Guides for Writing a Persuasive Letter

1. Think about your purpose. What do you want to persuade your reader to do? Think about your audience. Whom do you want to persuade?
2. Write your opinion in a clear topic sentence.
3. In the other sentences, give strong reasons to support your opinion. Choose reasons that are important to your audience.
4. List your reasons from the most important to the least important or the other way around.
5. Use the correct letter form. Include a heading, a greeting, a body, a closing, and a signature.

41 Woodstock Drive
Auburn, ME 04210
July 7, 1990

Dear Greg,

 I would like you to come and visit my family and me at Lost Lake. If you're thinking that spending a week here at Lost Lake might not be fun, you're wrong!

 Last year Kenji Sato visited and had a great time. We went swimming and fishing every day. We used my mother's rowboat and rowed to the island across the lake. We can do all those things when you visit. And guess what else? My uncle has a new motorboat! He wants to teach us to water-ski.

 I hope you decide to come. Write back soon!

Your friend,

Jacob

Writing Prompt

Directions: The classes in your school are taking part in a spring field day. You are planning some of the activities for that day. You need students to help you organize a few games and present awards. Write a letter to put on the bulletin board to persuade students to help with the field day activities.

How to Write a Research Report

A **research report** contains facts and information about a particular topic.

Guides for Writing a Research Report

1. Think about your purpose. What do you want your readers to learn? Think about your audience. For whom are you writing your report?
2. Choose a topic that is not too broad. Write questions about your topic that you will answer in your report.
3. Get information for your report. Use reference books, nonfiction books about your topic, and interviews. Use more than one source and the most recent books.
4. Take notes. Use a separate note card for each of your questions. Write just enough to remember the main ideas and important facts. Write your sources on each card.
5. Use your notes to write an outline. Put your questions in an order that makes sense. Turn each question into a main topic. Your notes will become the subtopics.
6. Turn your outline into a report. Use the main topic to write a topic sentence for each paragraph. Use the subtopics to write sentences that support the main idea.
7. Write a title and list your sources at the end.

Hummingbirds

The hummingbird is a very interesting bird. When it gathers food, the hummingbird hovers in the air like a helicopter, moving forward and backward. It uses its narrow head, slender bill, and tube-like tongue to collect nectar from flower blossoms.

Did you ever wonder why this tiny bird is called a hummingbird? When it flies, the hummingbird moves its wings very rapidly, causing a humming sound.

Writing Prompt

Directions: The store window below shows different kinds of sporting equipment. Which sport is your favorite? Use a reference source to find out more about that sport. How and where did the sport begin? How is it played? Who are its most famous players? Write several paragraphs about the sport to share what you have learned with a friend.

How to Write Instructions

Instructions tell what to do and explain how to do it. They are directions for doing or making something.

Guides for Writing Instructions

1. Choose an interesting topic. It should be something you know how to do or would like to know how to do. An art activity or a science experiment might make a good topic.
2. Make sure that you know who your audience is.
3. If your topic is something you do not yet know how to do, find out all you can about it.
4. List the steps you will include and put them in the correct order. Check to be sure the steps are all there.
5. Begin by explaining what the instructions are for. Then tell what kinds and amounts of materials are needed.
6. Write out the steps in order. Use words such as *first, next, then,* and *finally* to make the order clear.
7. Review your instructions to be sure they are clear and complete.

```
        A Puzzling Birthday Card

    Surprise someone with a birthday-card
puzzle! To make one, you need a large sheet of
cardboard. You also need some crayons, felt
markers, scissors, and an envelope.
    Write a birthday greeting on the cardboard.
Then decorate the whole sheet with drawings and
writing. Be sure to sign your name.
    When your decorating is finished, cut the
card into large, oddly shaped pieces. Then mix
up the pieces and put them in an envelope.
Finally, write the name of the birthday person
on the envelope. If you want to, you can
decorate the envelope too.
```

Writing Prompt

Directions: Look at what the children at camp are doing in this picture. Which things do you know how to do? Which things would you like to know how to do? Choose one camp activity and find out all you can about it. Then write instructions that explain how to do the activity.

How to Write a Biography

A **biography** is a true story of another person's life. It gives facts about what the person did and how the person acted.

Guides for Writing a Biography

1. Choose someone to write about. It can be a living person or someone who lived in the past. It might be a famous scientist, singer, ruler, or sports star.
2. Learn all you can about the person. Read newspaper reports, encyclopedia articles, and books about your subject. Take notes on important facts and details.
3. Use your facts to write the biography. Tell where and when the person was born and important things the person did and said. Show what the person was like. Begin with the person's early years and end with later years.
4. Tell something unusual the person did or said.
5. Write a good title and capitalize all important words.

A Scientist Who Dared to Speak

"What has already silenced the voices of spring in countless towns in America?" These words lead us into the book Silent Spring by Rachel Carson. Ms. Carson was one of the first people to tell us about the harm we are doing to our world.

Rachel Louise Carson was a marine biologist and science writer. She was born in Springdale, Pennsylvania, in 1907 and died in 1964. After her schooling, Ms. Carson went to work for the U.S. Fish and Wildlife Service.

Rachel Carson's life was devoted to protecting sea life and our seashores. Her two most famous books, The Sea Around Us and Silent Spring, stress how all living things depend upon one another.

Writing Prompt

Directions: Look at the people pictured below. Choose one of them and find out all you can about him or her. Then write a biography about the person. Tell important facts and interesting details. Begin in a lively way.

Dr. Elizabeth Blackwell

Queen Elizabeth II

Justice Thurgood Marshall

Albert Einstein

How to Write a News Story

A **news story** tells about a recent event. It reports **facts** about what happened. Facts give information that can be proved true.

Guides for Writing a News Story

1. Choose a subject for your news story. It might be something that happened at your school or in your neighborhood or town.
2. Find facts that answer these questions: *What* event took place? *Who* took part in it? *When*, *where*, and *why* did it happen? Talk to people who were there.
3. Write the most important facts at the beginning of your story. Put the least important facts at the end.
4. Write a beginning that captures your readers' interest.
5. Use the exact words of people who were at the event. Put their words in quotation marks.
6. Write a short, attention-grabbing headline for your news story. Capitalize each important word.

Ducks Take Over Local Swimming Pool

The new summer home of a wild duck and her duckling is a large swimming pool at the home of a local family. The Murphys, who live on Walnut Street in Linfield, state that the mallard hen arrived in June and promptly built a nest in a planter box. Before long, an egg appeared in the nest and hatched into a fuzzy little duckling.

The Murphy family is happy to have the ducks, because they eat insects that collect in the pool. "I don't have to clean out the bugs this year," reports Alan Murphy. "But you wouldn't believe how many people stop by. I should charge admission!"

Writing Prompt

Directions: Look at the picture. What event is taking place? Who is taking part in it? When, where, and why is the event taking place? Write a news story about the picture. In your story, answer the questions *What? Who? When? Where?* and *Why?*

How to Write a Shape Poem

A **shape poem** is a special kind of poem. Its shape helps readers understand the poem's subject and meaning. Shape poems are written for fun.

Guides for Writing a Shape Poem

1. Choose a subject that will be fun to write about such as a roller coaster or a kite. In a shape poem about a roller coaster, you can make the words go up and down like a roller-coaster ride. In a shape poem about a kite, you can write your words in the shape of a kite. Animals make good subjects for shape poems too.

2. Use sense words to describe things you see, hear, smell, touch, and taste. Your words as well as the shape of your poem will help to get your meaning across.

3. Think about how you will use sound in your poem. Will you use rhyme? Will your poem have a special rhythm? What sound words will you use? Will you repeat any beginning sounds?

4. Give your poem a title that tells what it is about. Capitalize each important word.

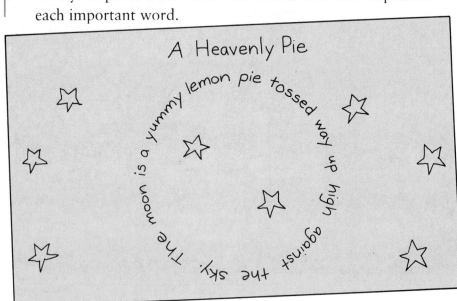

A Heavenly Pie

The moon is a yummy lemon pie tossed way up high against the sky.

Writing Prompt

Directions: Look at the pictures below. Each of them would make a good subject for a shape poem. What might the football, the sun, or the flower look like in such a poem? What words would make the poem appeal to the senses? Choose the item you think would be the most fun to write about. Then write your own shape poem about it.

■ SPELLING GUIDE■

Words Often Misspelled

accept	busy	fourth	nickel	to
ache	buy	Friday	ninety	too
again	by	friend	ninety-nine	tried
all right	calendar	goes	ninth	tries
almost	cannot	going	often	truly
already	can't	grammar	once	two
although	careful	guard	other	tying
always	catch	guess	people	unknown
angel	caught	guide	principal	until
angle	chief	half	quiet	unusual
answer	children	haven't	quit	wasn't
argue	choose	hear	quite	wear
asked	chose	heard	really	weather
aunt	color	heavy	receive	Wednesday
author	cough	height	rhythm	weird
awful	cousin	here	right	we'll
babies	decide	hers	Saturday	we're
been	divide	hole	stretch	weren't
believe	does	hoping	surely	we've
bother	don't	hour	their	where
bought	early	its	theirs	which
break	enough	it's	there	whole
breakfast	every	January	they're	witch
breathe	exact	let's	they've	won't
broken	except	listen	those	wouldn't
brother	excite	loose	though	write
brought	expect	lose	thought	writing
bruise	February	minute	through	written
build	finally	muscle	tied	you're
business	forty	neighbor	tired	yours

Spelling Guidelines

1. The /ă/ sound is usually spelled **a**. The /ā/ sound is often spelled **ai**, **ay**, or **a-consonant-e**.

hang	gain	pray
drag	drain	sale
hatch	gray	blade
maid	clay	shame

2. The /ĕ/ sound is usually spelled **e**. The /ē/ sound is often spelled **ee** or **ea**.

west	speed	tease
spent	need	least
desk	sweet	peach
edge	three	dream

3. The /ĭ/ sound is usually spelled **i**. The /ī/ sound is often spelled **i**, **igh**, or **i-consonant-e**.

lift	blind	shine
hint	sigh	crime
brick	flight	ripe
grind	fright	pride

4. The /ŏ/ sound is usually spelled **o**. The /ô/ sound is often spelled **o**. The /ō/ sound is often spelled **o**, **ow**, **oa**, or **o-consonant-e**.

stock	bold	crow
block	folk	coast
odd	bolt	goal
lost	shown	coach
cross	glow	globe
host	bowl	chose

5. The /ŭ/ sound is usually spelled **u**. The /yōō/ and /ōō/ sounds are often spelled **ew**, **u-consonant-e**, or **ue**. The /ōō/ sound may also be spelled **ui**.

dull	few	due
trunk	blew	glue
brush	tune	fruit
pump	tube	juice
threw	true	suit

6. The /o͞o/ sound is often spelled **oo**. The /o͝o/ sound is often spelled **oo** or **u**.	roof booth tool	wood brook poor	put bush pull
7. The /ou/ sound is often spelled **ow** or **ou**. The /ô/ sound is often spelled **aw**, **au**, or **a** before **l**.	howl gown proud	mount bounce dawn	sauce cause always
8. The /îr/ sounds are often spelled **ear** or **eer**. The /är/ sounds are usually spelled **ar**. The /âr/ sounds are often spelled **are** or **air**.	spear gear beard queer cheer	scarf alarm starve charm spare	glare stare square dairy hairy
9. The /ôr/ sounds are often spelled **or** or **ore**. The /ûr/ sounds are often spelled **ur**, **ear**, **ir**, or **or**.	horse worn chore	curve curl learn	firm thirteen world
10. The final /ər/ sounds in two-syllable words are often spelled **er**, **ar**, or **or**.	lad**der** bit**ter** prop**er**	cell**ar** begg**ar** sug**ar**	sail**or** doct**or** harb**or**
11. The final /l/ or /əl/ sounds in two-syllable words are often spelled **le**, **el**, or **al**.	mid**dle** bot**tle** bat**tle**	lev**el** mod**el** lab**el**	met**al** fin**al** tot**al**
12. Some words have unexpected spellings.	acre says	special guide	lamb knight

13. If a word ends in **e**, drop the final **e** before adding **-ed** or **-ing**. If a one-syllable word ends with one vowel and one consonant, double the final consonant before adding **-ed** and **-ing**.

faint**ed**	trac**ed**	ru**bb**ing
check**ing**	hik**ing**	ta**nn**ing
smell**ing**	danc**ing**	ski**pp**ed
land**ed**	pleas**ing**	stri**pp**ed
clos**ed**	phon**ing**	fli**pp**ed
strip**ed**	wast**ing**	sna**pp**ing

14. The final /ē/ sound in a two-syllable word is often spelled **y** or **ey**.

read**y**	hobb**y**	monk**ey**
lonel**y**	beaut**y**	vall**ey**
sorr**y**	turk**ey**	hock**ey**

15. The /k/ sound in a one-syllable word is often spelled **k** or **ck**. In a two-syllable word, it is often spelled **k**, **ck**, or **c**. The /ng/ sound before **k** is spelled **n**.

shar**k**	ja**c**ket	jun**k**
ris**k**	atta**ck**	drin**k**
stru**ck**	publi**c**	ran**k**
tra**ck**	musi**c**	blan**k**
la**ck**	a**c**tive	sin**k**
mista**k**e	topi**c**	blan**k**et

16. The final /j/ sound is usually spelled **dge** or **ge**. The /ĭj/ sound in a final, unstressed syllable is usually spelled **age**. The final /s/ sound is often spelled **ce**.

lo**dge**	chan**ge**	cott**age**
e**dge**	dama**ge**	chan**ce**
bri**dge**	ca**ge**	twi**ce**
ri**dge**	cabb**age**	glan**ce**
do**dge**	vill**age**	sin**ce**
stran**ge**	man**age**	fen**ce**

17. Prefixes are added to beginnings of words or roots. Suffixes are added to ends of words.

display	**un**aware	**re**form
pain**ful**	move**ment**	care**less**

CAPITALIZATION, PUNCTUATION, AND USAGE GUIDE

Abbreviations

Abbreviations are shortened forms of words. Most abbreviations begin with a capital letter and end with a period.

Titles	Mr. *(Mister)* Mr. Juan Albino Sr. *(Senior)* John Helt, Sr. Mrs. *(Mistress)* Mrs. Frances Wong Jr. *(Junior)* John Helt, Jr. Ms. Leslie Clark Dr. *(Doctor)* Dr. Janice Dodds
Words used in addresses	St. *(Street)* Blvd. *(Boulevard)* Rd. *(Road)* Ave. *(Avenue)*
Days of the week	Sun. *(Sunday)* Thurs. *(Thursday)* Mon. *(Monday)* Fri. *(Friday)* Tues. *(Tuesday)* Sat. *(Saturday)* Wed. *(Wednesday)*
Months of the year	Jan. *(January)* Apr. *(April)* Oct. *(October)* Feb. *(February)* Aug. *(August)* Nov. *(November)* Mar. *(March)* Sept. *(September)* Dec. *(December)*

Note: *May, June,* and *July* are not abbreviated.

States	The United States Postal Service uses two capital letters and no period in each of its state abbreviations.

AL *(Alabama)*	HI *(Hawaii)*	MA *(Massachusetts)*
AK *(Alaska)*	ID *(Idaho)*	MI *(Michigan)*
AZ *(Arizona)*	IL *(Illinois)*	MN *(Minnesota)*
AR *(Arkansas)*	IN *(Indiana)*	MS *(Mississippi)*
CA *(California)*	IA *(Iowa)*	MO *(Missouri)*
CO *(Colorado)*	KS *(Kansas)*	MT *(Montana)*
CT *(Connecticut)*	KY *(Kentucky)*	NE *(Nebraska)*
DE *(Delaware)*	LA *(Louisiana)*	NV *(Nevada)*
FL *(Florida)*	ME *(Maine)*	NH *(New Hampshire)*
GA *(Georgia)*	MD *(Maryland)*	NJ *(New Jersey)*

States (continued)			
NM *(New Mexico)*	PA *(Pennsylvania)*	VT *(Vermont)*
NY *(New York)*	RI *(Rhode Island)*	VA *(Virginia)*
NC *(North Carolina)*	SC *(South Carolina)*	WA *(Washington)*
ND *(North Dakota)*	SD *(South Dakota)*	WV *(West Virginia)*
OH *(Ohio)*	TN *(Tennessee)*	WI *(Wisconsin)*
OK *(Oklahoma)*	TX *(Texas)*	WY *(Wyoming)*
OR *(Oregon)*	UT *(Utah)*	

Titles

Underlining

Titles of books, newspapers, magazines, and TV series are underlined. The important words and the first and last words are capitalized.

Life on the Mississippi   Newsweek   Nova

Quotation marks

Put *quotation marks (" ")* around the titles of short stories, articles, songs, poems, and book chapters.

"The Necklace"   *(short story)*
"Home on the Range"   *(song)*

Quotations

Quotation marks

A *direct quotation* tells a speaker's exact words. Use *quotation marks (" ")* to set off a direct quotation from the rest of the sentence.

"Please put away your books now," said Mr. Emory.

Begin a quotation with a capital letter. When a quotation comes at the end of a sentence, use a comma to separate the quotation from the words that tell who is speaking. Put end marks inside the last quotation marks.

The driver announced, "This is the Summer Street bus."

Writing a conversation

Begin a new paragraph each time a new person begins speaking.

"Are your seats behind home plate or along the first-base line?" asked the voice on the phone.

"I haven't bought any tickets yet," said Mr. Williams. "I was hoping that you would reserve three seats for me now."

USAGE · PUNCTUATION · CAPITALIZATION

Capitalization

Capitalize the first word of every sentence.
What an unusual color the roses are!

Capitalize the pronoun *I*.
What should I do next?

**Capitalize every important word in the names of
particular people, pets, places, and things (proper nouns).**
Rover   District of Columbia   Elm Street   Lincoln Memorial

Capitalize titles and initials that are parts of names.
Governor Bradford   Emily G. Hesse   Senator Smith

**Capitalize family titles when they are used as names or as
parts of names.**
We visited Uncle Harry.   May we play now, Grandma?

Capitalize the names of months and days.
My birthday is on the last Monday in March.

Capitalize the names of groups.
Sutton Bicycle Club   National League

Capitalize the names of holidays.
Memorial Day   Fourth of July   Veterans Day

**Capitalize the first and last words and all important
words in the titles of books and newspapers.**
From Earth to the Moon   The New York Times

**Capitalize the first word in the greeting and the closing of
a letter.**
Dear Marcia,   Yours truly,

**In an outline, each Roman numeral and capital letter is
followed by a period. Capitalize the first word of each
main topic and subtopic.**
I. Types of libraries
   A. Large public library
   B. Bookmobile

End marks	**There are three end marks. A *period (.)* ends a statement or a command. A *question mark (?)* follows a question. An *exclamation point (!)* follows an exclamation.** The scissors are on my desk. *(statement)* Look up the spelling of that word. *(command)* How is the word spelled? *(question)* This is your best poem so far! *(exclamation)*
Apostrophe	**To form the possessive of a singular noun, add an apostrophe and *s ('s).*** baby's Russ's grandmother's family's
	For a plural noun ending in *s*, add only an apostrophe ('). sisters' families' Smiths' hound dogs'
	For a plural noun that does not end in *s*, add an apostrophe and *s ('s).* women's mice's children's
	Use an apostrophe in contractions in place of dropped letters. isn't *(is not)* wasn't *(was not)* I'm *(I am)* can't *(cannot)* we're *(we are)* they've *(they have)* won't *(will not)* it's *(it is)* they'll *(they will)*
Comma	**A *comma (,)* tells the reader to pause between the words that it separates.**
	Use commas to separate items in a series. Put a comma after each item in the series except the last one. Clyde asked if we had any apples, peaches, or grapes.
	You can combine two short, related sentences to make one compound sentence. Use a comma and the connecting word *and, but,* or *or.* Some students were at lunch, but others were studying.
	Use commas to set off the words *yes, no,* and *well* when they are at the beginning of a sentence. Well, it's just too cold out. No, it isn't six yet.

USAGE · PUNCTUATION · CAPITALIZATION

Comma (continued)	Use a comma or commas to set off the names of people who are spoken to directly.
	Jean, help me fix this tire. How was your trip, Grandpa?
	Use a comma to separate the month and the day from the year.
	Our nation was born on July 4, 1776.
	Use a comma between the names of a city and a state.
	Chicago, Illinois Miami, Florida
	Use a comma after the greeting in a friendly letter.
	Dear Deena, Dear Uncle Rudolph,
	Use a comma after the closing in a letter.
	Your nephew, Sincerely yours,

Problem Words

Words	Rules	Examples
a, an, the	These words are special adjectives called articles.	
a, an	Use *a* and *an* before singular nouns. Use *a* if a word begins with a consonant sound. Use *an* if a word begins with a vowel sound.	a banana an apple
the	Use *the* with both singular and plural nouns.	the apple the apples
	Use *the* to point out particular persons, places, or things.	The books that I like are long.
are	*Are* is a verb.	Are these gloves yours?
our	*Our* is a possessive pronoun.	This is our car.

Words	Rules	Examples
doesn't	Use *doesn't* with singular nouns, *he, she,* and *it.*	Dad <u>doesn't</u> swim.
don't	Use *don't* with plural nouns, *I, you, we,* and *they.*	We <u>don't</u> swim.
good	Use the adjective *good* to describe nouns.	The weather looks <u>good</u>.
well	Use the adverb *well* to describe verbs.	She sings <u>well</u>.
its	*Its* is a possessive pronoun.	The dog wagged <u>its</u> tail.
it's	*It's* is a contraction of *it is.*	<u>It's</u> cold today.
let	*Let* means "to allow."	Please <u>let</u> me go swimming.
leave	*Leave* means "to go away from" or "to let stay."	I will <u>leave</u> soon. <u>Leave</u> it on my desk.
set	*Set* means "to put."	<u>Set</u> the vase on the table.
sit	*Sit* means "to rest or stay in one place."	Please <u>sit</u> in this chair.
their	*Their* is a possessive pronoun.	<u>Their</u> coats are on the bed.
there	*There* is an adverb. *There* means "in that place."	Is Carlos <u>there</u>? <u>There</u> is my book.
they're	*They're* is a contraction of *they are.*	<u>They're</u> going to the store.
two	*Two* is a number.	I bought <u>two</u> shirts.
to	*To* means "toward."	A squirrel ran <u>to</u> the tree.
too	*Too* means "more than enough" and "also."	I ate <u>too</u> many cherries. Can we go <u>too</u>?
your	*Your* is a possessive pronoun.	Are these <u>your</u> glasses?
you're	*You're* is a contraction of *you are.*	<u>You're</u> late again!

USAGE · PUNCTUATION · CAPITALIZATION

Adjective and Adverb Usage

	Use adjectives to describe nouns. Use adverbs to describe verbs. This plant is <u>tall</u>. *(adj.)* It grew <u>fast</u>. *(adv.)*
Comparing	**To compare two people, places, or things, add -er to many adjectives and adverbs.** This plant is <u>taller</u> than the other one. It grew <u>faster</u>.
	To compare three or more people, places, or things, add -est to many adjectives or adverbs. This plant is the <u>tallest</u> of the three. It grew <u>fastest</u>.
Double comparisons	**Never combine -er with the word *more*. Do not combine -est with the word *most*.** She is a <u>better</u> (*not* more better) skier than he. The third book is the <u>longest</u> (*not* most longest).
good, bad	**When you use the adjectives *good* and *bad* to compare, you must change their form. Use *better* or *worse* to compare two. Use *best* or *worst* to compare three.** The weather today is <u>worse</u> than it was yesterday. The forecast for tomorrow is the <u>best</u> one of the week.
more, most	**With most long adjectives and with adverbs that end in -ly, use *more* to compare two people, places, things, or actions. Use *most* to compare three or more.** This song is <u>more beautiful</u> than the first one. Of the five songs, this one was sung the <u>most powerfully</u>.

Negatives

	A negative word or negative contraction says "no" or "not." Do not use two negatives to express one negative idea. **INCORRECT:** He can't see nothing. **CORRECT:** He <u>can't</u> see <u>anything</u>. **CORRECT:** He <u>can</u> see <u>nothing</u>.

Pronoun Usage

I and me	Use the pronoun *I* as the subject of a sentence. Use the pronoun *me* after action verbs and after words such as *to*, *with*, *for*, and *at*. When using *I* or *me* with other nouns or pronouns, name yourself last.
	Jan and <u>I</u> are going to the movies. She will telephone <u>me</u>.
	<u>Beth and I</u> will leave. Give the papers to <u>Ron and me</u>.
Subject and object pronouns	A pronoun used as a subject (*I, you, he, she, it, we,* or *they*) is called a subject pronoun.
	<u>She</u> did not disturb the grasshopper.
	A pronoun used as an object (*me, you, him, her, it, us,* or *them*) is called an object pronoun. Use object pronouns after action verbs and after words such as *to, with, for,* and *at*.
	The puppy likes <u>us</u>. Let's play with <u>him</u>.

Verb Usage

Tenses	Avoid unnecessary shifts from one tense to another.
	The trains <u>stopped</u>, and everyone <u>was</u> (*not* is) surprised.
Irregular verbs	Irregular verbs do not add *-ed* or *-d* to show past action. Because irregular verbs do not follow a regular pattern, you must remember their spellings.

Present	Past	Past with helping verb	Present	Past	Past with helping verb
be	was	been	have	had	had
begin	began	begun	know	knew	known
break	broke	broken	make	made	made
bring	brought	brought	say	said	said
come	came	come	sing	sang	sung
drive	drove	driven	take	took	taken
eat	ate	eaten	tell	told	told
give	gave	given	throw	threw	thrown
grow	grew	grown	wear	wore	worn

How to Use This Thesaurus

Why do you use a thesaurus? One reason is to make your writing more exact. Suppose you wrote the following sentence:

We had a nice day at the beach.

Is *nice* the most exact word you can use? To find out, use your Thesaurus Plus.

Look up your word Turn to the index on pages 485–489. You will find

nice, *adj.*

Because *nice* is in blue type, you can look up *nice* in the Thesaurus Plus.

Use your thesaurus The main entries in the thesaurus are listed in alphabetical order. Turn to *nice*. You will find

main entry word **nice** *adj.* pleasing or appealing.　　　part of speech

sample sentence → *Jean has a very **nice**, friendly, open smile.* meaning

agreeable to one's liking. *The lovely flowers were an **agreeable** sight.*

subentries ── *pleasant* giving enjoyment or delight. *The **pleasant** evening air felt good after the hot day.*

antonyms ── **antonyms:** awful, horrible, distasteful, terrible, unpleasant

Which word might better describe the day in the sentence above? Perhaps you chose *pleasant*.

Other index entries There are two other types of entries in your Thesaurus Plus Index.

1. The slanted type means you can find other words for *achieve* if you look under *do*.

   achieve do, *v.*
   actually really, *adv.*
   admirable good, *adj.*
   admire like, *v.*

2. The regular type tells you that *after* is the opposite of *before*.

   adore like, *v.*
   after before, *adv.*

Practice

A. Use your Thesaurus Index to write answers to these questions.

   1. What part of speech is helpful?
   2. What is the main entry word for expert?
   3. Where in the Thesaurus Plus is gorgeous listed?
   4. Is quiet listed as a main entry?
   5. What is an antonym for run?

B. Use the Thesaurus Plus. Choose a more exact word to replace each underlined word. Rewrite the sentence, using the new word.

   6. I told my friends a scary story.
   7. "A cat had climbed a tree," I said.
   8. Surprised at what it had done, the cat began to howl.
   9. Upset that the cat might fall, I called for help.
   10. I described the cat's yellow eyes to my neighbor.
   11. I think I should continue the story tomorrow.
   12. Everyone agreed to meet at my house.

■ Thesaurus Plus Index ■

A

able good, *adj.*
accomplish do, *v.*
achieve do, *v.*
actually really, *adv.*
admirable good, *adj.*
admire like, *v.*
adore like, *v.*
after before, *adv.*
agree, *v.*
agreeable nice, *adj.*
alarming scary, *adj.*
allow let, *v.*
amazed surprised, *adj.*
amethyst purple, *n.*
amusing funny, *adj.*
analyze think, *v.*
answer ask, *v.*
appealing pretty, *adj.*
appetizing good, *adj.*
appreciate like, *v.*
approve agree, *v.*
approximately nearly, *adv.*
aroma smell, *n.*
angry, *adj.*
ask, *v.*
associated related, *adj.*
assume think, *v.*
astonished surprised, *adj.*
astounded surprised, *adj.*
attractive pretty, *adj.*
awestruck surprised, *adj.*
awful good, *adj.*
awful nice, *adj.*

B

bad good, *adj.*
bark say, *v.*
be fond of like, *v.*
beautiful pretty, *adj.*

before, *adv.*
believe think, *v.*
bellow say, *v.*
beneficial helpful, *adj.*
bigger smaller, *adj.*
bigger, *adj.*
breezy easy, *adj.*
brief quick, *adj.*
brilliant pretty, *adj.*
bulkier bigger, *adj.*
bumpy rough, *adj.*
bumpy smooth, *adj.*

C

calm frighten, *v.*
calming scary, *adj.*
capable good, *adj.*
care for like, *v.*
carefree easy, *adj.*
caring good, *adj.*
carry out do, *v.*
casual easy, *adj.*
caught off guard
   surprised, *adj.*
cause effect, *n.*
cause reason, *n.*
challenging easy, *adj.*
charitable good, *adj.*
charming pretty, *adj.*
cheerful sad, *adj.*
cherish like, *v.*
chief main, *adj.*
clear easy, *adj.*
closely nearly, *adv.*
coarse rough, *adj.*
coarse smooth, *adj.*
cold, *adj.*
comfort frighten, *v.*
comfortable easy, *adj.*
comical funny, *adj.*

common strange, *adj.*
common, *adj.*
comply with agree, *v.*
conceal discover, *v.*
conceive think, *v.*
connected related, *adj.*
consent agree, *v.*
consequence effect, *n.*
consider think, *v.*
considerate good, *adj.*
correct right, *adj.*
costly expensive, *adj.*
courteous good, *adj.*
crawling, *v.*
creeping crawling, *v.*
cruel good, *adj.*
cry say, *v.*
cut off related, *adj.*
cute pretty, *adj.*

D

dash run, *v.*
dazed surprised, *adj.*
dazzling pretty, *adj.*
decent good, *adj.*
delicious good, *adj.*
demanding easy, *adj.*
deny agree, *v.*
dependable, *adj.*
desire want, *v.*
despise like, *v.*
detest like, *v.*
develop invent, *v.*
different common, *adj.*
different same, *adj.*
difficult easy, *adj.*
disagreeable good, *adj.*
discover, *v.*
disgusting good, *adj.*
dishonest dependable,
   adj.

dislike like, *v.*
distasteful nice, *adj.*
do, *v.*
dote on like, *v.*
dream up think, *v.*
dumbfounded surprised, *adj.*

E

earlier before, *adv.*
easy, *adj.*
easygoing easy, *adj.*
effect, *n.*
employment job, *n.*
enchanting pretty, *ad*
enjoy like, *v.*
enjoyment fun, *n.*
entertainment fun, *n.*
equal same, *adj.*
essential necessary, *adj.*
event, *n.*
evil good, *adj.*
exactly nearly, *adv.*
exalt like, *v.*
excellent good, *adj.*
exclaim say, *v.*
expect think, *v.*
expensive, *adj.*
experience event, *n.*
experienced good, *adj.*
expert good, *adj.*
explanation reason, *n.*
exquisite pretty, *adj.*

F

fair pretty, *adj.*
familiar common, *adj.*
familiar strange, *adj.*
fancy like, *v.*
fancy think, *v.*
fantasize think, *v.*
fast quick, *adj.*
fat thin, *adj.*

fatter bigger, *adj.*
few many, *adj.*
figure think, *v.*
fine good, *adj.*
fitting right, *adj.*
flabbergasted surprised, *adj.*
flavorful good, *adj.*
flighty dependable, *adj.*
foresee think, *v.*
fragrance smell, *n.*
friendly good, *adj.*
frighten, *v.*
frightening scary, *adj.*
frigid cold, *adj.*
fun, *n.*
funny, *adj.*
furious angry, *adj.*

G

generous good, *adj.*
gentle easy, *adj.*
gifted good, *adj.*
glad sad, *adj.*
gloomy sad, *adj.*
glorious pretty, *adj.*
gold yellow, *adj.*
good, *adj.*
gorgeous pretty, *adj.*
graceful pretty, *adj.*
grander bigger, *adj.*
grape purple, *n.*
greater smaller, *adj.*
gripe say, *v.*
groan say, *v.*
growl say, *v.*
grumble say, *v.*
grunt say, *v.*
guess think, *v.*

H

handsome pretty, *adj.*
happy angry, *adj.*

happy sad, *adj.*
hard easy, *adj.*
harmful good, *adj.*
harmful helpful, *adj.*
hate like, *v.*
have regard for like, *v.*
healthful good, *adj.*
heartless good, *adj.*
heavier bigger, *adj.*
heavy thin, *adj.*
helpful, *adj.*
hide discover, *v.*
hideous pretty, *adj.*
high tall, *adj.*
hinder let, *v.*
hiss say, *v.*
hobby job, *n.*
holler say, *v.*
homely pretty, *adj.*
honest good, *adj.*
honorable good, *adj.*
horrible nice, *adj.*
hot cold, *adj.*
howl say, *v.*
huger bigger, *adj.*
hurtful helpful, *adj.*
huskier bigger, *adj.*

I

icy cold, *adj.*
identical same, *adj.*
imagine think, *v.*
important, *adj.*
inaccurate right, *adj.*
inching crawling, *v.*
incident event, *n.*
incorrect right, *adj.*
indication sign, *n.*
inferior good, *adj.*
inquire ask, *v.*
invent, *v.*

J

jarred surprised, *adj.*
job, *n.*
joyful sad, *adj.*

K

kindhearted good, *adj.*

L

larger bigger, *adj.*
larger smaller, *adj.*
later before, *adv.*
lavender purple, *n.*
law-abiding good, *adj.*
lean thin, *adj.*
leisure job, *n.*
leisurely easy, *adj.*
lemon yellow, *adj.*
lenient easy, *adj.*
let, *v.*
lighthearted sad, *adj.*
like, *v.*
lilac purple, *n.*
littler bigger, *adj.*
littler smaller, *adj.*
loathe like, *v.*
loftier bigger, *adj.*
lofty tall, *adj.*
longer bigger, *adj.*
love like, *v.*
lovely pretty, *adj.*
loving good, *adj.*
low tall, *adj.*
luscious good, *adj.*

M

main, *adj.*
major important, *adj.*
make up think, *v.*
many, *adj.*
march walk, *v.*
masterful good, *adj.*

mauve purple, *n.*
mean good, *adj.*
meaningless important, *adj.*
merry sad, *adj.*
mightier bigger, *adj.*
mild easy, *adj.*
minor important, *adj.*
mistaken right, *adj.*
moan say, *v.*
moral good, *adj.*
more enormous bigger, *adj.*
more gigantic bigger, *adj.*
more massive bigger, *adj.*
more towering bigger, *adj.*
more tremendous bigger, *adj.*
mouth-watering good, *adj.*
mumble say, *v.*
murmur say, *v.*
muse think, *v.*
mutter say, *v.*

N

nasty good, *adj.*
nearly, *adv.*
necessary, *adj.*
nervous upset, *adj.*
nice, *adj.*
nourishing good, *adj.*
numerous many, *adj.*
nutritious good, *adj.*

O

obedient good, *adj.*
odd strange, *adj.*
operate, *v.*
orchid purple, *n.*
ordinary common, *adj.*
ordinary strange, *adj.*
originate invent, *v.*

outraged angry, *adj.*
outstanding good, *adj.*
overwhelmed surprised, *adj.*

P

peaceful easy, *adj.*
peculiar strange, *adj.*
perfectly nearly, *adv.*
permit let, *v.*
picture think, *v.*
plain easy, *adj.*
plain pretty, *adj.*
play job, *n.*
pleasant nice, *adj.*
pleased angry, *adj.*
pleasing pretty, *adj.*
pleasure fun, *n.*
plum purple, *n.*
plump thin, *adj.*
polished good, *adj.*
polished rough, *adj.*
polished smooth, *adj.*
polite good, *adj.*
ponder think, *v.*
poor good, *adj.*
praiseworthy good, *adj.*
precisely nearly, *adv.*
predict think, *v.*
pretty, *adj.*
prevent let, *v.*
previously before, *adv.*
principal main, *adj.*
prize like, *v.*
proper good, *adj.*
punier bigger, *adj.*
purple, *n.*
puzzling easy, *adj.*

Q

qualified good, *adj.*
question ask, *v.*
quick, *adj.*

T
H
E
S
A
U
R
U
S

P
L
U
S

THESAURUS PLUS

R

race run, v.
really, adv.
reason, n.
reflect think, v.
refuse agree, v.
related, adj.
relaxed easy, adj.
reliable dependable, adj.
relish like, v.
reply ask, v.
repulsive pretty, adj.
required necessary, adj.
responsible dependable, adj.
restful scary, adj.
result effect, n.
reveal discover, v.
right, adj.
roar say, v.
rough smooth, adj.
rough, adj.
roughly nearly, adv.
run walk, v.
run, v.

S

sad, adj.
same, adj.
say, v.
scare frighten, v.
scary, adj.
scorn like, v.
scream say, v.
screech say, v.
scrumptious good, adj.
second-rate good, adj.
separated related, adj.
serious funny, adj.
several many, adj.
shocked surprised, adj.
shocking scary, adj.
short tall, adj.
shorter bigger, adj.
shout say, v.
sigh say, v.
sign, n.
significant important, adj.
simple easy, adj.
skilled good, adj.
skinny thin, adj.
sleek smooth, adj.
slender thin, adj.
slighter bigger, adj.
slim thin, adj.
slow-paced easy, adj.
smaller bigger, adj.
smaller, adj.
smell, n.
smooth rough, adj.
smooth, adj.
snap say, v.
snarl say, v.
soothe frighten, v.
soothing scary, adj.
special common, adj.
speechless surprised, adj.
splendid pretty, adj.
sputter say, v.
stammer say, v.
stand still walk, v.
startled surprised, adj.
stop let, v.
strange, adj.
stride walk, v.
stroll run, v.
stroll walk, v.
stunned surprised, adj.
stunning pretty, adj.
suitable right, adj.
superior good, adj.
surprised, adj.
symptom sign, n.

T

taken aback surprised, adj.
talented good, adj.
tall, adj.
taller bigger, adj.
task job, n.
tasty good, adj.
terrible nice, adj.
terrify frighten, v.
thin, adj.
think, v.
thoughtful good, adj.
thunderstruck surprised, adj.
tinier bigger, adj.
tinier smaller, adj.
treasure like, v.
truly really, adv.
trust think, v.
trustworthy dependable, adj.

U

ugly pretty, adj.
uncomplicated easy, adj.
unearth discover, v.
uneven rough, adj.
unhappy sad, adj.
unimportant main, adj.
unimportant necessary, adj.
unkind good, adj.
unlike same, adj.
unneeded necessary, adj.
unpleasant nice, adj.
unselfish good, adj.
unsightly pretty, adj.
untroubled easy, adj.
unusual strange, adj.
unworthy good, adj.
upright good, adj.
upset, adj.
upstanding good, adj.
use operate, v.
useful helpful, adj.
useless helpful, adj.

V

valid right, *adj.*
valuable expensive, *adj.*
vaster bigger, *adj.*
violet purple, *n.*
visualize think, *v.*

W

walk run, *v.*
walk, *v.*
want, *v.*
warm cold, *adj.*
weigh think, *v.*
weird strange, *adj.*
well-mannered good, *adj.*
whimper say, *v.*
whine say, *v.*
whisper say, *v.*
wicked good, *adj.*
wider bigger, *adj.*
wish for want, *v.*
wonder think, *v.*
work job, *n.*
work operate, *v.*
worried upset, *adj.*
worship like, *v.*
wrong right, *adj.*

Y

yell say, *v.*
yellow, *adj.*
yummy good, *adj.*

A

agree *v.* to express willingness. *My parents* **agreed** *to get a dog for my brother and me.*

consent to say yes. *Did Judy* **consent** *to your plan?*

approve to say officially that something is correct or should be done. *The principal* **approved** *of the field trip.*

comply with to follow a request or a rule. *Please* **comply with** *the rules when you visit the museum.*

antonyms: deny, refuse

angry *adj.* feeling or showing displeasure. *My sister was* **angry** *when I stained her favorite skirt.*

furious feeling or showing rage. *I was* **furious** *when my bicycle was stolen.*

outraged feeling or showing offense to. *He was* **outraged** *at the jury's verdict.*

antonyms: happy, pleased

ask *v.* to put a question to. *I will* **ask** *Donna to come with me.*

question to try to get information from. *Please* **question** *him about his plans.*

inquire to try to find out certain information. *We* **inquired** *about the price of the bicycle.*

antonyms: reply, answer

B

before *adv.* in the past. *He was excited about his trip because he hadn't been to Texas* **before.**

earlier sooner or at a past time. *Since the game ended* **earlier** *than usual, we had time to spare.*

previously taking place in the past. **Previously** *she wore her hair long, but now it is short.*

antonyms: after, later

Word Bank

bigger *adj.* of greater size.

grander	fatter
larger	loftier
huger	taller
bulkier	heavier
huskier	more towering
mightier	more massive
vaster	more enormous
wider	more tremendous
longer	more gigantic

antonyms: smaller, tinier, littler, shorter, punier, slighter

C

cold *adj.* at a low temperature. *The snowy mountaintops are* **cold.**

icy feeling as chilled as ice. *My hands become* **icy** *when I get nervous.*

frigid at a very low temperature. *The North Pole has a* **frigid** *climate.*

antonyms: hot, warm

common *adj.* found or occurring often. *A dog is a* **common** *pet, but a monkey is not.*

familiar well known because it is often seen or heard. *The bus route home is very* **familiar.**

ordinary usual or regular. *She wished that she had not worn her* **ordinary** *dress to the fancy party.*

antonyms: special, different

crawling *v.* moving slowly by dragging oneself. *The baby was **crawling** across the room.*

inching moving by small degrees. *The worm was **inching** toward its home.*

creeping moving with the body close to the ground. *The cat was **creeping** up on the mouse.*

D

dependable *adj.* able to be trusted or relied on. *Mrs. Li hired Al because she knew he was **dependable**.*

trustworthy deserving other people's confidence. *Share your secrets only with **trustworthy** friends.*

reliable able to be trusted to keep one's word. *The **reliable** worker always arrived on time.*

responsible able to be counted on. *The **responsible** baby sitter checked the baby every hour.*

antonyms: dishonest, flighty

discover *v.* to find out or learn of. *When I turned around, I **discovered** that a cat was following me.*

unearth to find. *The detective searched the room and **unearthed** several important clues.*

reveal to make known. *Karen did not **reveal** the secret tree house to any of her friends.*

antonyms: hide, conceal

do *v.* to carry out an act or action. *Nate **does** his homework right after school.*

accomplish to perform a task. *Can you **accomplish** the job before dark?*

achieve to succeed in doing something. *Emily **achieved** good grades this year.*

carry out to put into practice. *My dog **carried out** my command to sit.*

E

> ### Shades of Meaning
>
> **easy** *adj.*
>
> 1. not hard to understand: *simple, plain, clear, uncomplicated*
>
> 2. free from worry or pain: *comfortable, carefree, breezy, untroubled, peaceful*
>
> 3. not strict or hard to please: *gentle, mild, easygoing, lenient*
>
> 4. not hurried or forced: *slow-paced relaxed casual leisurely*
>
>
>
> antonyms: hard, difficult, puzzling, challenging, demanding

effect *n.* something brought about by a cause. *The burnt leaves on the plant are the **effect** of too much sunlight and lack of water.*

consequence the outcome of something. *One **consequence** of being sick yesterday is that I have to miss the game tomorrow.*

result something that is produced by an action or happening. *The flood was the **result** of too much rain and very poor drainage.*

antonym: cause

event *n.* a happening. *Ronald's wedding was a happy **event**.*

➡️

THESAURUS PLUS

event (continued)

incident a brief or unimportant happening. *There was a funny* **incident** *at school today.*

experience a happening that one has lived through. *Making that speech was an unforgettable* **experience.**

expensive *adj.* costing a great deal of money. *She kept her* **expensive** *jewels in a safe.*

costly having a high price. *Meals at fancy restaurants are often* **costly.**

valuable worth a lot, in quality or money. *Museums usually contain* **valuable** *paintings.*

F

frighten *v.* to alarm or scare. *Thunder and lightning* **frightens** *me.*

startle to fill with sudden shock. *The knocking at the door* **startled** *me.*

terrify to fill with horror. *Scary movies* **terrify** *me.*

antonyms: comfort, calm, soothe

fun *n.* a good time. *Marlene has* **fun** *at the circus.*

pleasure a feeling of happiness. *Lou smiled with* **pleasure.**

entertainment amusement. *The puppies provide us with more* **entertainment** *than the TV does!*

enjoyment delight. *Jill's greatest* **enjoyment** *is playing soccer.*

funny *adj.* causing amusement or laughter. *The joke was so* **funny** *that we could not stop laughing.*

amusing pleasantly entertaining. *The polka-dotted bear was* **amusing.**

comical producing laughter; silly. *A clown is supposed to be* **comical.**

antonym: serious

G

Shades of Meaning

good *adj.*

- - - - - - - - - - - - - - - - - - - -

1. well-behaved:
   polite, proper, obedient, well-mannered, courteous

2. trustworthy:
   honest, decent, honorable, law-abiding, upstanding, upright, moral

3. aiding one's health:
   healthful, nutritious, nourishing

4. pleasant-tasting:
   delicious, tasty, flavorful, mouth-watering, yummy, appetizing, luscious, scrumptious

5. having much ability:
   skilled, able, capable, talented, gifted, masterful, expert, qualified, polished, experienced

6. kind:
   considerate, caring, thoughtful, generous, unselfish, friendly, loving, charitable, kindhearted

7. better than average:
   outstanding, excellent, fine, superior, praiseworthy, admirable

- - - - - - - - - - - - - - - - - - - -

antonyms: awful, unkind, harmful, bad, evil, wicked, disagreeable, disgusting, unworthy, cruel, mean, nasty, heartless, inferior, poor, second-rate

H

helpful *adj.* providing aid or assistance. *Thank you for being so* **helpful** *when I lost my keys.*

useful being of service; handy. *A hammer is a* **useful** *tool.*

beneficial favorable or helping out. *The right amount of rain and sunlight is* **beneficial** *to the crops.*

antonyms: harmful, hurtful, useless

I

important *adj.* strongly affecting the way things happen. *For healthy teeth, it is* **important** *to brush them.*

major larger or greater. *Because it rained for the* **major** *part of the day, the game was canceled.*

significant having a great deal of meaning. *June 2 is* **significant** *for me because it is my birthday.*

antonyms: meaningless, minor

invent *v.* to make something that did not exist before. *Thomas Edison* **invented** *the phonograph.*

develop to bring or come into being. *Henry Ford* **developed** *a new way to build cars.*

originate to start or be responsible for starting. *Spaghetti* **originated** *in ancient China, not in Italy.*

J

job *n.* something that must be done. *Would you prefer the* **job** *of scrubbing or waxing?*

work things that must be done. *You have enough* **work** *to keep you busy.*

task an assignment or a chore. *Adam's* **task** *was to sweep the hall.*

employment an activity by which one earns money or to which one devotes time. *Teaching is a wonderful form of* **employment.**

antonyms: play, hobby, leisure

L

let *v.* to give permission to. *Ron took the leash off his dog and* **let** *her run free in the field.*

allow to say yes to. *Please* **allow** *me to go to Jenny's party.*

permit to consent to. *The state law* **permits** *sixteen-year-olds to drive cars and motorcycles.*

antonyms: prevent, stop, hinder

How Much Did You **Like** It?

like *v.* to find pleasant or attractive.

1. to like quite well:
   enjoy, appreciate, have regard for, care for, be fond of, admire, fancy

2. like very well:
   love, cherish, relish, prize, treasure

3. like extremely well:
   adore, worship, dote on, exalt

antonyms: dislike, hate, scorn, detest, despise, loathe

M

main *adj.* most important or primary. *The* **main** *street in our town is called Main Street!*

➡

main (continued)

chief leading all others. *Wheat is the* **chief** *product of the state.*

principal first in rank or importance. *The* **principal** *violinist played a solo.*

antonym: unimportant

many *adj.* adding up to a great number. *The show was so good that* **many** *people bought tickets.*

several more than two but not a large number. *Kathy lives within walking distance, only* **several** *blocks away.*

numerous made up of a large number. *Colds and other illnesses are more* **numerous** *in the winter.*

antonym: few

N

nearly *adv.* almost but not quite. *John had* **nearly** *finished the test when the bell rang and he had to stop.*

closely almost equally or evenly. *They ran so* **closely** *together that I did not know who had won.*

roughly more or less. *The room can hold* **roughly** *twenty people.*

approximately close to or about. *A yard is* **approximately** *the same as a meter.*

antonyms: exactly, perfectly, precisely

necessary *adj.* having to be done. *It is* **necessary** *to study for good grades.*

essential impossible to do without. *Breathing is* **essential** *to life.*

required needed or called for. *Sneakers are* **required** *in the gym.*

antonyms: unimportant, unneeded

nice *adj.* pleasing or appealing. *Jean has a very* **nice**, *friendly, open smile.*

agreeable to one's liking. *The lovely flowers were an* **agreeable** *sight.*

pleasant giving enjoyment or delight. *The* **pleasant** *evening air felt good after the hot day.*

antonyms: awful, horrible, distasteful, terrible, unpleasant

O

operate *v.* to run. *Can you* **operate** *a bulldozer?*

work to perform a function. *Who knows how to* **work** *the computer?*

use employ for some purpose. *Did you* **use** *my saw to build the bookcase?*

P

Word Bank

pretty *adj.* pleasing to the eye or ear.

cute	attractive	pleasing
fair	enchanting	charming
lovely	appealing	handsome

exquisite	gorgeous	brilliant
graceful	beautiful	dazzling
stunning	glorious	splendid

antonyms: homely, plain, unsightly, ugly, hideous, repulsive

Shades of Purple

purple *n.* a color that is a mixture of red and blue.

- - - - - - - - - - - - - - - - - - -

lilac: a pale purple, like the tiny flowers on a lilac bush

lavender: a pale bluish purple, like the flowers of the sweet–smelling lavender plant

plum: a dark reddish purple, like the color of purple plums

grape: a dark grayish purple, like the color of purple grapes

amethyst: a medium purple, like the gem

orchid: a pale pinkish purple, like the petals of an orchid

violet: a bright bluish purple, like the purple in a rainbow

mauve: a light grayish purple, like a cloudy sky at twilight

Q

quick *adj.* fast. *She ran with* **quick** *steps.*

brief short in time. *The senator's speech was* **brief.**

fast swift; rapid. *Hockey is a* **fast** *game.*

R

really *adv.* certainly. *We* **really** *had a good time when you visited.*

truly indeed. *It was* **truly** *wonderful to see the Grand Canyon.*

actually in fact. *Did a double rainbow* **actually** *appear in the sky after the storm?*

reason *n.* something that explains why something else happens. *The* **reason** *we took no pictures is that I forgot my camera!*

cause something that makes something else happen. *Was lightning the* **cause** *of the fire?*

explanation something that reveals why something else is so. *There is a logical* **explanation** *for why iron is heavier than wood.*

related *adj.* having something in common; linked to something. *A paragraph is made up of* **related** *ideas.*

connected joined. *The two* **connected** *houses share a yard.*

associated having a link or a relationship. *Turkeys and Thanksgiving are* **associated** *ideas.*

antonyms: cut off, separated

right *adj.* in agreement with fact or reason. *Andy was* **right** *when he said that it would rain, for it just started to pour.*

correct free from error. *Since all her answers were* **correct,** *her grade was one hundred.*

fitting suited to the occasion. *It was* **fitting** *that Lynn spoke because she is class president.*

suitable appropriate or right for the purpose. *Which are more* **suitable** *to jog in—shorts or sweat pants?*

valid having facts or evidence as support; sound. *Her reason for being absent is* **valid**—*she is sick.*

antonyms: wrong, incorrect, mistaken, inaccurate

rough *adj.* full of bumps and ridges. *The carpenter sanded the* **rough** *wood until it was smooth.*

bumpy covered with lumps. *The* **bumpy** *road made us bounce in our seats.*

coarse not polished or fine. *The surface of sandpaper is* **coarse.**

uneven not level. *Because the floor was* **uneven,** *the bookcase would not sit straight.*

antonyms: smooth, polished

run *v.* to move quickly on foot. *Please walk, not* **run** *in the halls.*

dash to move with sudden speed. *We* **dashed** *out the door when the alarm sounded.*

race to rush at top speed. *Leon* **raced** *to catch the bus.*

antonyms: walk, stroll

S

sad *adj.* showing or filled with sorrow. *Mark was* **sad** *when his uncle moved far away.*

unhappy without pleasure or joy. *The* **unhappy** *girl walked with her head down.*

gloomy feeling low in spirits. *The soccer team felt* **gloomy** *after their third loss.*

antonyms: happy, cheerful, joyful, merry, glad, lighthearted

same *adj.* having all qualities in common. *My best friend and I get along well because we have the* **same** *interests.*

equal exactly alike in some measured quality. *A foot is* **equal** *to twelve inches.*

identical exactly like something or someone else. *I could not tell the* **identical** *twins apart.*

antonyms: different, unlike

Shades of Meaning

say *v.* speak aloud.

- -

1. to say quietly or unclearly:
   whisper
   murmur
   mutter
   sigh
   mumble
   grunt

2. to say in an excited or nervous way:
   exclaim, cry, stammer, sputter

3. to say loudly:
   yell, scream, screech, shout, holler, bellow, roar, howl

4. to say in an angry way:
   snarl, snap, growl, bark, hiss

5. to say in a complaining way:
   whine, moan, groan, grumble, whimper, gripe.

scary *adj.* causing alarm or fear. *The monsters in the movie were* **scary.**

frightening making one afraid. *The ugly,* **frightening** *mask made me scream.*

alarming causing great worry or concern. *The news of a possible tornado is* **alarming.**

shocking very upsetting or surprising. *The* **shocking** *news of the accident disturbed everyone.*

antonyms: calming, restful, soothing

sign *n.* something that reveals a fact, quality, or condition. *The paw prints were a* **sign** *that a large animal had come by.*

indication something that shows that something else has happened or may happen. *Dark clouds are an* **indication** *of rain.*

symptom something that signals or is associated with something else. *Yawning can be a* **symptom** *of boredom.*

smaller *adj.* of a more limited size or amount. *Do you want the* **smaller** *sandwich or the larger one?*

littler less in size or amount. *The* **littler** *paw prints were made by the puppy, not the dog.*

tinier much less in size. *Doll clothes are even* **tinier** *than baby clothes.*

antonyms: larger, bigger, greater

smell *n.* an odor or scent. *The* **smell** *of fresh paint makes Laurie sneeze.*

fragrance a sweet or pleasant scent. *Allan breathed deeply to get the full* **fragrance** *of the roses.*

aroma a pleasant odor. *Jess loved to smell the* **aroma** *of fresh bread.*

smooth *adj.* even, level, and without bumps. *Glass usually has a* **smooth** *surface.*

polished made shiny, especially by rubbing. *He could see his face in the* **polished** *table top.*

sleek very even, glossy, and shiny. *She put gel in her hair to make it* **sleek.**

antonyms: rough, coarse, bumpy

strange *adj.* not known or familiar; different. *We turned down a* **strange** *street and realized that we were lost.*

odd out of the ordinary. *I read a funny story about an* **odd** *animal that had three humps!*

peculiar hard to understand or explain. *There is nothing* **peculiar** *about a green apple, but what do you think about a purple orange?*

unusual rare or different from what might be expected. *Her* **unusual** *name was hard to say.*

weird not common or usual; mysterious. *A purple shirt, orange pants, and a green hat make a* **weird** *outfit.*

antonyms: common, ordinary, familiar

How **Surprised** Were You?

surprised *adj.* feeling the effect of a sudden, unexpected happening.

- - - - - - - - - - - - - - - - -

1. quite surprised:
startled, jarred, caught off guard, taken aback

2. very surprised:
amazed
shocked
astonished
astounded
overwhelmed

3. extremely surprised:
speechless, stunned, dazed, flabbergasted, dumbfounded, awestruck, thunderstruck

---

T

tall *adj.* having greater than ordinary height. *A basketball player does not have to be extremely* **tall** *to be good.*

high at a great distance above the ground. *The apples were too* **high** *in the tree to reach.*

lofty towering. *The mountains had many* **lofty** *peaks.*

antonyms: short, low

thin *adj.* having little fat. *Exercise helps you stay* **thin.**

skinny very thin. *The cat was so* **skinny** *that you could see its ribs.*

lean containing little or no fat. *I prefer to eat* **lean** *meat rather than fatty meat.*

➡

thin (continued)

slim small and narrow around. *After Carla lost weight, she looked good in the **slim** skirt.*

slender having little width. *The **slender** tree bent in the strong wind.*

antonyms: fat, plump, heavy

Shades of Meaning

think

- - - - - - - - - - - - - - - - -

1. to suppose:
   believe, expect, trust, guess, fancy, figure, assume, predict, foresee

2. to examine in the mind:
   ponder, consider, reflect, wonder, muse, weigh, analyze

3. to form ideas or visions in the mind:
   *imagine
   make up
   fantasize
   visualize
   dream up
   conceive
   picture*

W

walk *v.* to move on foot at a steady pace. *Gabriel can **walk** to the store to get milk.*

march to move forward with regular and measured steps. *The band **marched** around the stadium as they played.*

stride to take long steps. *You **stride** so fast I cannot keep up with you.*

stroll to go forward in a slow relaxed way. *Shall we **stroll** through the park after dinner?*

antonyms: run, stand still

want *v.* to long for. *Sue **wanted** to go to San Francisco so that she could see her sister again.*

desire to have a strong longing for. *In hot weather, I always **desire** cool watermelon.*

wish for to hope for strongly. *It is not enough just to **wish for** good grades.*

Y

yellow *adj.* having the color of the sun. ***Yellow** sunflowers dotted the field.*

gold having a deep yellow color. *Wheat turns **gold** when it is ripe.*

lemon having a bright yellow color named for the fruit. *The **lemon** walls seemed to fill the room with sunshine.*

U

upset *adj.* sad or unsettled. *I was **upset** when I heard the bad news.*

worried uneasy because of fear. *Janet was **worried** about getting lost in the big city.*

nervous shaken and jittery because of fear or challenge. *Dean was very **nervous** because he had to give a speech in front of the class.*

■ LITERATURE VOCABULARY ■

A

absence /ăb′səns/ *n.* To be away from someone or away from a place. *I brought a note to explain my absence from school.*

absentminded /ab′sənt **min**′dĭd/ *or* absent-minded *adj.* Forgetful; not paying attention. *Because I am absent-minded, I often misplace my keys.*

advertiser /ad′vər tīz ər/ *n., pl.,* advertisers A person or agency that calls public attention to a product or service. *Our school newspaper needs more advertisers.*

adviser /ăd vī′zər/ *n.* One who informs, or offers help in solving a problem. *My neighbor is my adviser when I have problems.*

affection /ə fĕk′shən/ *n.* Fondness or love for a person, animal, or thing. *I feel deep affection for Aunt Sarah.*

alligator /ăl′ĭ gā′tər/ *n.* A large reptile with sharp teeth and long, broad, powerful jaws. *An alligator has a wider jaw than a crocodile.*

almanac /ôl′mə năk′/ *n.* A book published once a year filled with lists, charts, and tables of information about seasons, tides, stars, and crops. *Look in the almanac to find the time of today's high tide.*

anvil /ăn′vĭl/ *n.* A heavy block of iron or steel with a smooth, flat top. Metals can be hammered and shaped on an anvil. *The blacksmith pulled the iron from the fire and hammered it on the anvil.*

aspen /ăs′pən/ *adj.* A tall, thin poplar tree with small leaves. *The leaves of the aspen tree fluttered in the wind.*

B

background /băk′ground′/ *n.* The part of a picture, scene, or view that seems far away. *You cannot see me in the background of this picture.*

beckon /bĕk′ən/ *v.* beckoned, beckoning To signal with a movement of the head or hand. *He beckoned to me from across the room.*

C

chamberlain /chām′bər lən/ *n.* An official who manages the household of a king or noble. *We asked the chamberlain for permission to visit the king.*

citizen /sĭt′ĭ zən/ *n., pl.* citizens A person who is a member of a city, state or country. *They were proud citizens of a new homeland.*

comet /kŏm′ĭt/ *n., pl.* comets A mass of material that travels around the sun in a long, slow path; at night it can be seen as an object with a long, bright tail. *The word comets, in Greek, means "long-haired stars."*

comment /kŏm′ĕnt′/ *n., pl.* comments Something spoken or written that explains or gives an opinion. *His comments about my report were helpful.*

commercial /kə mûr′shəl/ *n.* An advertisement on television or radio. *There were too many commercials during this TV program.*

conclude /kən **klo͞od′**/ *v.* concluded, concluding To think about something carefully and then reach a decision or form an opinion. *I have concluded that the best way to make a friend is to be one.*

contrary /**kŏn′**trĕr′ē/ *adj.* Going against; acting completely different. *Don't act contrary to your parents' wishes.*

crocodile /**krŏk′**ə dīl′/ *n.* A large reptile with thick skin, large teeth, and a long, narrow jaw. *A crocodile has a longer jaw than an alligator.*

cushion /**ko͝osh′**ən/ *n.* A soft pad or pillow used to sit or lie on. *The emperor relaxed on a puffy, velvet cushion.*

D

delicate /**dĕl′**ĭ kĭt/ *adj.* 1. Very fine in quality. 2. Easily broken or damaged; fragile. *These silk flowers are very delicate.*

diplomat /**dĭp′**lə măt′/ *n.* A person whose job it is to represent a government in its dealings with other countries. *During the Revolutionary War, Ben Franklin was sent to France as a diplomat.*

dispose /dĭ **spōz′**/ *v.* To get rid of by destroying or throwing away. *After the party, please dispose of the paper plates.*

domed /dōmd/ *adj.* Rounded like the top half of a ball. *Eskimos live in domed ice houses called "igloos."*

dormouse /**dôr′**mous′/ *n.* A small animal like a squirrel, that sleeps by day and is active at night. *I can hear a dormouse moving under the floor boards.*

E

embarrass /ĕm **băr′**əs/ *v.* embarrassed, embarrassing To cause to feel nervous. *I was embarrassed when I dropped my lunch tray.*

entertainment /ĕn′tər **tān** mənt/ *n.* A performance such as a show that is intended to amuse. *The circus was great entertainment.*

F

fantastic /făn **tăs′**tĭk/ *adj.* Something amazing or wonderful. *My sister gave me a fantastic birthday present.*

fiery /**fīr′**ē/ *adj.* Glowing like fire. *The fiery sunset lit up the sky.*

forecast /**fôr′**kăst′/ *n., pl.* forecasts A guess in advance of what will happen, especially about the weather. *All the weather forecasts predict a big storm.*

frantically /**frăn′**tĭ kəl ē/ *adv.* In an excited manner, as from fear or worry. *My father frantically searched for his car keys.*

H

hover /**hŭv′**ər/ *v.* hovered, hovering To stay in one place in the air. *A hummingbird was hovering over a blue flower.*

humorous /**hyo͞o′**mər əs/ *adj.* Funny or amusing. *Comedians tell humorous stories.*

hurricane /**hûr′**ĭ kān′/ *n., pl.* hurricanes A very powerful storm with strong winds over 75 miles an hour and heavy rains. *Two hurricanes hit the coast of Florida last year.*

I

interrupt /ĭn'tə **rŭpt'**/ *v.* interrupted, interrupting To stop by breaking in. *I'm sorry I **interrupted** your conversation.*

inventor /ĭn **věn'**tər/ *n.* A person who makes or produces something that didn't exist before. *Thomas Edison was the **inventor** of the light bulb.*

J

jolt /jōlt/ *v.* To move or ride in a jerky, shaking way. *This old car **jolts** down bumpy roads.*

L

limpid /**lĭm'**pĭd/ *adj.* Very clear; easy to see through. *We counted many fish swimming below the **limpid** pool's surface.*

M

meander /mē **ăn'**dər/ *v.* meandered, meandering To go along a curved, winding path. *A cow was **meandering** through our yard.*

mechanical /mə **kan'**ĭ kəl/ *adj.* Done or performed by a machine. *I wound up my **mechanical** toy rabbit.*

memorize /**měm'**ə rīz'/ *v.* memorized, memorizing To learn by heart. *I spent the afternoon **memorizing** my speech.*

modest /**mŏd'**ĭst/ *adj.* 1. Quiet and humble in appearance. 2. Not large or showy. *We live in a **modest** five-room house.*

mustache /**mŭs'**tăsh'/ *n.* 1. The hair growing on a man's upper lip. 2. Something similar to a mustache in looks and position. *The thatched roof's **mustache** dripped with rain.*

N

naturally gifted /**năch'**ər ə lē **gĭf'**tĭd/ *adj.* Well suited for an activity because of ability that is present from birth. *Carlos is a **naturally gifted** athlete.*

nuisance /**noo'**səns/ *n.* Someone or something that is annoying; a bother. *The children were a **nuisance** to their baby sitter.*

O

octopus /**ŏk'**tə pəs/ *n.* A sea animal with a round body and eight long arms. *When he juggled oranges, he looked like an **octopus**.*

operate /**ŏp'**ə rāt'/ *v.* To work or to run something such as a machine. *I learned how to **operate** my computer.*

outing /**ou'**tĭng/ *n., p.* outings An outdoor pleasure trip. *My family enjoys Sunday **outings** by the river.*

P

pantry /**păn'**trē/ *n.* A small room near the kitchen where food and dishes are kept. *Lucy came out of the **pantry** with a can of soup.*

peg /pěg/ *n., pl.* pegs A pin used as part of a musical device or instrument. ***Pegs** pluck the strings inside this music box.*

permission /pər **mĭsh'**ən/ *n.* Consent given by someone in authority; allowed. *Our parents gave us **permission** to go skating.*

pincers /**pĭn'**sərz/ *n.* A metal tool with handles and jaws used for grasping; a large pair of pliers. *He held the two pieces of metal together with **pincers**.*

porcelain

LITERATURE VOCABULARY

porcelain /pôr′sə lĭn/ *n.* A hard, white material made by baking a fine clay. *Mother keeps the porcelain cat on the top shelf.*

portion /pôr′shən/ *n.* The amount of food served at a meal; a helping. *Jenny always gets the biggest portion of corn.*

praise /prāz/ *n.* To show warm approval. *Praise from my coach meant a lot to me.*

prey /prā/ *n., pl.* prey An animal hunted or caught by another for food. *Small mice are often prey for snakes.*

R

restaurant /rĕs′tər ənt/ *n.* A place where meals are served to the public. *We ate at Dad's favorite restaurant.*

rivulet /rĭv′yə lĭt/ *n., pl.* rivulets A small stream. *Tadpoles swam in the muddy rivulets.*

rush /rŭsh/ *n., pl.* rushes Tall, grassy marsh plants with long green leaves and hollow stems. *Small birds hopped from stem to stem in the rushes by the river.*

rustly /rŭs′lē/ *adj.* To move with soft whispering sounds. *The rustly pond grass bent in the wind.*

S

scarlet /skär′lĭt/ *adj.* A bright red color. *The leaves on our maple tree turn scarlet in autumn.*

schedule /skĕj′ool/ *n.* A written or printed list of times when things occur; a list of times for arrivals and departures. *Check the schedule to tell me when the train will come.*

self-discipline /sĕlf′dis′ə plĭn/ *n.* Training and controlling of oneself for personal goals. *It takes a lot of self-discipline to learn to write well.*

shallow /shăl′ō/ *adj.* Not deep; lacking depth. *The river became so shallow that our boat touched bottom.*

shock /shŏk/ *v.* To surprise greatly. *The bright sun shocks my eyes.*

shudder /shŭd′ər/ *v.* shuddered, shuddering To shake or tremble suddenly from fear or cold. *She was shuddering in the cold snow.*

silken /sĭl′kən/ *adj.* 1. Made of a fine, glossy fiber that is made by silkworms. 2. Like silk in feeling or looks. *The silken scarf looked lovely over her shoulders.*

slab /slăb/ *n.* A flat, thick piece such as bread, stone, or cheese. *I spread jam all over a slab of bread.*

specialty /spĕsh′əl tē/ *n.* A special study, skill, or occupation. *A writer's specialty is words.*

stealthy /stĕl′thē/ *adj.* Moving in a way to avoid being noticed. *A stealthy lion crept up on a zebra.*

T

tango /tăng′gō/ *n.* A Latin-American dance. *We danced the tango all night.*

terror /tĕr′ər/ *n.* Someone fierce or one who creates fear in another person. *My sister becomes a terror when I wear her clothes.*

tiger lily /tī′gər lĭl′ē/ *n.* A plant with curved, black-spotted orange flowers. *A single tiger lily floated in a bowl of water.*

tortoise /tôr′tĭs/ *n.* A large land turtle with thick, scaly limbs and a hard, rounded shell. *The* **tortoise** *looked like a huge rock.*

U

ungrateful /ŭn **grāt′**fəl/ *adj.* Not thankful for kindness shown or something received. *I helped him with his work, but he was* **ungrateful.**

V

vestry /**vĕs′**trē/ *n.* A room in a church where robes and holy objects are kept. *I spoke to the priest in the* **vestry.**

visible /**vĭz′**ə bəl/ *adj.* Able to be seen; clear to the eye. *The Statue of Liberty is* **visible** *from miles away.*

W

warming-pan /**wôrm′**ĭng păn/ *or* warming pan *n., pl.* warming-pans A metal pan with a cover and a long handle; holds hot coals and was used to warm a bed. *In the past, people used* **warming-pans** *to heat their beds.*

whimper /**hwĭm′**pər/ *v.* whimpered, whimpering To cry or sob with weak, soft, whining sounds. *My friend's dog* **whimpered** *as she showed me her hurt paw.*

wolverine /**wo͞ol′**və rēn′/ *n.* An animal related to the weasel with thick fur, a bushy tail, and sharp claws. *The* **wolverine** *survives by hunting small forest animals.*

LITERATURE VOCABULARY

LANGUAGE TERMS

abbreviation   a short form of a word.

action verb   a word that tells what people or things do.

adjective   a word that describes a noun and can tell *what kind* or *how many*.

adverb   a word that describes a verb and tells *how, when,* or *where*.

apostrophe   takes the place of any missing letters in a contraction and is used to form possessive nouns.

command   a sentence that tells someone to do something. It ends with a period.

common noun   names any person, place, or thing.

complete predicate   includes all the words in the predicate.

complete subject   includes all the words in the subject.

compound predicate   made by using *and* to combine the predicates of two sentences with the same subject.

compound sentence   two related, short sentences that have been combined, using a comma and the connecting word *and, but,* or *or*.

compound subject   formed by using *and* to join the subjects of two sentences with the same predicate.

contraction   a shortened form of two words joined together. An apostrophe replaces the missing letter or letters.

direct quotation someone's exact words.

exclamation   a sentence that shows strong feeling. It ends with an exclamation point.

future tense   a verb that shows action that will happen.

helping verb   a verb that comes before the main verb.

irregular verbs   verbs that do not add -*ed* to show past action.

main verb   the most important verb.

negative   a word that means "no."

noun   a word that names a person, a place, or a thing.

object pronouns   used after action verbs and words such as *to, with, for, at (me, you, him, her, it, us, them)*.

past tense   a verb that shows action that has already happened.

plural noun   names more than one person, place, or thing.

plural possessive noun   shows ownership. It is formed by adding an apostrophe to a plural noun.

possessive noun   shows ownership. It is formed by adding an apostrophe and *s* to a singular noun.

possessive pronoun   may be used in place of a possessive noun (*my, your, her, his, its, our,* and *their*).

present tense   a verb that shows action that is happening now.

pronoun   a word that replaces one or more nouns.

proper noun   names a particular person, place, or thing and is capitalized.

question   a sentence that asks something. It ends with a question mark.

quotation marks   used before and after a direct quotation.

run-on sentence   has two complete thoughts that run into each other.

sentence   a group of words that tells a complete thought.

simple predicate   the main word in the complete predicate. It tells exactly what the subject does or is.

simple subject   the main word in the complete subject. It tells exactly whom or what the sentence is about.

singular noun   names one person, place, or thing.

special verb forms   forms of the verb *be* that tell what someone or something *is* or *is like*.

statement   a sentence that tells something. It ends with a period.

subject pronouns used as the subjects of sentences (*I, you, he, she, it, we, they*).

■ INDEX ■

Numbers in **bold type** indicate pages where skills are taught.

A

a, an, the. See Articles
Abbreviations, 266–267, 280, 286, 398, 475–476
Adapting language, 64, 124, 192, 248, 310, 372, 432
Addresses, 266–267, 280, 286, 315, 398, 475–476
Adjectives
  combining sentences with, **214**
  comparative forms of, **208–209,** 210–211, 212–213, 217, 221, 227–229, 398, 481
  diagraming, **446–448**
  identifying, **204–205,** 216, 221, 224, 397
  irregular, **212–213,** 217, 221, 229, 398
  predicate, **206,** 216, 221, 225, 397
  superlative forms of, **208–209,** 210–211, 212–213, 217, 221, 227–229, 398
  See also Usage, adjectives
Adverbs
  comparative forms of, **386–387,** 394, 399, 403, 481
  diagraming, **448–449**
  identifying, **384–385,** 394, 399, 402
  superlative forms of, **386–387,** 394, 399, 403
  See also Usage, adverbs

Affixes. *See* Prefixes; Suffixes
Agreement, subject-verb, 142–143, 158, 165, 220, 397
Alliteration, 433–434, 468
Almanac, 363
Alphabetical order, 407–408
Antonyms, 441, 483–484
Apostrophes
  in contractions, **154–155,** 159, 171, 221, **332–333,** 339, 346, 397, 399
  in possessive nouns, **86–87, 88–89,** 93, 95, 102, 103, 397
  rules for, 478
Applying writing skills
  comparison and contrast, 130–131
  description, 254–255
  persuasive letter, 316–317
  research reports, 378–379
  story about yourself, 70–71
  story writing, 198–199
Appositives, 90
are, our, **479**
Art, writing about, 33, 91, 157, 215, 255, 279, 337, 393
Articles, 207, 216, 221, 226, 397, 479
Atlas, 363
Audience, adapting to, 64, 124, 192, 248, 310, 372, 432, 450, 452, 454, 456, 458, 460, 462

B

Base words, 438–439
be, **forms of, 152–153,** 159, 170, 220, 397, 482
Biographical fiction, 350–353
Biography, 354–356, **464–465**
Book report
  book jacket as, 256–257
  interview as, 380–381
  letter as, 318–319
  puppet play as, 200–201
  television commercial as, 132–133
  writing a, **72–73**
Books
  finding information in, **363**
  finding in the library, **413–416**
  parts of, **418–421**
  recommended, 73, 133, 201, 257, 319, 381
  titles of, capitalizing and underlining, **276–277,** 281, 291, 398, 476
Brainstorming, 62, 63, 122, 190, 246, 308, 361–362, 368

C

Call numbers, 415–416
Capitalization
  of abbreviations, **266–267,** 280, 286, 398, 475–476
  of first word in sentence, **16–17, 18–19,** 34, 38, 39, 94, 218, **260–261,** 280, 283, 396, 398, 477

INDEX

letters
  friendly, 303–304
  parts of, **303–304,**
    305, 458
  persuasive, 303, 304,
    308–317, 458–459
note-taking, **364,** 460,
  464
opinions, writing and
  supporting, **306–307,**
  458
outline, writing from,
  366–367, 460
outlining, **365–366,**
  460
parts of a story
  (beginning, middle,
  end), **186–188,** 454
plot, **186–188,** 454
purpose, 450, 452, 454,
  456, 458, 460
senses, using, 239, 240,
  242, 456
setting, **188–189,** 454
titles, writing, **59,** 450,
  454, 460, 464
  topic sentences, writing,
  118–119, 243–244,
  452, 456, 458, 460
steps in writing
  prewriting, **4–5,** 62–63,
    122–123, 190–191,
    246–247, 308–309,
    368–369
  planning, **370–371**
  first draft, **6,** 64, 124,
    192, 248, 310, 372
  revising, **7–9,** 65–66,
    125–126, 193–194,
    249–250, 311–312,
    373–374
  proofreading, **10,**
    67–68, 127–128,
    195–196, 251–252,
    313–314, 375–376

publishing, **11,** 69, 129,
  197, 253, 315, 377
types. *See* Biography;
  Comparison and
  Contrast; Descriptions;
  Instructions; Letters;
  News story; Personal
  narrative; Persuasive
  writing; Research
  reports; Shape poem;
  Stories
Composition Strategies,
  450–469
Compound sentences,
  26–27, 35, 43, 94, 218,
  396, 478
Compound words, 54
Comprehension, literal, 49,
  52, 110, 112, 180, 235,
  236, 297, 298, 353,
  356. *See also* Critical
  thinking; Inferences,
  making
Conclusions, drawing, 110,
  184–185, 298, 353,
  356
Conferences, writing. *See*
  Writing conferences
Conjunctions (*and, but, or***),**
  26–27, 28–29, 35, 43,
  94, 214, 218, 396, 478
Content area, writing in,
  71, 131, 199, 255, 317,
  379
Context clues, 182
Contractions
  with *not,* **154–155,** 159,
    171, 221, 397
  with pronouns, **332–333,**
    339, 346, 399
Copyright page, using, 418
Creative activities, 36, 53,
  63, 96, 113, 149, 160,
  161, 181, 209, 222,
  237, 282, 299, 340,
  357, 379, 400, 401. *See*

also Book report;
  Publishing
Creative writing, 13, 15, 17,
  19, 21, 25, 27, 29, 31,
  33, 36, 53, 70, 73, 77,
  79, 81, 83, 85, 87, 89,
  91, 113, 130, 137, 139,
  141, 143, 145, 147,
  153, 157, 161, 181,
  190–199, 203, 205,
  206, 207, 209, 211,
  213, 215, 222, 237,
  254, 255, 261, 263,
  267, 269, 271, 275,
  279, 299, 316, 319,
  323, 325, 329, 331,
  335, 337, 357, 378,
  385, 387, 389, 391,
  393, 400, 401, 451,
  455, 457
Critical listening, 66, 126,
  183, 194, 250, 301,
  312, 374, 430–431,
  433–434
Critical thinking, 49, 52, 56,
  64–66, 110, 112, 117,
  124–126, 180,
  184–185, 192–194,
  235, 236, 248–250,
  297, 298, 302,
  310–312, 353, 356,
  361–362, 372–374,
  435–436

D

Descriptions
  activities for writing, 79,
    89, 91, 145, 205, 206,
    215, 231, 254, 255,
    261, 279, 337, 340,
    357, 456
  skills
    details, choosing,
      243–244, 456
    exact words, using,
      244–245, 456

(Acknowledgments continued.)

"Ululation," from *It Doesn't Always Have to Rhyme* by Eve Merriam. Copyright © 1964 by Eve Merriam. All rights reserved. Reprinted by permission of Marian Reiner for the author.

"Understanding," from *A Song I Sang to You* by Myra Cohn Livingston. Copyright © 1984, 1969, 1967, 1965, 1959, 1958 by Myra Cohn Livingston. Reprinted by permission of Marian Reiner for the author.

"We Invent the Franklin Stove," from *Ben and Me* by Robert Lawson. Copyright 1939, 1951 by Robert Lawson. By permission of Little, Brown and Company.

"What Is Orange?" from *Hailstones and Halibut Bones* by Mary O'Neill. Copyright © 1961 by Mary Le Duc O'Neill. Reprinted by permission of Doubleday & Company, Inc., and William Heinemann Limited.

"What's the Big Idea, Ben Franklin?" from *What's the Big Idea, Ben Franklin?* by Jean Fritz. Text copyright © 1976 by Jean Fritz. Reprinted by permission of Coward, McCann and Geoghegan, and Russell & Volkening, Inc. as agents for the author.

"The Yak" (verses one and two) from *Zoo Doings* by Jack Prelutsky. Copyright © 1967, 1983 by Jack Prelutsky. By permission of Greenwillow Books (A Division of William Morrow & Company).

Brief Quotations

from *Someday You'll Write* by Elizabeth Yates McGreal. Copyright © 1962. Reprinted by permission of the author. (p. 1)

from "Country Window" in *Out in the Dark and Daylight* by Aileen Fisher. Text copyright © 1980 by Aileen Fisher. Reprinted by permission of Harper & Row, Publishers, Inc., and William Heinemann Limited. (p. 12)

from "Crocodile" in *Animal Encyclopedia* by Robin B. Cano and Irving Wasserman. Copyright © 1973 by Robin B. Cano and Irving Wasserman. Reprinted by permission of the authors. (p. 104)

from "How Big Is a Foot?" (excerpt) by Rolf Myller. Copyright © 1962 Rolf Myller. Reprinted with permission of Atheneum Publishers. (p. 172)

from "Chums," in *The Laughing Muse* by Arthur Guiterman. Copyright © 1915 by Arthur Guiterman. Reprinted by permission of Louise H. Sclove. (p. 320)

from *Lightning and Thunder* by Herbert S. Zim. Copyright © 1952 by Herbert S. Zim. Reprinted by permission of the author. (p. 348)

from *The Story of Ben Franklin* by Eve Merriam. Copyright © 1965 by Eve Merriam. All rights reserved. Reprinted by permission of Marian Reiner for the author. (p. 364)

from "Sunning" in *Crickety Cricket! The Best-Loved Poems of James S. Tippett*. Copyright 1933 by Harper & Row, Publishers, Inc. Renewed 1961 by Martha K. Tippett. Reprinted by permission of Harper & Row, Publishers, Inc., and William Heinemann Limited. (p. 382)

Entries from *Houghton Mifflin Intermediate Dictionary*. Copyright © 1986 by Houghton Mifflin Company. Adapted and reprinted by permission Houghton Mifflin Company.

Glossary excerpt from *Houghton Mifflin Reading Program* "Flights" copyright © 1989. Reprinted by permission of the publishers.

Title and copyright page from *The Remembering Box* by Eth Clifford, illustrated by Donna Diamond. Copyright © 1985 by Eth Clifford Rosenberg. Reprinted by permission of Houghton Mifflin Company and Scott Meredith Literary Agency, Inc.

Pronunciation Key from *Houghton Mifflin Spelling Program*, copyright © 1985. Used by permission of the publishers.

Table of Contents from *This Is an Orchestra* by Elsa Z. Posell. Copyright © 1973 by Elsa Z. Posell. Reprinted by permission of Houghton Mifflin Company. (p. 419)

Index from the book *Turkeys, Pilgrims, and Indian Corn: The Story of the Thanksgiving Symbols* by Edna Barth. Published by Clarion Books, Ticknor & Fields, A Houghton Mifflin Company, New York. Copyright © 1975 by Edna Barth. Reprinted by permission of Houghton Mifflin Company and Curtis Brown Ltd. (p. 420)

Grateful acknowledgment is given to Nathaniel Worden, Mandy Art, Joby Gelbspan, Brian Gilmore, and Daniel Bauer for permission to adapt and reprint original material as student writing models in The Writing Process lessons.

The publisher has made every effort to locate each owner of the copyrighted material reprinted here. Any information enabling the publisher to rectify or credit any reference is welcome.

Credits

Illustrations
Leo Abbet: 199
Anthony Accardo: 301
Alan Baker: 78, 82, 89, 106–114, 118, 130, 140, 149, 204, 210, 211, 273–275, 326
Mary Jane Begin: 20, 21, 24, 136, 262, 322, 324, 328, 330, 332, 441, 442
Higgins Bond: 294–299, 316, 318, 433
Boston Graphics/Paul Foti: 423
John Butler: 232–239, 243, 254, 435
Penny Carter: 450–469
Dan Collins: 26, 438
Bonnie Gee: 48–54, 60, 70, 245
Leigh Grant: 390
Graphics Etcetera: 424
Alexander Farquharson: 2–3
Ellen Harris: 143
Mary Keefe: 62, 64, 65, 67, 122, 124, 125, 127, 190, 192, 193, 195, 246, 248, 249, 251, 308, 310, 311, 313, 368, 370–373, 375
Meg Kelleher Aubrey: 7, 11, 200, 266, 413, 415, 417
Dave Kelley: 71
Robert Lawson: 350 (illustration), 378 (illustrations)
Mitchell and Malik: 350–353 (borders)
Linda Phinney: 138, 139
Kristina Rodanas: 174–182, 187, 198
Claudia Sargent: 36, 56, 96, 160, 161, 222, 223, 241, 282, 308, 326, 340, 400, 401, 439, 440
Carol Schwartz: 63, 73, 80, 87, 123, 144, 152–154, 191, 201, 206, 208, 247, 256, 257, 309, 319, 369, 381, 384
Michael Smith: 14, 16, 22, 260, 264
Mark Tetreault: 354, 363
George Ulrich: 483, 490–498

Hand marbleized English Cockerell paper from Andrews/Nelson/Whitehead Corporation, Long Island City, New York: 32, 33, 90, 91, 156, 214, 215, 278, 279, 336, 337, 392, 393

Photographs
1 Dave Philips.   13 Dr. E. R. Degginger.

15 David Muench Photography.   7 The Bettmann Archive.   19 (top) Jan Halaska/Photo Researchers Inc.   19 (bottom) Luis Villota/The Stock Market.   30 Robert Frerck 1984/Woodfin Camp & Assoc.   46–47 Dallas & John Heaton/Click/Chicago.   74–75 Brian Seed 1981/Click/Chicago.   76 Voscar The Maine Photographer/Southern Stock Photos.   77 Helen Marcus/Photo Researchers Inc.   79 G. Tomsich/Photo Researchers Inc.   84 (bottom) Animals Animals/D. R. Specker.   84 (top) Luis Villota/The Stock Market.   104–105 Tad Goodale.   111 Walter Chandoha Photography.   112 both John R. Hamilton/Globe Photos.   120 both Dr. E. R. Degginger.   134–135 Guido Alberto Rossi/The Image Bank.   137 Breck P. Kent.   151 R. Rowan/Photo Researchers Inc.   172–173 D & J Heaton/Click/Chicago.   189 Jonathan Barkan/The Picture Cube.   202–203 Stephen P. Parker/Photo Researchers Inc.   205 Youngblood.   213 J. Rawle.   230–231 Miguel Castro/Photo Researchers Inc.   255 David Meunch Photography.   258–259 Peter Menzel.   261 Michael Freeman.   265 (top) Bruno J. Zehnder/Peter Arnold Inc.   265 (bottom) Clyde H. Smith/Peter Arnold Inc.   269 Los Angeles County Museum.   271 Skylar Hansen/West Stock.   292–293 Ed Cooper.   298 (top) Van Phillips/Leo deWys Inc.   298 (left) Photo Researchers Inc.   298 (right) David Overcash/Bruce Coleman Inc.   317 Kathy Squires.   320–321 Elliot Varner Smith.   323 R. Steedman/The Stock Market.   325 John Shaw/Tom Stack & Assoc.   327 Jay Lurie/West Stock.   329 Stephanie Maze/Woodfin Camp & Assoc.   331 Tom McHugh/Photo Researchers Inc.   335 (top) Gregory K. Scott/Photo Researchers Inc.   335 (bottom) F. Gohier/Photo Researchers Inc.   348–349 Barry Parker/Bruce Coleman Inc.   356 Eliot Elisofon, Life Magazine © 1959 Time Inc.   360 Chicago Historical Society.   366 Eliot Elisofon, Life Magazine © 1959 Time Inc.   379 James Mason/Black Star.   382–383 Nancy Sheehan.   385 David Smith.   387 Charles Gupton/Southern Light.   388 Daemmrich.   465 Ken Heinan.   465 Matthew McVay/Picture Group.   465 The Bettmann Archive.   465 The Granger Collection.

Charlie Hogg: 62, 65, 68, 69, 122, 125, 127, 128, 190, 193, 196, 197, 246, 249, 252, 253, 308, 311, 314, 315, 370, 373, 376, 377

Fine Art

33 *Carrie and Cocoa*, by Robert Vickrey, Private Collection, Courtesy of Midtown Galleries. Photo by Russ Lappa.   91 *The Banjo Lesson*, by Henry O. Tanner (1893), Oil on Canvas, 49 in. x 35½ in. Photo by Mike Fischer, Hampton University Museum.   157 *Breezing Up*, by Winslow Homer, National Gallery of Art, Washington, Gift of the W. L. and May T. Mellon Foundation.   215 *Tres Riches Heures du Duc de Berry: May*, Musée Condé Chantilly. Photo by Giraudon/Art Resource.   279 *La Gare Saint-Lazare Arrivee d'un Train*, by Claude Monet, Courtesy of The Harvard University Art Museum, The Fogg Art Museum, Bequest—Collection of Maurice Wertheim, Class of 1906. 337 *Trail Riders*, by Thomas Hart Benton, The National Gallery of Art, Washington.   393 *The Great Wave*, by Katsushika Hokusai, From the Series: Fugaku Sanjuroki, Japanese, 1760–1849, Woodblock print, Spaulding Collection, courtesy Museum of Fine Arts, Boston.

Cover Photographs

Cover and title page photograph: Mike Yamashita/Woodfin Camp

The photograph shows Natural Arches, a cave in Bermuda.

Back cover: Jon Chomitz